General de Gaulle's Cold War

BERGHAHN MONOGRAPHS IN FRENCH STUDIES

Editor: **Michael Scott Christofferson,** Adelphi University

France has played a central role in the emergence of the modern world. The Great French Revolution of 1789 contributed decisively to political modernity, and the Paris of Baudelaire did the same for culture. Because of its rich intellectual and cultural traditions, republican democracy, imperial past and post-colonial present, twentieth-century experience of decline and renewal, and unique role in world affairs, France and its history remain important today. This series publishes monographs that offer significant methodological and empirical contributions to our understanding of the French experience and its broader role in the making of the modern world.

Volume 1
The Populist Challenge: Political Protest and Ethno-nationalist Mobilization in France
Jens Rydgren

Volume 2
French Intellectuals against the Left: The Antitotalitarian Moment of the 1970s
Michael Scott Christofferson

Volume 3
Sartre against Stalinism
Ian H. Birchall

Volume 4
Sartre, Self-Formation and Masculinities
Jean-Pierre Boulé

Volume 5
The Bourgeois Revolution in France 1789–1815
Henry Heller

Volume 6
God's Eugenicist: Alexis Carrel and the Sociobiology of Decline
Andrés Horacio Reggiani

Volume 7
France and the Construction of Europe 1944–2006: The Geopolitical Imperative
Michael Sutton

Volume 8
Shades of Indignation: Political Scandals in France, Past and Present
Paul Jankowski

Volume 9
Mitterrand, the End of the Cold War and German Unification
Frédéric Bozo

Volume 10
Collective Terms: Race, Culture, and Community in a French New Town
Beth S. Epstein

Volume 11
France in the Age of Organization: Technicians, Culture and Politics from the 1920s to Vichy
Jackie Clarke

Volume 12
Building a European Identity: France, the United States, and the Oil Shock, 1973–1974
Aurélie Élisa Gfeller

Volume 13
General de Gaulle's Cold War: Challenging American Hegemony, 1963–1968
Garret Joseph Martin

Volume 14
At Home in Postwar France: Modern Mass Housing and the Right to Comfort
Nicole C. Rudolph

GENERAL DE GAULLE'S COLD WAR

Challenging American Hegemony, 1963–1968

Garret Joseph Martin

berghahn
NEW YORK · OXFORD
www.berghahnbooks.com

First published in 2013 by
Berghahn Books
www.berghahnbooks.com

Library of congress cataloging-in-publication data

Martin, Garret Joseph, 1980–
General de Gaulle's Cold War : challenging American hegemony, 1963–
1968 / Garret Joseph Martin.
   pages cm. — (Berghahn monographs in French studies; volume 13)
   Includes bibliographical references and index.
   ISBN 978-1-78238-015-3 (hardback — ISBN 978-1-78533-031-5 (paperback)
ISBN 978-1-78238-016-0 (ebook)
   1. France—Foreign relations—1958–1969. 2. Gaulle, Charles de, 1890–1970.
3. World politics—1945–1989. 4. Cold War. I. Title.
   DC420.M3753 2013
   327.44009'046—dc23

2013005579

British Library cataloguing in publication data

A catalogue record for this book is available from the British Library.

ISBN: 978-1-78238-015-3 hardback
ISBN: 978-1-78533-031-5 paperback
ISBN: 978-1-78238-016-0 ebook

CONTENTS

Acknowledgments   vii

List of Abbreviations   ix

Introduction   1

Part I. The Quest for Great Power Status, 1963–1965

Chapter 1
All (not so) Quiet on the Western Front   17

Chapter 2
The Long Road to Moscow   51

Chapter 3
A "Shining Light" for the World?   74

Part II. The Rise and Fall of the Gaullist Design, 1966–1968

Chapter 4
1966, Gaullist Zenith   97

Chapter 5
Illusion of Independence Part 1, January–June 1967   123

Chapter 6
Illusion of Independence Part 2, July–December 1967   149

Chapter 7
The Fall, January–August 1968   171

Conclusion   192

Annexes   199
Endnotes   207
Bibliography   251
Index   266

Acknowledgments

I am deeply indebted to the many individuals and institutions that made this book possible. A scholarship from the Arts and Humanities Research Council in the United Kingdom, various research studentships from the International History Department of the London School of Economics and Political Science, and a Moody Grant from the Lyndon Johnson Library provided much-needed financial support throughout the research process. The archivists and staff at the Ministère des Affaires Etrangères, Paris; the Archives Nationales, Paris; the Fondation Nationale des Sciences Politiques, Paris; the United Kingdom National Archives, Kew Gardens; the John F. Kennedy Presidential Library, Boston; the Lyndon B. Johnson Presidential Library, Austin; the U.S. National Archives II at College Park, Maryland; and the International Monetary Fund Archives, Washington, DC, were extremely patient and invaluable sources of advice for locating the many documents that went into this book.

Throughout the writing and editing process, I was fortunate enough to receive help and advice from many colleagues. Various chapters of this book were reviewed by Dr. Toshihiko Aono, Dr. Elizabeth Benning, Dr. James Ellison, Dr. Tanya Harmer, Prof. Tsuyoshi Hasegawa, Dr. Helen Parr, Dr. Gil-li Vardi, Dr. Alex Wieland, and Prof. Salim Yaqub. All were very generous with their comments and feedback. I would also like to thank Ann DeVita, Adam Capitano, Melissa Spinelli, Elizabeth Berg, and Marion Berghahn of Berghahn Books, as well as Professor Irwin Wall, the editor of this series. Of course, my greatest academic debt is to my supervisor, Dr. Piers Ludlow, who never faltered in his encouragement of my work over the years. I am lucky to count him as a friend. Any errors of fact or interpretation are, of course, my own.

Finally, none of this would have been possible without the unwavering love of my family. My wife, Dr. Louise Woodroofe, was throughout this process a calming and uplifting presence, whether I needed feedback or simply a fine bottle of wine! My parents, John and Jacqueline Martin, and my siblings, Neil and Eimear, have always remained by my side and never ceased to support me in my various endeavors. "Ní minic a bhíonn an seans againn a chur in iúl an méid ghrá a bhfuil againn lenár n-ansachtaí." It is therefore to my family, passed (Hilary, Vera, Sarah, Joseph, and Deirdre) and present, that I humbly dedicate this work.

ABBREVIATIONS

ANF	Archives Nationales Françaises
ASP	American Selling Price
CAP	Common Agricultural Policy
CDU	Christian Democratic Union
COMECON	Council for Mutual Economic Assistance
CRU	Collective Reserve Unit
DDF	Documents Diplomatiques Français
DF	Documentation Française
DPC	Defence Planning Committee
EEC	European Economic Community
FFA	Forces Françaises d'Allemagne
FNSP	Fondation Nationale des Sciences Politiques
FO	Foreign Office
FRUS	Foreign Relations of the United States series
G10	Group of Ten
GATT	General Agreement on Tariffs and Trade
GNI	Gross National Income
HAWK	NATO's body in charge of production and logistic organization
ICBM	Intercontinental Ballistic Missiles
ICC	International Control Commission
IMF	International Monetary Fund

LBJL	Lyndon Baines Johnson Library
MAEF	Ministère des Affaires Etrangères Français
MLF	Multilateral Force
NAC	North Atlantic Council
NADGE	NATO Air Defense Ground Environment
NAMSO	NATO's Maintenance and Supply Organization
NARA	National Archives Record Administration
NATO	North Atlantic Treaty Organization
NDAC	Nuclear Defense Affairs Committee
NLF	National Liberation Front
NPG	Nuclear Planning Group
NPT	Non-Proliferation Treaty
OAS	Organisation de l'Armée Secrète
OAU	Organization of African Unity
OECD	Organization for Economic Co-operation and Development
PCF	Parti Communiste Français
PRC	People's Republic of China
PTBT	Partial Test Ban Treaty
SALT	Strategic Arms Limitation Talks
SDR	Special Drawing Rights
SEATO	Southeast Asia Treaty Organization
SECAM	Séquentiel Couleur Avec Mémoire
TEA	Trade Expansion Act
U.K.	United Kingdom
UK-NA	United Kingdom National Archives
UN	United Nations
UNEF	United Nations Emergency Force
UNR	Union pour la Nouvelle République
U.S.	United States
WEU	Western European Union

INTRODUCTION

[General Charles] de Gaulle is a European and the head of a metropolitan country. In addition, he has the advantage of being able to act irresponsibly. The United States, on other hand, is a world power while France is not.
—George Ball, Summary Record of NSC Executive Committee Meeting
   number 39, 31 January 1963

Only General de Gaulle, Mikhail Gorbachev, and Pope John Paul II made constructive proposals to address the problem of East-West relations in Europe with regard to peace, equilibrium, and Europe's destiny.
—Alain Larcan, L'Europe de l'Atlantique à l'Oural

On 11 March 2009, during a speech at l'Ecole Militaire, French President Nicolas Sarkozy announced that his country would fully reintegrate into the North Atlantic Treaty Organization (NATO), forty-three years after General Charles de Gaulle had withdrawn France from NATO's integrated military structure.[1] Despite the objections from officials within Sarkozy's party, who decried the betrayal of the Gaullist legacy, and the criticisms from the main opposition parties, Sarkozy's decision hardly amounted to a major turning point for French policy.

Since the end of the Cold War, military ties between NATO and France had continuously strengthened. Sarkozy's decision to fully reintegrate France into NATO was less of a dramatic break with the past, and more of a culmination of a progressive rapprochement that had gained momentum in the last two decades. In other words, the contrast between 2009 and 1966 could not have been greater. While the 2009 return of the "prodigal son" to the NATO family proved low-key and consensual, de Gaulle's 1966 decision to withdraw France from NATO's integrated military structure had marked a traumatic moment for the Alliance.

The departure from NATO would come to symbolize French President General Charles de Gaulle's turbulent relationship with his Western allies throughout the 1960s. During this period, the General came to be regarded as the scourge of Atlantic unity and the biggest threat to American leadership of the Western Alliance in an era still dominated by the Cold War.[2] When the former leader of the Free French and postwar head of state returned to power in June 1958 to tackle the Algerian War, France's Western allies hoped that he would end the conflict and restore stability and prosperity to his country. They could not anticipate that de Gaulle would not only fulfill those aims, but also pursue an ambitious foreign policy agenda in the following eleven years that would seriously challenge the structure of the Atlantic Community.

The General's bold diplomacy generally received the support of French public opinion, but caused grave chagrin to Paris's Western partners.[3] The latter often cursed the French president, whose masterful sense of timing and cultivated air of secrecy turned him into a formidable opponent. Even his bitter critic, the Belgian politician Paul-Henri Spaak, reluctantly acknowledged that:

> He [de Gaulle] is, however, in daily politics a tactician with an exceptional and undeniable talent. He is a great diplomat, but more by the variety of the means that he used than by the grandeur of the aim he had. He hides his intentions, suddenly reveals them, generally with panache. He creates uncertainty in the mind of those he negotiates with … There is no one better when it comes to giving importance to what he does, and to hide, behind his assurance, the fluctuations of his thought.[4]

De Gaulle's attachment to secrecy followed from his personality traits of autonomy and aloofness, with even his closest advisers declaring that it was impossible to achieve familiarity with him.[5] It also stemmed from the General's conception of authority and leadership. The leader needed to be distant, since he believed authority depended on status, and status required distance. Without mystery there could be no prestige, since one could not revere what one knew too well.[6]

Throughout his career, de Gaulle never hesitated to resort to deliberate ambiguity, as vagueness and a certain blurring of categories generally suited his purposes; he frequently conflated tactics and aims.[7] What he meant by expressions such as a "European Europe," a "Europe from the Atlantic to the Urals," or the neutralization of Vietnam, was never clearly spelled out. He kept his allies second guessing about his ultimate intentions, much to their frustration. That goes a long way toward explaining why the General has remained to this day a captivating yet controversial figure of postwar European history.

The vast number of memoirs, biographies, and scholarly works focusing on de Gaulle—which exceeds three thousand—is a testimony to this enduring fascination, but also reveals very sharp divisions when it comes to assessing the overarching objective of his foreign policy. Three key fault lines stand out in the literature. The first group of historians have echoed frustrated Kennedy and Johnson administration officials in their denunciations of de Gaulle as irrational, and complained that his policy was "largely animated by anti-US prejudice." United States (U.S.) officials often viewed de Gaulle as the ultimate free rider, a "highly egocentric" leader, "with touches of megalomania," who welcomed confrontation with the U.S. as a way to regain France's identity as a Great Power; as U.S. President Kennedy claimed, "these bastards [the French] just live off the fat of the land and spit on us every chance they get."[8]

Other scholars agree that the French president could be considered anti-American in the sense that he challenged U.S. leadership and harbored strong antipathy for U.S. society.[9] Various authors and former French officials, however, reject the idea that de Gaulle was somehow obsessed with Washington. In their view, France and the U.S. strongly disagreed during the 1960s, but there was nothing that could be construed as systematic hostility on the French side. The tension resulted instead from conflicting national goals, and if anything, the General was driven more by anti-hegemonic than anti-American feelings.[10]

Additionally, authors and former officials disagree on whether or not de Gaulle possessed some kind of grand design. If Spaak took the most categorical approach when he claimed that "I see in his [de Gaulle's] action neither doctrine nor grand design that he pursued with continuity," others have also tried to downplay the idea that the French president followed a broader vision for his diplomacy.[11] They have pointed out that behind the blustering and ambitious rhetoric, the General sought to achieve more modest aims, such as restoring his country's pride and independence or guaranteeing commercial benefits for France when it came to European integration.[12]

Other officials and scholars acknowledge that de Gaulle had a design, but define it as essentially negative, narrow, and selfish. For instance, they argue that the General's diplomatic agenda aimed to establish a continental system led by France and that he deployed his strength only to advance some largely irrelevant claims to greatness.[13] Alternatively, a final group of scholars recognizes the French president's foreign policy as an ambitious and genuine attempt to overcome the bipolar Cold War order. They point out that de Gaulle viewed the Cold War order as a dangerous system where all states were permanently threatened by two contradictory, but equally dangerous, prospects: either superpower conflict or a superpower joint hegemony. Driven by "global revisionism," he sought to fashion a more stable and balanced multipolar world order, based on the multiplicity of nation-states and responsive to their individual needs.[14]

Furthermore, even those who accept that de Gaulle sincerely wanted to overcome the prevailing bipolar Cold War system struggle with the feasibility of such an objective. Observers sympathetic to the ideas of the General, such as German politician Franz Josef Strauß, could not understand why his grand design downplayed the existing power relationships.[15] As in Aesop's fable "The Frog and the Ox," many believed that vanity and envy blinded the French president to the moral that not all countries can become as great as they think they can.

In the eyes of his detractors, the General was living in a state of denial, as an odd and antiquated figure who refused to accept the extent to which the Cold War had transformed the international system. As Canadian Prime Minister Lester Pearson confided to U.S. Under Secretary of State George Ball, "he was impressed as the president [Lyndon Johnson] had been with de Gaulle's eighteenth and nineteenth century confidence and rigidity. He said, of course, de Gaulle was one hundred and fifty years behind the times, but he was not bothered by any problems about keeping up with the times."[16]

This book contributes to our understanding of de Gaulle and of the international history of the 1960s, by tackling the three main fault lines in the literature described above. It provides a more balanced account of the General, going beyond the misleading views of him as either a visionary or an irresponsible and anti-American nationalist. Although the French president was not systematically driven by anti-American hostility, the aim of countering U.S. power still became increasingly pervasive and central to his policies as relations between the two countries deteriorated during the 1960s.

Moreover, the book argues that de Gaulle did pursue a somewhat coherent and ambitious grand design, centered on the two key and interrelated aims of recapturing France's Great Power status and overcoming the bipolar Cold War order. Rather than simply reforming transatlantic relations, he wanted to transform Europe's security system.[17] Even taking into account his global aspirations, the General's grand design was essentially Eurocentric. The Third World remained at the periphery of his design, confined as an area of competition for Great Powers keen to spread their spheres of influence.

This book argues for a Gaullist grand design by relying on an original methodology. Instead of focusing on various policy areas in isolation, it provides a comprehensive overview of French foreign policy that treats different geographic regions, as well as different spheres of the economy, political relations, and security, in the same analytical orbit. It explains how closely connected France's policies toward its Western allies became with its opening to the Eastern bloc, and how its strategy with regard to the Third World became increasingly subordinated to Franco-American relations. It also underlines the close ties between France's security and monetary policies. By adopting this methodology, this book outlines a better understanding of de Gaulle's grand strategy.

Finally, this book suggests that the French president's grand design was far from quixotic, that it was not doomed to fail, but rather that de Gaulle made important mistakes that contributed to the undoing of his diplomatic agenda.[18] It does so by approaching the General's foreign policy from an international perspective, drawing on wide-ranging archival research in France, the United Kingdom (U.K.), and the U.S., as well as private papers, interviews, and extensive secondary literature on France, Europe, and the Cold War. It places de Gaulle in his international historical context by arguing that as the Cold War system became more multipolar by the early 1960s, middle powers like France gained a greater margin of action. France could have a significant impact on the world stage during the 1960s because it took advantage of a more fluid international context, and because de Gaulle's ideas seemed in phase with the changes affecting the Cold War order. In other words, this is the story of the meeting of a man and a moment.

When de Gaulle returned to power in June 1958, he already boasted an illustrious career that had included leading the Free French during World War II. While the Cold War dominated international affairs, the General could draw inspiration from the main tenets of his political philosophy, which he had developed well before the emergence of the East-West conflict. These principles would shape his approach to the world stage and his diplomatic grand design during his presidency.

The General naturally placed France at the heart of his thinking. He believed France could only be itself in its rightful rank as a Great Power, and that in turn depended on establishing a strong leadership that could fiercely protect the state's independence in its actions. This commitment to France fit with another central aspect of de Gaulle's understanding of international affairs, as described by the U.S. ambassador to France, Charles Bohlen: "[The] fundamental and basic element in de Gaulle's foreign policy is his strongly held and unchangeable conviction that the nation (the state and not the people) represents the permanent unit in international affairs."[19]

De Gaulle ascribed a central role to the nation-state because of his understanding of history, which deeply influenced his overall thinking. He interpreted history as an essentially tragic developmental narrative, with violence and war as forces continually shaping the world. Amid such a tough environment, where only power counted, nations remained the main players of history and international life reflected the struggle between competing national interests, their opposition, or their temporary agreement.[20]

Conversely, the General's emphasis on historical *longue durée* led him to downplay ideology, which he defined as "temporary and mortal,"[21] and nowhere would this become more obvious than in de Gaulle's pragmatic attitude toward the Soviet Union and communism. His philosophy of history pushed him to believe in "Russia" and to call for dialogue with the country many times during his career, despite his firm opposition to communism.[22]

When the German threat reemerged, he wrote to his mother in 1936 that Soviet Russia still provided the best fallback alliance for France, regardless of what one thought of its regime. Thirty years later, he would again refer to a "political and affectionate reality as old as our two countries [France and Russia], which is linked to their history and geography."[23] Ideological differences, for de Gaulle, did not impede cooperation if that suited the national interests of both parties, nor could ideological solidarity forever mask conflicting national policies.[24]

Struggle equally played an intrinsic part in de Gaulle's vision of history, a Bergsonian competition in which nations—rather than ideologies—strove to flourish, and which required visionary leadership exercised by a strong state in order to succeed. But, alongside competition and leadership, balance also played a vital role in the General's philosophy.[25] Balance constituted a moral imperative for de Gaulle, who equally feared excessive power in states, because it almost always led to hubris, and excessive feebleness, because of his conviction that deference and weakness could become bad habits.[26]

De Gaulle looked to historical precedents to support his belief in balance: "There was, though, a notion that was mentioned in no treaty and that is called equilibrium, and that was then the European equilibrium. All nations agreed tacitly to prevent anyone from acquiring excessive power at the expense of others. It is in the name of European equilibrium that Europe made war first to Louis XIV, then to the French Revolution, then to Napoleon.... Thanks to this notion, smaller states like the Netherlands and Belgium had their existence guaranteed."[27]

The quest for balance was intended as a means, not an end, and could be characterized in different ways by the General: a moderation of power, a refusal of hegemony and alignment, and the sharing of a community of values. All of these principles were aimed at achieving the end goal of peace, which depended on a continuous commitment to the idea of balance.[28] And from de Gaulle's perspective, balancing German power and solving the "German problem" appeared to be a vital precondition for peace and stability in Europe.

Thus, the fundamental pillars of de Gaulle's political philosophy— struggle, the deep influence of history, the notion of balance and the centrality of states in international affairs—predated the Cold War. This does not mean, however, that the General's ideas were not influenced by the onset of the East-West conflict. In 1947, for example, he worried about the danger posed by the Soviet Union's extension of its control over two-thirds of the European continent, and the fact that it controlled a bloc less than five hundred kilometers away from France's border.[29] Years later, when the threat seemed to fade away, he remained wary of the Soviet Union.

Nonetheless, the profound anchoring of the General's political philosophy in history shaped the fact he did not view the Cold War as a permanent state of affairs, or even a real break with the past. He increasingly came to regard the 1945 Yalta Conference as a catastrophe that had completely undermined the interests of France and Europe. Besides deciding Europe's fate without involving the European powers, Yalta was responsible, he believed, for dividing the continent into two blocs, thereby undermining the balance of the old European system.[30] But, driven by his views deeply rooted in history, de Gaulle believed that the legacy of Yalta could be undone, that the Cold War represented nothing more than a transient phenomenon that could and should be overcome.

De Gaulle's opposition to the Cold War and the bipolar order became more pronounced in the years before his return to power. Despite initially supporting the signing of the Atlantic Pact in 1949, he shifted to a more lukewarm stance during the 1950s, especially after the crisis surrounding the European Defence Community and the Suez Canal. He resented the objective deterioration of France's position within the Atlantic Alliance and the "subordination" of French leaders to their American counterparts.[31] At the same time, the General lambasted Paris's failure to reach out to the other side of the Iron Curtain. Following his first reference in March 1950 to a Europe extending from the Atlantic to the Urals, he called on France to take a more active role in East-West affairs, seeing its position as "the most qualified historically, geographically and politically to create a bridge with the East."[32]

While de Gaulle deplored the detrimental impact of the Cold War on France's status, he welcomed the fact that the risks of war in Europe seemed to be declining. Not only did he feel that the chances of a Soviet invasion of Western Europe were receding in the 1950s, as the Soviets faced internal challenges, but he also came to the conclusion that the superpowers were not willing to start a nuclear war, and if one did not resort to war, then one had to make peace sooner or later. This in turn, according to de Gaulle, undermined the main raison d'être of the existing military alliances in Europe.[33]

Additionally, a number of signs suggested that the scales of power were tipping away from both superpowers, although the international order in the 1950s and 1960s remained structured around the U.S.-Soviet competition. The Cold War system was becoming more diffuse.[34] This applied first and foremost to the Atlantic Community. The dramatic recovery experienced by Western Europe in the first postwar decade raised a number of challenges for a transatlantic partnership that had initially rested on American military, economic, and monetary supremacy.[35]

The creation of the European Economic Community (EEC) in 1957—a customs union that included France, West Germany, Italy, Belgium, the Netherlands, and Luxembourg (the six)—symbolized the resurgence of the old continent, but also caused mixed reactions in the U.S. On the one hand, Washington welcomed regional integration as a way of strengthening the European economies and increasing their unity. On the other hand, it feared that the EEC might raise protectionist barriers, shut out U.S. exports, and undermine the cohesion of the Western Alliance.[36]

The Western European economic revival also affected the international monetary system set up at Bretton Woods in 1944, which was centered on dollar-gold parity. By the late 1950s, the structural weaknesses of Bretton Woods were becoming apparent. U.S. international accounts were being drained by a variety of developments, including the country's overseas military commitments related to the Cold War, its support for free trade, and the European economic recovery that was pushing American companies to invest offshore. The world also depended on continued U.S. balance-of-payments deficits for the growth of its reserves, but an increase in the quantity of dollars in circulation carried the risk of fostering worldwide inflation and undermining international faith in the dollar.

Yet, if U.S. deficits were eliminated, the world would be deprived of its major source of reserve growth. In turn, this could put a limit on the overall amount of liquidity in the system, thereby hindering multiple transactions that had little to do with central bank reserves, such as international trade transactions, many of which are carried out in dollars. Many Europeans complained about these deficits and worried that they would lead Washington to end dollar convertibility. If this were to happen, the billions of dollars in foreign government treasuries would drastically decline in value. At the same time, European officials could not push the U.S. too far. The easiest way for the U.S. to end its balance-of-payments deficits was to eliminate or significantly decrease its defense commitments to Europe.[37]

Tied to this, the erosion of the credibility of the American nuclear deterrent posed a serious dilemma for the transatlantic Alliance. Once the Soviet Union developed Intercontinental Ballistic Missiles (ICBM) in 1957, American territory was no longer invulnerable to Soviet nuclear attacks.

This raised the question of whether the U.S. government was still prepared to sacrifice, for instance, New York to defend Hamburg. That was the heart of the problem, and one that prompted Washington to switch NATO's nuclear strategy from one of massive retaliation to flexible response. It hoped to reduce the Alliance's dependence on nuclear weapons and develop a variety of responses to any Soviet invasion, which included a buildup of the member-states' conventional capabilities in warfare. Yet, for many Europeans, this appeared to be a sign that the U.S. was decoupling itself from the defense of Western Europe.[38]

While de Gaulle welcomed Western Europe's resurgence, he also anticipated that changes within the Eastern bloc would one day make it favorable to détente.[39] He outlined his perspective during a press conference in November 1959: the Soviet leaders understood the dangers created by nuclear weapons and the need for peace; the Russian people aspired to freedom and a better life; and Moscow could see the desire for independence among the peoples of Eastern Europe who craved emancipation without necessarily wanting to give up their social regime. Moreover, the General believed that the communist camp would fragment because of the likely rivalry between Russia and communist China. Considering all these factors, he reached the conclusion that the communist world could not escape fundamental change.[40]

Thus, when de Gaulle returned to office in June 1958, he was determined to reclaim France's Great Power status and optimistic about the prospects of overcoming the Cold War order in Europe. He came back to office with a clear grand design that focused first on restoring French independence, especially in the military field. As he made clear in his famous September 1958 memorandum to U.S. President Dwight Eisenhower and British Prime Minister Harold Macmillan, "France cannot consider that NATO, in its current form, satisfies the conditions of the security of the Free World and, especially, its own security."[41] Instead, he called for a reform of the Atlantic Alliance through the establishment of a tripartite directorate. When Eisenhower and Macmillan failed to follow up on his suggestion, the General began to progressively disengage French troops from NATO's integrated military structure.[42]

De Gaulle hoped that a stronger France could help create a new balance in Europe that would overcome the Cold War divide. That implied, initially, the development of a more independent Western Europe. Thus, Paris accepted the Rome Treaty and fully invested itself in the development of the EEC. This partly reflected economic self-interest, since France hoped to guarantee the establishment of the Common Agricultural Policy (CAP) as compensation for the creation of a common industrial market. Yet, de Gaulle also saw the EEC as a means to achieve his long-held objective of establishing a Western European political entity centered on a Franco-German partnership.[43] The latter would remain allied with, but independent from, the U.S. To this end, French leaders proposed the Fouchet Plan in 1961 for an intergovernmental political union of the six.[44]

This more assertive Western Europe would not only become more independent from the U.S., but would also achieve peace with the Eastern bloc. During his first years in power, de Gaulle sent a number of signals to the Soviet leaders. In 1959, the French president recognized the Oder-Neisse line and referred to a "Europe from the Atlantic to the Urals." In 1962, he publicly claimed that close Franco-German cooperation would make possible the establishment of a new European equilibrium between East and West. Convinced that Russia would eventually discard communism, he believed it would accept the idea of playing a role in a new post–Cold War European security system.[45] As for the Empire, de Gaulle envisaged a sort of "Eurafrique" that would maintain privileged ties between France and its African colonies, including Algeria, thereby safeguarding France's sphere of influence.[46] Thus, in 1958, the General established the French Community, a federal body that granted wide autonomy to France's African colonies and established structures of cooperation.

However, between 1958 and 1962, a number of domestic and international obstacles prevented the General from fully pursuing or achieving his diplomatic grand design. Aside from the fact that he needed to prioritize economic recovery and the divisive Algerian War, the renewed period of East-West tension over Berlin and Cuba removed any opportunity for a meaningful dialogue between those on both sides of the Iron Curtain. By the end 1962, however, many of these same obstacles had receded or were no longer so threatening.

On the international stage, the Cuban Missile Crisis in October 1962 marked the high point of East-West tensions. While de Gaulle gave his unconditional support to Washington during the crisis, the lessons he drew from it would have a lasting impact on French strategy. The Cuban episode convinced him that neither superpower wanted to fight a nuclear war. Moscow would not dare to attack Europe, which meant that there was a chance that it would be interested in peace in the future. Additionally, the crisis confirmed to the General that the U.S. would not be willing to risk a nuclear conflict to defend Europe. This provided the best justification for his policy of independence and the need to develop a nuclear arsenal, or force de frappe.[47]

Domestically, 1962 also proved a key turning point for France and de Gaulle. Thanks to his success in the referendum of 28 October, which modified the constitution and ensured that the president would be elected by universal suffrage, and the victory of the Gaullist Party Union pour la

Nouvelle République (UNR) in the parliamentary elections of 18–25 November, the General had consolidated his domestic position. He could now look ahead to three years free from electoral constraints. At the same time, the Evian Accords in March finally ended the Algerian War, removing a major constraint on French diplomacy.[48] With the collapse of the French Community in 1961, and with the page of colonization now turned, Paris would have more leeway to redefine its foreign policy, including in the Third World.

Indeed, at the start of 1963, the situation was ripe for a more ambitious Gaullist diplomacy. France now had the means to pursue a more independent policy within a more favorable international environment. In the space of four years, its economy had grown remarkably, and the government had managed to repay its debts and stabilize its currency.[49] Despite the failure of the Fouchet Plan in April 1962, the Franco-German rapprochement was making great strides forward. As both sides discussed the option of signing a reconciliation treaty, the creation of a Paris-Bonn axis, as the basis of a more independent Western Europe, seemed a distinct possibility.

De Gaulle wanted to pursue a bolder diplomatic agenda and he also had a pretext to act quickly and decisively in the form of U.S. President John F. Kennedy's grand design. Outlined in a speech in Philadelphia on 4 July 1962, Kennedy's vision aimed to establish a large Atlantic Community that threatened the General's goal of developing a more independent Western Europe. Under Kennedy's plan, the U.S. and Western Europe would "develop coordinated policies in all economic, political and diplomatic areas." This essentially amounted to a proposal for interdependence under U.S. guidance, centered around three key initiatives.[50]

First, Washington supported the U.K.'s application to join the EEC, which had been on the table since July 1961.[51] Second, Kennedy pushed for a new, more extensive round of tariff cuts under the General Agreement on Tariffs and Trade (GATT)—dubbed the Kennedy Round—to prevent the Atlantic Community from dissolving into separate trade systems. Thanks to the Trade Expansion Act (TEA) passed by Congress, he was granted extensive power to conduct trade negotiations for a five-year period ending on 30 June 1967. Two notable provisions allowed the president to negotiate a reciprocated and across-the-board 50 percent reduction in tariffs on both sides of the Atlantic, as well as to completely eliminate tariffs when the U.S. and the EEC combined accounted for at least 80 percent of world exports. This was the "dominant supplier" provision, which would only be meaningful if the U.K. joined the European Community.[52]

Finally, the U.S. sought to create a Multilateral Force (MLF). First proposed in December 1960 at the North Atlantic Council by U.S. Secretary of

State Christian Herter, the MLF project sought to establish an integrated nuclear force for NATO. The aim was to restore European confidence in the American nuclear umbrella, while conceding some limited European role in matters of nuclear strategy.[53] This was the situation that the General faced as he prepared to give his semiannual press conference on 14 January 1963.

This book is thus a study of de Gaulle's foreign policy in the Cold War context of 1963–1968, with a primary focus on the international stage. Domestic factors are certainly taken into account, since they often either impeded or influenced de Gaulle's approach to foreign policy, not to mention that pursuing an ambitious diplomatic agenda also allowed the president to harness the energies of French citizens, distracting them from other concerns and mutual animosities.[54] But, it would be equally misleading to suggest that domestic goals provided the central motivation for the General's foreign policy.

Moreover, while this book adopts a comprehensive overview, covering economic, monetary, and military affairs, it still centers on a diplomatic and political perspective. As such, it clearly places de Gaulle at the heart of a wider decision-making process, which included a variety of other sources: ambassadors, diplomatic advisers, as well as Étienne Burin des Roziers, secretary-general of the Elysée between 1962 and 1967, and of course Maurice Couve de Murville, the foreign minister between 1958 and 1968.

Nonetheless, the General still played a predominant role in defining France's grand strategy. His distrust of Quai d'Orsay (French Foreign Ministry) officials and their tendency to compromise meant that he often kept them in the dark when it came to key decisions—as would happen, for instance, with the recognition of communist China or the withdrawal from NATO.[55] Similarly, the weekly Council of Ministers meeting remained a very formal affair, and rarely led to any substantial decision-making. According to Jean Charbonnel, a junior minister between January 1966 and March 1967, there were only four instances of roundtable debates during his time in government.[56] Instead, decisions were generally taken in small committees, especially during Inner Council meetings.[57] Considering the small circle of people involved in decision-making, it makes sense therefore for this study to focus primarily on de Gaulle.

This book is divided into two broad chronological sections. The first part, covering the period between 1963 and 1965, is organized thematically and geographically. Since the General followed multiple paths in his quest to restore France's Great Power status, this allows for the examination of the separate strands of his policy and the specific goals he pursued in each of them. It is also a useful way to detail the various challenges that Paris faced. Thus, the opening chapter will focus on France's policy toward the Western world, chapter 2 will concentrate on the relations between France and the communist world, and the third chapter will highlight Paris's policies toward the developing states in the postcolonial era.

The second part of the book, which deals with the period following the General's reelection as president in December 1965 up to August 1968, is organized in chronological fashion. It brings together the broad threads of the first three chapters and provides a more convincing explanation of the rise and fall of the Gaullist grand design. Chapter 4 covers de Gaulle's bold and spectacular initiatives in 1966, including the withdrawal from NATO, his trip to the Soviet Union, and his Phnom Penh speech. Chapters 5 and 6 detail the major challenges faced by Paris throughout 1967, and in particular its attempt to tackle the complex challenge of interdependence. Finally, chapter 7 chronicles the demise of the General's ambitious diplomatic agenda during the first eight months of 1968. His grand design, this book argues, was in shambles well before he resigned in April 1969.

Part I

THE QUEST FOR GREAT POWER STATUS, 1963–1965

Chapter 1

ALL (NOT SO) QUIET ON THE WESTERN FRONT

Introduction

In early 1963, French president General Charles de Gaulle was about to start a very serious crisis within the Western world. Granted he had proven a thorn in his allies' side before, but the virulence and unilateral nature of his new challenge against the Anglo-Saxons came as a complete shock. Through his brutal veto against the United Kingdom joining the EEC and his refusal to integrate France's nuclear force into the MLF, he would single-handedly ruin Kennedy's grand design for a partnership between Western Europe and the U.S. Although the hysterical reactions to the General's challenge would temper quickly, the events of January 1963 nevertheless created serious scars within the Atlantic Community that would take years to heal.

January 1963 thus signaled a defining moment for the Western Alliance and for French foreign policy. With his domestic and international positions secure, de Gaulle believed the time was ripe to pursue a bolder agenda on the international stage. He wanted specifically to focus on France's Western policy, which centered on three key goals: defending France's independence and claim to Great Power status; developing a more independent Western Europe through the Franco-German axis; and reforming transatlantic relations by creating a more equal partnership between Western Europe and the U.S.

This new direction was well summed up by French Prime Minister Georges Pompidou in early January 1963. "If the United Kingdom entered the EEC, nothing could stop the American firms from invading the continent.... We are the only ones defending Europe against the American invasion.... We have decolonized the French empire. We now have to shake off the Anglo-Saxon colonization."[1]

January–May 1963: *Le Double Non* and Its Consequences

De Gaulle's 14 January 1963 press conference, along with the Franco-German Treaty signed eight days later, marked a dramatic turning point in French foreign policy. This seminal period was characterized by the very forceful way that the General outlined his vision for the Western world, rather than the ideas he exposed, which were not necessarily novel. Facing no elections until December 1965 gave him a unique opportunity to focus on foreign affairs, and he could do so with greater confidence thanks to the more favorable domestic and international context in late 1962.

Indeed, the French president brought a new sense of purpose to his ambitious agenda to reform the Western world, starting with his country's claim to Great Power status. He wanted to send a signal to his allies about his determination to vigorously defend France's independence and its right to act unilaterally to protect its interests, even if this angered them. Thus, during the 14 January press conference, de Gaulle unambiguously rejected the American offer to integrate the force de frappe into the MLF. Without an independent nuclear deterrent, he feared that France could not be considered a Great Power. At the same time, he also viewed the nuclear arsenal as a means to an end. By vetoing the United Kingdom's entry into the EEC during the same press conference, the General could guarantee that France remained the sole power in the EEC with an independent nuclear force.[2]

The "double non" of the press conference reflected de Gaulle's obsession with France's independence and his rejection of subordination to the Anglo-Saxon powers. It also underlined his desire to safeguard the process of Western European integration and to make sure it developed along lines that were consistent with his convictions. This meant, in the economic sphere, ensuring the integration of agriculture in the European Community and the eventual establishment of a CAP. The General regarded this latter aim as a sine qua non of French membership: "We cannot conceive of a Common Market where agriculture would not receive its rightful place and we feel that we are the country that needs this the most amongst the six."[3] The United Kingdom's lukewarm attitude toward the CAP provided further justification for de Gaulle's decision to veto its application to the EEC.

Politically, the General hoped to revive the Fouchet Plan—for an intergovernmental union between the states of the EEC—through the Franco-

German Treaty of 22 January 1963. Three main aspects defined the treaty: it represented the solemn act of reconciliation between the French and German people; it promised bilateral cooperation in the fields of foreign policy, defense, and education—with de Gaulle attaching great impor- tance to defense;[4] and in a more subtle manner, it also hinted at a Europe which progressively emancipated itself from the U.S.[5]

Both the French president and the West German Chancellor Konrad Adenauer actively supported the treaty, but not for the same reasons. Adenauer emphasized the crowning achievement of Franco-German rec- onciliation and thought the treaty could restrain de Gaulle's tendency to undermine NATO.[6] The General, for his part, wanted to fully implement all three aspects of the treaty. If both states developed a common policy, he believed this could create a powerful magnet around which the other EEC partners would gravitate, thereby fostering the development of a more independent Western Europe.

As de Gaulle had outlined in his war memoirs, written before he came back to power in 1958, he envisioned a Western European organization that would eventually become "one of the three world powers, and if pos- sible one day the arbiter between the Soviet Union and the Anglo-Saxon powers."[7] He thus considered the emergence of a more independent West- ern Europe as a vital development, not only to help overcome the division of Europe but also to establish a new peaceful equilibrium on the conti- nent. That ambition, more than anything else, explains why the General vetoed the United Kingdom's entry into the Common Market. As long as London maintained a special relationship with Washington, he feared that the U.K.'s adhesion would inevitably jeopardize the EEC's fragile equilib- rium, undermining its cohesion and distinctive European nature. The end result of British membership could only be the emergence of a "colossal Atlantic Community under US direction and leadership ... [that would] quickly absorb the European Communities."[8]

Instead of subordinating Western Europe to the U.S., de Gaulle aimed, as he explained during his press conference, to reform transatlantic re- lations along the principles of "independence and alliance."[9] Obviously, the ongoing Soviet menace justified the continuing partnership between Western Europe and the U.S., but he added that "alliances do not have absolute virtues."[10] Western Europe needed to maintain its distinctiveness and to be prepared to take charge of its own fate, since its interests would not always coincide with those of the U.S.

Only by being prepared to stand up to its powerful ally could Europe develop a separate identity: "The national feeling has always been ex- pressed against other nations.... The European idea, since the end of the war, progressed thanks to the existing threat in Europe. Now that the Russians are less threatening, and this is good, we have an opportunity to harden our attitude towards the US, and it is our duty; if not, integrated Europe will be dissolved in an Atlantic, that is to say American, whole like sugar in coffee!" the General confided to his then Minister of Information Alain Peyrefitte.[11]

The French president's attachment to a more assertive Western Europe, or European Europe as he called it, was also essentially tied to his conflicted thinking about the long-term role the U.S. would or should play in Europe. On the one hand, he believed that the American presence on the continent resulted from the abnormal circumstances after World War II, and he expected it would not last forever. He could not, however, forecast when such a departure might happen. On the other hand, he feared that America, because of its might, might be tempted to prolong its stay indefinitely and might end up dominating its European allies.[12] Either scenario, be it disengagement or hegemony, justified creating a European entity that could resist either the Soviet menace or America's leadership.

The January 14 press conference and the Franco-German Treaty had thus enabled de Gaulle to outline in a forceful way the principles of his Western policy. The General appeared less candid, however, when it came to explaining how he planned to achieve these ambitious objectives. Since he anticipated that his vision could only materialize over the long term, he probably assumed that it made sense not to reveal too much about tactics; in the short term, however, his two January initiatives created major uproar within the Western world, starting in the EEC.

Community rules required unanimity for any enlargement, and France was not alone in feeling that the negotiations with the U.K. were getting bogged down. But, the brutal and unilateral manner in which de Gaulle vetoed the U.K. candidacy came as a complete shock to the other EEC members.[13] Despite their disbelief, the other five ("the five") refused initially to accept the General's fait accompli, and instead pressured the French government into attending another meeting in Brussels on 28 January.[14] They were encouraged by Washington and London, which believed that the five could force Paris to change its mind if they remained united. For good measure, U.S. Secretary of State Dean Rusk reminded West German Foreign Minister Gerhard Schroeder that "if this negotiation [EEC] should fail, there would result a most serious injury to Western cohesion in the cooperation across the Atlantic."[15]

This vigorous resistance surprised the French government, causing significant divisions during the Council of Ministers meeting on 24 January. Whereas French Foreign Minister Maurice Couve de Murville worried about his country's isolation and advocated dilatory tactics, de Gaulle wanted a confrontation.[16] The president's view eventually prevailed and

France adopted a hard line during the Brussels meeting. Once Couve de Murville confirmed that France considered the negotiations with the U.K. suspended, the EEC had no choice but to end negotiations with London on 29 January. The five's anger and frustration with France at that moment would seldom be matched again.[17]

Nonetheless, even though the five were livid with the General over the U.K. question, the integration of agriculture in the EEC continued in the aftermath of the Brussels split. In part, this success reflected the clever strategy adopted by French officials. They made a number of gestures to appease their partners and diffuse tension, including both supporting various tariff cuts and external tariff alignments planned for 1 July and claiming that they approached the forthcoming Kennedy Round trade negotiations in a positive spirit.[18] They went to great lengths to reassure the Allies that the door of the Common Market was not closed to the U.K., and that France did not want an autarkic Western Europe.[19] At the same time, this conciliatory behavior alternated with more brazen tactics when needed. De Gaulle did not hesitate, for example, to confront the Netherlands. He complained about their government's obstructionist behavior toward the Common Market after the Brussels split and accused them of displaying a total loss of interest in the EEC's development.[20]

Moreover, the five had their own reasons not to punish the French. Since they believed de Gaulle opposed additional integration between the U.S. and Western Europe, it made little sense to further endanger the EEC; instead, they attempted to revive the Community while maintaining a close bond with the U.K. West Germany, under fire for the Franco-Germany Treaty, took a leading role in this process. During the 2 April 1963 meeting of the EEC Council of Foreign Ministers, Schroeder presented his "synchronization" plan—a broad agenda for the future development of the Community—to restore momentum to the EEC.[21]

France had thus adopted a cautious attitude in the aftermath of the Brussels crisis in the hope that in time, the hostile attitude of its partners would lessen and the six could move on; the 2 April meeting highlighted the relative success of this strategy. For Jean-Marc Boegner, French permanent representative to the EEC, the improvement in atmosphere had been progressive, a result of both the five's unwillingness to paralyze the Common Market and France's reassurances that it was committed to developing an outward-looking EEC. Tension did not disappear altogether, but all parties saw benefits in getting back to work.[22]

Similarly, the agreements reached during the 9 May meeting on the Community's future agenda represented another success for France. The Council opted to define the basic elements of the CAP before entering into any negotiation on agriculture in the Kennedy Round framework, rejecting the German-Dutch thesis that advocated simultaneous progress on both fronts. The Council also emphasized the need to reach an agreement on the next three sets of CAP regulations—on beef, rice, and dairy products—by 31 December 1963, rather than Germany's preferred deadline of 1 July 1964.[23] The French had managed to impose their view that the six should first complete the tasks they had set themselves, including implementing the CAP. In the longer term, they counted on the Franco-German axis to stimulate political cooperation within Europe.[24]

Yet, French accomplishments in pushing their economic goals in Europe were not matched by similar achievements in the political sphere. Indeed, the Franco-German Treaty had thrown the U.S. government into a state of panic. Kennedy viewed it as a "very unfriendly act," or evidence that de Gaulle wanted to kick the U.S. out of Europe and break up NATO.[25] It occurred in a context where the American government already felt vulnerable because of the potential monetary power of the Franco-German bloc. Possessing more dollars in reserves than other countries, France and West Germany could potentially expose the U.S.'s monetary weaknesses by running down the American gold supply, thus shaking confidence in the dollar.[26]

All these concerns convinced the U.S. that it needed to immediately neutralize the threat posed by the Franco-German Treaty. Despite the temptation to teach de Gaulle a lesson, the Kennedy administration avoided an open battle with the French president. Washington feared that this would give credence to the General's attacks against the U.S. and adversely affect the unity of the Atlantic Alliance.[27] Additionally, the American government doubted it could really influence Paris's policies. It chose instead to target Bonn, considered the weakest link in the Franco-German axis. In a barely hidden threat, Kennedy warned Adenauer that continuing European hostility might convince the American people and Congress to return to isolationism. The message was unmistakable: if West Germany ratified the Franco-German Treaty in its present form, it would be putting its relations with the U.S. at risk.[28]

Washington's pressure found a receptive audience, since many members of the German political class were very angry about the failure of the U.K.'s application to the EEC. To repair the damage in German-American relations, Schroeder sent Karl Carstens, his secretary of state for foreign affairs, to Washington in early February. Following talks with American officials, Carstens agreed to accompany the ratification of the Franco-German Treaty with a "resolution" of the Bundestag.[29] How the treaty would be affected was not immediately clear, but under the influence of Jean Monnet and Christian Democratic Union (CDU) member Kurt Birrenbach the idea of a preamble quickly gained support.

Adenauer, despite his commitment to the Franco-German Treaty, could not oppose the adoption of a preamble. Having agreed to resign in October 1963, the old chancellor had lost most of his political leverage and despite his best efforts he could not prevent Ludwig Erhard, his minister of finance, from being named his successor.[30] On 16 May 1963, the Bundestag ratified the treaty with a preamble that unambiguously reaffirmed Bonn's loyalty to NATO, the Atlantic Alliance, and the EEC. If France raised no objections to the addition publicly, privately de Gaulle fumed against the preamble for emptying the Franco-German Treaty of its content.[31]

By May 1963, therefore, the considerable tension within the Western world had abated significantly. The preamble had tempered many of the American concerns about the Franco-German Treaty, while the EEC had somewhat recovered from the Brussels split. De Gaulle, for his part, avoided further escalating the situation after the January uproar. Despite strong domestic support for his foreign policy, he was not ready for an all-out offensive against the Anglo-Saxon powers;[32] even had he tried to follow that course, he would have been impeded by urgent domestic problems that were seriously denting his popularity in spring 1963, in particular a large miners' strike.[33]

The progress achieved in the Kennedy Round talks also benefited the Western Alliance. De Gaulle had already dealt a crushing blow to Kennedy's grand design for a partnership between Western Europe and the U.S. By vetoing the U.K.'s entry into the EEC, he had managed to limit the scale of the Kennedy Round and make the "dominant supplier" provision meaningless.[34] Despite that disappointment, the American government wanted to keep the tariff negotiations on track. The U.S. feared that if the Kennedy Round failed and it did not obtain a bigger trade surplus to make up for its balance-of-payments deficit, it would have to cut its economic and military expenditures—i.e., probably reduce the number of American soldiers serving abroad.[35]

France's EEC partners generally supported Kennedy's trade aims, and despite fears to the contrary, France did not categorically oppose the Kennedy Round either. Paris realized that the five's strong attachment to the success of the tariff negotiations—especially Bonn's—could be instrumentalized to obtain compensation on other issues, especially the CAP.[36] The Kennedy Round also forced the EEC states, very divided after the January 1963 crisis, to work toward a common effort in order to conciliate their often diverging interests.[37] For the first time, the six would negotiate as one. Finally, the Kennedy Round was not incompatible with the larger French goal of balancing transatlantic relations, as long as the EEC received fair benefits.

In order to ensure that balance, France wanted the Community to adopt the following three main principles in the negotiations: "a) while accepting a linear reduction of tariffs, we [the EEC] have to look for ways to guarantee a strict reciprocity and removal of excessive differences; b) non-tariff elements of protection should be included in negotiations; c) and in the agricultural field, we need a synchronization between the work of the six in Brussels and the Geneva talks."[38] Not only did Paris convince its European partners on agriculture, but it also made inroads on the question of tariff disparities. Speaking to U.S. officials, Belgian Foreign Minister Paul-Henri Spaak "confessed that he was personally impressed by the arguments put forward by France that our equilinear approach did not in itself represent an entirely satisfactory or equitable solution for the high-tariffs problem."[39] Since the U.S. and the U.K. had far more very high rates than the Community, the latter argued that these high tariffs would remain protective even after being cut in half, whereas the Community's moderate tariffs would be reduced to impotence.

Indeed, the French appealed to legitimate concerns of the EEC members over the tariff-cutting formula. If the Community seemed to accept the procedural implications of linear tariff reductions, "they would not trust them to produce the kind of reciprocity they had sought in past negotiations and still continued to seek"; the EEC instead suggested a formula for automatic and unequal cuts.[40] When it came to adopting its positions for the industrial component of the Kennedy Round on 9 May, the Council eventually settled on principles that fitted nicely with the three aims the French were hoping to achieve with the tariff negotiations.[41]

After intense discussions during the 16–21 May Kennedy Round ministerial meeting in Geneva, the goodwill among all parties involved helped facilitate a breakthrough. Noticeable differences remained between the various parties, with the talks over agriculture deadlocked. But thanks to postponement and ambiguity, the ministers agreed that "in those cases where there are significant disparities in tariff levels, the tariff reductions will be based upon special rules of general and automatic application."[42] The battle over tariff disparities was not over, but the negotiations in this rule-making stage could now move forward before the planned official opening of the Kennedy Round in May 1964.

June 1963–July 1964: The Rise and Fall of the Western Strategy

As the crisis abated by mid June 1963, de Gaulle pursued his ambitious foreign policy agenda amid a calmer atmosphere, which meant first and foremost focusing on Western matters. Despite misgivings about the preamble added to the Franco-German Treaty, the General's core strategy remained the development of an independent Western Europe centered on the Franco-German axis. A more assertive Western European organization could, as a first step, help place transatlantic relations on a more equal footing; later, if the Soviet Union evolved enough, it could then aim to establish a new East-West equilibrium in Europe.[43]

The focus on a Western European organization went hand-in-hand with France protecting its independence. By resorting to spectacular initiatives, France knew it could strengthen its claim to Great Power status and provide a model for other countries to follow. As Couve de Murville explained, France could not only speak in Europe with great authority, but could show that solidarity with the U.S. did not equate with systematic alignment.[44] Yet, as long as France prioritized its Western European strategy, it did show restraint and only acted unilaterally in domains in which it believed it could not compromise—specifically nuclear and defense questions.

Thus, Paris refused to be bound by the Partial Test Ban Treaty (PTBT), which was first signed by the U.K., the U.S., and the Soviet Union on 5 August, and which banned all above-ground nuclear tests. Had they signed and forgone additional tests, French leaders would have jeopardized the development of an autonomous nuclear arsenal, which they considered to be the core element of their policy of independence.[45] Failure to develop an adequate deterrent, as long as the Soviet Union posed a threat, would mean "attracting thunder while not being protected," and entrusting France's survival to a "foreign protectorate"—a veiled attack from de Gaulle against the presence of American troops on French soil—that could not necessarily protect it adequately.[46]

The force de frappe, therefore, could defend the French territory in case of a Soviet invasion, but also compel the U.S.—still the only plausible defender of Western Europe—to react before it was too late.[47] This latter concern drove France in autumn 1963 to block attempts by the Atlantic Alliance to adopt flexible response as its new nuclear strategy.[48] French leaders not only feared that flexible response might "gravely undermine" the Alliance's deterrent effect, as the Soviet Union would interpret it as hesitation to use nuclear weapons, but also that the Americans might hide behind flexible response in order to determine their engagement according to their own interest.[49] For de Gaulle, this clear difference in strategy did not automatically invalidate the alliance with the U.S., but it certainly made "integration" within NATO even more unjustifiable.[50]

Consequently, French leaders pursued the policy initiated in 1959, with the withdrawal of its Mediterranean fleet, of reclaiming national control over their armed forces, since they believed that a national community needed to be in charge of its own defense in order to keep control of its fate.[51] On 21 June 1963, Paris announced the withdrawal of its Atlantic fleet from NATO, and on 4 March 1964, de Gaulle decided that French naval ships would no longer be under the organization's command.[52] Both actions aimed to safeguard France's autonomy of action, a vital component in its quest for Great Power status. But they were also a sign, as Jean de la Grandville, head of the Quai d'Orsay's Service des Pactes, confided to U.K. officials, that the General's attitude was hardening as he prepared France for a complete break with NATO.[53] The French president was undoubtedly the driving force behind this incremental withdrawal, and neither Couve de Murville nor the French navy managed to soften his instructions regarding the role of French ships within NATO.[54]

Despite this animosity against NATO and integration, French leaders still sought to avoid a major public "conflict" with the organization. In part, this reflected their desire not to alienate their main allies, especially Bonn. De Gaulle reminded Adenauer that a future reform of NATO might be possible one day if European cooperation developed sufficiently, but "for the moment there is no alternative to US omnipotence."[55] NATO was simply not ripe for reform, Couve de Murville hinted to Kennedy in October 1963: "NATO, as it is now, corresponds less and less to realities. Western Europe needs a bigger share of responsibilities." However, he also added that it was preferable to "leave the situation as it is and not talk about it."[56] France saw no reason to shift its aloof attitude toward NATO.

At the same time, the unwillingness to start an open confrontation within NATO reflected tactical considerations. During the mid May 1964 ministerial meeting in The Hague, Couve de Murville did not deny that a split existed between France and its allies in regard to NATO reforms. While France wanted more military freedom, other members called for more integration. He concluded, nonetheless, that it would be vain to open a debate about the future of the Atlantic Alliance, considering the irreconcilable differences among the various parties.[57] As Spaak later surmised, the French foreign minister avoided all controversial questions during this meeting, because maintaining mystery about France's intentions would better serve its long-term goals toward NATO.[58]

The restraint France showed toward NATO also applied to other transatlantic domains, as it sought to place U.S.-European relations on a more equal footing. This applied first to the tariff negotiations, which progressed smoothly between mid 1963 and May 1964. The debate over tariff disparities was shelved when all parties agreed to disagree on the subject.[59] Moreover, thanks to a generalized desire to avoid confrontations, the formal opening of the Kennedy Round on 4 May 1964 proved a relaxed affair. All participants agreed unanimously on two important points: adopting

50 percent linear cuts as a working hypothesis and setting 10 September as a deadline to table exception lists—or items not subject to a 50 percent cut.[60]

France played its part in this breakthrough by showing goodwill during negotiations, which reflected the parallel achievements regarding the CAP. At the same time, de Gaulle still feared that a Western Europe without a common tariff might invite an invasion of U.S. products.[61] This only reinforced the need for the six to maintain their cohesion, so as to ensure that they received adequate benefits in the Kennedy Round negotiations.[62] Yet, despite the General's concerns, no evidence surfaced that Paris was seeking to turn the EEC into an autarkic community. As Emile Noël, the European Commission's executive secretary, confirmed to American officials, the French negotiators showed no desire to torpedo the tariff negotiations, although he felt this could change if future CAP talks faltered.[63]

Progress in the Kennedy Round talks coincided with intensifying discussions regarding the international monetary system. As Margaret de Vries argues, by spring 1963, most central bankers and monetary officials had begun to seriously question whether the world's supply of liquidity would remain sufficient, especially as the world economy expanded further. Two important developments had brought about a heightened interest in the liquidity problem. Official reserves of International Monetary Fund (IMF) members had not grown in 1962, as opposed to the previous three years, and central bankers along with financial officials understood that a successful American effort to reduce the country's balance-of-payments deficit would cause a slowdown in the growth of world reserves.[64]

As quoted by Susan Strange, this prompted Kennedy to mention, in a message to Congress on 18 July 1963, that the U.S. would "continue to study and discuss with other countries measures which might be taken for a further strengthening of the IMS over the longer run." He feared the "growth of international liquidity to finance expanding world trade," and the fact that the closing of the deficit would "cut down our provision of dollars to the rest of the world."[65] This statement indicated a clear shift in U.S. policy toward considering reform, which was caused partly by the persistence of the payments figures and by the influence of a Brookings Institute report.

Commissioned by the government, the report, published in July 1963, provided a long-term study of the U.S. balance-of-payments situation that foresaw a continuation of the U.S. deficit until 1968. The authors also concluded that closing the deficit could lead to a liquidity shortage and world deflation unless prompt action was taken. The Europeans, dismayed by the prospect of a continued outflow of dollars from the U.S., were also pushing for a better balanced and more effectively managed system.[66]

De Gaulle shared this concern about the running of the international monetary system and the role of the dollar. As he told Peyrefitte on 27 February 1963, "US imperialism, no field can escape it. It takes all forms, but the most insidious one is the dollar ... Luckily, we prevented the UK from joining the EEC. If not, American investments in the UK would have multiplied. It would have been the bridgehead of the American invasion of capital in Europe." He added to Peyrefitte on 30 April that "the Americans are engaged in a process of dominance of all the political, financial, economic and military circuits. ... That is why we must create the irreversible. The irreversible, for currencies, would be the gold standard."[67] The General, however, kept these harsh words about the U.S. and the dollar private.

His discretion reflected his lack of expertise in the monetary field, and in fact he only slowly developed firm views on the subject.[68] It also reflected his awareness of the strong divisions within the French government. Jacques Rueff, the influential economic adviser to de Gaulle, had for long argued to the president about the need for a deep reform of the Bretton Woods system.[69] Rueff could count on the support of Couve de Murville, a close friend since the 1930s when Couve de Murville was Rueff's protégé in the finance ministry.[70] Both men pushed the General to challenge the Bretton Woods status quo: Couve de Murville called for an increase in the price of gold, whereas Rueff wanted France to convert its dollar reserves into gold so as to indicate his displeasure with American abuses of the reserve-currency system. Pompidou and Finance Minister Valéry Giscard d'Estaing, however, clearly disagreed. They believed that the French national interest lied in stabilizing the existing international monetary situation.[71] In the short term, Giscard and Pompidou's line prevailed, convincing the president that the time was not right to denounce the international monetary system.[72]

This allowed Giscard to present a less confrontational line at the annual IMF meeting. On the one hand, he did underline the structural weaknesses of the international monetary system, including the lack of mechanisms to correct balance-of-payments deficits and the asymmetry between the reserve-currency countries and the rest of the world. On the other hand, he also declared his country's readiness to help improve the system, including supporting increased liquidity should developments in world trade make this necessary.[73] The goodwill at the meeting enabled the ministers and governors of the Group of Ten (G10)—a select group of eleven IMF states comprising the U.S., Canada, West Germany, Japan, Italy, France, the U.K., Switzerland, Sweden, the Netherlands, and Belgium—to agree that their deputies should "undertake a thorough examination of the outlook for the functioning of the international monetary system and of its probable future needs for liquidity."[74] In parallel, the IMF staff decided to pursue a similar study.

Robert Roosa, U.S. Under Secretary of Treasury, chaired the G10 meetings between November 1963 and June 1964. The deputies exchanged views on the international monetary system in a conciliatory manner, with the French and American representatives defending opposite views and other deputies falling somewhere in the middle.[75] The goodwill could not altogether hide the two main disagreements within the group: should liquidity be increased or not? And if so, who should exercise control over the process? While Roosa argued that a greater use of credit facilities would probably be necessary in the future and pointed to the IMF as a potential forum, the Europeans were reluctant to grant the power to create and allocate a new reserve asset—or form of international money—to the U.S.-dominated Fund. They favored instead a new system of rules that could be operated automatically.

The discussions revealed two clashing conceptions of monetary affairs. The French underlined the fundamental equality of states' rights and duties in the international system. No one had a divine right to a deficit. The opposite view, defended by the U.S., could be called the "center country" view. It argued that the state with the dominant national economy in the system could not be treated in the same way as other countries.[76]

Considering the existing divergences, the talks ended unsurprisingly with a compromise report presented by the deputies to their ministers in mid June 1964. Published two months later, it essentially defended the international monetary system and argued that the current stocks of gold and reserve currencies could cover liquidity needs. However, it also pointed out that future growth in world trade and payments would increase demand for liquidities, which could be covered either by expanding credit facilities or by establishing new reserve instruments. Since both proposals raised complex questions, Rinaldo Ossola, of the Bank of Italy, was asked to chair another group to examine the different options.[77] Even though the French criticisms of the international monetary system had been softened in the report thanks to Anglo-Saxon pressures, de Gaulle found the compromise acceptable during an Inner Council meeting on 9 June.[78]

Overall, Paris performed a balancing act in regard to transatlantic relations. It remained cooperative in the monetary and tariff fields, avoiding obvious challenges against American leadership for fear of alienating its European partners. Concurrently, French leaders encouraged their Western European counterparts to act more assertively so as to push the U.S. to transform its "leadership" into a more equal "partnership." While French leaders felt this evolution would surely occur, they acknowledged that it would happen over a long period of time.[79] Only by achieving European economic and political unity could they guarantee such an outcome.

Indeed, consolidating the EEC remained a vital focus of France's Western strategy. This meant first that the six had to complete their economic union before they could deal with military matters, political cooperation, and trade relations with the rest of the world.[80] It also implied moving forward on the CAP and making sure that Paris's partners respected the deadline of 31 December 1963 for comprehensive agricultural agreements. Unfortunately, this required overcoming a fierce German resistance to the CAP, which escalated in the weeks after the 9 May 1963 agreement.[81] Bonn disliked the CAP because it would compel Germany to buy EEC goods at prices that were more expensive than those outside the Community, and they approached the CAP believing that de Gaulle might block the Kennedy Round. In other words, the CAP was an important lever for the Germans.[82]

The General opted to confront his German partners during the Franco-German summit in July 1963, as he wanted to show that the Franco-German entente would be meaningless unless both countries could overcome their differences at the Community level.[83] At the summit, French leaders adopted a mixed strategy that included both pressuring Bonn on the CAP and expressing empathy with its position. Thus, de Gaulle accused Bonn of not really wanting to complete the Common Market. Couve de Murville, for his part, cajoled his counterparts when he agreed with the West Germans that they could not accept exaggerated sacrifices. He also reminded his counterparts that completing the CAP was vital for any common trade policy, and a prerequisite for the Kennedy Round talks.[84]

Neither de Gaulle's nor Couve de Murville's approach proved successful. Bonn distrusted Paris and doubted its commitment to the Kennedy Round. The July meeting achieved little, as the German government stuck to its positions. The German government complained about the inherent flaws of the CAP, including how it would affect its trade with the outside world, and wanted the EEC to agree first on a common position for the upcoming Kennedy Round. France's response to this deadlock was swift and threatening. In his press conference of 29 July 1963, de Gaulle reminded all that France considered an agreement on the CAP to be essential for its agricultural interests and for the upcoming tariff negotiations with the U.S. Failure to respect the self-imposed deadlines could cause the Common Market to completely disappear. The General then added that success in the economic field could significantly increase the chances of developing a common European policy, which was particularly key since the Anglo-Saxon powers were negotiating with the Soviet Union over vital nuclear issues that involved the fate of Western Europe.[85]

For the rest of 1963, French leaders stuck to their hard line according to which the Common Market could only survive if the six respected their deadlines. De Gaulle repeatedly dropped hints that France could live without the Common Market.[86] This amounted more, however, to brinkmanship tactics than a genuine threat. If Paris sometimes feigned indifference toward the Common Market, privately it remained strongly committed to its completion. Therefore, the French president still showed flexibility in his attempt to win over the West Germans. He accepted the possibility of a temporary solution for grain prices, so long as Germany agreed to reach an agreement for the other three settlements by the end-of-year deadline.[87]

Even in late December, France was still working hard toward a solution. Meeting Manfred Klaiber, West German ambassador in Paris, on 21 December, de Gaulle again hinted that France could live without the Common Market. He also confronted the West Germans and questioned their commitment to the EEC. He mentioned that France had compromised on the Kennedy Round and added that doing the same for the European Community would not mean Bonn had capitulated.[88]

French cajoling and pressuring played an important role, but in the end Sicco Mansholt, the European Commissioner responsible for agriculture, helped break the deadlock with his plan presented on 5 November 1963. Attempting to resolve both the Community's internal and its external problems, Mansholt put forward three main proposals to the member-states: selecting 1 July 1964 as the deadline to agree on a common set of grain prices; the main lines of the EEC's agricultural offer in the Kennedy Round; and a Community position on disparities in industrial tariffs for the Kennedy Round.[89]

This plan convinced Bonn to compromise on the three outstanding CAP regulations—regarding beef, rice, and dairy products. Not only was the West German government isolated on this issue, but it also realized that the Mansholt Plan, especially on grain prices, presented a graver threat.[90] On 23 December, the six reached a package deal for the CAP and the Kennedy Round, while agreement on a common price for grains was postponed. The French were thrilled, with Boegner convinced that "the December 23 deal has erased the immediate consequences of the crisis caused by the breaking off of negotiations with the UK."[91]

De Gaulle welcomed the 23 December agreement as significant for the EEC, but he did not lose sight of his larger objectives. As he reminded his European partners in his press conference of 31 January 1964, failure to complete the other elements of the CAP would lead his country to "reclaim its freedom." The General also drew attention to the more important tasks that could lie ahead once the six accomplished their economic goals. These would include negotiations with other states—especially the U.S.—and the vital question of political cooperation, as long as it did not involve subordination to a wider Atlantic framework or supranational integration.[92] French leaders remained committed to the principle of European political unity, which had essentially meant Franco-German cooperation since the failure of the Fouchet Plan two years earlier.

Fulfilling the potential of the Franco-German partnership, or turning it into the nucleus of a more independent Western Europe, remained the cornerstone of de Gaulle's Western strategy in this period. Undoubtedly, the preamble and the early efforts to consolidate Franco-German cooperation had disappointed the General,[93] but it is easy to overstate the preamble's immediate impact. It hardly constituted a complete turning point for French foreign policy. Georges-Henri Soutou seems closer to the mark when he argues that the failures of the Franco-German Treaty did not become immediately apparent to the French leaders.[94] Despite initial misgivings, de Gaulle continued to place high hopes on the Franco-German partnership.

Paris's restraint in transatlantic and European relations and its unwillingness to openly challenge Washington stemmed from its efforts to avoid alienating Bonn. French leaders resented the fact that their German partners had apologized to the U.S. so soon after the signing of the Franco-German Treaty.[95] Equally, de Gaulle had sent a clear warning to Bonn by deciding to withdraw France's Atlantic fleet from NATO without prior consultation, a mere four days before Kennedy's triumphant visit to West Berlin in late June 1963.[96] Yet, as long as Paris remained committed to Franco-German cooperation, it sought to avoid giving the impression that it was fighting Washington over Bonn's loyalty.

Privately, de Gaulle reassured Adenauer that he was not hostile to the U.S., and later—during a talk with Adenauer's successor Erhard—dismissed as a "bad joke" the idea that Bonn had to choose between Paris and Washington.[97] At the same time, Couve de Murville agreed with U.S. officials that Bonn could easily maintain good relations with both Paris and Washington.[98] France wanted to play down its conflict with the U.S., while not necessarily ignoring all existing problems. During his press conference of 29 July 1963, the General pointed out that while changes in France's political, economic, and military situation had affected Franco-American relations, they certainly had not undermined the alliance between the two countries.[99]

In the short term, moreover, France had no incentive to force West Germany to make a choice between its two key allies. The change of leadership in autumn 1963 in both West Germany and the U.S.—Erhard succeeding Adenauer as chancellor and Lyndon Johnson replacing Kennedy after the latter's assassination—had naturally created uncertainty with regard to both countries' future policies. If de Gaulle did not think much of the new American president, he believed that Erhard's pro-American inclination could be reversed.[100]

Nonetheless, these private and public reassurances could not hide the fact that the U.S. and France remained suspicious of each other's intentions with regard to West Germany. De Gaulle could dismiss the competition as a "bad joke" in front of Erhard, but he still entertained the hope that Bonn would eventually side with Paris rather than Washington. As he confided to Peyrefitte: "It is important for West Germany to understand that its destiny is Europe, and Europe is mainly its union with France."[101]

Moreover, West Germany's failure to tilt in France's direction eventually caused a serious confrontation. Tension had been slowly simmering between both countries ever since they had signed the Treaty in January 1963. Within the Treaty's first year, the preamble, France's withdrawal of its Atlantic fleet from NATO, Kennedy's triumphant visit to West Berlin, and tough negotiations over the EEC and the Kennedy Round had all dampened enthusiasm for the Treaty, including within German public opinion.[102] Differences persisted throughout the first half of 1964 thanks to France's unilateral recognition of communist China and the Argoud affair. In the latter case, French secret services had kidnapped a member of the Organisation de l'Armée Secrète (OAS)—who had been involved in assassination attempts against de Gaulle but was roaming free in West Germany—without informing the relevant West German authorities.

These episodes combined to undermine confidence in the Treaty's usefulness. In West Germany, any hope that the Treaty could act as a restraint on French foreign policy appeared more and more illusory. As Secretary to the Chancellery Ludger Westrick complained to Roland de Margerie, French ambassador in Bonn, Paris's unilateral decision to recognize the People's Republic of China (PRC) had only made life more difficult for the German "Gaullists" who advocated closer cooperation with France.[103] De Gaulle, similarly, voiced his concerns when he spoke of "trying to give a new basis to our relations with Germany" during a speech on 31 December 1963. While they felt the Treaty worked with regard to procedures and holding regular meetings, French officials were convinced it could have worked better if Bonn had not constantly looked toward Washington.[104]

This was the heart of the problem for the French. In all fields, American influence presented an insurmountable obstacle for the closer cooperation that the French aspired to with their German neighbor. This was true for defense, where projects to develop and build common weapons, such as tanks, and to establish common strategic and tactical concepts faltered quickly. Undoubtedly, the significant arms deal Kaï-Uwe von Hassel, the

German defense minister, signed—without consulting the French—in August 1963 with his American counterpart Robert McNamara, did very little to help Franco-German military cooperation.[105]

Moreover, while de Gaulle questioned America's commitment to defend Western Europe in case of a Soviet aggression, Erhard had total faith in the U.S. nuclear umbrella.[106] The Franco-German divergence became more pronounced once Erhard became chancellor in 1963. Taking a more independent stance toward de Gaulle, the new chancellor quickly moved to strengthen relations with the U.S. and increasingly based his political fortunes on the assumed steadfastness of the American commitment in Europe. He promised his American partners several times that his government accepted full offset for American troops stationed in Germany, despite the concerns of his officials.[107]

Differences in policies highlighted the lack of individual chemistry between the new German leader and de Gaulle. As Schoenborn argues, the new chancellor Erhard felt closer politically to Lyndon Johnson than he did to de Gaulle. Erhard had no real affinity with France, and his economic philosophy drove him to be very critical of the French statist model in effect since World War II. The German chancellor did not share Adenauer's attachment to the historical and political significance of Franco-German friendship, nor to de Gaulle's European discourse.[108] On a personal level, Erhard found it hard to connect with the General. The pragmatic West German chancellor was often exasperated by the cryptic French president, while the latter never viewed his counterpart as a true leader.[109] Since Erhard had clearly chosen Washington over Paris, a crisis appeared inevitable.

When a clash occurred, it was, surprisingly, triggered by Vietnam—as yet only a marginal concern for Bonn—rather than over European issues.[110] On 12 June 1964, a few days after Schroeder had mentioned Bonn's lack of interest in the situation in Indochina to Couve de Murville, Erhard offered U.S. President Johnson full support for the war effort in Vietnam.[111] According to Klaiber, de Gaulle viewed Erhard's statement as a "slap in the face" and further proof of Bonn's inability to stand up to the U.S. on any issue at all.[112]

If Bonn could not show independence from Washington on an issue marginal to German interests like Vietnam, how could it cooperate closely with France on more significant matters? Disappointed by West Germany's excessive friendliness toward the U.S. and the fact that "they [Germans] do not want it [the Franco-German Treaty] to be a treaty of friendship and cooperation," de Gaulle chose to confront the German chancellor during the 3–4 July summit in Bonn.[113]

The General's first meeting with his German counterpart set the tone for the following discussions. After announcing "he had no illusions regarding the results of this meeting with West Germany," he presented Bonn with a clear choice: "either you [West Germany] follow a policy subordinated to the US or you adopt a policy that is European and independent of the US, but not hostile to them."[114] Erhard and his colleagues, unsurprisingly, rejected the French president's ultimatum by pledging total loyalty to Washington. After that, French leaders spared no efforts to convey their irritation toward their German counterparts and displayed none of the diplomatic restraint normally exhibited at these summits. They also abandoned their moderate stance toward the U.S. and showed little flexibility on the project of a European political union, despite the fact it was a subject close to Erhard's heart.[115]

The summit ended in failure, as de Gaulle expected.[116] If he still hoped that Bonn would eventually adopt France's independent stand in the long run, he could see no such possibility as long as Erhard remained chancellor. The French government had hoped that the January 1963 Treaty could foster a common European policy, which could serve as a model for other EEC states and provide the basis for an independent Western Europe. Yet, the previous eighteen months had confirmed that Bonn had not adopted the Treaty in the same spirit and, instead of working toward a united Europe, had chosen to side with Washington. The consequences were very clear for Couve de Murville. Without a common European policy, there was no prospect of reforming the Western alliance and therefore no more reason for France to tolerate integration into NATO.[117]

July–December 1964: Toward a New Strategy

The July 1964 Bonn summit proved a major disappointment for de Gaulle, as he bitterly acknowledged: "West Germany is an American protectorate in political, military and economic terms. There is no way of developing a common Franco-German policy."[118] The shortcomings of the Franco-German partnership undermined immediate hopes of establishing a more independent Western Europe and reforming transatlantic relations, although the General did not abandon these objectives altogether in the long term.

Furthermore, the failures of the Treaty forced de Gaulle to reconsider his grand strategy, since he had previously set relations with West Germany as the cornerstone of his foreign policy. While a new cornerstone did not become immediately clear, Paris certainly wasted no time in modifying its relations with its neighbor. No longer compelled to appease Bonn, Paris instead focused on protecting its independence and promoting its claim to Great Power status. French leaders still supported cooperation with West

Germany, especially when it came to finalizing the CAP, but they no longer considered the Treaty a priority of French foreign policy.

Relations further deteriorated between Paris and Bonn in the aftermath of the July summit, especially after de Gaulle's press conference of 23 July 1964. After referring to the "minor successes" of the Franco-German Treaty, the president listed the numerous areas where both states had failed to agree on a common policy.[119] The German government firmly rejected these criticisms. In response to the press conference, Schroeder reminded his French counterparts that Bonn had not signed the treaty to "adopt France's policy."[120] Relations had thus reached a stalemate, with each side blaming the other for the existing tensions.

In turn, Bonn's subservience to Washington also hardened Paris's attitude toward the U.S. As de Gaulle complained to Hervé Alphand, his ambassador in Washington, "… the Americans have to realize they are not the dictators of Western Europe. It is clear for France, but others will surely follow, even if they do not seem to for the moment."[121] Until that happened, France increasingly sought to underline its independence vis-à-vis the U.S., starting with pressure against NATO: "the Americans have to leave France.… Not a single American uniform must remain," de Gaulle privately confided to Peyrefitte just a few days after the July Franco-German summit.[122]

Moreover, France began to vocalize its hardening stance toward the Atlantic organization. During a meeting with Manlio Brosio, the new secretary-general of NATO, de Gaulle forcefully rejected integration as obsolete, and hinted that it would no longer apply to his country by 1969 — the year when member-states could theoretically denounce the April 1949 North Atlantic Treaty.[123] News of the discussion filtered through to Charles Bohlen, U.S. ambassador in Paris, who considered it far more brutal and specific than any previous de Gaulle statements on the subject; he also believed the French president wanted to send a clear message to his allies, since he knew Brosio would repeat the content of their talk.[124]

The relative failure of the Franco-German Treaty thus drove France to adopt a more independent and confrontational stance toward Washington and Bonn, but only after autumn 1964 did France make significant changes to its Western strategy, as a consequence of a sharp dispute with its allies. Tension erupted when the fates of a series of unrelated negotiations, that is to say over the MLF, the CAP, and the German plans to relaunch talks on European political union, became closely intertwined.

The MLF had received renewed support from the U.S. administration in spring 1964, and especially from its more "Europeanist" members like George Ball, the under secretary of state for European affairs. Ball believed the MLF presented multiple advantages. Aside from granting West Germany a legitimate role in the Alliance's defense, albeit "on a leash," it also provided "an Atlantic solution to the problem of the nuclear defense of the West" and weakened "French and British determination to hold on to their national nuclear establishments."[125] Erhard committed enthusiastically to this project, and after meeting Lyndon Johnson on 12 June 1964, both pledged to reach an agreement on the MLF by the end of the year. During an interview on 6 October, Erhard went a step further when he publicly mentioned the possibility of a German-U.S. bilateral agreement over the MLF.[126]

In parallel to these nuclear developments, the West German government outlined its plan for European political cooperation on 4 November. The proposal listed several stages and involved the establishment of a consultative commission to help governments.[127] Bonn's willingness to advance political union stood in stark contrast to its obstructive policies toward the CAP. Despite the European Commission's repeated pressure, backed by France and the Netherlands, West Germany steadfastly refused to agree on a common price for grains throughout 1964, speaking instead of postponement until the following year. Since it feared hurting the income of its farmers before the parliamentary elections of 1965, the Bonn government saw no reason to hurry.[128]

France responded forcefully to Bonn's delay tactics. On 21 October, reverting to the brinkmanship tactics adopted the previous year, Peyrefitte issued a firm warning to France's partners in an official communiqué: "The president and the French government stressed that France would cease to participate in the EEC if the agricultural market was not organized as had been previously agreed." He further added, "France maintains in this regard the position it has always taken. There is no possibility of negotiating usefully with the US as long as the EEC—including agriculture—is not completely organized and this will not be the case as long as the Common Market for agriculture is not established."[129] To convey its seriousness, France made sure to link the CAP with other key issues besides the Kennedy Round.

As it raised the stakes over the CAP, Paris also launched a major offensive against the MLF. Previously, French officials had barely objected to the nuclear project because they felt that it had little support among NATO members.[130] Once it became a concrete possibility, however, they stepped up their opposition to the MLF.[131] Moreover, once de Gaulle returned from his month long trip to Latin America in mid October, his advisors immediately informed him of the latest developments in the MLF negotiations. Describing the force as an American tool to "block French diplomacy," they pushed the president to address this issue on the political level; failure to do so would mean France "accepted the indefinite postponement of a political Europe in line with its views, and the supremacy of the US in Western Europe."[132]

Spurred by this argument, de Gaulle and his colleagues immediately attacked the MLF by specifically targeting their German partners. During a meeting with Secretary of State for Foreign Affairs Karl Carstens, Couve de Murville tied the European political project to the CAP and the MLF. A European political union required prior agreement on aims and policy, but the discussions on the nuclear force confirmed the lack of such accord; how could the six agree on a political organization if they could not agree on the economic bases of the Common Market?[133] Pompidou ratcheted up the pressure when he claimed, in early November 1964, that the MLF would not be compatible with the Franco-German Treaty.[134] This tense atmosphere in fall 1964 appeared to echo that of January 1963, as Olivier Wormser, head of the Quai's Direction Economique, pointed out to American officials.[135]

France's offensive also reflected a growing mistrust of the U.S. and increasingly interpreted the events of October and November as part of a wider Franco-American struggle over the future of the Western world. Wormser believed that the Americans were clearly undermining the CAP by insisting to the Germans that they did not consider the common price of grains to be important for the Kennedy Round;[136] these agricultural questions appeared to represent an "open and resolute conflict between France and the US."[137] In the same way, Paris denounced the MLF, like the Kennedy Round, as an American weapon aiming to divide Europe.[138] France also resented the MLF since it would allow West Germany to indirectly possess nuclear weapons, thereby threatening France's status as the sole country possessing nuclear weapons among the six.[139]

Eventually, the October–November turmoil petered out quickly. Strong pressure from the Commission and its partners forced West Germany to accept a common price for grains.[140] This in turn facilitated progress on the Kennedy Round: on 16 November, sixteen countries, including the U.S., Japan, the six, and the seven members of the European Free Trade Association, submitted their exceptions list to an otherwise across-the-board cut to industrial tariffs.[141] As for the MLF, American interest in the project faded in late November. Noting the swelling opposition both at home and abroad, President Johnson acknowledged: "I worked like hell to get to be president and I don't want to set it off all at once … If we're inciting the Russians, if we've set de Gaulle on fire … if we're forcing the British and not satisfying the Germans, and only getting thirty votes in the Senate — then the hell with it."[142]

The crisis faded quickly but its consequences proved far-reaching. Strong German resistance made France even more determined to finalize the establishment of the CAP by reaching a quick agreement on the financial settlement, the last step required for its implementation. Achieving that outcome, however, would be challenging considering the deteriorating atmosphere within the European Community. Both the Commission and France's partners expected future compensation in exchange for the agreement on grain prices. In particular, the Erhard government felt it had made great sacrifices, and expected concessions in other domains, noticeably with regard to its plan for political union.[143] Bonn was effectively less likely to compromise on the CAP, and its disappointment over Paris's opposition to the MLF hardly helped. Thus, the margin for agreement in future EEC discussions had dangerously narrowed.

Furthermore, the events in the autumn dramatically affected France's Western strategy. They confirmed to French officials the shortcomings of Franco-German cooperation stemming from Bonn's constant subservience to the U.S., much to de Gaulle's chagrin.[144] They also caused a serious deterioration in Franco-American relations. While these had been poor to start with, French leaders believed they now faced a different challenge: with the MLF, it seemed that the American government was trying to create a firm German-American axis, which would forever prevent the emergence of a more independent Western Europe.[145]

The consequences for France's Western strategy—and for its policy toward the Soviet Union, as will be outlined in the next chapter—proved fundamental. Completing its economic goals in Europe and preserving its independence remained important, but France's priority shifted toward systematically challenging U.S. leadership within the Western world, starting with NATO. Thus, de Gaulle wanted to accelerate the timing for withdrawal, and he now privately hinted at making a move in 1967, instead of 1969.[146] Disappointed by the unwillingness of his European partners, especially West Germany, to stand up to the U.S., the General hoped France could act as a trailblazer and shatter the notion of a necessary European dependence on its powerful ally: "between us and the Americans, behind the courteous conversations, it is a struggle. We are the only ones resisting," he confided to Peyrefitte.[147]

January–December 1965: Challenging America

On 31 December 1964, de Gaulle announced to his compatriots his determination to protect France's independence and reject "all systems which ... would hold us under the hegemony that we know."[148] Throughout 1965, the French president would engage in a systematic challenge against America's political, economic, and military leadership in the Western world, at a time when the Johnson administration was dramatically escalating the country's involvement in Vietnam. Public opinion in France largely supported this new direction for French foreign policy, as well as de Gaulle's attitude toward the U.S.[149]

Fireworks first surfaced in the monetary field, where the fragile compromise of mid 1964 progressively unraveled because of the growing political and economic differences between France and its Anglo-Saxon partners. The two sides disagreed on the question of international liquidity. Whereas the U.K. and the U.S. sought to create more liquidity, France wanted to establish a system of sound international finance and focused on the dangers of European inflation resulting from the American balance-of-payments deficit. Politically, France wanted to enlarge its own role in monetary affairs but distrusted international organizations, while the U.S. wanted to improve the IMF mechanisms.[150]

By the 1964 annual IMF meeting in September in Tokyo, the fundamental argument over who should control any new reserve asset had come to the fore. Many European states, including the Netherlands and France, wanted a restricted group—such as the G10—to be in charge rather than the IMF.[151] Giscard also used his platform to attack the Bretton Woods system for its inflationist tendencies and for its lack of a corrective mechanism for the deficits of the reserve-currency states. He suggested instead an international monetary system organized in concentric circles, with gold at the heart of international payments.[152]

Douglas Dillon, U.S. secretary of the treasury, rejected Giscard's criticisms and supported the IMF plan to increase national quotas within the organization so as to solve the liquidity problem for the next few years. Paris opposed such a quota increase because it would remove some of the pressure on the U.S. currency by allowing IMF members to pay in dollars. Despite its opposition, France could not stop the adoption of the plan advocating a 25 percent quota in early 1965. The battle lines were now clearly drawn, with France keen to see gold replace the dollar as the cornerstone of the monetary system and the Anglo-Saxon powers defending the existing organization.[153]

Developments in late 1964 only reinforced Paris's objections, as explained by de Vries. The U.S. balance of payments had, in early 1964, moved closer to equilibrium for the first time since 1961. By the end of the year, however, the U.K.'s balance of payments was facing a setback, the American account showed a sizeable deficit, and the combined balance of payments of the EEC states displayed a large overall surplus.[154] The context thus appeared favorable for a more forceful French stance in monetary matters, especially as France now possessed the means to adopt such a stance: its economy was growing faster than those of its main Western partners, and its dollar reserves had increased by $5 billion between 1959 and 1963.[155] Moreover, de Gaulle, prompted by Rueff, also blamed the international monetary system for France's inability to control domestic inflation and for helping U.S. multinationals buy French assets—such as computer manufacturer Bull—which he viewed as another form of imperialism.[156] The press conference on 4 February 1965 provided de Gaulle with the perfect platform to go on the offensive.

Throughout his speech, the French president denounced the Bretton Woods dollar-centered system in an eloquent manner. Not only did it no longer fit the current situation—if the U.S. possessed most of the world's gold reserves after World War II, by 1965, the six's total gold reserves nearly matched those of the Americans—but the dollar's special status granted the U.S. unfair privileges. It could run balance-of-payments deficits with impunity and export its inflation abroad, while all other states needed to rigorously maintain their economic equilibrium.[157] The only alternative solution was to establish a system in which international exchanges would be tied to gold, "a monetary basis that is not controversial and bears the sign of no country in particular."[158]

De Gaulle was moving closer to Rueff's ideas. But, as David Calleo argues, a system centered on gold also appealed to him because it mirrored the requirements of a healthy international order, meaning a multipolar world system based on interdependence without hegemony, where everyone obeys the same rules.[159] Additionally, the General realized that through his very public and political denunciation of the dollar and Washington's monetary predominance, he could promote French independence and place his country at the forefront of the debate about the international monetary system. Self-assured, he had outlined his main principles and announced a very public program to convert most of France's dollar reserves into gold, convinced that the flawed dollar-based system would not survive in the long run.[160]

As de Vries details, Giscard elaborated on French objections to the existing international monetary system during a speech on 11 February 1965. First, in his view, the Bretton Woods system lacked reciprocity, since the need to quickly correct payments deficits was not the same for all countries. Second, it lacked strength because the assumption that dollars held by foreigners could be converted into gold had become increasingly questionable. Third, it was essential to guarantee a better mechanism for balance-of-payments adjustment than currently existed. Finally, the Bretton Woods system could not provide sufficient international liquidity to permit the growth of the world economy without inflationary pressures.

Giscard also added flesh to de Gaulle's proposal for a return to a system based on gold by suggesting that: (1) big countries should declare publicly that they would henceforth settle their payments deficits only in gold and not through the creation of additional reserve monies, (2) additional liquidity should be provided only through the use of IMF's resources, (3) and the creation of additional international liquidity should be made dependent on a reform of the present system. On June 15, he reiterated the French view that gold should be the center of the international monetary system and suggested the establishment of Collective Reserve Units (CRUs). CRUs were artificial reserve units representing a certain amount of gold, which would be distributed according to the reserves of all states. They would be used outside the IMF, where the U.S. exercised great influence, and among a select group of states—preferably the G10. They would also address French concerns about curbing global inflation, while meeting the demands for expanded international liquidity.[161]

In parallel to his public attacks against the dollar and the international monetary system, de Gaulle privately planned France's departure from NATO. He chose to keep his cards close to his chest when it came to the timing of his plans and his ultimate intentions. Maintaining mystery and keeping his allies guessing was an integral part of his strategy because it would dramatize his eventual initiative. For example, during a meeting with Brosio on 27 February 1965, the French president confided that he firmly intended to withdraw France from the NATO organization by 1969; but he cryptically added that he would not attack the organization between then and 1969 "as long as matters remained substantially as they are."[162] Similarly, Couve de Murville advised the relevant ambassadors to inform allies that Paris sought a complete reshaping of the organization by 1969.[163]

What would follow the withdrawal was less clear, as de Gaulle considered various scenarios, including a project for a bilateral Franco-American Treaty or, as he hinted to Alphand, a series of bilateral accords to replace the Atlantic Alliance altogether. The latter option, though, sounded more like a trial balloon than a serious option.[164] When it came to timing, the General proved more forthcoming. Confiding to Alphand, he expected France would make an announcement in early 1966—or after the presidential election scheduled for December 1965.[165]

De Gaulle's increasing willingness to challenge American leadership led him to accelerate preparations for the eventual withdrawal from NATO. In March 1965, he instructed Couve de Murville to prepare a study on "the political, legal and practical implications of a reconsideration of the decisions taken, which have the effect of inserting France into the military integrated structure of NATO." According to concerned Quai officials, this marked the first time they had been asked to write such a comprehensive paper in conjunction with military authorities.[166]

Additionally, American interventions in Vietnam and in the Dominican Republic hardened the General's attitude, and further encouraged him to move quickly toward NATO. Not only did he fear the consequences of U.S. actions for world stability, but he also worried that America had now reached a level of power where it could do whatever it pleased.[167] After a meeting with de Gaulle in early May, U.S. Ambassador Bohlen commented that he "had never heard him before state so flatly that all foreign military installations would have to leave French soil."[168]

France's challenge against American hegemony and its coming withdrawal from NATO contributed indirectly to the outbreak of another very serious crisis within the EEC. Paris had not been planning a major attack against the Community like it was in the transatlantic sphere. The turmoil instead resulted from the interaction between three normally independent disputes: the battle over the CAP, the divisions surrounding political cooperation, and the growing gap—especially since January 1963—between France's vision of transatlantic relations and that of its partners.

Indeed, the lack of trust between France and the five, symbolized by the failure of talks on European political union, played an important role in the crisis. The prospects for closer European political cooperation had improved in early 1965, especially as the new Labour government in the U.K. showed limited interested in the European Community at that time.[169] Additionally, during their talks in Rambouillet in early 1965, de Gaulle and Erhard had reached an agreement in principle to have a future meeting of the six heads of state to discuss political cooperation.[170]

Any enthusiasm caused by these events, however, soon dissipated. The Erhard-de Gaulle accord rested on a fragile foundation: if the French government supported the idea of a meeting in principle, it would only agree to participate if it witnessed genuine political will among its partners to establish a common policy.[171] The French president, though, doubted these talks could succeed as long as the six continued to disagree on all essential issues.[172] He feared his partners were driven by cynical motivations, like Erhard's eyeing of forthcoming elections, and regretted that France was isolated in its criticisms of American actions in Vietnam and the Dominican Republic.[173] Furthermore, the French government no longer considered the development of an independent Western Europe an immediate priority and so preferred to do nothing rather than pursue a futile process.[174] On 27 March 1965, Couve de Murville firmly rejected the Italian proposal for a meeting of the EEC foreign ministers to discuss political cooperation.

France's decision angered the five, especially West Germany. Whereas Bonn had expected concessions from Paris after agreeing to higher grain prices in December 1964, Paris downplayed its neighbor's sacrifices.[175] Erhard was furious and confused by de Gaulle's seeming change of mind on political cooperation following the Rambouillet meeting.[176] He saw this refusal as yet another proof that France only wanted to impose its priorities on the Community. Already frustrated by France's confrontational approach toward the U.S. and flirtations with the Soviet Union, Bonn decided in early May that it was time to challenge Paris over the CAP's financial settlement. It thereby hoped to force Paris to accept progress on other EEC matters that were of interest to the five.[177]

Besides West Germany, the Dutch and Italians also had grievances against the French, and perceived the CAP's financial settlement as a golden opportunity to exert pressure on Paris. The atmosphere was ripe for conflict as the EEC approached the 30 June 1965 deadline for the financial settlement negotiations. As Ludlow sums up, "never before had the Community encountered a situation in which so many national delegations had decided independently that the outcome of a particular negotiation was a vital issue of national interest and something on which compromise and concession might undermine the very bases of the integration process."[178]

Tensions between member-states became intertwined with a dispute involving the European Commission, led by Walter Hallstein and centering on the thorny question of supranationalism. Since 1958, the relationship between the Commission and French representatives resembled that between the Pope and the Holy Roman Emperor, a tribute to their competitive and cooperative relationship.[179] Their interests had converged when it came to establishing the CAP, and France had even supported the allocation of important powers of control to the Commission in that domain. As Ludlow points out, supranationalism suited Gaullist France when it served the interests of its farmers.[180] Yet, the General always suspected that Hallstein and his colleagues wanted to make France "suffer over the agricultural Common Market and push Europe in the direction of a federation."[181] Directed to make proposals for the financial settlement covering the period between July 1965 and 1970, Mansholt and Hallstein believed they had a last chance to exploit the leverage stemming from de Gaulle's desire to finalize the CAP.

Breaking with precedent, they prepared their proposals in secret and then presented them on 24 March 1965 to the European Parliament rather than the Council of Ministers, a procedure considered unacceptable by Couve de Murville.[182] The truly controversial aspect of the plan, however, was the suggested increase in both the budgetary powers of the European Parliament and the Commission's funds.[183] De Gaulle immediately grasped the implications. This plan would grant the Commission control of the financial administration of agricultural matters and in turn would make the whole of the EEC a supranational entity, handing significant funds to an organization without responsibility.[184]

In the aftermath of the Commission's proposals, the situation worsened as Paris's partners sought to take advantage of the confusion to block an agreement on the financial settlement.[185] The five did not necessarily fully support Hallstein's plan, but they, especially the Dutch, saw it as an opportunity to make the French pay for the January 1963 veto of Britain's entry into the EEC.[186] Thus, with the Commission's challenge to integration and the five's obstruction of the financial settlement, the French government believed they faced a new and radical threat to the CAP. Until then, neither de Gaulle nor French officials expected that the Rome Treaty provision for the implementation of majority voting by 1 January 1966 would be implemented, or that it would substantially affect EEC decision-making.[187] Now, however, Paris ran the risk of being outvoted by this institutional procedure, which could undermine its previous hard-earned successes in the agricultural sphere.

Paris reacted to this threat with a mixture of anxiety and anger. On the one hand, until the 30 June deadline expired, French officials did their best to make sure that the negotiations would succeed.[188] In particular, they tried to cooperate closely with their German partners to end the deadlock. On the other hand, the threat to their national interest pushed the French leaders to be less flexible and to consider more dramatic solutions.

In late May, Couve de Murville first suggested to de Gaulle the possibility of a generalized boycott if the six failed to accept the financial settlement, which as a bonus would block the adoption of majority rule in January 1966.[189] When negotiations actually collapsed in Brussels on 30 June, the General did not hesitate: the following day, after the French Council of Ministers meeting, the government officially announced its decision to recall its representatives from Brussels and abstain from any future meeting until a solution was found.

Coming on the tails of the public attacks on the dollar and France's growing estrangement from NATO, the country's decision to boycott the EEC—the "empty chair" crisis—naturally appeared very ominous to its allies. The move seemed to be part of a combined offensive against the principle of integration at both the European and Atlantic levels.[190] Yet, despite the rampant anxiety, several considerations convinced de Gaulle to tone down his policies in the second half of 1965. He had to contend with the upcoming presidential elections, scheduled for 5 December. While the General only made his candidacy official on 4 November, the prospect of facing the electorate led him to postpone all crucial decisions to the following year.

Moreover, the president saw significant benefits in keeping his allies guessing about his ultimate intentions toward NATO. It would only add importance to his initiative once he pulled the trigger. Finally, the "empty chair" crisis changed French priorities. De Gaulle preferred not to fight "on several fronts" at the same time, and he decided to deal first with the turmoil within the European Community. This crisis presented a more urgent challenge because of the Treaty of Rome's provision to introduce majority voting on a grand scale from 1 January 1966 onward. Additionally, with the French presidential elections looming in the near future, it made sense to focus more on European matters, which resonated more with the electorate than NATO did.[191]

The French government could not, however, ignore other policy areas altogether. Giscard d'Estaing reminded American officials that his government had already put forward ideas on how to reform the international monetary system and would continue to do so.[192] French leaders still largely adopted a wait-and-see attitude, right when the American government finally shifted to a more proactive stance in the monetary field. Responding to de Gaulle's challenge against the dollar, Henry Fowler, the new U.S. secretary of the treasury, confirmed in a speech on 10 July that his government now embraced reform and proposed the convening of an international monetary conference.

Fowler did not convince his European partners. France turned down the suggestion because it believed a conference could only happen once two key conditions had been fulfilled: a return to equilibrium of the balance-of-payments of reserve-currency countries, and a minimum agreement between the main states on the modalities for reform of the current system. The other European states were not wildly enthusiastic either, preferring to have an agreement among the major powers before convening another Bretton Woods.[193]

Indeed, the transatlantic gap on monetary issues remained fairly substantial, as confirmed by the report written under the chairmanship of Rinaldo Ossola of the Bank of Italy. Completed in May and published in August 1965, the report quickly demonstrated a lack of support for Giscard's CRU proposal among the G10.[194] It also highlighted four main points of contention—mainly between France and the U.S.—regarding the creation of reserve assets and on which a range of views existed: (1) the link between gold and the new reserve asset, (2) how many countries would be involved in the management and distribution of the asset, (3) the role of the IMF in the creation of the reserve, and (4) rules for decision-making concerning the creation of reserve assets.[195]

These differences surfaced during the 1965 IMF annual meeting in Washington in September. The Europeans argued again that countries in deficit should give priority to attaining balance-of-payments equilibrium and that there was no urgent need for more liquidity. While both the Europeans and the Anglo-Saxons agreed that liquidity negotiations would eventually include states outside the G10, the U.S. and the U.K. seemed in much more of a hurry than their European allies were to see that happen. Nevertheless, despite these disparities, all parties agreed to cooperate to improve the international monetary system and accepted the principle of contingency planning should a need for liquidity arise. The ministers and governors of the G10 countries thus instructed their deputies to "determine and report to the ministers what basis of agreement can be reached on improvements needed in the international monetary system, including arrangements for future creation of reserve assets, as and when needed, so as to permit adequate provision for the needs of the world economy."[196]

As with monetary matters, the American government adopted a more proactive stance when it came to nuclear strategy. Robert McNamara, U.S. secretary of defense, sought in spring 1965 to give a less radical formulation to flexible response. He hoped to reestablish the strategic consensus in NATO by factoring in European reservations and isolating France. McNamara's approach succeeded, even if his original idea of a select committee with four or five representatives eventually underwent some changes. On 27 November 1965, ten of the fifteen defense ministers of the Atlantic Alliance formally established a special committee in charge of nuclear consultation, which was meant to be ad hoc.[197]

Unsurprisingly, de Gaulle confirmed that France would not participate in this committee, largely because it provided no substantial improvement to the Alliance strategy and would tie France down when it came to the use of its force de frappe.[198] Paris, however, could do very little to stop McNamara's proposal from going forward. During the NATO ministerial meeting on 14–16 December, Couve de Murville was isolated as France's allies were not only determined to see the Alliance "moving on again," but more comfortable with the idea of a NATO without France.[199]

Indeed, the General's NATO policy now focused solely on the imminent disengagement, while misleading his allies as to the exact timing of his move. As de la Grandville secretly notified American officials, de Gaulle, because of his advanced age, was in a hurry; privately, he had instructed the Quai to send him the dossiers on the "US occupation of France," which he had requested back in February, by mid December.[200] The French president and his collaborators, however, took a different line when they dealt with foreign officials. They sounded reassuring by claiming that the NATO Treaty remained valid until 1969 and that there was no rush to modify it.[201]

Publicly, de Gaulle adopted the same tactic of criticizing NATO, while remaining vague in regard to timing. During his 9 September 1965 press conference, electoral concerns pushed the president to outline French independence in even more forceful terms than usual. Referring to France's rapid economic expansion, the General condemned the "subordination that is integration" and stuck to the line that integration "would end by 1969 at the latest."[202] As 1965 came to an end, America's increasing involvement in Vietnam only fueled de Gaulle's desire to rapidly disengage from NATO. He feared that the U.S. had become unreasonable and too powerful, and with the risks of war between China and the U.S. increasing in Asia, he felt that France's membership in NATO might drag it into a war it had not chosen.[203]

The eventual timing of the challenge against NATO, however, would depend to a large extent on what happened within the European Community—de Gaulle would not move until he had sorted out the "empty chair" crisis. Failure to agree on the CAP's financial settlement had initially triggered the French boycott of the EEC, but the motivations of the French government went beyond agricultural matters: "we have to take advantage of this crisis to deal with political problems in the background. It is not acceptable that on 1 January 66, our economy could be submitted to a majority rule, which could impose on us the will of our partners ... As for the Commission, it proved partial ... and needs to be completely replaced," the General explained on 7 July.[204]

Besides calling for the completion of the CAP, Paris pushed for a revision of the Treaty of Rome. De Gaulle made this point clear during his press conference of 9 September. Going to great lengths to appear to voters as the ultimate defender of French independence, he placed full responsibility for the crisis on his partners and on the Commission and warned that this crisis could last for a very long time.[205]

Nonetheless, beneath the surface, the crisis within the EEC was not quite as dramatic as suggested by de Gaulle's tone. The French did not completely boycott Community institutions and their chair did not remain empty for all meetings. Maurice Ulrich, Boegner's deputy, stayed in Brussels to make sure that his government remained well informed of any developments.[206] Moreover, the General relied on threats and warnings for his strategy of brinkmanship. As he explained to Peyrefitte, "last time, you gave the impression it would all work out in the end. You must not use that tone! You have, instead, to worry everyone. It is the best way to defeat our opponents. If they are not afraid, they will figure that it will all be fine ... In reality we will win, won't we? We will not win immediately because we want a total victory."[207]

Furthermore, Couve de Murville confided to Bohlen early on that the crisis would probably last a few months, but he was confident that they would find a solution.[208] After all, France could afford to stall for a while, but it could not delay the EEC crisis indefinitely because it planned to move against NATO. Moreover, behind the firm rhetoric, de Gaulle was actually ready to show some flexibility if need be. Speaking to Peyrefitte a few days after the September press conference, he implied that France could settle for a formal agreement instead of a revision of the Rome Treaty.[209]

Until the presidential elections, though, the French leaders mostly adopted a carrot-and-stick policy toward their partners. During a meeting with Baron Adolph Bentinck, the Netherlands ambassador in Paris, the General stuck to a hard-line strategy. He explicitly accused the five of causing the split, by both ignoring past promises and accepting the Commission's proposals. He implied that the ball was in the five's court when it came to renewing talks, but added that no discussion could take place within the Brussels framework. Furthermore, de Gaulle reminded Bentinck that the supranational question took priority because the planned voting procedures could undermine any agreement on the CAP at any time. Considering the importance of the matter, France could only accept written engagements.[210] De Gaulle was still happy to use a potential revision of the Rome Treaty as a negotiating card, but he also revealingly ended the meeting by mentioning that France did not object to a meeting of the EEC's foreign ministers as long as it did not take place in Brussels.

Couve de Murville's speech to l'Assemblée Nationale a few days later adopted the same approach. He paid lip service to the motto of independence, and again demanded guarantees to prevent a recurrence of the crisis that the EEC was experiencing. At the same time, he also appealed to Bonn by underlining how the latter had fought against the principle of majority rule during the talks on a common price for grains. Lastly, Couve de Murville dangled the promise of progress on political union if the six managed to solve the current crisis.[211]

The diplomatic waiting game eventually came to an end, since all sides had strong incentives to end the crisis. There was no doubt that France had benefited economically from its membership in the EEC. As for the five, they needed to get the French back in line if they wanted to push forward the Kennedy Round negotiations, which had been effectively stalled since the start of the "empty chair" crisis.[212] By late October, de Gaulle had made up his mind that France would restart talks with its European allies in January 1966, after the presidential elections.[213] Thus, on 23 December, Couve de Murville confirmed to Giovanni Fornari, Italian ambassador in Paris, that France would meet the five for talks in Luxemburg on 17–18

January.[214] The crisis was not over, but a settlement appeared imminent, meaning de Gaulle could now concentrate on his move against NATO.

Conclusion

The General was reelected president in December with 54.5 percent of the popular vote, but the strength of the opposition, and the fact he needed a second round, surprised many observers. Aside from the EEC row, de Gaulle's domestic difficulties did not stem from his foreign policy, which still received wide support from the public.[215] Rather, the elections and the television medium had provided new exposure for a series of rival candidates, including François Mitterrand, who appeared far more novel and modern in comparison to the General. The results had confirmed, additionally, a certain erosion of support for Gaullism in public opinion, weakening the image of the president as an extraordinary leader and emboldening the opposition for the upcoming parliamentary elections of 1967.[216]

Between 1963 and 1965, France's Western strategy had experienced a similar disenchantment. In January 1963, de Gaulle seemed very optimistic as he pursued his three key aims of promoting France's Great Power status, developing a more independent Western Europe centered on the Franco-German axis and using the latter to balance transatlantic relations. Yet, as the Franco-German partnership faltered, it rapidly became apparent that building a more European Europe was not feasible in the medium term. Instead, growing disaffection with West German subservience to the U.S. led de Gaulle, especially after 1964, to start an "all-out war" with Washington in all fields of transatlantic relations. Chapter 4 will chronicle how France's Western policies evolved in 1966. The next chapter, however, will explain how and why de Gaulle's pan-European strategy, along with relations with the communist world, became the focal point of his foreign policy by the end of 1965.

Chapter 2

THE LONG ROAD TO MOSCOW

Introduction

During the crisis that rocked the Western Alliance in January 1963, rumors surfaced in London that de Gaulle was planning a major deal with the Soviet Union.[1] Based on his writings and political philosophy, as outlined in the Introduction, this scenario certainly appeared plausible. The General believed that the establishment of an independent Western European entity, along with the expected evolution of the Soviet bloc in a peaceful manner, would allow the emergence of a "Europe from the Atlantic to the Urals." This new Europe could overcome its division inherited from the Cold War based on a new equilibrium between its Western and Eastern parts.[2]

Relying solely on de Gaulle's philosophy and writings, the rumor in January 1963 that France would soon reach an agreement with Russia made sense. That the rumor proved false—which quickly became clear—could have been easily surmised, however, by studying the recent history of Franco-Soviet relations. Between 1958 and 1962, Franco-Soviet relations were tense, with the Berlin crisis and the Algerian War as the main bones of contention. Confrontation dominated ties between Paris and Moscow in 1963 and 1964.[3] Only in late 1964 and 1965 did a rapprochement between both states become possible.

Obstacles

Trade, cultural, and scientific relations between Paris and Moscow proved an exception, showing modest improvement in the latter part of 1963 and into 1964. While Valéry Giscard d'Estaing headed to Moscow in January 1964, Konstantin Rudnev, Soviet state president for scientific and technical coordination, went to Paris the following month. Giscard discussed with his hosts a possible five-year commercial agreement starting the following year, whereas Rudnev argued that France and the Soviet Union should develop their cultural and scientific exchanges.[4] These initiatives created a more favorable atmosphere for talks and were complemented by hopes on both sides for further progress in the future. Soviet Premier Nikita Khrushchev renewed his invitation to the General to visit Moscow, while de Gaulle reassured Soviet Ambassador in Paris Sergei Vinogradov that relations between France and the Soviet Union would eventually improve.[5]

The political value of these initiatives, however, remained very limited, and it is hard to agree with Thomas Gomart's claim that summer 1963 marked the beginning of a Paris-Moscow rapprochement.[6] The French government had no objections to improving practical relations with its Soviet counterpart, but it displayed no urgent desire to provide preferential treatment. Before Giscard's trip to Moscow, Couve de Murville clearly insisted to him that France would not break solidarity with other Western nations by granting favorable long-term credits to the Soviet Union.[7] Moreover, political considerations did not motivate the push to expand commercial links. Paris wanted to develop economic relations with and sell food to the Soviet Union because it was normal trade and good business.[8] Moscow, for its part, was driven by necessity. Facing serious economic problems, especially in the agricultural sector, it sought help from the West. Appeals to France paralleled similar requests to the U.S. and West Germany.[9]

Nonetheless, improvements in trade, cultural, or scientific relations could not offset the many obstacles that prevented a Franco-Soviet rapprochement during this period, starting with the lingering mistrust on both sides. French leaders fluctuated between short-term fear and long-term optimism in their attitude toward the Soviet Union. They acknowledged that the Soviet Union faced severe problems, with de Gaulle adamant that Russia "understands its time has passed."[10] Besides the split with Beijing, which according to the General would inevitably result in open struggle, Moscow had to contend with internal challenges and its failure to assimilate the populations of the Eastern bloc.[11] These difficulties, combined with the belief that the nationalist element in Russia was becoming more predominant at the expense of ideology, raised hopes that one day Western Europe might no longer face a communist threat.[12]

But, long-term expectations aside, de Gaulle still considered the Soviet Union an imminent threat, as shown by its actions during the Berlin and

Cuban crises.[13] Russia's significant nuclear arsenal meant that only a major change in Moscow's attitude could ensure peace.[14] As long as the Soviet leaders tried to impose their will on the world, de Gaulle doubted that their small efforts to improve relations with the West and France would change the European situation.[15] Despite some promising changes within and outside the Soviet Union, France did not appear forthcoming and adopted a wait-and-see approach. The General still had strong reservations about political negotiations with Khrushchev and consequently turned down Vinogradov's invitation to visit Moscow.[16]

The Quai d'Orsay shared this strong skepticism in regard to the prospect of any meaningful change in Soviet policy. A note written in early March 1964 outlined three complementary reasons to explain Moscow's motivations for fostering better relations with Paris: a desire to take advantage of tensions between Paris and its main Western allies; a need for Western aid to offset its serious economic problems; and a reaction to France's recognition of communist China.[17]

The Soviet leadership, for its part, remained divided when it came to courting France. Aware of the ever-worsening Franco-American relations, certain Soviet foreign policy strategists paid closer attention to France and pointed out that Moscow could gain from de Gaulle's centrifugal pull away from NATO and Washington.[18] Even the Franco-German rapprochement, while considered a danger for world peace, could potentially contribute to the decline of the U.S. in Europe. In other words, these Soviet strategists called for a more flexible policy toward Western Europe that would play on existing divisions within the Atlantic Alliance.[19]

These arguments did influence the Soviet leaders to a certain extent, encouraging them in 1963 and 1964 to moderate their criticisms of France and to try instead to benefit from any tensions between France and its Western allies. Thus, on 17 May 1963, the Soviet government sent an accommodating note to France. While still condemning the Franco-German partnership, the note referred to past Franco-Soviet cooperation against Germany during World War II and expressed hope that both countries might cooperate once again for the sake of European peace.[20] In July, Khrushchev repeated similar arguments during a conversation with French Ambassador in Moscow Maurice Dejean.[21]

This strategy to drive a wedge between France and its Western allies, however, had only a limited impact because it never fully convinced the Soviet premier. While happy to exploit differences within NATO, Khrushchev remained essentially an "Atlanticist": he never lost sight of American dominance and did not believe that Western Europe would ever abandon its powerful protector.[22] Considering this perspective, France presented only a limited appeal for the Soviet Union, and this was reinforced by

Khrushchev's ambivalent feelings toward the French president. Khrushchev feared de Gaulle's view of détente as a means of undoing Soviet ideology and worried about Gaullism as a symbol of the growing centrifugal forces in the world. But he also often showed contempt for the General, likening him to the emperor without clothes in the old story.[23]

Furthermore, differences in grand strategy presented a fundamental obstacle to a Franco-Soviet rapprochement. Even if for different reasons, Bonn and Paris both considered the January 1963 Franco-German Treaty a useful bulwark against the communist threat in the East. For Adenauer, signing the treaty allowed him to prevent a recurrence of a Franco-Russian alliance.[24] As for the French leaders, they viewed the Franco-German axis as the key to establishing a Western European organization that could one day become independent from both superpowers. Only then, and only after Russia had evolved sufficiently, could they envisage reaching a settlement with the Eastern bloc in order to end the Cold War in Europe and achieve a new continental equilibrium.[25]

Despite the early difficulties in connection with the Franco-German Treaty, de Gaulle initially refused to give up on cooperation with Bonn, and showed little inclination to appease Moscow: "we [France] decided to make a policy of entente with the Germans to the detriment of our relations with Russia, with Poland, with Czechoslovakia, with Yugoslavia," he reminded Peyrefitte on 11 December 1963.[26] As long as de Gaulle viewed the axis with West Germany as the cornerstone of his foreign policy, an entente with Russia remained more of a potential fallback option than a serious alternative.[27]

The negative reaction of the communist bloc to the Franco-German Treaty also acted as a major brake on any meaningful Franco-Soviet cooperation. Vinogradov reported home that the Paris-Bonn axis was unequivocally hostile to the Soviet Union. The Soviet's Eastern European allies were equally critical, with Czechoslovakia denouncing the Treaty for its dangerous repercussions on international relations.[28] But, Moscow and its allies were certainly more fearful of West Germany than of France. As Soviet Foreign Minister Andrei Gromyko argued to Dejean, the Franco-German Treaty was essentially a military pact and a tool in West Germany's policy of revenge.[29] It worsened Soviet fears that West Germany might one day gain access to nuclear weapons, either through the MLF or through cooperation with France. In either case, such an outcome would pose a grave threat to Soviet interests.[30]

Paris's close ties to West Germany presented a significant obstacle to better relations with Moscow, but the French government did not see this as a loss since it felt the Soviet Union only wanted a dialogue with the U.S.[31] Indeed, with superpower relations in 1963–64 at their closest since the start of the Cold War, Franco-Soviet cooperation was not a feasible option.[32] The priority allocated by Soviet diplomacy to the U.S. seemed obvious during the talks leading up to the Partial Test Ban Treaty (PTBT).[33] In the aftermath of the Cuban Missile Crisis, nuclear discussions had moved slowly at first as Khrushchev worried about possible criticism from communist China. With the Sino-Soviet rift reaching a critical stage, he decided to make another effort at conciliating the Chinese by inviting them for talks in Moscow in July 1963.[34]

The breakthrough occurred in June–July. Whereas the Sino-Soviet talks ended in acrimony, President Kennedy's speech on 10 June, calling for a new attitude toward the Soviet Union, and Khrushchev's speech in Berlin on 2 July—where he expressed Soviet readiness "to conclude an agreement on the cessation of nuclear tests"—created an opening.[35] On 5 August 1963, the U.K., the U.S., and the Soviet Union signed the PTBT, thereby agreeing to end all above-ground nuclear tests. A week before, during his 29 July press conference, de Gaulle signaled very publicly that France would not sign the PTBT.[36]

The PTBT highlighted the significant divergence of interests between Paris and Moscow in summer 1963. France opposed the test ban treaty because it needed additional tests to finalize the development of its force de frappe, the core pillar of its policy of independence.[37] Additionally, Paris calculated that a strong opposition would appeal to Bonn and work to its advantage. The West German government had reluctantly signed the PTBT, but had been very upset by the "upgrading" of East Germany to a signatory to this same treaty.[38] De Gaulle seized the opportunity to warn Adenauer that the blossoming relations between the Anglo-Saxon powers and the Soviet Union threatened both France and West Germany.[39]

Moreover, France opposed the PTBT as a symbol of a dangerous form of détente. According to the General, peace could only occur if the Soviet Union abandoned its aggressive ideology and loosened its grip on the satellite states.[40] The superpower talks, however, were an illusion because they gave the impression that East-West relations could improve without a meaningful change of atmosphere, and were a threat because they risked consolidating the Cold War bloc logic.[41] French leaders worried that following the PTBT, the U.S. and Soviet Union might acquire the habit of deciding the fate of the world without consulting other states.[42]

French fears about superpower détente continued in the aftermath of the test ban treaty and created an important obstacle to any rapprochement between Paris and Moscow. While the Soviet Union hoped to keep the momentum in its talks with the U.S., France fought to prevent the bipolar Cold War from developing into a bipolar process of détente.[43] French leaders tried to undermine the U.S.-Soviet dialogue by emphasizing its inherent dangers to other NATO members, who were already divided on the question of post-PTBT détente initiatives.[44]

France warned—again to appeal to Bonn—that the talks between the Anglo-Saxon powers and the Soviet Union, especially the proposed project of a non-aggression pact, might lead to the neutralization of West Germany and hence be catastrophic for Western Europe.[45] Instead, it advocated a more cautious stance on East-West relations, as Couve de Murville outlined during his speech at the December 1963 NATO ministerial meeting. If he welcomed the signs of change in the communist world, he added that détente could only happen if the Soviets desired it and if they adopted a less menacing attitude. Paris was willing to wait, as it believed that détente with the East would inevitably happen once it became clear that the latter did not want a war.[46]

At the same time, the PTBT and superpower détente also pushed France to seek a rapprochement with communist China. Since the end of the Algerian war—previously the main bone of contention between Paris and Beijing—de Gaulle had seriously considered the possibility of establishing diplomatic relations with the PRC. Such an initiative would present the double advantage of annoying the Americans and strengthening France's position vis-à-vis the Soviet Union: "We need fall-back allies. It has always been the policy of France ... One day I will make an alliance with China to strengthen us against Russia. Well, alliance, we are not there yet. We will first renew relations."[47] As the General showed a growing interest in communist China, Chinese officials in Berne were repeatedly pointing out to French counterparts that their government wanted to establish official relations with France.[48]

When China also refused to sign the test ban treaty, it provided further evidence for de Gaulle that both countries shared a common opposition to the U.S.-Soviet hegemony and that China could become an element of equilibrium between both superpowers.[49] As will be detailed in the next chapter, other factors drove de Gaulle as well, but the PTBT incident certainly convinced the French president that the time was right to approach the Chinese.[50] In late September 1963, he secretly instructed former President of the Council Edgar Faure, who was about to go to Beijing, to explore the possibility of a mutual recognition with the Chinese leaders.[51] Once Faure reached a provisional understanding with the Chinese regarding the establishment of diplomatic relations, Couve de Murville instructed Jacques de Beaumarchais, head of the Quai d'Orsay's European department, to finalize the agreement with the Chinese officials in Berne.[52] The establishment of diplomatic relations was finally announced on 27 January 1964.

Convergence

Significant obstacles, including mutual mistrust, incompatible grand strategies, and differing conceptions of détente, had prevented any meaningful rapprochement between France and the Soviet Union in 1963 and parts of 1964. In the second half of 1964, however, the gap separating both countries narrowed considerably.

The Southeast Asian conflict emerged as the first area of agreement for Paris and Moscow. As will be detailed in the following chapter, the conflict in former Indochina escalated in 1964, particularly in Vietnam after the August Gulf of Tonkin incident. France increasingly opposed American policy as the U.S. stepped up its military involvement in Indochina. Like the Soviet Union, France advocated a political solution to the crisis based on the 1954 Geneva accords. As a consequence, Soviet leaders repeatedly praised French policy and expressed hope that both countries might unite their efforts to ensure Indochina's independence.[53]

That approach won French assent. As de Gaulle told Vinogradov, French and Soviet policy might converge since the Soviet Union did not want to cause trouble in Southeast Asia.[54] Granted, these remained very tentative steps and were not enough to offset the other obstacles preventing a rapprochement. Yet, they marked a small change in Franco-Soviet relations. While the Soviet leaders still disapproved of French policy toward West Germany, they emphasized that this should not prevent entente on other questions.[55]

Additionally, Paris and Moscow were encouraged to adopt a more open attitude because of significant developments in their respective grand strategies. After the highs of 1963, superpower relations lost momentum in the following year. Despite a series of small measures to ease international tension, like the U.S.-Soviet Consular Convention signed in June, events in Vietnam adversely affected other spheres of U.S.-Soviet relations. Moreover, Kennedy's successor, Lyndon Johnson, chose to push the dialogue between Moscow and Washington to the side as he focused on the upcoming presidential election.[56]

As for Paris, the shortcomings of the Franco-German axis, very apparent during the 3–4 July 1964 summit, would dramatically alter French foreign policy. The consequences for France's relations with the communist bloc were not immediate, apart from some small progress in practical talks. Negotiations for a new Franco-Soviet trade agreement continued during the summer, while France considered, despite Bonn's protests, breaking Western solidarity and granting longer-term trade credits to the Soviets. Additionally, Gaston Palewski, French minister for scientific research, nuclear, and spatial questions, discussed with Khrushchev possible scientific exchanges and cooperation on French color television technology, i.e., Séquentiel Couleur Avec Mémoire (SECAM).[57] The failures of the Franco-German Treaty, though, had the General quickly searching for alternative policies: if in the future there was no progress with West Germany, France would seek an entente with Eastern Europe, he warned Peyrefitte a few days after the July summit.[58]

French frustration with West Germany and the cooling of superpower relations created new opportunities for Paris and Moscow, but their rapprochement also resulted from changes in their mutual perceptions. French leaders were specifically influenced by seeming developments in Eastern Europe, which appeared to downplay the Soviet threat. De Gaulle, as he explained to the French people during a televised address on 31 December 1963, expected that the gap between the respective sides of the Iron Curtain would eventually lessen: "we have to ... envisage the day when, maybe, in Warsaw, Prague, Pankow, Budapest, Bucharest, Sofia, Belgrade, Tirana, Moscow, the totalitarian communist regime, which still rules captive populations, would progressively evolve in a direction compatible with our own transformation."[59]

De Gaulle attributed a high importance to this sociology of development in his vision of the future of communist states, as argued by Paul-Marie de la Gorce. He believed that the industrial growth of the Soviet Union—and its satellites—would create a larger demand from its population for consumer goods, but also for more peaceful, freer, and quieter living conditions.[60] This raised the possibility of a convergence of the two sides of the European divide. After all, de Gaulle felt that the free world was becoming less capitalist, while the Soviets were becoming a bit more liberal. As he told Harold Wilson: "There are fewer differences than before with Eastern Europe in the economic and social spheres."[61]

Western states capitalized on the growing desire of the Eastern European states to establish contacts with them. President Johnson, in a 23 May 1964 speech, had emphasized the need to build bridges with Eastern Europe.[62] West Germany, for its part, had established a series of trade missions in the East between fall 1962 and spring 1964. Bonn relished the chance to increase trade with Eastern Europe and to try to isolate East Germany within the Warsaw Pact.[63] Paris also looked eastward: on 28 February 1964, it signed a cultural agreement with Poland, followed by one with Yugoslavia on 19 June.[64] French leaders welcomed these agreements because they felt any future dialogue with the East would be meaningless if limited to the Soviet Union alone.[65]

French leaders also believed that these contacts symbolized the beginnings of a more profound transformation within the Eastern bloc—in particular when looking at Romania. Soviet-Romanian tensions had increased markedly since 1962 because of disputes over modernization plans and because Romania leveraged the Sino-Soviet split to act more independently.[66] This new orientation was confirmed by the Romanian Communist Party's April 1964 resolution: "It is the sovereign right of all socialist states to decide, to choose and change the forms and methods of their social construction. No state has the right to present its own interests as the general interest…"[67]

Romanian officials repeatedly signaled to their French counterparts that they wanted more extensive contacts.[68] This included practical relations, especially trade, but also, significantly, talks at the highest levels. In early June, Bucharest contacted the French ambassador and confirmed Prime Minister Ion Maurer's desire to visit Paris. This marked an important breakthrough because it would be the first visit of a Romanian prime minister to any Western capital and it provided further evidence for Paris that Bucharest wanted to free itself from Moscow's dominance.[69]

Maurer eventually arrived in Paris in late July and met with de Gaulle. Aside from a discussion of possible economic, cultural, and scientific agreements, the striking part of their conversation centered on Maurer's analysis of the situation within the Eastern bloc. He argued that the communist world was changing, as a consequence of Russia's own evolution and the Sino-Soviet split. This allowed Romania to strive for more independence, especially in the economic sphere, while remaining part of the socialist bloc. Consequently, Bucharest wanted to improve relations with the Western world, but Maurer also noted that France held a special status because it was not trying, as the U.S. was, to detach the Eastern European states from the socialist camp.

When de Gaulle asked Maurer why he had gone to Moscow before coming to Paris, the Romanian prime minister replied that he had done so to dissipate Soviet worries that he wanted to go to France to criticize them. Despite difficulties, Maurer felt he had eventually alleviated Soviet mistrust.[70] The meeting had a significant impact on French leaders. Despite his customary caution, Couve de Murville regarded Maurer's visit to Paris as "a spectacular sign of the beginning of new relations between European states of both camps, [which] opens up some interesting perspectives for a thaw of the situation created twenty years ago."[71]

De Gaulle endorsed this view, as Alphand noted two days after the Maurer meeting: "he can feel the world is changing, and as a proof of this, the conversations he just had with the Romanian representative. He was in Moscow before his visit to France. Khrushchev was incapable of imposing his will on Romania because he is weakened by internal problems and his conflict with Mao."[72]

Maurer's visit crystallized the French president's assumptions that Russia's weaknesses were symptomatic of broader failures of the communist bloc, as he detailed in a personal note in summer 1964:

> 1. The demise of nations under a common ideology. But that has not happened. Some nations are under the rule of the communist system. They remain and are even powerful. We can see those two opposing each other; 2. The growth and victory of communism in other industrialized countries besides Russia. There are occupations (Eastern Europe and Central Europe). Nowhere have we seen a modern country spontaneously giving in to communism; 3. The establishment of communism in countries of the Third world and straight obedience. China did receive communist rule. But it rejected obedience ...; 4. The economic and social success of the system as opposed to others. Despite some successes and great efforts, the system has failed.[73]

Significantly, de Gaulle anticipated that Russia's numerous internal and external problems would compel it to take a less threatening stand in Europe, a precondition for a future establishment of a new equilibrium and security order on the continent. The General felt confident enough to instruct Philippe Baudet, his new ambassador in Moscow, to show the Russians that "we are not afraid of them anymore."[74]

Although Baudet had reservations about the implication that Russia no longer posed a threat, the Quai d'Orsay agreed with de Gaulle's perceptions of the Eastern bloc. Previously, the Foreign Ministry had been split on that same question. On the one hand, many diplomats shared the view that Moscow was incapable of resolving the problems of the world communist movement and that the process of differentiation among communist parties was irreversible. On the other hand, Soviet specialists Jean Laloy, the directeur-adjoint des affaires politiques, Jean-Marie Soutou, the director of the European department, and Henri Froment-Meurice, head of the Eastern Europe desk, were more skeptical and doubted that Moscow had lost full control over Eastern Europe. But, in 1963–1964, Laloy was demoted, while Soutou and Froment-Meurice were moved to other departments.[75]

While France saw the Soviet threat as fading, the Soviet Union increasingly viewed France as a more appealing partner. The recognition of communist China, which France expected would embarrass the Soviet government, instead played an important role in changing Moscow's attitude.[76] When Dejean informed Vasilii Kuznetsov, Soviet deputy foreign minister, that his government planned to establish diplomatic relations with the PRC, Kuznetsov actually congratulated France for its reasonable decision.[77]

According to Wolton, the positive Soviet reaction can be partly explained by the fact that officials were not surprised by the announcement. Faure, without de Gaulle's assent, had informed Vinogradov on 3 December 1963 about the forthcoming decision to normalize relations with

China, and added that the move owed more to Franco-U.S. relations and had nothing to do with the Sino-Soviet split. Moscow welcomed Paris's decision because it believed that the decision consolidated the socialist camp and worsened Franco-American relations.[78] At the same time, if the surprise effect failed, the recognition of the PRC pushed the Soviet Union to pay more attention to France's role on the international scene.[79]

Growing Soviet interest became evident soon after when Nikolai Podgorny, a senior member of the Presidium, suddenly replaced a lesser figure to head a delegation of Soviet parliamentarians for a long-planned visit to Paris.[80] Podgorny used the opportunity to meet Couve de Murville, Pompidou, and de Gaulle. He hailed the recognition of China as a positive initiative, underlined past Franco-Soviet cooperation, and referred to the lack of conflicts between the two countries. De Gaulle, for his part, also expressed relative optimism for future Franco-Soviet relations, especially in his suggestion that the Soviet Union was changing in a direction that suited France.[81] The rest of the French diplomatic establishment, however, remained somewhat more cautious than the General.[82]

Changes in Soviet perception of France were also tied to Khrushchev's fate. As mentioned before, the Soviet leader had never considered France a serious player, dismissing de Gaulle as having "little influence in world affairs and ... know[ing] it."[83] Instead, in 1964, Khrushchev had focused his efforts on trying to improve relations with West Germany. He hoped to get trade benefits for the ailing Soviet economy and a modus vivendi with Bonn so as to have a free hand with China.[84]

On 2 September, a seeming breakthrough occurred when the West German government formally invited Khrushchev to visit Bonn in January 1965. However, this trip would never take place. On 14 October, the Soviet Central Committee toppled Khrushchev and replaced him with a collegial leadership dominated by the new secretary-general of the Communist Party, Leonid Brezhnev; the new prime minister, Alexei Kosygin; and the new president, Anastas Mikoyan.

Turning Point

By late 1964, the context was thus more favorable for a Franco-Soviet rapprochement. Common views on Southeast Asia, Franco-German tensions, and the cooling of superpower relations, as well as the glimpses of change within Eastern Europe, had all combined to narrow the gap between Paris and Moscow. Additionally, for the French, the fall of Khrushchev appeared to signal a return to collegial rule in the USSR and to promise more tranquility in Soviet foreign policy.[85] But, a more favorable environment did not necessarily guarantee that France and the Soviet Union would strengthen their cooperation.

The new Kremlin rulers—Brezhnev, Kosygin, and Podgorny—lacked clear goals when it came to foreign policy. Besides urgent domestic problems, the leadership faced divisions over Europe and Asia between the advocates of hard-line policies and those who supported a moderate approach.[86] It tried to reverse some of the decisions of its predecessor, starting with an attempt to repair relations with China. In regard to Vietnam, Moscow opted for the middle path of sending more aid to North Vietnam, while at the same time undertaking efforts to end the conflict.[87] The Soviet leaders also decided to end Khrushchev's attempted rapprochement with Bonn. Beyond that, the Soviet Union's policies seemed confused, and its leaders hesitated over fully exploiting the growing tensions between the U.S. and some of its Western European allies.[88]

Moscow's attitude toward Paris thus alternated between criticism and flattery. On 17 and 20 October 1964, *Pravda* attacked French positions on Vietnam and Latin America, but a week later, it devoted a lengthy article to underlining France's indispensable role in solving European problems.[89] On 27 October, the fortieth anniversary of the establishment of diplomatic relations between France and the Soviet Union, Gromyko also suggested that "concrete possibilities" existed for further improvement in Franco-Soviet relations.[90]

The French leaders were uncertain about what to make of the changes happening in Moscow. They welcomed the new five-year trade agreement signed on 30 October, but neither the Quai d'Orsay nor de Gaulle believed they were witnessing any major changes in Soviet policy after Khrushchev's removal. The foreign ministry, in particular, argued that the latest Soviet statements resembled previous efforts to exploit French tensions with the U.S. and West Germany.[91] Nonetheless, de Gaulle encouraged Peyrefitte to visit Moscow to sound out the new Soviet leaders, using the pretext of cooperation on SECAM.[92]

The MLF crisis, not the change of Soviet leadership, provided an important impetus for the Franco-Soviet rapprochement. Both states came together in their fierce opposition to West Germany gaining access to nuclear weapons. Moreover, the MLF episode led France and the Soviet Union, albeit for different reasons, to consider future cooperation as potentially beneficial. It convinced Moscow to pay more attention to the opportunities offered by de Gaulle's policies to undermine American influence in Europe and isolate West Germany.[93] Starting with Vinogradov on 18 November, Soviet officials systematically asked their French counterparts for more regular consultation on issues where they converged, including Southeast Asia, the MLF, and Germany's borders.[94]

In late December 1964, during a meeting with Baudet, Kosygin repeated the appeal for closer collaboration. Not only did he suggest giving a contractual form to the growing Franco-Soviet entente, but he also emphasized the numerous areas of Franco-Soviet agreement and highlighted the dangers associated with a U.S.-German partnership.[95] Similarly, in early January 1965, during Peyrefitte's visit to Moscow to discuss potential cooperation on SECAM, Kosygin hinted that his government had chosen the latter project for political rather than technological reasons.[96]

As for France, the MLF episode seriously contributed to the deterioration of relations with West Germany. De Gaulle, in particular, felt very bitter against the Germans and, according to Belgian Foreign Minister Paul-Henri Spaak, his mood toward them was reminiscent of that toward the British in January 1963.[97] In his public and private words, he subscribed once again to the view of Germany as a permanent problem, which had poisoned Europe since Charles V.[98]

Furthermore, the General saw the pronounced dispute over the MLF as further evidence of the shortcomings of the Franco-German Treaty and the fact that it would not become the basis of a more independent Western Europe in the foreseeable future. As a result, "automatically we [France] are getting closer to the Russians to the extent that the Germans are moving away from us," he confirmed to Peyrefitte.[99] Resentment toward the West Germans and the fear of a German-American axis were pushing the French president to revert to the traditional alliance with Russia to contain Germany. French leaders declined to hide this fact, such as when Couve de Murville warned that the MLF would be unacceptable for the Soviet government.[100]

Despite their similar views on the question of German nuclear armament, de Gaulle remained wary of Soviet intentions and did not know what value to give to their openings at the end of 1964.[101] On the one hand, he believed both countries had a lot in common and that Russia was taking into account France's growing prestige in China and the Third World. On the other hand, he feared that the Soviets were only interested in France in order to gain an edge over the U.S.[102]

Yet, at the same time, the ongoing changes in Eastern Europe, especially the ever-growing list of Eastern European visitors to Paris, helped to counter de Gaulle's fears about Soviet intentions.[103] After the foreign ministers of Bulgaria, Yugoslavia, and Czechoslovakia all came to Paris in November, the Hungarian representative soon followed in January 1965. If discussions centered mostly on commercial and cultural relations, French officials still considered these meetings a confirmation that important developments were taking place within the Eastern bloc. Couve de Murville was cautious enough to speak of an evolution rather than revolution and dismissed the idea that France should seek to detach the Eastern European states from Russia.

But, Couve de Murville also believed that a general normalization of relations among all European states was possible and that the satellite states were drawn to France because of its exceptional prestige throughout the world.[104] Similarly, de Gaulle assumed that the situation in Europe was moving in the right direction and, even if this was not irreversible, France needed to encourage the Eastern bloc states to reclaim their national sovereignty. Depending on the results of the evolution, German reunification might even become feasible in the near future.[105]

Thus, any misgivings that the General had in regard to the sincerity of the Soviet intentions were more than offset by the effects of the growing emancipation of the satellite states. Even if the Soviet Union's apparent internal evolution was less than genuine, according to de Gaulle, it simply could not stop the process of fundamental transformation that was developing in Europe: "There is a trigger lately. We can feel it everywhere. The Cold War is out of date. … The Soviet bloc is crumbling, China is separate. Romania, Poland are also detaching themselves. The Soviet Union is becoming something else. As to the Western bloc, it is also crumbling. France has recovered its freedom. It is independent once again."[106] The momentum of French foreign policy was swinging in the direction of greater independence. As France prepared to challenge U.S. leadership in monetary and military matters, better relations with the Soviet Union offered another means to challenge American hegemony and its claim to speak for its allies in their relations with the other superpower.[107]

De Gaulle's willingness to initiate Franco-Soviet cooperation was not shared by the rest of the foreign policy establishment. The Quai d'Orsay remained very mistrustful of the Soviet Union, doubting that the latter saw France as the best interlocutor, and argued that the Soviets' main goal was to exploit divisions within the Atlantic Alliance.[108] Couve de Murville supported the principle of more extensive talks with Moscow, but only as long as they did not ignore the existing differences on many key subjects, including Europe. As such, according to a well-placed source, he had to alter a telegram of instructions to Baudet, originally drafted by the Elysée, so that it conformed more fully to the requirements of Western orthodoxy.[109]

De Gaulle, though, overrode these objections and acted as the driving force for better relations with the Soviet Union. Meeting with Vinogradov on 25 January 1965, he signaled that he would be happy to visit Moscow if bilateral relations continued to progress. But, he also warned his interlocutor that Franco-Soviet collaboration would fail if the Soviet Union sought to divide France from its allies, or if the Soviets sought to obtain French recognition of East Germany.[110] This amounted to a conditional green light to kick-start a dialogue between Paris and Moscow. It was in this context that the General gave his all-important press conference on 4 February, twenty years after the start of the Yalta Conference.

The press conference gave the president an opportunity to reflect on developments in East-West relations and to outline his vision of how the division of Germany could be overcome within a European framework.[111] He argued that the German problem could not "be solved by the confrontation of the ideologies and forces of the two camps opposed to each other"; it needed to be considered from the perspective of "the entente and conjugated action of the peoples that are and will remain most interested in the fate of Germany, the European nations."[112]

He carefully added that such an outcome could only occur in the long term and depended on many conditions. The Eastern bloc would have to evolve, meaning that Russia would first have to move away from totalitarianism and allow the once-satellite states to play a more significant role in Europe. The states of Western Europe would have to extend their organization to cover political and defense matters. West Germany would have to consent that any reunification would involve acceptance of its borders, including the Oder-Neisse frontier with Poland, and restraints acceptable to all its neighbors on its possession of weapons. Finally, a solution to the German question could happen once a general "détente, entente and cooperation" had developed among all the European states.[113]

A source in the Quai confided to American officials that the German section of the press conference marked a major turning point in the evolution of French foreign policy.[114] De Gaulle's overarching aim—overcoming the Cold War in Europe and creating a new continental security system centered on the Soviet Union and a French-led Western Europe—remained, but he was changing strategies.[115] Since his return to power in 1958, the General had given priority to a Western approach because Khrushchev's Soviet Union had still posed a threat. He had hoped to contain West Germany through a close partnership, which in turn would form the embryo of a more independent Western Europe. The latter could then hope to establish a new continental balance once Russia had changed sufficiently.

By early 1965, though, de Gaulle was shifting to a pan-European approach. His anger at the failure of the Franco-German Treaty led him to revive the traditional alliance with Russia to contain Germany. Moreover, the internal and external weaknesses of the Soviet Union, combined with the growing assertiveness of Eastern Europe, convinced the French president that Europe was ripe for East-West détente and for overcoming its division inherited from the Cold War. If Europe could restore its unity and achieve peace, the other states of Western Europe would be less reticent to take their distances from the U.S. and establish a political union to balance the Soviet Union. The U.S., for its part, would revert to its traditional role of underwriting this European concert.[116]

Entente

The General had offered a long-term vision of a post–Cold War Europe, but he had provided few details about how to achieve this evolution. His political future appeared uncertain, with his presidential mandate coming to an end in December 1965. He approached his new pan-European strategy with caution, aware that success would require a delicate balancing act among various aims: better relations with the Soviet Union were vital, but he hesitated to fully commit before overcoming his lingering doubts about its intentions; in parallel, he wanted to combine the rapprochement with the Soviet Union with increasing contacts with Eastern Europe, while not seeming to openly challenge Soviet control; finally, he wanted to avoid the impression that his policy of détente was directed against his Western allies.

The international context in 1965 facilitated Franco-Soviet cooperation. Paris and Moscow shared an opposition to the U.S. stepping up its involvement in the Third World with interventions in Vietnam and the Dominican Republic. As such, Peyrefitte's official statement on 24 February expressed his government's willingness to "consult with the Soviet Union" in seeking "peace in Southeast Asia thanks to an international conference"; following the Dominican Republic incident, French and Soviet representatives enjoyed frequent contacts.[117] The escalating war in Vietnam proved particularly significant because it seriously compromised any superpower dialogue.[118]

Moreover, 1965 also witnessed serious disputes between France and its Western allies. The conflict between France and America reached new heights over NATO and the international monetary system. The brewing crisis within the EEC finally erupted on 30 June when France opted to boycott the Community institutions. It is no surprise that France's Western allies viewed de Gaulle's openings toward the Eastern bloc with great suspicion at a time when he seemed to be challenging the fabric of the Western Alliance. But equally, it made sense for France to look eastward in this period. Isolated and at odds with its allies in the West, with no prospect of establishing a more independent Western European union in the immediate future, France saw greater opportunities to consolidate its Great Power status through cooperation with the East.[119]

The eastward drift received further impetus from the deterioration of Franco-German relations. Aside from the struggles within the EEC, Bonn's refusal to abandon the MLF project drew Paris and Moscow closer together. During summer 1965, officials from the Quai d'Orsay had downplayed West Germany's renewed demands for involvement in nuclear matters. They felt, like the head of the European department François Puaux, that many of the West German statements on the MLF were calculated for the upcoming German general elections scheduled in September.[120] Bonn's stubborn push for the MLF after the elections, however, really angered French leaders. West Germany's nuclear ambitions, de Gaulle warned American Senator Mike Mansfield, could impede any real peace between Western and Eastern Europe.[121]

By late 1965, the French president's disillusionment with West Germany seemed complete: "The Germans have taken a dissident position towards our treaty of cooperation and friendship. We cannot stop them. Germany follows its way, it is not ours. They look for reunification at all costs and without delay; they will not get it as long as the Soviets resist."[122] Facing an apparent resurgence of German nationalism and its desire to participate in nuclear defense matters, Couve de Murville concluded that France's best option was to revert to the historic policy of an alliance with Russia.[123]

Indeed, following de Gaulle's 4 February press conference, France intensified its cooperation with the Eastern bloc, starting with the Soviet Union. Initially, the rapprochement produced more results in the scientific and commercial spheres than in the political field.[124] On 23 March 1965, the Soviet Union officially adopted the French SECAM technology for its TV system, and on 12 May, both states signed a protocol of cultural exchanges. Six days later, they signed an agreement regarding the peaceful use of nuclear energy.

While less dramatic than in other domains, progress also occurred at the political level. Paris and Moscow, keen on high-level consultations, agreed that Gromyko would visit Paris in April and that Couve de Murville would visit Moscow in the autumn.[125] Additionally, the appointment in March 1965 of Valerian Zorin, as Soviet ambassador in Paris, signaled a new phase in Franco-Soviet relations. Whereas Vinogradov had been active in cultural and technical matters, Zorin, a former deputy minister for Foreign Affairs and expert on European and German policies, would be expected to focus on the latter fields.[126]

The Kremlin leaders believed that improving Franco-Soviet relations did not involve big risks and that they could benefit by sending signals in response to de Gaulle's speeches. It cost the Soviet Union little to thank France by upgrading their embassy in Paris or by sending their Foreign Minister Gromyko.[127] As for the French, they seemed pleased that a dialogue could take place not only on Vietnam, but also on the crucial question of Germany, despite their differing viewpoints on East Germany.[128]

Both French and Soviet leaders approached their relations with great optimism. Zorin mentioned to Pompidou that his government "really wants to improve its friendly relations with France, as a great European power itself," while Pompidou replied that as in the past, good Franco-Soviet relations could provide a solid base for European peace.[129] Gromyko's visit in late April reinforced French confidence, convincing de Gaulle that "it is obvious the Russians have a strong desire to develop contacts with us."[130] Believing that Russia faced a combination of serious problems, the General confided to Gromyko that his country no longer appeared so threatening.[131]

In this favorable context, and despite the fact that France officially supported German reunification, de Gaulle sought to capitalize by making an important concession to the Soviet leaders. While he viewed the partition of Germany as "abnormal" and not permanent, he was "in no hurry" to overcome it and accepted that partition was "an accomplished fact" for the moment. With Gromyko replying that Moscow did not oppose reunification per se, provided both German states agreed, there was now growing overlap—beyond their shared acceptance of the Oder-Neisse frontier—between the French and Soviet positions.[132]

Convergence on the German question, common opposition to American involvement in the Third World, and France's conflicts with its Western allies all combined to significantly improve Franco-Soviet relations. But, various developments kept the pace of the rapprochement under control. As a U.S. State Department report pointed out, neither France nor the Soviet Union could move too far in its relations without causing unpredictable consequences with regard to its allies.[133] France, in particular, did not rush its dialogue with Moscow, denying the accusation that its policy of détente sought to cause serious disruption within the Western alliance. De Gaulle's 4 February press conference had already stirred anxiety in the West: Washington feared that the General's "European" approach to the German problem aimed to exclude the U.S. from any settlement, while Schroeder believed it was not up to the French president to discuss the fate of Germany.[134]

French officials worked to reassure their Western colleagues that they were not seeking any "reversal of alliances" and to show that they were not departing from Western orthodoxy on East-West matters. De Gaulle told Bohlen that he saw no differences in principle between the American and French approaches to détente, while he explained to Brosio that a European approach to the German question would only be appropriate if significant changes were made within the Eastern bloc.[135] Likewise, France made a gesture toward West Germany when it issued a tripartite declaration with the U.K. and the U.S. on 12 May 1965. Stressing that German unification could only occur via peaceful means and in agreement with the Soviet Union, the declaration reaffirmed the responsibility of the four major powers in the German question.[136] Even on the MLF, Puaux reminded Yuri Doubinin, Soviet counselor in the Paris embassy, that while France and the Soviets held similar views, they belonged to different alliances and thus it would be difficult for Paris to take a common stand with Moscow against Bonn.[137]

This tentative progress in Franco-Soviet relations did not please the Soviet Union. Doubinin complained to Puaux that his government had expected France would "respond" more rapidly to Gromyko's visit "by taking an initiative on the German problem."[138] The Soviet government had to a certain extent misunderstood the implications of de Gaulle's February press conference. When the General had claimed that a solution to the German question needed the agreement of all Germany's neighbors, Moscow had wrongly assumed that this included East Germany. It was later surprised to hear that France's position on not recognizing East Germany had not changed.[139]

Paris welcomed the slow pace of the Franco-Soviet rapprochement. Its lingering doubts about Moscow's intentions meant it wanted to continue probing the Soviet government before intensifying cooperation. France made it clear that it expected actions, not just words, from the USSR before it would strengthen bilateral ties. As Pompidou emphasized to Zorin, any improvement in Franco-Soviet relations would depend on solid foundations in all spheres, not just the political field. He underlined the low level of Franco-Soviet trade and Soviet delays in fully implementing the October 1964 agreement.[140]

De Gaulle also remained wary of Moscow. Speaking to Alphand soon after Gromyko's visit, he explained that Russia was "trying to take advantage of our disagreements with the U.S.," but "for the moment it is not really going anywhere."[141] He was not far off the mark. Speaking to an American diplomat, Igor Usachev, a Soviet chargé d'affaires in the Paris Embassy, barely hid the fact that his government was mainly engaging in a dialogue with France to annoy the U.S.[142]

Caution drove the French leaders to keep their cards close to their chests in their dealings with their Soviet counterparts. When Gromyko questioned de Gaulle about a possible Franco-Soviet treaty, the president's reply was purposefully ambiguous: he excluded no possibilities in the future, but added that this was not an immediate priority.[143] During a later meeting with Zorin, he stuck to his "wait-and-see attitude." After the Soviet ambassador pointed out that France and the Soviet Union had failed to reach common positions despite similar views on many international problems, the French head of state concurred that both countries had similar views on Vietnam and Germany. He added, though, that these questions would take a long time to solve.[144]

This does not mean de Gaulle showed no interest in a high-level dialogue with the Soviet Union, and he certainly attached great importance to Couve de Murville's upcoming visit to Moscow that autumn. He believed, though, that a prudent attitude would better serve France's interest: "our position is unique: Russia is courting us and China congratulates us for our courage and independence," he told Alphand.[145] Enjoying good relations with several Great Powers, it was wiser for France not to appear desperate to respond to Russian advances.

Paris hoped also to balance its rapprochement with Russia through growing contacts with Eastern Europe.[146] In June 1965, following a commercial agreement with Romania, France signed a scientific and trade cooperation agreement with Czechoslovakia and a new trade and industrial cooperation agreement with Poland. Several French ministers visited Eastern Europe, including Minister for Administrative Reform Louis Joxe, who went to Belgrade and Prague, and Giscard d'Estaing, who traveled to Bucharest.

French officials welcomed the evolution on the other side of the Iron Curtain. According to a Quai D'Orsay analysis, the Soviet Union surely disapproved of the growing exchanges between Western Europe and Eastern Europe, but they felt that Moscow already had its hands full with its own economic and external problems. These weaknesses effectively prevented the Soviets from stopping the changes in Europe.[147] De Gaulle agreed with the Quai d'Orsay's analysis and did not doubt that the satellite states would inevitably recover their complete independence: "Eastern Europe will start moving," so "it is our role to help and nobody can do it better than France."[148]

While France could offer nothing more than other Western powers could on the economic and cultural fronts, even lagging behind in terms of trading with Eastern Europe, the Quai d'Orsay remained optimistic. Its officials banked on the fact that France possessed a certain political credit within the Eastern bloc and that this might allow it to eventually become the main interlocutor of the satellite states.[149]

France worked to establish that position through continual discussions at the highest levels. The September 1965 visit of Polish Prime Minister Josef Cyrankiewicz to Paris appeared to be a particularly important step in Eastern Europe's shift toward greater independence, as the first visit of a Polish prime minister to an Atlantic Alliance state since World War II. French officials also considered it an excellent opportunity to improve their country's cultural, commercial, and political presence in Poland. As for de Gaulle, he gave Cyrankiewicz a finer reception than the one given to

Romanian Prime Minister Maurer in 1964 because of his deeper personal interest in Poland—dating from his time spent in Warsaw in 1920—and Poland's more significant role in the overall European picture.[150]

The French leaders, however, placed limits on how much they would court Eastern Europe. They accepted that détente could not happen against Moscow's will and that it would be counterproductive to try to remove the satellite states from the Soviet sphere of influence.[151] The General, despite his optimistic belief in the inexorable changes within the Eastern bloc, also acknowledged that any improvement in France's relations with the satellite states had to go hand in hand with better relations with Russia. As long as "you [Poland] keep your national personality ... we have no problems with your alliance with the Soviet Union," de Gaulle explained to Cyrankiewicz after wishing for greater contacts between Poland and France. He later added that France wanted to cooperate more with Russia, which it saw as beset with problems and no longer bent on dominating Europe.[152]

Happy with the parallel progress of relations with Eastern Europe, the General could approach Couve de Murville's autumn trip to Moscow with less concern. His stance contrasted significantly with that of Quai officials, who expressed more skepticism about the prospects of Franco-Soviet cooperation. A note drafted before the visit acknowledged the growing Soviet interest in France and the tenser relations between the superpowers. It suggested, however, that the U.S. and the Soviet Union had enough common interests to make it likely that they would engage in a close dialogue in the future.[153]

Despite that warning, Couve de Murville's positive talks with his Russian hosts played a key role insofar as they reassured de Gaulle about Russian intentions and made the goal of an East-West rapprochement in Europe seem more plausible. These first meetings with the new leadership of Brezhnev and Kosygin produced no clear changes in the countries' respective viewpoints. Nevertheless, the repeated discussions between French and Soviet officials—after Gromyko's visit in April and Gromyko's meetings with Couve de Murville in Vienna in May and at the UN in October—provided striking evidence of the new friendlier atmosphere between France and the Soviet Union.[154] Couve de Murville, who tended to get on better with Russians than with Anglo-Saxons, came back particularly impressed with Kosygin, who seemed more liberal than his colleagues.[155]

The Kremlin leaders went to great lengths to flatter Couve de Murville, often complimenting de Gaulle and his policies, and suggested the latter should visit the Soviet Union. Brezhnev promised Couve de Murville that the General "would be warmly welcomed."[156] Kosygin also mentioned that de Gaulle's trip could offer the opportunity to "draft a serious document to organize our relations for the coming years." The French foreign minister admitted that de Gaulle would be interested in the invitation, but added that he could only reply after the December presidential elections.[157]

Couve de Murville's trip to Moscow appeared to be a significant confirmation of the incremental improvements in Franco-Soviet relations throughout 1964–65. Furthermore, it helped to overcome some of the lingering doubts on both sides. The Soviet foreign policy community remained undecided and caught up in the "great debates" about peaceful coexistence. Thus Brezhnev paid a skimpy tribute to Franco-Soviet relations as being merely "not bad" during the Central Committee plenum in September 1965.[158] But, an increasing number of officials, including Zorin, who was delighted by the spirit of Franco-Soviet cooperation, pushed for closer ties with Paris.[159] As the 1965 political report from the Soviet Embassy in Paris argued, "the political orientations of the French government present for us undeniable advantages in regards to the general aims of Soviet foreign policy, because, first and foremost, this tendency destabilizes the Western camp in its current organization, weakens objectively the United States—our main imperialist enemy—and compromises West Germany's chances for military and political progress."[160]

As for France, it stuck with its prudent stance toward the Soviet Union. De Gaulle mentioned to British conservative leader Edward Heath that although the Soviets appeared more reasonable, the West still needed to be cautious. French leaders shied away from hasty and adventurous positions, which explained their lukewarm reaction to the Soviet proposal for a European security conference.[161] Nevertheless, this caution increasingly gave way to a growing sense of optimism because, according to Couve de Murville, his trip had shown that Paris could "objectively cooperate" with Moscow.[162] He came back extremely pleased and impressed with the results of the talks, and as he told Schroeder, struck by the changes in the Soviet Union since his last visit in 1947.[163] In late 1965, as a source from the Quai d'Orsay confirmed to American officials, there was no doubt that de Gaulle considered the East-West rapprochement in Europe to be his main strategic objective.[164]

Conclusion

Between 1963 and 1965, France's attitude toward the communist bloc had undergone a major evolution. The relative failure of the Franco-German Treaty and its Western strategy, combined with the growing emancipation of Eastern Europe and a seemingly declining Russian threat, had proven instrumental in dramatically altering France's approach toward the East-

ern bloc. By the end of 1965, Paris was fully committed to East-West détente in Europe and its pan-European strategy to overcome the Cold War
division of the continent.

After his victory in the second round of the presidential elections on 19
December, de Gaulle lost no time in turning to relations with the communist bloc. During a meeting with Zorin on 12 January 1966, he announced
that he accepted Brezhnev and Kosygin's invitation to visit the Soviet
Union later in the year.[165] Up to then, French public opinion supported
the rapprochement with the Soviet Union, and chapter 4 will consider
whether that remained so after de Gaulle's trip. First, though, chapter 3
will focus on how French policy toward the Third World evolved between
1963 and 1965.[166]

Chapter 3

A "Shining Light" for the World?

Introduction

The four years following de Gaulle's return to power in 1958 marked the end of the French empire. Paris eventually granted independence to its Sub-Saharan African colonies in 1960. The French Community collapsed soon after, before France ended the Algerian War with the Evian Accords in March 1962. The loss of colonies removed a major burden and freed France to focus on its quest for Great Power status, but it left many questions unanswered about how France should redefine its role in the Third World. What did it seek to achieve with its policy of cooperation? How important a role should the Third World play in de Gaulle's overall grand strategy?

Furthermore, France had to contend with the urgent challenge of what involvement, if any, it should have in the Third World following decolonization. This simple question divided French public opinion. Strong voices on both sides of the political spectrum argued in favor of a broad disengagement from the extra-European world. On the one hand, journalist Raymond Cartier had long denounced the exorbitant costs of maintaining colonies, and his view, dubbed Cartiérisme, only hardened after the former territories were granted independence.

Cartier's blunt slogan of financing "la Corrèze avant le Zambèze" emphasized his preference for spending money on France rather than Africa, as well as his view that France could not afford both a nuclear arsenal and aid to its former colonies. On the other hand, cooperation was also criticized by those opposed to the de Gaulle the government and to liberal economics. Socialist politician François Mitterrand complained that aid was doled out according to the fitful fancies of the quasi-monarchic head of state.[1] These arguments did not go unheeded. In 1963 and 1964, a majority of the public wanted to reduce France's aid to the Third World.[2]

The Rhetoric of Cooperation

The French president participated actively in these debates. But, unlike the proponents of imperial disengagement, he believed that decolonization offered France a chance to reclaim lost influence and status in the Third World. No longer a bastion of colonialism, France could now try to appear as a liberating state to the rest of the world.[3] In order to justify, both domestically and internationally, France's continuous role outside of Europe, de Gaulle and his collaborators relied on rhetoric that emphasized history, their country's unique nature, and its humane motivations.

Aside from its colonial past, the General often underlined France's traditional links of friendship with many states throughout the world when he met foreign leaders.[4] This, in turn, allowed French leaders to argue that their country, through its history, could claim an authoritative standing on extra-European affairs. On the thorny issue of Vietnam, Couve de Murville would regularly remind American officials that France had spent more than ninety years in Indochina, so as to emphasize its superior understanding of the region.[5] By referring to its blend of tradition and experience, Gaullist rhetoric thus sought to present France as a qualified and desirable interlocutor for Third World states.

Yet, even discounting history and tradition, French leaders underlined that their country's specific nature drove it to seek closer cooperation with developing states.[6] The spirit, the soul, and the genius of France, Couve de Murville would explain in his memoirs, pushed it toward the universal: it stood as the flag bearer of the fundamental principles of the time, that is to say national independence, peace, and cooperation among peoples.[7] Because of its values and its ability to stand up to the superpowers, French officials believed that an independent France could be a major source of inspiration for all states fighting foreign intervention.[8]

In other words, they felt that France's nature and values compelled it to play a special role in the world: "France's authority is moral … Our country is different than others because of its disinterested and universal vocation … France has an eternal role. That is why it benefits from an immense credit; because France was a pioneer of American independence, of the abolition of slavery, of the rights of people to dispose of their own fate; because it is the champion of nations' independence against all hegemonies. Everyone realizes that: France is the light of the world, its genius is to enlighten the universe," de Gaulle explained to Peyrefitte.[9]

Gaullist rhetoric also sought to justify France's involvement in the Third World by highlighting how much its contributions benefited developing states. In order to break with its colonial past, Paris could not simply focus on states that had once been part of its empire. A new policy demanded grander ambitions, as highlighted by the rapport Jeanneney. Published in July 1963, it proved instrumental in determining the scope of French aid and whether it should be limited. Influencing de Gaulle's thinking, the report emphasized that France "should remove all geographical limits. Wanting to set up a list of states with which to cooperate would lead to wrongful exclusions and inclusions. Cooperation must be directed globally...."[10] Between 1963 and 1967, the share of French aid for states outside the franc zone—especially in Asia, the Middle East, and Latin America—actually doubled.[11]

The General clearly invoked France's generosity when he tried to convince citizens to support his policy of cooperation with Third World states. Speaking during his all-important press conference on 31 January 1964, he presented France as at the vanguard of the effort to assist developing states by reminding his audience that it dedicated a greater percentage of total gross national income (GNI) to development aid than did any other state.[12] The General added that the material gains France received from helping these states were very insignificant compared to what France spent in terms of aid.

Moreover, he argued that France's cooperation policy was not a cynical effort, but rather a humane and disinterested effort. Beyond the financial aid it provided, he talked of France's duty to "educate and train" the people of the Third World so as to enable them one day to follow their own path toward progress.[13] This obligation could be applied to all states irrespective of their ideologies, as shown by Paris's ties with socialist Algeria or its recognition of communist China.[14]

As Gaullist rhetoric ceaselessly repeated, the policy of cooperation was underpinned by four core principles: non-intervention in the internal affairs of other states; the right of peoples to self-determination; the independence of nations; and respect for other states.[15] This solemn stand allowed de Gaulle to create a sharp contrast between France and the superpowers, as he pointed out during his trip to Latin America in September–October 1964. France, unlike the two hegemons, did not want to dominate other states. It only wanted to walk "la mano en la mano" with Third World states on their journey toward progress.[16] France thus sought to appear as a state with pro–Third World sensitivities. Its support for stable and fixed prices for raw materials, so as to protect the exporting countries of the Third World, projected concern for their development.[17]

France's stated commitment to the cause of Third World progress was intrinsically connected to its broader goal of promoting world peace. The official discourse repeatedly emphasized the government's active steps to further that noble cause. French leaders presented themselves as reasonable leaders who advised moderation to belligerent states, like when they dealt with their counterparts from the Middle East.[18] They constantly condemned war as solving nothing and advocated political solutions to conflicts.

Gaullist rhetoric claimed that France could and should play a role in the Third World, by virtue of its experience and its ability to help developing states. But, it also used the cooperation policy to foster France's overarching aim of challenging the bipolar Cold War order. Indeed, for de Gaulle, the end goal of peace depended on a commitment to the idea of balance, whereas "a simplistic division of the world into two blocs invariably led to opposition and conflict."[19] Paris essentially viewed the Cold War as a dangerous system. Instead, global equilibrium required the participation of the whole world and could not depend solely on agreements between Moscow and Washington.[20]

For the French president, the emergence of many new independent states represented a profound change in modern civilization, but one that could be easily jeopardized by the Cold War.[21] The global spread of the ideological competition threatened to turn developing states into pawns of the superpower rivalry. In that respect, French leaders were convinced that the policy of neutralization would benefit the interest of small, less-developed states caught between the great free nations and the communist powers.[22]

Promoting neutrality, in other words, sought to encourage Third World independence and less-developed nations' attempts to resist subordination to the superpowers. As de Gaulle explained to the Laotian Prime Minister Prince Souvanna Phouma, "a state can have friends and receive aid. But, it has to solve its own problems without foreign intervention."[23] This reflected the central Gaullist creed according to which nationalism, rather than the sterile (and self-serving) struggle between the U.S. and the Soviet Union, constituted the driving force in world affairs.[24]

The General rejected the Cold War order as abnormal because the bipolar system did not fit with historical precedents. As he told Senator Nelson Rockefeller: "It has never happened in modern times that one or two nations hold all the power. The US and the Soviet Union have all the means of power. All my life, I saw the power of the UK, France, Germany, Russia, a bit Italy, Japan before. It created equilibrium. Today all has changed. Yet, France cannot accept that all the power of the world is shared between two countries. Deep down, all countries agree with us."[25] Influenced by his views deeply rooted in history, de Gaulle essentially perceived the Cold War as a transient phenomenon.

It was a transient phenomenon, and in any case, that hardly mattered when compared to the true global challenge of "two billion people aspiring for progress, well-being and dignity."[26] It was just not possible to let the universe "be divided into haves and have-nots. The whole world is part of a common civilization," de Gaulle explained to Peyrefitte.[27] He refused to consider all international relations, including French policy toward the Third World, through the prism of the East-West conflict.[28] Instead of the Cold War's divisive ideologies, Gaullist rhetoric outlined an ambitious alternative model for relations between developed and developing states. The dominating fact in the world, de Gaulle claimed during a speech at Mexico University, was the unity of the universe and the need for fraternal relations among states, which implied that richer states should help those requiring aid.[29]

Thus, Gaullist rhetoric outlined a coherent and unselfish French presence in the Third World by virtue of its experience and unique nature, so as to contribute to the greater goal of promoting North-South cooperation. This discourse obviously targeted a domestic audience, but it also expressed some of de Gaulle's core ideas about the international system and the artificial and transient nature of the Cold War divide. Yet, this idealistic and long-term view of France's role in the extra-European world also clashed with the short-term necessities and contradictions tied to the country's claim to Great Power status.

The Benefits of Cooperation

Notwithstanding the idealistic Gaullist rhetoric, France's policies toward the Third World proved far less coherent, humane, and pro–Third World in practice. Policy-making with regard to the former African colonies, for instance, was hardly harmonious because it remained the preserve of not one but three different governmental authorities. The Ministry of Cooperation, established in June 1961 and headed by Raymond Triboulet since late 1962, reported to the prime minister and focused on economic affairs. It assumed specific responsibility for aid and cooperation missions in sub-Saharan Africa and for the Aid and Cooperation Fund (Fonds d'Aide et de Cooperation), which sought to foster development in the new countries through investment subsidies.[30] Michel Habib-Deloncle, secretary of state for foreign affairs, represented the Quai d'Orsay and dealt with political affairs and defense accords. Finally, Jacques Foccart, the head of the secrétariat général pour les affaires africaines et malgaches, spoke for the Elysée. The three met every week, along with the director of the competent department of the Quai d'Orsay and an adviser of the prime minister, in order to coordinate policies.[31]

The attempt to establish consensus, however, succumbed to fierce turf wars that primarily involved the Ministry of Cooperation and the Quai d'Orsay. From the start, Couve de Murville conveyed to Triboulet his negative feelings about the Ministry of Cooperation.[32] Triboulet believed that the Foreign Ministry resented the competition from his new ministry. The Quai d'Orsay, for its part, resented that Triboulet tried to use his special funds, behind its back and that of Foccart, to undermine Guinea's leader, Sékou Touré.[33] This struggle was only settled in 1966 when the Ministry of Cooperation lost out and became subordinated to the Quai d'Orsay for the following eight years.

Moreover, aside from the less than harmonious policy-making process, French leaders relied heavily on symbols, as opposed to concrete measures, to mask some of the limitations of their Third World policy. France, after all, had pursued unpopular actions with regard to developing states, including the intervention in Gabon and the termination of aid to Tunisia—to which we could add de Gaulle's disdainful attitude toward the United Nations (UN), one of the sacred cows of anti-colonialism. But, the General, aware of his enormous popularity in the Third World that stemmed from his acts of decolonization and his constant nose-thumbing at the superpower hegemonies, relied on his prestige to gloss over the contradictions of French policy.[34]

Visibility, additionally, allowed the General to dramatize many of his policies in the Third World. His extremely theatrical trips abroad, in particular the tour of South America in autumn 1964 when he made a stop in every country of the continent, were generally accompanied by very ambitious rhetoric, if only to add effect. Yet, they also offered stark evidence of the gap between de Gaulle's aspirations for France and its actual achievements.

A visible policy certainly helped to reinforce France's global prestige. It also gave credibility to the Gaullist rhetoric that France paid close attention to the concerns of developing states and pursued a policy that sought cooperation with these states rather than domination. In turn, substantiating that claim largely depended on establishing good relations with Algeria. After the trauma of the Algerian War, Paris needed to recast its ties with Algiers along the lines of equality and friendship, as symbolized by the agreement of 29 July 1965 that set up a cooperative partnership for the joint exploitation of Algeria's oil reserves.[35]

Algeria would be the "door through which we [France] can penetrate the Third World."[36] Not only would it help remove the stain of France's colonial past, but it would give credibility to the policy of cooperation that sought a fairer model of relations between developed and developing states. The importance of Algeria cannot be overstated since it received 75 percent of France's aid to North Africa, and 22 percent of all money

France sent to developing states for the period 1962–1969.[37] Additionally, de Gaulle proved more lenient with Algeria than with other countries. Despite the difficulties in implementing the Evian Accords, he did not cancel aid, unlike what happened with Tunisia in May 1964 after it breached a bilateral agreement.[38]

The overreliance on symbols and presenting Franco-Algerian relations as model of cooperation helped mask the shortcomings of France's Third World policies, with financial limitations chief among them. Since it already dedicated more than 2 percent of its national wealth to cooperation, de Gaulle could only offer limited additional help to states requesting more aid,[39] and as the 1960s progressed, the share of France's GNP dedicated to aid decreased rather than increased.

Thus, Paris's cooperation policy proved far less disinterested than Gaullist rhetoric suggested, since financial pressure compelled it to seek concrete benefits, especially in the domain of trade. In the case of Algeria, for example, French officials did not view the aid they sent as a gift, but instead as a currency for significant benefits in return. These included a military base, a location for nuclear tests, a significant amount of oil for domestic consumption, a decent market for French exports, and an opportunity to maintain influence.[40] Equally, the military agreements signed with the former sub-Saharan colonies included clauses that gave France priority in the purchase of strategic raw materials and equipment, while these new states also provided markets for the French weapons industry.[41]

Indeed, despite the good deeds and the many advisers and teachers sent to help developing states, France's Third World policy often failed to live up to the humane standards outlined by Gaullist rhetoric. Moral considerations rarely stood in the way of good business, and France handsomely benefited from selling weapons to Third World states.[42] As such, Paris happily supplied arms to both Algeria and Morocco, even though these states had fought each other in 1963; it also provided weapons to both Israel and Arab states.

Moreover, ignoring UN recommendations, France also engaged in military trade with pariah states like Portugal and South Africa, becoming the latter's main supplier until the mid 1970s. Pik Botha, a former South African defense minister, later described the importance of these deliveries: "All these helicopters and the aircraft, coming from France, at a time in our history when we were totally isolated; you must not forget the impact of that; it is tremendous. If you are alone on the ocean, and your boat is about to sink, then another ship goes along; that is quite something."[43] Paris justified these sales by claiming its attachment to the principle of non-interference in domestic affairs and by repeating the promises South Africa made to not use these weapons for internal repression. However, the concrete benefits Paris received in exchange for providing weapons—gold and uranium from South Africa and a satellite station in the Azores from Portugal—easily overcame any qualms it might have had.[44]

The nature of France's aid program was also less disinterested than Gaullist rhetoric suggested. On the one hand, it involved a "conceptual shift from direct aid for friendly allies to a more 'infra-structural' form of assistance based on the sending of teachers, technical advisers and so on."[45] French leaders repeatedly emphasized this evolution, claiming that France sought solely to "train" Third World elites and facilitate their states' development.

On the other hand, by sending teachers and advisers to Third World states, de Gaulle undoubtedly hoped to channel these states' development along a path favorable to French interests. He expected that the promise of cultural, technical, commercial, and linguistic aid could entice the former African colonies to develop according to a French model.[46] This reasoning also extended to other developing states. Training Latin American engineers and elites, in the General's view, would encourage them to speak French and to look to France on a human and material level. Technical assistance was thus not an end in itself, but was expected to result in concrete economic benefits.[47]

This meant that France's policy of cooperation with the Third World amounted to less of a break than it might seem with the colonial period: the aid provided shifted "from the direct and administrative forms of domination specific to colonialism to more indirect forms of control that are more appropriate for neo-colonialism," and by doing so it safeguarded "the monopolies' control on the resources of under-developed states, maintaining them in a position of providers of raw materials and clients for industrial goods."[48]

Additionally, the interests of France and Third World states hardly coincided when it came to economic goals. As an advanced industrial power, France essentially sought to maintain its supplies of raw materials, to spread its political influence, and to gain access to new markets, objectives in stark contrast with the demands of poorer states.[49] These diverging economic aims highlighted the intrinsic limits of the collusion between Paris and the developing world. While France championed universal nationalism, it also aspired to a role of world police officer with the other nuclear powers.[50] Even if de Gaulle described France as sympathetic to the cause of developing states, his conception of the world remained aristocratic; he hardly endorsed the principle of equality between states.[51] When France courted Third World states, it did so on the understanding that it would never jeopardize its independence of action.

Relations with former colonies only strengthened France's desire to maintain a certain distance and relative condescension toward developing states. Since France had granted independence to its colonies, the General felt that it was no longer its duty to solve all their problems. But, at the same time, he saw these same states as utterly dependent on France, constantly asking for more financial aid.[52] As a consequence, he often looked down on them: "They say Fulbert Youlou [president of Congo-Brazzaville until August 1963] is independent. But I am paying for him. So for me, Youlou is not independent" de Gaulle once exclaimed to Peyrefitte.[53]

The General's aristocratic conception of the world, combined with his aspirations to give France a global role, cemented his vision of the Third World as an area of Great Power competition. This did not mean, however, that Gaullist calls for North-South cooperation were entirely cynical, but they certainly downplayed the importance of power politics in France's policy toward the developing world. That the Third World was viewed as an area of struggle for influence emerges very clearly when comparing how Paris dealt with states attempting to "free" themselves from superpower hegemony—like Vietnam, as we will see later—with how it treated its former African colonies.[54]

From 1962 onward, Africa dropped down de Gaulle's priority list once he focused more on global affairs, whereas Couve de Murville had never paid close attention to the continent;[55] this allowed the all-powerful Foccart to exert huge influence on policy. Foccart had laid the foundation for his "bureaucratic predominance in all things African" thanks to his family's import-export company, which had primarily traded with the African colonies prior to World War II. He had also established close contact with the politico-military and intelligence establishment through his involvement in the French resistance, becoming a confidant of the General.[56] Once named secretary general to the presidency of the republic for African and Malagasy Affairs in 1961, Foccart used his position, and his direct access to the French secret services, to pursue goals that were far less magnanimous than those implied by Gaullist rhetoric.[57] The policy toward Africa became largely based on handouts that caused serious distortions: dependency, clientelism, and irresponsibility.[58]

Since Foccart perceived Africa as France's backyard, he mainly sought to protect this French sphere of influence from other Great Powers. In that respect, he shared de Gaulle's inclination to "refuse any American attempts towards harmonization [of policy], that is to say 'leadership' in Africa."[59] He feared that any cooperation with the U.S. might undermine France's prime position in Africa and subordinate it to American interests. Equally, Quai d'Orsay officials feared the spread of communism on the continent. Officially, they stuck to the view that France did not object to Algeria being socialist. In private, however, the same officials emphasized the importance of making sure that Algeria did not join the Eastern bloc.

France did not want a hostile power on its doorstep that could adversely affect the other North African states.[60]

France's military agreements with certain former African colonies served to protect its sphere of influence. These accords claimed to guarantee the internal and external security of the former colonies, since according to Pierre Messmer, the French minister for armed forces, de Gaulle saw instability and anarchy as "the biggest threat to these new states."[61] Even after withdrawing most of its troops from Africa—from 35,000 in West Africa and 12,000 in Equatorial Africa in 1960, down to 9,000 and 6,600, respectively, in 1964—Paris was still in a position to protect its sphere of influence.

Progress in transport enabled troops based in France to quickly intervene in Africa if and when needed. Moreover, by recalling most of its troops, France had reduced its financial burden, maintained its freedom of action, and countered the criticisms made by the Organization of African Unity (OAU) in regard to the presence of foreign troops.[62] France had fewer troops stationed in Africa, but it would not hesitate to intervene at the expense of other states' sovereignty if this would suit its interests.

The Gabon episode in 1964 confirmed this. On 17–18 February, Gabon's army toppled President Léon M'Ba, which immediately prompted the French government to send troops to rescue him. The Quai d'Orsay played no role in the decision-making process. Instead, Foccart authorized the intervention before informing de Gaulle and without M'Ba's request.[63] Gabon was rich in mineral resources such as oil, manganese, and uranium, a powerful incentive to act. On top of that, France wanted to send a signal to its other African partners that it could be trusted to guarantee general order and their security.[64]

Foccart and other French officials would later claim that American intrigues were behind the military putsch in Gabon, and they pointed to companies such as U.S. Steel trying to exploit the mineral resources of the country.[65] Recent research, however, does not back up the claim of American involvement in the Gabon coup. The alleged U.S. involvement essentially played the role of a founding myth for France's Africa policy, a confirmation and a pretext for French authorities for their anti-American policy in Africa.[66] In other words, Paris acted in Gabon of its own accord and to maintain order and protect its influence, not because of external competition from other Great Powers.

France's Third World policy thus followed a variety of motivations that coexisted uneasily. On the one hand, the cooperation policy reflected the universalist aims of human solidarity. France dedicated a significant share of its GNP to help developing states and sent many experts and teachers. On the other hand, cooperation served as another manifestation of France's traditional role as a world power.[67] Besides Foccart's African intrigues, Paris expected self-interested benefits—such as extending its influence or promoting its language, culture, and trade—from its Third World policy and did not hesitate to deal with unsavory partners like South Africa.

Moreover, despite his calls for North-South cooperation, de Gaulle was no Tiers-Mondiste. While he believed that facilitating the progress of the developing states was crucial for global stability, he still believed that Great Powers had special responsibilities in international affairs. He objected to spreading the Cold War into the Third World because it would threaten the independence of smaller states, but primarily, he feared that the extension of the superpower struggle outside of Europe would undermine France's prestige, its influence, and the cause of peace. Instead, peace depended on a regulated competition and the establishment of a new equilibrium between the five great nuclear powers of the time—the U.S., the Soviet Union, France, the U.K., and communist China.

The Third World in France's Grand Strategy

France's ambition to play a greater role on the world stage, along with its pursuit of economic and political benefits, did not always complement its stated aim of helping the developing states and preventing them from becoming pawns in the U.S.-Soviet rivalry. Furthermore, the policy of cooperation had to compete for time and resources with other foreign policy priorities. If de Gaulle had hoped to engage more with the Third World after 1962, within a few years it was clear that this focus could not compete with France's Western and Eastern policies in Europe.

Despite French strategy's firm focus on Western affairs in 1963, decolonization freed France to pay closer attention to the wider world, starting with Latin America. As a State Department analysis noted, de Gaulle turned his attention to the region in 1962, sending former Ambassador Jean Chauvel on a fact-finding mission. It was widely believed that Chauvel came back advocating a more active presence for France. Doing so would buttress its claim to world power status and restore its cultural influence in a region that had declined since World War II.[68] The General also believed that there might be a "great card to play" in the aftermath of the Cuban Missile Crisis, considering the complex relations between the U.S. and its southern neighbors.[69] The idea of "nose-thumbing" Washington in its own backyard certainly encouraged the French president to develop relations with Latin America.[70]

The visit of Mexico's president, Adolfo Lopez Mateos, in March 1963, culminating with the announcement of a $150 million credit from France to Mexico for the building of a petrochemical industry, confirmed France's growing interest in Latin America. But, occurring so soon after the divisive January 1963 crisis, de Gaulle made sure Mateos's visit would not further inflame Franco-American relations. During a toast to his counterpart, he underlined France's desire to cooperate "without changing your [Mexico's] relations with the US."[71] He similarly reassured Juan Bosch, president of the Dominican Republic, that France and America remained friends despite their temporary differences. While de Gaulle did not want to criticize the U.S., he still felt that an exclusive dialogue between the latter and the Latin American states was not desirable.[72]

In private, the General talked much more candidly about his designs toward the region. Acknowledging that Mexico and its neighbors were extremely dependent economically on the U.S., he explained to Peyrefitte that "France could enable them to a certain extent to escape American dominance" and this could start with his plans for a trip to Latin America in 1964.[73] Nevertheless, ambitious rhetoric aside, the Third World was a peripheral concern for France in its overall grand strategy.

Indochina also remained low on the list of France's priorities during this period. As with Latin America, French leaders avoided a confrontational stance; when meeting their American counterparts, they generally expressed minimal solidarity with their policies toward the region. De Gaulle reassured American Secretary of State Dean Rusk that "if Southeast Asia turned against the West, we would act in common with you and the allies of the Southeast Asia Treaty Organization [SEATO]."[74]

Behind closed doors, however, de Gaulle and his colleagues appeared less supportive. Couve de Murville complained about France's exclusion from affairs in South Vietnam, while the General described the situation in Indochina as rotten, as he had warned President Kennedy it would become in 1961. France had "no interest in taking sides ... and even less in siding with the US," he pointed out to his ministers.[75] In part, de Gaulle's lukewarm attitude toward the U.S. stemmed from his resentment at the way it had replaced France in Vietnam, following the humiliating withdrawal in 1954 after the battle of Diên Biên Phû.[76]

The historic ties to Indochina led de Gaulle to consider the region part of the French "sphere," even though it had lost a lot of its past influence. Additionally, his policy toward the former French colony rested on a number of well-established principles, including his belief that the forces of national self-determination unleashed since World War II could not be ignored. He doubted that the conflict in Southeast Asia could be solved by force, and the Algerian War had only strengthened this feeling.[77] Instead, the General and Couve de Murville pushed for a political solution through a return to the 1954 Geneva accords—which had sought to establish an independent Vietnám, free from foreign interventions—and they regularly criticized the American and communist failures to live up to these agreements.[78]

Despite its ambiguity as a concept, the French president considered neutralization the best the West could hope for. As Logevall argues, de Gaulle envisaged a situation whereby the Vietnamese would settle their conflict without external interference, possibly leading to reunification. Even if he saw the most likely outcome of an American withdrawal as a reunified Vietnam under communist control, he did not fear this outcome. Vietnam's traditional animosity toward Beijing would prevent China from controlling Indochina.[79]

The strength of his convictions, combined with the historic connections with the former colony, compelled de Gaulle to seek to restore France's influence in Indochina. Significant developments in 1963 gave him the opportunity to do just that. Roger Lalouette, French ambassador in Saigon, constantly reported to Couve de Murville that the American presence in South Vietnam was causing friction between President Ngo Dinh Diem and his patrons. In May 1963, Diem's brother, Ngo Dinh Nhu, even called for the withdrawal of half of the American advisers.[80] French officials also received reports from Hanoi that the North Vietnamese leaders felt increasingly squeezed between Moscow and Beijing. The moderates were calling for relief from fighting in the South as a means of reducing Chinese pressure.[81]

Lalouette, along with his friend Mieczyslaw Maneli, the Polish representative to the International Control Commission (ICC), believed there was a real opportunity for a political solution. They had been acting more or less as informal mediators between Diem and the North Vietnamese leadership.[82] With Hanoi less intransigent toward Saigon, and with a change in the South's power structure seeming more likely, a new environment was emerging that appeared more favorable for French action; in addition, both South and North Vietnamese officials continually suggested that Paris could play an important role in the future evolution of their country.[83] It is in this fluid context that de Gaulle chose, on 29 August, to publicly come out in support of a reunified and independent Vietnam.[84]

This declaration, an important moment for Gaullist policy, sought to fulfill three different objectives. In the aftermath of the PTBT, de Gaulle wanted to underline France's independence vis-à-vis the superpowers and demonstrate its ability to have an impact on world affairs. He was ready to give the Third World a bigger role in his grand strategy, in reaction to the shortcomings of his European policy and the partnership with Bonn. Finally, as the General told Peyrefitte, the declaration marked the beginning of France's great return in Asia.[85] It is no surprise that Paris's growing focus on Indochina went hand-in-hand with the rapprochement with Beijing. De Gaulle's stand on Vietnam, more so than the PTBT or the common opposition to the superpowers, convinced him that the time was right to send Faure on a negotiating mission to China.[86]

France could no longer ignore the PRC as it sought more influence in Indochina. When Prince Norodom Sihanouk of Cambodia unilaterally denounced American aid on 20 November 1963, he turned to Paris. The French government swiftly obliged and agreed to send Messmer in early January 1964 to discuss future cooperation. Helping Cambodia, for de Gaulle, was essential for Indochina's neutrality and independence, but he also believed that contacts with Beijing would help relations with Phnom Penh.[87]

Thus, the establishment of diplomatic relations between France and communist China derived in part from Paris's growing involvement in Southeast Asia. However, the connection worked both ways. De Gaulle wanted France and the PRC to understand each other and possibly co-operate.[88] Indochina was the obvious area of collaboration, and de Gaulle hoped that the recognition of communist China would yield benefits and provide a great asset for his Vietnam diplomacy, although, unknown to the General, the Chinese leaders viewed the situation very differently and actually feared that the normalization of relations with Paris would prove a liability in their dealings with Hanoi.[89]

The French president believed that Beijing played a pivotal role in the region. There could be no political reality in Asia, he argued in his 31 January 1964 press conference, "regarding Cambodia, Laos, Vietnam, or India, Pakistan, Afghanistan, Burma, Korea or Soviet Russia or Japan which does not include nor involve China … Therefore, it would be impossible to have a neutralization agreement for Southeast Asia without China."[90]

The rapprochement with the PRC acted essentially as a prerequisite for a more active role in Asia. De Gaulle, though, also expected the initiative to have global repercussions. As a Quai d'Orsay source confirmed to a British official, the General had chosen to officially recognize communist China just before his 31 January 1964 press conference in order to draw attention to the announcement of his trips to Mexico and Latin America later that year.[91] In other words, the master of the Elysée believed that the rapprochement with China would act as a stepping stone for a more active French policy toward the Third World.

When Peyrefitte claimed that the forthcoming trips to Latin America would be the most important events of 1964, he was not just engaging in hyperbolic rhetoric.[92] With his European policies stalling somewhat at that time, de Gaulle turned to the Third World path as a means to boost France's prestige as a global power. It needed to make its presence felt in

Latin America, and frustrating the Americans provided an added bonus; "plant a French flag there, on the US doorstep," de Gaulle reminded Raymond Offroy, French ambassador in Mexico City.[93] Additionally, the General counted on his visits to Latin America to define an international order that was not solely defined by the two superpowers.[94]

While he cautiously distinguished between the Soviet tyranny and U.S. as a country respectful of freedom, the central message of his public and private speeches centered on the need for Western Europe and Latin America to cooperate in order to prevent the division of the world between the two hegemons.[95] De Gaulle assumed that denouncing the double hegemony of Moscow and Washington would appeal to his hosts and reinforce the image of France as a truly independent power. But, the main purpose of these trips was to sow seeds for future developments, rather than to achieve any immediate concrete goal. The General confided to former Prime Minister Michel Debré that he was going to Latin America "without a clear diplomatic program, but in some ways instinctively."[96]

Furthermore, French leaders also sought to use Latin America to provide a renewed impetus to the stalling Paris-Bonn axis. During the February 1964 Franco-German summit, de Gaulle tried to convince West German Chancellor Ludwig Erhard that the French and American policies toward Latin America were compatible. He explained that France and West Germany could become alternative partners for these states, thereby reducing the risks of an exclusive U.S.-Soviet competition that could end up with Latin America choosing Moscow.[97] Bonn's help would be particularly welcome if it participated in a joint aid effort, since that would allow France to respond to critics who suggested its policy toward Latin America was solely driven by anti-American aims.[98]

The escalating focus on the Third World during 1964 led France in parallel to push for peace in Indochina along the principle of neutralization.[99] According to the General, as he outlined in his 23 July press conference, force would not solve the conflict in Southeast Asia and there was no other choice but peace along the lines of the 1954 Geneva Accords. The Great Powers, in turn, would have to promise not to intervene, and instead provide substantial economic and technical aid to the region.[100] This plan offered few details, and French leaders did not publicly explain how exactly neutralization would come about. Vagueness, as Logevall points out, certainly suited de Gaulle's purposes. He saw no reason to provide too many specifics because negotiations required a certain blurring of categories and he preferred to see how the situation would develop.[101]

Behind closed doors, however, the General's views were more defined, as Césari explains. France hoped to neutralize Cambodia, Laos, and South Vietnam, under international guarantee and with the cooperation of China, which would gain a buffer-zone free from American presence.[102] This would not necessarily lead to Vietnamese reunification in the short term, and privately, French leaders believed that Hanoi would refuse neutralization; instead it should first be applied to the South in the hope that a truly Vietnamese government would emerge in Saigon.[103] De Gaulle also aimed to convince the PRC to stop providing North Vietnam with the means to lead a struggle in the South. He counted on the fact that China would concentrate on its internal development if the security of its southern flank was assured.

Washington would not lose anything, since the existence of an international guarantee in Southeast Asia, to which the U.S. and the PRC were parties, could maintain the "credibility" of U.S. engagements: it would leave each party free to engage in reprisals if accords were not respected. As for South Vietnam, France believed that the establishment of a pluralist political regime would undermine the popularity of the National Liberation Front (NLF), while military escalation would instead lead opponents to adopt a rigid attitude. In the longer term, de Gaulle bet on the traditional animosity of Vietnam toward China to ensure that Hanoi would prefer neutralization over being absorbed in Beijing's sphere of influence.[104]

These long-term considerations aside, Paris did pursue more immediate actions in favor of peace. De Gaulle actively encouraged Lucien Paye, his first ambassador in Beijing, to sound out the Chinese leaders and determine whether they would support a peaceful solution for Indochina.[105] France wanted a dialogue with China, but without siding with it. In their respective meetings with Huang Chen, the Chinese ambassador in Paris, Couve de Murville and de Gaulle both pointed out that for all the preconditions and recriminations put forward by China, the U.S. responded with similar accusations and conditions. The most important issue was to convene an international conference with participants who were keen to reach a settlement for Southeast Asia.[106]

To this end, France's policy focused on all of Indochina, not just Vietnam. It went to great lengths to prevent Cambodia from abandoning its neutral foreign policy; in March 1964, Paris believed that its strong lobbying alone had convinced Sihanouk not to break relations with London and Washington.[107] Paris continued to promote the idea of an international conference to guarantee Cambodia's independence and territorial integrity, while simultaneously advocating an international conference for Laos after the coup in April that had shaken its fragile equilibrium. France later hosted the representatives of the three Laotian factions—the Pathet Lao, the neutralists, and the rightists—in August–September 1964 in an attempt to save the 1962 Geneva Accords that had established Laos's neutrality.

France's turn to the Third World, however, would not last and instead increasingly succumbed to Great Power considerations. As the situation in Indochina gradually deteriorated, so did relations between Paris and Washington. The tension existed primarily at the higher levels of government, since Quai d'Orsay officials often disagreed with de Gaulle's Vietnam policies; some even suspected that he was working deliberately against U.S. policies.[108] Moreover, differences between Paris and Washington remained somewhat muted until late 1963, with French leaders showing restraint when dealing with their American counterparts.

For example in a talk with President Kennedy, Couve de Murville had strongly denied that de Gaulle's August 1963 declaration sought to create further problems for America in Indochina.[109] Similarly, de Gaulle expressed a certain outward solidarity with the U.S. when Cambodia unilaterally repealed the latter's aid.[110] Behind closed doors, of course, his assessment of American policy sounded more damning. After the coup against Diem in November 1963, he warned Peyrefitte that the U.S.'s involvement would only end in catastrophe if it became more engaged in the region.[111]

As the situation in Vietnam worsened throughout 1964, the General's attitude toward Indochina hardened noticeably.[112] Disagreements came to a head during the SEATO meeting in April 1964, when only France refused to publicly support America's policy.[113] Couve de Murville did not hide his skepticism about the prospects of the U.S. ever achieving a solution via military means. Instead, he warned that only a political settlement could be successful and prevent a serious escalation of the conflict with North Vietnam and China.

Couve de Murville rejected Rusk's view of China as a fully expansionist power. He believed that the U.S.'s dominance in the Pacific, along with China's internal problems, could push the latter to welcome a political settlement.[114] De Gaulle seemed even more forthright during a talk with Under Secretary of State George Ball in June 1964: "I do not believe you can win in this situation [Vietnam] even though you have more canons, more planes, etc.... The more the U.S. becomes involved in the actual conduct of military operations, the more the Vietnamese will turn against you, as will others in Southeast Asia."[115]

Furthermore, Paris's frustrations with Washington's Vietnam policy spilled over to other topics, including Latin America. When de Gaulle visited Mexico in March 1964, he proved more willing to criticize the American attitude toward Latin America than he had the year before, and this even in public speeches. During a toast to Mateos, after repeating his usual comment that France did not want to undermine Mexico's relations with the U.S., he described Franco-Mexican cooperation as a force for good "in opposition to older axes and pacts seeking domination," a clear attack against the Monroe doctrine.[116] De Gaulle's rhetoric confirmed his desire to appeal to Latin American frustrations with the U.S. and to encourage them to take their distances from their powerful neighbor in the North. He deplored America's failure to recognize new changes in the world, such as the emergence of a "Third World with its own ambitions and views," and to accept independent policies from its allies.[117]

By the time of his autumn 1964 trip to Latin America, de Gaulle had shifted to an even higher gear. He still denounced the two superpowers, but his criticism of the blocs now possessed an undeniably strong anti-Yankee tone.[118] He called for the emergence of both Latin America and Europe on the world scene, but he also made it clear that they needed to develop as allies of America, not subordinate entities.[119] The General no longer simply criticized American hegemony in Latin America, he wanted to undermine it. According to former Chilean President Jorge Alessandri: "He [De Gaulle] had described the US as an octopus which had exploited the Latin American countries, was sucking them dry of their natural resources, and which controlled their foreign policy. He called on Alessandri to free Chile from the US grasp and regain its liberty in both the economic and political spheres."[120]

Moreover, growing Franco-American differences also played a crucial role as de Gaulle's assessment of the nature of the conflict in Indochina was evolving. He seemed increasingly inclined to view the conflict in Southeast Asia through Great Power lenses, with the war appearing more like a Sino-American struggle than a battle about Vietnam.[121] In such a context, the tensions with Washington contributed to the French leaders' perceptions that the U.S. held more responsibility for the current problems in Indochina. Describing Moscow as less virulent and Beijing as generally cautious, de Gaulle stressed that American illusions concerning military force threatened to cause a universal crisis.[122] Paris mainly based its assessment of Chinese intentions on the meetings between its officials and their Chinese counterparts. The Chinese leaders, such as Foreign Minister Chen Yi, repeatedly proclaimed their attachment to peace and hoped France could help in that endeavor.[123]

Evidence, however, suggests that China's attachment to peace was tenuous at best. The PRC had an interest in war, not in peace. A persistent people's war in South Vietnam would be more desirable than Vietnamese reunification, which would create a powerful neighbor on its southern flank.[124] Thus, during a trip to Hanoi in July 1964, Chinese Prime Minister Zhou En-lai advocated a combined military and political struggle: in the military area they would strengthen forces, and on the political front, they would adhere to the Geneva Accords and seek to exploit Franco-American differences.[125] France "bought" into this Chinese rhetoric somewhat and perceived China as more defensively minded that it actually was. France believed that American interventionism bore the most responsibility in the escalation of the conflict, a perspective further strengthened after the Gulf of Tonkin incident in August 1964. Franco-American relations embodied such a level of mistrust by then that Couve de Murville would describe the incident as a conspiracy inspired by an America keen to stop communist insurgencies.[126]

By late 1964, France's Third World policy, as well as the situation in Indochina, had reached a turning point. France's shift toward prioritizing its pan-European strategy had major implications. With the emphasis on Europe, the Third World became a lesser concern for de Gaulle. Moreover, as 1964 ended, the gap between Washington and Paris on Indochina had become significant. Couve de Murville openly denounced American policy in South Vietnam as the equivalent of a colonial occupation.[127] De Gaulle, for his part, had given up on helping Washington in the region: "In the last two years, the US has accumulated mistakes. What do you want me to do? They should have been less stupid. I did what I could to push them towards a reasonable path. If they do not want to understand, it is too bad."[128] While the fighting escalated, the chances of convening a conference on Vietnam faded away.[129]

Finally, the worsening crisis in Southeast Asia affected France's approach toward developing states in other crucial ways. While the Third World played a lesser role overall in French strategy, the escalation of the crisis in Vietnam meant that it became France's principal extra-European area of interest, to the detriment of other regions. Additionally, as Devillers argues, the growing American involvement in the war pushed de Gaulle to consider his Asian policy as an extension of his general attitude toward the U.S.[130]

Unsurprisingly, Washington's decision to launch a prolonged bombing campaign against North Vietnam in February 1965, strengthened by a massive dispatch of troops in the following months, intensified the Indochinese conflict and caused a further deterioration in Franco-American relations. After the initial bombing of Hanoi on 7 February, France still pursued the diplomatic option. On 10 February, Peyrefitte officially repeated France's desire to urgently convene an international conference so as to settle all the outstanding problems in Indochina.[131] Couve de Murville also went to Washington a few days later to rally U.S. leaders to the conference plan,[132] and France made it clear to the Soviet government that they would be ready to consult and cooperate, as long as Moscow agreed to convene a conference on Indochina without preconditions.[133]

This diplomatic initiative failed, however, once it became clear that certain protagonists did not want to achieve a settlement. In particular, France increasingly regarded American intransigence as the main obstacle to peace; for Couve de Murville, Beijing and Hanoi wanted to negotiate, but the U.S. did not.[134] With a conference unlikely to happen in the near future, de Gaulle decided to step back and wait: "At one moment, we will say 'That is enough!' We have already said what we needed to at the right moment. The Americans still went to war. And there will be a moment when everyone will have enough of this war. Then, we will say so."[135] During the Council of Ministers meeting on 14 April 1965, he added that if America did not withdraw from Indochina, the war would last for many years and inevitably end in shame.[136]

While France put its peace efforts on hold, it became more vocal in its criticism of the U.S.'s war effort. During the NATO Ministerial Council in May 1965, Couve de Murville launched a scathing attack against America. Claiming that he regretted America's failure to listen to any advice on Indochina, Couve de Murville denounced the American vision of the conflict. In his view, South Vietnam faced a civil war, not a manifestation of world communism as suggested by Washington. To Vietnam, Couve de Murville disingenuously contrasted the example of Algeria, underlining how France had successfully settled the conflict and maintained acceptable relations with its former colony.

The French foreign minister ended by lamenting that it was impossible in current conditions to convene an international conference to negotiate peace.[137] America's intervention in the Dominican Republic in April further exasperated de Gaulle: "The policy the US is leading in Vietnam, in South America and elsewhere is provoking the hostility of peoples of Asia and elsewhere. It is the same thing in South America after sending troops to the Dominican Republic. We are against those operations, which are supposedly part of a crusade against communism, but which in fact seek to defend economic interests."[138]

The Vietnam War symbolized, for the General, all that was wrong with American foreign policy: naïve self-righteousness, a readiness to quash smaller nations' independence, a tendency toward military actions that threatened to drag France into war, and a stubborn persistence in containing "communist" expansion while underestimating the Sino-Soviet split and Vietnamese nationalism.[139] Nevertheless, for all this harsh criticism, France temporarily pushed the issue of the Vietnam War to the side after May 1965, as other policy disputes became more urgent in that period. Moreover, de Gaulle saw no possibilities of ending the conflict in the near future as the war continued to escalate in the second half of 1965.[140]

Meeting with Arthur Goldberg, Lyndon Johnson's special envoy, in December 1965, de Gaulle did not hide his prediction that Indochina might succumb to communism one day, albeit an Asian form of communism. He added that since Hanoi would never accept the American presence in the South, only an American withdrawal could lead to negotiations.[141] But until then, the General believed it was preferable for France to refrain from further intervention in the conflict and instead develop relations with all the other protagonists in the region.[142] Paris pursued a serious dialogue with Moscow and Beijing in this period, while it moved closer to North Vietnam after Saigon broke off diplomatic relations in June 1965.[143] Quai d'Orsay officials also established an initial contact in Algiers with representatives of the South Vietnamese NLF during summer 1965.[144] Maintaining ties with all the main players would be essential if the situation in Indochina became ripe for diplomacy.

Conclusion

Despite its efforts to play a more active role in the Third World after the demise of its empire, France could never match the ambitious aims of the Gaullist rhetoric of cooperation with the developing states. There was always an inherent tension between Paris's genuine desire to help these emerging states and its Great Power ambitions. Moreover, with the exception of 1964, the Third World never quite became a central priority for French leaders. As Franco-American relations deteriorated during this period, particularly over Vietnam, the acrimony ended up pervading all aspects of French policy. By late 1965, France's Third World policy appeared essentially to be an extension of its relations with the other Great Powers, rather than a policy distinct from the Cold War and the East-West conflict.

Thus, from 1963 to 1965, two pillars had dominated de Gaulle's foreign policy, namely restoring his country's Great Power status and overcoming the Cold War bipolar order. If he had given priority to the former goal in that period, he had shown an ability to explore different means to achieve it, including the Franco-German Treaty in the West, the spectacular trips in the Third World, and, finally, détente with the Eastern bloc. Freshly reelected president for seven years in December 1965, the General could now pursue an even more revisionist foreign policy, whereby he would actively challenge the international system led by the superpowers.

Part II

THE RISE AND FALL OF
THE GAULLIST DESIGN, 1966–1968

Chapter 4

1966, Gaullist Zenith

Introduction

On 31 December 1965, in a television address to the French people, de Gaulle announced that, "starting from our rediscovered independence, and not wishing to reverse our alliances and friendships … it is the year of ardor. It is the end of doubts, hesitations and renunciations."[1]

Since returning to power in 1958, the General had sought to restore his country's confidence, power, and prestige. Despite setbacks, he had ended the Algerian War, strengthened the economy, and succeeded in making France's voice heard on the international stage. As he reflected to Peyrefitte: "This septennat, it was primarily une liquidation. La liquidation of the Algerian affair, which was painful and terrible in many ways. … And also the liquidation of subordination to the Americans. … Independence, it is done, at least virtually, there are only a few formalities left. We will no longer be integrated."[2]

In 1966, freshly reelected president, he intended to pursue an even more ambitious foreign policy agenda. No longer content to simply show that France still mattered, he wanted to transform the international order. Keeping his cards close to his chest, de Gaulle was planning major initiatives toward NATO and the Eastern bloc. With France a more assertive player, and with the emerging East-West détente in Europe, the General believed the timing was right to pursue the key objective of his grand design: striving to overcome the Cold War order in Europe.

Disengaging in the West

Since 1959, de Gaulle had progressively withdrawn French forces from NATO's integrated military structure. As he explained to Adenauer, this policy derived from his cardinal belief that any country that was not in charge of its own fate eventually risked losing its self-confidence;[3] by 1966, the General wanted to take the final step in disengaging from NATO, marking the culmination of his quest to restore his country's independence.

Domestic considerations helped convince de Gaulle that he needed to act quickly. Freshly reelected president in December 1965, he now possessed a clear mandate from the French people, but, according to Bruno de Leusse, French representative to NATO, the General probably feared that he might not stay in office for more than a few years. It was now or never, since rising domestic opposition threatened to reduce his margin of action even further after the parliamentary elections scheduled in 1967. Additionally, the French president believed that no leader other than him would be capable of carrying out such a policy.[4]

De Gaulle's determination, however, did not make him more forthcoming with his allies or Quai d'Orsay officials when it came to timing or sharing his ultimate objectives.[5] He continued to blow both hot and cold, so as to purposefully sow further anxiety among the other NATO members. During a meeting on 20 January with Manlio Brosio, NATO's secretary general, the president claimed that France intended to denounce the 1949 Atlantic Pact and effectively withdraw from the Atlantic Alliance altogether.[6] On 10 February, however, de Gaulle reassured Bohlen that his policy would only affect the Organization, not the Atlantic Pact, before falsely suggesting that France was in no hurry to act.[7] He maintained this fiction during his 21 February press conference, when he stated that France would progressively end its subordination to NATO before April 1969.[8] At that time, the North Atlantic Treaty would be up for renewal twenty years after its establishment, with Article Thirteen allowing member-states to denounce the treaty altogether.

Did the General seriously plan to denounce the Atlantic Pact, or was it a ploy? And if he was serious, why did he change his mind between his conversation with Brosio and his talk with Bohlen? A definitive answer to the first question remains elusive but, interestingly, his former collaborators provided conflicting perspectives. Whereas Alphand claimed that the French president decided not to denounce the Atlantic Pact after Couve de Murville and others intervened, Couve de Murville denied that leaving the Atlantic Alliance was ever a serious option.[9]

For the second question, Soutou suggests that in mid January 1966, both les Services de l'Elysée and the Quai d'Orsay's Service des Pactes were looking for formulas whereby France would cease its participation in NATO but not the Atlantic Alliance. He adds that the Quai recommended this formula because France might lose its right to station its troops in West Germany if it left the Atlantic Alliance.[10] As a source from the French administration confirmed to American officials, the Quai d'Orsay had sent a paper to de Gaulle just after his meeting with Brosio, repeating their warnings about the troops in West Germany. The source believed that this had probably convinced the French president to change his mind.[11]

Yet, if the German factor mattered, it did not necessarily play a decisive role. It seems more likely that the General never seriously contemplated withdrawing from the Atlantic Alliance—at least not in 1966—because this would not really advance his other key foreign policy goals. His claim to Brosio appears instead as a typical example of his strategy of causing anxiety among his allies about his intentions. De Gaulle skillfully made people expect the worst, and when he settled on a less excessive position, they breathed a sigh of relief thinking they had won a concession from him.[12] The fact that he authorized Brosio to repeat the contents of the conversation to the representatives of other NATO states tends to substantiate the previous argument.

On 7 March 1966, de Gaulle ended the cat-and-mouse game. In a letter to U.S. President Lyndon Johnson, he confirmed that France would stay in the Atlantic Alliance, but he also announced that France would "recover the entire exercise of its sovereignty on its territory, … terminate its participation in the 'integrated' [NATO] commands, and no longer place its forces at NATO's disposal."[13] Domestically, the initiative made few waves. The government easily won support for its policy in parliament, with the Gaullists defending the move, the socialists condemning it, and the communists not following the socialists. As for public opinion, it reacted with unease and in contradictory ways, confirming the limited importance it attached to NATO matters.[14]

The calm domestic response contrasted completely with the uproar in diplomatic circles. Quai d'Orsay officials, typically more Atlanticist than the General, often disapproved of the policy toward the U.S., but the withdrawal from NATO came as a shock, nearly provoking a revolt from the heads of the main departments. Lucet, the ambassador in Washington, contemplated resigning in disgust over the fact he was not given any forewarning.[15] Even the French military leadership showed some reserve. While it supported in principle the withdrawal from NATO and the idea of challenging the American yoke, it feared that the exit was occurring too abruptly.[16] Finally, while the disengagement from NATO was in line with the enduring French position toward the Atlantic Alliance, the unilateral decision and the forceful method of negotiation shocked the Alliance's other member-states and caused a major crisis.[17]

The other member-states faced a difficult challenge. How could they maintain the cohesion of the Western alliance, while not completely alienating France? Paris primarily aimed to redefine its relations with the Organization, rather than simply "leave" NATO, in order to underline its Great Power status and increase its influence.[18] It remained a member of the Atlantic Alliance and ultimately did not reject some degree of collaboration with its allies, which raised the complex problem of establishing a new framework for this cooperation.[19] In the short term, however, France appeared more interested in dramatizing its break from NATO rather than negotiating, if only to give more weight to its challenge to U.S. leadership.

From the start, Paris presented its Allies with a fait accompli that left little room for compromise. In an aide-mémoire sent to its partners in late March, the French government announced the following measures: it would no longer assign its troops located in Germany to NATO command from 1 July 1966 onward, it would withdraw French personnel from the Allied Integrated Command, and it would demand the evacuation from its territory of all foreign troops and organizations by 1 April 1967.[20] Similarly, France informed the Johnson administration that it no longer recognized the five Franco-American agreements signed in the 1950s: the agreement covering the Châteauroux military base (1951), the agreement covering the Donges-Metz pipeline (1953), the U.S. Military Headquarters Agreement (1953), the Air Bases Agreement (1952), and the System of Communications Agreement (1958).[21]

France relied on this forceful style to send the message to its Allies that they should abandon any hopes of undermining its decisions. According to a Quai d'Orsay source, the government, and de Gaulle especially, stubbornly refused any compromise. The same source, during a talk with Bohlen, confirmed that the General was determined to see the American forces begin their evacuation from France immediately. If Washington tried to delay their departure, the president's reaction could be violent.[22]

France possessed, as Bozo argues, many advantages in the early stages of negotiations. Considering its geostrategic situation, a profound break with the rest of NATO would be more disadvantageous for its allies than for itself. France also had a clear idea of the type of relations it wanted with the Organization, and it sought in priority to reach agreements on cooperation with the Allied forces in case of war. The Allies, America especially, wanted to guarantee maximum collaboration with France, and that placed them in a position of petitioner. Additionally, Washington seemed uncertain about France's ultimate intentions, which it estimated ranged somewhere between a neutral position and support for a "diluted NATO."[23]

Moreover, de Gaulle used all available leverage to pressure his Allies: "if our partners prove difficult, we can make life complicated for them. We can refuse to provide vital services for the survival of their bases, we can deny them authorizations to fly over France," he explained to Hervé Alphand, now secretary general of the Quai d'Orsay.[24] The French military agreed that French airspace could be used as a trump card, in particular to secure continued participation in the Alliance's early warning system—the NATO Air Defense Ground Environment (NADGE).[25] On 3 May 1966, the French president proved true to his word. Paris announced that any authorization for military planes to overfly France would now be renewed on a monthly basis rather than an annual one. For the Service des Pactes, this move sought to emphasize to France's partners the precarious nature of their current situation. Any change in the overflight regime would depend on the evolution of the negotiations linked to France's withdrawal from NATO.[26]

These uncompromising tactics sent a clear warning to the other NATO members: they needed France more than France needed them. As de Gaulle added during the Council of Ministers meeting on 31 March 1966: "… Our allies will realize that it is in their interest to be accommodating, just to be able to benefit from the North-South air communications. No plane going from Germany to Italy can do so without flying over our territory."[27] The General and his officials did not doubt that they were negotiating from a position of strength, and so felt they could afford to act tough.

Thus, France's decision to no longer commit its Forces Françaises d'Allemagne (FFA) to NATO created uncertainty about their future: would they leave West Germany, or would they remain there under a new status? And if so, what would be their mission? Schroeder insisted that the October 1954 convention—which had set the legal ground for the presence of foreign troops in West Germany—became null once France withdrew from NATO, and that both states would need to agree on a new legal status whereby France recognized the sovereignty of the host state.

Paris, however, rejected this argument. In an aide-mémoire, it declared its readiness to withdraw its troops from West Germany by July 1967 unless the German government made it clear it wanted to keep the FFA.[28] Privately, de Gaulle was more forthcoming about his desire to see French troops remain in West Germany, as their presence symbolized their victory in World War II and had nothing to do with NATO.[29] In talks with foreign officials, though, the General threatened to withdraw the FFA so as to put pressure on Bonn.[30]

By summer 1966, French leaders believed that they had won their show-down with NATO.[31] Their reaction was only reinforced by the limited U.S. reaction to the withdrawal. President Johnson had counseled restraint, to the obvious displeasure of his collaborators. Johnson's "soft" treatment of the General had particularly angered Dean Acheson, who complained that the president had "made the greatest imperial power the world has ever seen kiss de Gaulle's arse."[32] Moreover, with the negotiations concerning the withdrawal about to start—France only selected its teams at the Inner Council meeting on 2 June—the General felt he had accomplished his first aim of imposing a redefinition of France's relations with NATO.[33]

Delaying negotiations helped French interests in many respects. It dramatized the symbolic split between France and the Organization and forced the Allies to accept France's new status. Paris had achieved its main objective, but the situation was far from completely resolved, as de Gaulle told his collaborators during the same 2 June meeting: "This NATO busi-ness is both simple and complex. Simple, because we know what we want and where we are going. Complex, because there are in fact several nego-tiations."[34] The withdrawal from NATO culminated France's quest to re-claim its independence, promoted its Great Power status, and challenged U.S. leadership, but it also stood as the cornerstone of a more ambitious foreign policy agenda. The disengagement from NATO thus closely inter-acted with other vital domains of France's international action.

The international context, especially the Vietnam War, compelled de Gaulle to quickly withdraw from NATO. Few scholars have pointed out that he sent his letter to Lyndon Johnson on 7 March 1966, or five weeks after the U.S. ended a truce on bombing North Vietnam.[35] Couve de Mur-ville later confirmed this this influenced the General's decision, stating "he [De Gaulle] took the resolution just after the renewal of his presiden-tial mandate, and even more firmly as the Vietnam War was becoming bloodier."[36] Leaving NATO's integrated military structures at a time when America was seriously escalating its involvement in Vietnam benefited France. It added more weight to France's criticism of U.S. leadership and to the arguments that NATO no longer seemed relevant in a changing world in which Asia, rather than Europe, was the main field of Cold War conflict.[37]

The initiative against NATO also interacted with the EEC crisis. Boycot-ting the Community since 30 June 1965, France had agreed in late Decem-ber to restart talks with its five partners. After more acrimonious debates, France finally agreed to end its "empty chair policy" after the Luxemburg compromise of 30 January 1966.[38] Crucially, France chose not to initiate the disengagement from NATO as long as the EEC crisis was not settled. The General usually shied away from dealing with two crises simultaneously.

Moreover, attacking NATO while the EEC remained deadlocked would give the impression that France intended to destroy the whole organization of the Western world.

Instead, by first ending the Community boycott, France could try to project the image of an independent but loyal ally, solely targeting American leadership within the Atlantic Alliance rather than the European project. In practice, the French leaders were pleasantly surprised that the NATO showdown did not cause further disruption to the European Community.[39] As the Atlantic Organization faced a severe test, the EEC secured its future through the three agreements of 11 May, 14 June, and 27 July. Not only did these accords finalize the CAP's financial regulation and set 1 July 1968 as the date when the common industrial and agricultural markets would come into force, but they also defined part of the Community's stance on agricultural questions for the Kennedy Round.[40]

The NATO crisis effectively shielded the EEC. After France announced its withdrawal from the Atlantic Organization, the latter stage became the main point of focus for government officials, with beneficial consequences for the Community. As Emile Noël, the European Commission's executive secretary, suggested, the French administration took advantage of de Gaulle's preoccupation with NATO to push ahead on the CAP and the Kennedy Round in Brussels. Similarly, according to Jean Dromer, an adviser in the Elysée, the absence of the anti-French Schroeder from the Belgian capital certainly facilitated Franco-German cooperation.[41]

Both France and the five believed they benefited by compromising on EEC matters, or what U.S. officials labeled the "double trap" theory. While France assumed the five might act more softly on the NATO front if they were sucked into having a vested interest in the maintenance of the EEC, the five believed they were trapping France into greater enmeshment in the Community.[42] This would significantly lessen the danger of a total break between France and its Western partners. Rather than being communicating vessels, as Ludlow points out, "the Community and NATO spheres were hence more like separate billiard balls, liable at times to touch and affect each other's advance but otherwise subject to independent stimuli and dynamics."[43]

The withdrawal from NATO was also closely connected to de Gaulle's key upcoming trip to the Soviet Union in June 1966, despite Couve de Murville's claims to the contrary.[44] The General needed to finalize the disengagement before going to Moscow. As Roussel argues, this would only strengthen de Gaulle's position in his talks with the Soviet leaders.[45] Conversely, if the initiative against NATO had come after the trip to the Soviet Union, this might have led some of France's allies to suggest that de Gaulle's policy had been the result of a deal with the Kremlin.[46]

Moreover, besides bolstering France's Great Power status during the Moscow trip, the president aimed for balance in his policy. By withdrawing from NATO, de Gaulle believed he was anticipating future changes in East-West relations that would eventually make the military alliances obsolete; in the short term, though, he chose not to leave the Atlantic Alliance as a guarantee against any resurgence of the Soviet threat. Additionally, he planned to use the withdrawal from NATO as a tool in his dealings with the states of the Eastern bloc and as a motor for his key objective of East-West détente in Europe.[47] Thus, de Gaulle wanted his policy toward the Atlantic organization to serve his overarching goal of overcoming the Cold War order in Europe.

Extending a Hand to the East

Indeed, East-West détente in Europe and disengagement from the Atlantic Alliance were intrinsically connected. On the one hand, Paris argued that the new international context, marked by a growing thaw between states on either side of the Iron Curtain, justified its departure from NATO. As Couve de Murville emphasized during a radio interview: ... within each camp, the Western and the Communist camps, things have changed and ... the various members of both camps have rebuilt their economies and reclaimed their personalities. All this means that the situation is very different today [than it was in 1949]. It is under this angle that we have to consider the recent decision taken by France towards NATO."[48] De Gaulle subscribed to this viewpoint when he stated, during the Council of Ministers meeting on 31 March 1966, "it is natural for us to loosen in times of détente a [military] system established for periods of tension."[49]

On the other hand, the disengagement from NATO did not solely result from the changing East-West relations in Europe. As François Puaux, head of the European department of the Quai d'Orsay, argued in an internal note, France's policy toward NATO could only be understood by looking beyond the context of the Atlantic Alliance. It followed instead the ideas expressed by de Gaulle on Europe's long-term future in his seminal press conference of 4 February 1965.

Ending military integration, Puaux added, constituted a vital precondition for the East-West rapprochement pursued by France, since integration prevented European states from reclaiming their independence. To the criticism that France's policy toward NATO played into Moscow's hands, Puaux countered that France's move could prove equally contagious within the Eastern bloc. Romania, after all, also relied on French policy to resist the Soviet integration efforts through the Warsaw pact.[50]

France's withdrawal from NATO and the opening toward the Eastern bloc were therefore not separate policies, but two sides of the same coin; both aimed to end the division of Europe and restore full sovereignty to all its states.

French leaders pointed to the withdrawal from NATO when encouraging their Eastern bloc counterparts to reassert their independence. This strategy featured very prominently during the French diplomatic offensive aimed at the satellite states during spring–summer 1966. Between April and July 1966, Couve de Murville successively visited Bucharest, Sofia, Warsaw, Prague, and Budapest. During his talks with communist officials, he reiterated the argument that France's policy toward the Atlantic Alliance could serve the cause of détente in Europe. Thus, he told Ion Maurer, Romanian prime minister, "we [France] took a certain decision towards NATO, which will constitute another step on the path towards the normalization of political conditions in Europe."[51] Couve de Murville shared these same thoughts with the more orthodox Bulgarians and Poles: "That is why we left NATO. This policy is part of our plans for the whole of Europe, which aims to have Western European and Eastern European states living in normal conditions ..."[52]

Nevertheless, the Soviet Union and some of its allies worried about the impact of de Gaulle's diplomacy within their own bloc, as Puaux confided to American officials: "the Romanian Ambassador [in Paris] Victor Dimitriu informed me that de Gaulle's efforts to 'unfreeze' the Cold War and to force reconsideration of the NATO organization were having a beneficial effect in Romania, but constituted an embarrassment to the Soviets."[53] Romania benefited from the French example, but it was an exception within the communist bloc. Other states, in particular Poland, tended to instinctively adopt a cautious approach when it came to undermining the status quo.[54] Poland seemed happy in theory to destroy the military pacts in Europe, but acknowledged in practice that this was not a realistic policy.[55]

Paris still hoped that its diplomatic offensive of spring and summer 1966 could help to develop contacts and cooperation with all satellite states, which it considered a vital component of its East-West policy. Couve de Murville used his visits to Eastern Europe to finalize cooperation agreements, such as the new cultural and scientific agreements of cooperation that he signed in Poland with his counterpart Adam Rapacki.[56] By dealing with all Eastern bloc states, the French foreign minister sought to increase French prestige and remind his hosts that détente should involve all states, not just the superpowers.[57]

France, however, was not trying to detach the satellite states from their powerful Soviet protector. In the long run, the General wanted them to show more independence vis-à-vis Moscow, because as he told Zenon

Kliszko, vice-marshal of the Polish Diet, "an ideology does not prevent a state from being a state, with its own ambitions and policies."[58] A more assertive Eastern Europe would also encourage Western Europe to take its distance from the U.S. But, de Gaulle did not object to the satellite states maintaining ties with their Soviet patron. While the French president opposed blocs, he viewed spheres of influence in a more nuanced way, even tolerating them when they resulted from historical roots or affinities.[59]

The General thus chose the Soviet Union for his first trip behind the Iron Curtain, because he wanted France to show that it "started with the essential, and to avoid giving the impression to the Russians that it was trying to detach them from their satellites."[60] Paris acknowledged that serious progress in East-West relations could only occur with Moscow's agreement. But even with that caveat, de Gaulle's trip to the Soviet Union still represented the crowning moment of France's pan-European strategy.[61] He wanted it to appear as a defining moment in his quest to foster an East-West rapprochement in Europe.

The General could not move too quickly at a time when his imminent visit to the Soviet Union, occurring so soon after the withdrawal from NATO, caused great anxiety in the West.[62] Paris's allies feared that it might be breaking away from the Atlantic Alliance, but de Gaulle and his collaborators did their utmost to deny that claim. France needed the support of its Western partners as long as the Soviet Union remained a potential threat. Thus, French leaders went to great lengths to reassure their Allies and public opinion in regard to the aims of the visit.[63] Addressing the French Parliament, Pompidou emphasized that the General's trip to the Soviet Union did not signal a reversal of alliances and presented no danger to the European and American allies.[64] French officials also sought to downplay the possible impact of the trip. During a dinner with his West German, British, and American counterparts, Couve de Murville described the president's upcoming voyage to Moscow as a normal development of French policy and predicted that nothing dramatic would emerge from it.[65]

Additionally, since he believed Western Europe would play a key role in any post–Cold War system and he hoped to encourage them to follow in his footsteps, de Gaulle wanted to convince his European allies that he was acting in their interests by going to the Soviet Union: "it is not at the moment when the two blocs are cracking up that I am going to think of leaving one bloc for the other ... I will speak for Western Europe," he explained to Alain Peyrefitte, now minister for scientific research, nuclear, and spatial questions.[66] Consequently, by presenting France as Western Europe's leading spokesperson when it came to relations with the Eastern bloc, the General defended many key Western ideas. He adamantly opposed any recognition of East Germany, in part to reassure Bonn that his trip to Moscow would help the cause of German reunification. In other words, France wanted to keep one hand firmly tied to its Western allies and to extend the other one to the states of the Eastern bloc.

By reaching out to the Soviet leaders, the General planned to probe and test Soviet intentions. He wanted "to see where the Soviets are going, and what they can agree on; or at least where they are going and what they cannot agree on."[67] De Gaulle and his collaborators still remained suspicious of their Soviet counterparts, and they sought to develop cooperation with Moscow within certain boundaries. When Soviet ambassador in Paris, Valerian Zorin, again suggested a possible Franco-Soviet treaty, the General refrained from giving any categorical answer.[68] He did not want any far-reaching agreement with Moscow, as he confided to Adenauer: "the Russians are very polite, which is line with their policy. I am not refusing their politeness, but I will not make any fundamental agreements with them. Maybe we will improve scientific and cultural relations. Surely, we will speak about Germany as we have done in the past."[69]

Instead, de Gaulle envisioned the trip as involving a sort of *diplomatie du témoignage* (testimony diplomacy). He would tell the Soviet leaders that France wanted to talk, despite differences in regimes.[70] He intended to discuss any subject or region with his Soviet counterparts.[71] But, equally, he had no clear idea of how the conversations would develop, nor what they would achieve. As he told Danish Prime Minister Otto Krag, he did not know what to expect from his trip, but the Soviet leaders had repeatedly invited him and he wanted to repay the visit made by Khrushchev in 1960.[72] What was clearer, though, is that the French president did not want German reunification to happen quickly. He also realized that the Soviet Union pursued détente for its own interests, but he still viewed it as less bellicose than in the past and more interested in reaching some sort of general détente with the West.[73]

Even though de Gaulle downplayed the importance of the trip, it did not mean that he had no precise idea of how the latter could serve his ambitious long-term plans for Europe. As Soutou explains, the end goal of the General's pan-European strategy was a Europe-wide security system in which American troops would eventually leave the continent. In exchange for their departure, the Soviet Union would abandon East Germany and allow German reunification, which in turn would also restore the independence of the satellite states. The two main pillars of the system would be France and the Soviet Union, as nuclear powers, but security would be guaranteed by an interlocking set of checks and balances.

Paris and Moscow would contain Bonn, while a closer union between the states of Western Europe would contain Soviet power. The U.S. would play its traditional role of underwriter and ultimate arbiter of the European order. This amounted, in other words, to a modernized version of the Concert of Nations of the nineteenth century.[74] In this context, withdrawing from NATO just before going to Moscow made complete sense. As Pierre Maillard, former diplomatic adviser to de Gaulle, confirmed to Zorin, the French president wanted to have something to offer the Soviets in order to ask for their support for his views on German reunification.[75]

The General expected his trip to play a central role in his long-term goal of transforming the European order and to signal that the Soviet Union, rather than West Germany, had become France's main partner.[76] As Couve de Murville explained in an interview for Soviet radio on 4 June 1966, Franco-Soviet cooperation on European matters could act as a role model for their respective allies and encourage them to follow a peaceful path.[77] He reinforced that message during his speech at the NATO ministerial meeting in Brussels in early June 1966. While calling for détente without illusions, he attacked the principle according to which the East-West rapprochement should be the competence of the military alliances, that is to say, the responsibility of the superpowers.[78] Détente needed to take place within a European framework.

De Gaulle's optimism in regard to Franco-Soviet cooperation benefited from Moscow's effort to seek better relations with Western Europe—except West Germany—and exploit U.S. vulnerability on Vietnam.[79] In previous years, as detailed in chapter 2, Soviet leaders had been greatly divided over the desirability of peaceful coexistence.[80] Conservative figures, like Politburo members Aleksandr Shelepin and Mikhail Suslov, assumed that centrifugal forces in the West would intensify independently of Soviet actions. They called for increased military spending because they still considered NATO a threat, and they feared that peaceful coexistence could undermine the cohesion of the socialist alliance.

The so-called "instrumental Europeanists" disagreed with this conservative analysis and instead argued that the rise of centrifugal trends had resulted from the combination of Soviet overtures and the decrease in international tension. They saw serious benefits in de Gaulle's campaign to reduce, and perhaps eliminate, the American presence in Europe. Finally, a third group, that included Gromyko, supported peaceful coexistence but appeared less hostile to the U.S. They viewed West Germany as the main threat and feared that a more independent Western Europe could undermine the bipolar strategic order, making international relations more dangerous and unpredictable.[81]

These debates came to a head in March 1966 at the Twenty-Third Party Congress of the Communist Party of the Soviet Union and were solved by a compromise. Brezhnev's speech emphasized vigilance, with only a secondary emphasis on peaceful coexistence. He stressed Soviet-European cooperation as a counterweight to the American and West German menace, whereas Gromyko put more emphasis on German "revanchism" and sang an Americanist tune. France was singled out as the centerpiece of this combined strategy, with Brezhnev highlighting Soviet-French ties and ordering a "further improvement of these relations."[82] For the Kremlin leaders, Paris's policy corresponded to Soviet interests because it sought to weaken the links between Bonn and Washington. Some officials even hoped that Paris might denounce the Atlantic Pact in April 1969.[83]

Thus, both Paris and Moscow wanted de Gaulle's trip to be a success, even if for different reasons. On his arrival, the General went out of his way to praise Russia and the possibilities for further cooperation. He repeatedly emphasized the fact that both Russia and France had a long past — implicitly opposing them to the rootless America — and that history dictated an important role for Russia in Europe.[84] This claim that the Soviet Union needed to take part in the peace process in Europe pleased the Kremlin leaders.[85] The three high-level conversations that took place during the trip highlighted many areas of agreement, ranging from Vietnam to a shared opposition to any speedy German reunification. The General also took a step in the Soviet direction when he praised the idea of a European security conference, even if he added that this was not an immediate prospect.

On the other hand, during the first talk with Brezhnev, Kosygin, and Podgorny, de Gaulle made no efforts to hide their differences. He refused to depart from Western orthodoxy and recognize East Germany. He also highlighted France's independence, pointing out that he accepted Soviet power as a balance against American hegemony, like he accepted American power as a guarantee against Soviet hegemony. His key aim, ultimately, was to probe Soviet intentions. With his very first question, he confronted his hosts about whether they perceived the situation in Europe as definitive or whether they accepted the possibility of change, in particular with regard to Germany.[86] The General wanted to know whether the Soviet Union could go along with his vision for a new European system, which was why he constantly argued for taking the German question away from the U.S.-Soviet rivalry.

De Gaulle left the Soviet Union very pleased with the results of his trip, as he explained during the Council of Ministers meeting of 2 July 1966: "The [Soviet] regime survives but is transforming itself. It is becoming less ideological and more technocratic. The meetings went well. The differences of opinion on the German question are clear, but were pointed out without insistence ... They consider that the dialogue with Western Europe must go through France. They want to keep up these contacts. Our policy, which consists in breaking up the Cold War, is coherent with their feelings and interests."[87] The masters of the Kremlin had remained pretty inflexible on the German question, but they had not ruled out reunification either. Additionally, both states signed various agreements, including a common declaration on their relations, established economic commissions, and promised to set up a "hot-line" between the two capitals for regular consultations.[88] The "hot-line," in particular, really appealed to de Gaulle's global ambitions.[89] After all, the only other existing "hot-line" was the one set up in 1963 between Moscow and Washington.

Moreover, the General appreciated the welcome he received throughout his time in the Soviet Union, the opportunity to directly address the people directly via Soviet television, and how his trip was received domestically.[90] De Gaulle wanted his policy of détente to appeal to the people of the Eastern bloc, not just its leaders.[91] Thus, by summer 1966, considering Moscow's tense relations with Bonn and Washington, Paris could legitimately claim to be the principal mediator in East-West relations.[92]

A Platform in Cambodia

The trip to the Soviet Union marked a high point for de Gaulle. Combined with France's withdrawal from NATO, it had provided an ideal platform to promote his foreign policy grand design, namely overcoming the Cold War order in Europe. Additionally, it had further confirmed the extent to which Europe had become the General's essential area of concern. The dominant focus on Europe largely shaped France's stance on the Vietnam conflict, since the latter appeared to be an obstacle to Paris's goal of fostering East-West détente in Europe.

France's attitude toward the Vietnam War had already crystallized in the preceding years. It believed that the fighting in Indochina threatened the independence of the states in the region, in line with de Gaulle's views about the detrimental effect of the Cold War on the Third World, but it also feared that the conflict might escalate into a serious confrontation between the U.S. and communist China. That is partly why de Gaulle warned Lyndon Johnson that peace talks could only start once the U.S. government had decided to withdraw its troops and end its intervention in Vietnam.[93]

France opposed American policies, although it refrained from overly publicizing its criticism. During talks with their American counterparts, French officials were more candid, highlighting their differing assessment of the nature of the conflict. While Washington blamed North Vietnam, sponsored by communist China, as the aggressor, Paris believed that South Vietnam was in the midst of a civil war where the local population was fighting against a government imposed from the outside.[94] French diplomats also disagreed with their American colleagues over the motivations of the main belligerents, preferring to emphasize national rather than ideological considerations. Couve de Murville, for example, often underlined existing differences between Beijing and Hanoi. He judged Hanoi to be more receptive to negotiations and believed Beijing would be unable to stop its ally should it choose to press forward with peace talks.[95]

Furthermore, during his 21 February 1966 press conference, de Gaulle outlined what he considered to be the key guiding principles for any peaceful settlement. After claiming that war would not solve the conflict, he added that peace demanded a political solution among all parties involved and a return to the provisions of the 1954 and 1962 Geneva Conferences. Locally, all foreign interventions would have to end, allowing for the establishment of neutrality for Vietnam as a whole; in the international sphere, the Great Powers—the U.K., the U.S., the Soviet Union, communist China, and France—would then act as guarantors of the agreement.[96]

Even though a peaceful settlement did not seem feasible in 1966, French leaders worked hard behind the scenes. They knew that their views on Indochina resonated with many states throughout the world and that this provided them with a good card to play. Thus, the Eastern bloc states consistently applauded France for its criticism of American policy, and Couve de Murville certainly used that to his advantage during his extended tour of the satellite states.[97] French positions on the Vietnam War also appealed to officials from the Third World, although French leaders did try to distance themselves from the anti-American tone of some of the more outspoken critics.[98] Couve de Murville, for instance, disagreed with some of the attacks against the U.S. delivered by the Chinese ambassador in Paris, Huang Chen, expressing his doubts that Washington had any plans to wage war against the PRC.[99]

The similarity of France's views with those of communist and Third World states strengthened France's claim to play a mediating role if peace talks ever became more likely, as de Gaulle explained to Alphand in early January 1966: "The war will continue and get worse. We must not intervene, but instead establish and develop our relations with all the actors."[100] This was true in regard to the Great Powers. De Gaulle confirmed to Huang Chen that he wanted to welcome Chinese Prime Minister Zhou En-lai to France.[101] At the same time, French officials maintained contacts with all local parties. Étienne Manac'h, head of the Asie-Océanie department of the Quai d'Orsay, regularly met with the South Vietnamese General Consul in Paris, Nguyen Huu Tan.[102]

In parallel, Paris strengthened its ties with Hanoi. On 24 January 1966, Ho Chi Minh sent a letter to all socialist, non-aligned, neutral, and Western states. Significantly, France was the only state of the Atlantic Alliance to reply to Ho's message. De Gaulle's missive helped develop a new chapter in the relations between the two countries.[103] On 13 May 1966, Couve de Murville hosted Mai Van Bo, the commercial delegate of North Vietnam in France, for the first time, and on 2 August, the French government upgraded this commercial representation to the status of general delegation, thereby fulfilling Hanoi's desire to have equal status with Saigon for their representation in Paris.[104] Moreover, France continued its secret diplomacy with non-state actors, especially the South Vietnamese NLF (National Liberation Front). Manac'h agreed to the opening of an NLF "press bureau" in Paris, despite knowing that it would act as a cover for political action.[105]

Despite France's ultimate ambition to act as a peace broker, the escalation of the conflict in 1966 and the overall direction of its foreign policy pushed France to sharpen its criticism of Washington's rising involvement in Indochina after the end of the short bombing truce in late 1965, and the restart of the bombing campaign of North Vietnam in late January 1966 only added more fire to the smoldering Franco-American relations. The French government issued a communiqué on 2 February deploring the recent course of action and emphasized that "this renewed bombing ... compromises even more the cause of peace";[106] France partly justified its withdrawal from NATO by stating its refusal to become involved in a war against its will.[107]

This period crystallized the General's desire to head to Asia with the intention of taking a public stand against the U.S. war effort. On 24 February, he summoned Jean Sainteny to the Elysée and instructed him to visit Beijing, Hanoi, and Phnom Penh on a fact-finding mission. Thanks to his past in the French Resistance and his experience as general delegate to Hanoi, Sainteny presented the advantage of being trusted by both de Gaulle and many Vietnamese communist leaders. He would eventually complete his visit in the early summer.[108] De Gaulle, for his part, prepared his trip to Asia in complete secret. As Manac'h confided to a British colleague, the Quai d'Orsay only heard of the plan in mid June, just before the trip to Moscow, when they received a telegram drafted by the Elysée. The message, intended for Phnom Penh, confirmed the General's intention to go to Cambodia in early September.[109]

By the time the General had returned from the Soviet Union and turned his attention back to Indochina, the situation on the ground appeared even more dangerous. America's first bombings of Hanoi and Haiphong had just taken place in late June, coinciding with Sainteny's mission in Southeast Asia.[110] Not surprisingly, the latter's reports painted a grim picture of the region, suggesting that communist China seemed ready to launch a massive intervention in Vietnam and that all the elements were in place for a "new Korean war."[111] Additionally, Ho Chi Minh claimed to Sainteny that Hanoi would never surrender to America, which only further convinced de Gaulle that the U.S. needed to seek peace through negotiations.[112]

Throughout summer 1966, French leaders increasingly worried about the developments in Indochina. Couve de Murville complained to Schroeder that the "general situation in the world will depend on those developments [in Indochina]"; de Gaulle later warned Ethiopian Emperor Haile Selassie that the threat of a universal catastrophe was growing as a result of the Southeast Asian war.[113] The General, in particular, feared that the Vietnamese conflict might seriously thwart his blossoming détente with the communist bloc.[114]

In some respects, France did not necessarily mind seeing America trapped in the Vietnamese quagmire, since it meant that it would focus less on Europe and thereby allow France more leeway in continental affairs. But, as long as the U.S. stayed in Indochina, there was also the risk that the conflict might escalate and lead to a dangerous increase in U.S.-Soviet tension, which could undermine France's rapprochement with the Eastern bloc. As Sullivan points out, the success of the General's objectives relied on the correct balance between superpower cooperation and conflict; too much of either might restrict France's margin of action.[115]

In any case, the French president's frustration with American policy in Vietnam reached its peak by summer 1966. De Gaulle perceived the U.S. government as holding nearly all the cards, and that it alone could end the war once it finally decided to withdraw its troops.[116] By doing so, the U.S. could remove a significant obstacle to the French pursuit of East-West détente in Europe. So, beset by resignation and anxiety, de Gaulle was not going to Cambodia with the hope of facilitating the settlement of the Vietnamese conflict.[117] Rather, as he confided to U.S. Ambassador to Ethiopia Edward Korry during a stopover in Addis Ababa, he planned to speak his mind. He added that Americans would later thank him for it.[118]

The General's views on the Vietnam War were not always shared by the wider French administration. The more Atlantic-minded diplomats in the Quai d'Orsay often complained about their colleagues who wished for a humiliating American surrender.[119] Even at the top level, de Gaulle appeared far more uncompromising than Couve de Murville.[120] According to Manac'h, in a letter he wrote to the new ambassador in Washington Charles Lucet, Couve de Murville did not support the Sainteny mission, which echoed his own pessimism: "Showing that a channel remains open between Paris and Hanoi, that is something, but we have not much to convey ... Unless the General has decided to finally leave the domain of ritual declarations on Southeast Asia and make concrete proposals."[121]

Yet, as with other key foreign policy decisions of 1966, de Gaulle took sole charge of policy toward Indochina in the summer and barely consulted with his officials. The speech given in Phnom Penh on 1 September, written during de Gaulle's plane trip to Djibouti, reflected, according to Couve de Murville, the General's deepest feelings about the Vietnam War.[122] Without a doubt, it would prove his most complete and dramatic statement on the subject of Indochina.[123]

Delivered to a crowd of near 100,000 people, the speech read as a solemn and scathing one-sided criticism of the American involvement in Vietnam, which the General described as a growing threat to the world. If it was "unlikely that the American war machine would be destroyed, there was no chance, at the same time, that the peoples of Asia would submit to the law of a foreigner from the other side of the Pacific, regardless of his intentions or the power of his weapons." There could be no military solution to the conflict and the opening of negotiations depended on the eventual withdrawal of American forces.[124]

The speech provoked strong and varied reactions across the world. Press articles were typically welcoming in the Third World, systematically favorable in European Communist countries, and mitigated in the West. U.S. officials protested vigorously to their French counterparts, denouncing Paris's "stab in the back."[125] The speech would later be the subject of disputes among scholars, who could not agree on what the General was trying to achieve. Whereas Roussel describes the Phnom Penh address as a violent denunciation of the American presence in Vietnam and part of a wider global strategy to make France's voice heard in the world, Lefort argues that de Gaulle was keen to show his American friends the errors of their ways.[126] Lacouture emphasizes the fact that the French president took advantage of the great platform provided by Cambodian leader Prince Norodom Sihanouk to speak to the Third World. De Gaulle indeed confirmed to his aide-de-camp, Jean d'Escrienne, that France would draw great benefits in the Third World thanks to his oration.[127]

These interpretations certainly have some merit. The General understood that his fierce criticism of the U.S. would play well domestically and abroad. Moreover, by speaking in neutral and independent Cambodia, he could take advantage of an ideal stage from which to defend his ideas on neutrality in the Third World and contrast them with the detrimental impact of Cold War interventions. As he told Peyrefitte, "we had to tell the world that there will only be peace in Indochina if the two superpowers do not transform it into a field of their rivalry."[128] The speech also underlined France's moral authority, with the reference to the Algerian War enabling de Gaulle to stress his credentials as a commentator on the Vietnam War.[129] In his narrative, France had ended the conflict in Algeria without losing its prestige and had subsequently managed to establish a new chapter in the cooperation with developing states.

Yet for all the merit of these interpretations, the evidence suggests that de Gaulle's Phnom Penh speech was mostly driven by his European strategy. The condemnation of the U.S.'s war effort reflected the General's sincere views, but the timing of the speech resulted from the imperatives of his larger foreign policy objectives. As Paris promoted East-West détente and overcoming the Cold War order in Europe, it considered the Vietnam War a vital obstacle to that goal. It is also for this reason that the president singled out America for blame, since he believed Washington held all the cards for ending a conflict that impeded France's goals.

Staying the Course

While France had pursued an ambitious foreign policy agenda for most of 1966, in the aftermath of Phnom Penh it focused on consolidating these previous initiatives. This included finalizing the negotiations on France's new status within the Alliance, a subject which Paris had somewhat put on the back burner since June 1966. Once the talks started, however, de Gaulle knew exactly what he wanted. As long as the other NATO allies respected France's independence of decision, meaning it would not be automatically committed if a war broke out, some form of cooperation could be established.[130] This approach surfaced clearly in the three main negotiations surrounding the disengagement from NATO: the future use granted to Americans for the facilities located in France, the status of the FFA, and the possible cooperation between the FFA and NATO troops.

For all these topics, Paris adopted a firm, but not inflexible, stand and made strenuous efforts not to appear as a petitioner. The French president rejected the presence on French soil of any American troops or supplies or any agreement that guaranteed an automatic French intervention in case of a war. Yet, he seemed open to letting the French and NATO Chiefs of Staff discuss possible cooperation scenarios, which might include providing facilities to American troops in case of a war in which France participated.[131] Similarly, de Gaulle wanted to keep the FFA stationed in West Germany, but he did not want to interpret the agreement of 23 October 1954—which gave a legal basis for the presence of foreign troops—as subordinating their maintenance to the desires of the Bonn government.[132]

The dispute over the FFA benefited from the slight improvement in Franco-German relations following the EEC agreements in the summer and de Gaulle's trip to Moscow where he had advocated German reunification. During the July summit meeting with de Gaulle, Erhard diffused the issue when he declared his desire to keep the French troops stationed in Germany.[133] Bonn wanted to find a way out of the deadlock once it became worried about the threat of the U.K. and the U.S. reducing the number of their troops stationed in West Germany.[134] Once the July summit had helped to clear the air, it was left to the *Directeurs Politiques* of the two Foreign Ministries, Jacques de Beaumarchais and Hermann Meyer-Lindenberg, to hammer out the details of a new agreement for the FFA. On 21 December 1966, the dispute ended after Couve de Murville exchanged letters with Willy Brandt, the new foreign minister of the just formed grand coalition government, headed by Kurt Georg Kiesinger.

Talks on possible cooperation between the FFA and NATO troops remained deadlocked for a long time since France and the fourteen disagreed on whether a political agreement should precede the discussions on military arrangements. Despite seeming initially favorable to the idea of settling political questions first, France soon changed its stance and insisted that any agreement should remain strictly limited to the military sphere.[135] De Gaulle undoubtedly imposed this change of policy. In his view, the "missions [of French forces] were to be decided by the French government only, and the French and NATO chiefs of staff could only discuss possible links or common actions in case of war."[136]

Nevertheless, the General remained open to wartime cooperation with NATO. He confirmed on 14 November 1966 to General Charles Ailleret, chief of the general staff, that, in case of a major war, "France could take part immediately; this would likely mean that our forces would fulfill missions similar to their present ones."[137] Under the influence of Brosio, the fourteen relented on 26 October, allowing talks between France's and NATO's military chiefs of staff—Ailleret and General Lyman Lemnitzer respectively—to go ahead without any preestablished positions.[138] All parties appeared willing to make concessions in order to solve the NATO crisis.

By autumn 1966, modest success in the various negotiations had helped to establish a de facto "14+1" Atlantic Alliance, whereby France remained a full member but stayed away from most of the common military decisions.[139] Moreover, under pressure from the French military leadership, Prime Minister George Pompidou had also conceded after meetings on 22–23 August 1966 that France would continue to participate in a number of NATO bodies and agencies that were international but not integrated. These included NADGE, NATO's Maintenance and Supply Organization (NAMSO), and NATO's body in charge of production and logistic organization (HAWK).[140]

Lyndon Johnson's commitment, despite divisions within his government, to avoid a "war" with the General certainly helped to keep the NATO crisis under control.[141] He refused, as he told George Ball, to get into a "pissing match" with the French president because it "would serve to build de Gaulle and France up."[142] A public dispute would accomplish little, since according to Francis Bator, Johnson's adviser on European affairs: "... the central point about the NATO crisis is that de Gaulle has no real cards. If we play our hand skillfully, we can manage to carry on with NATO without him. In many ways, he is like a lightweight jujitsu artist. All his leverage comes from our over-exertion."[143] Johnson and his collaborators understood that they could not force the General to change his mind. Geographical realities meant that any threat to deprive France of American protection was either not credible or plain silly. It would be similar to "threatening to abandon Kentucky in the face of a land attack by Canada. It is hard to do unless one is prepared to throw in Ohio."[144]

Yet, while avoiding a futile struggle with de Gaulle, NATO, British Minister of Defense Denis Healey suggested, could now move ahead on projects that France had previously blocked.[145] In other words, Paris's disengagement from NATO provided the other members with an opportunity to improve not only the mechanisms of the Atlantic Alliance, but also its cohesion through a multilateral response to the French threat.[146] That included the U.S. government consolidating Secretary of Defense Robert McNamara's proposals for the Alliance's nuclear strategy, following his efforts in the previous year.

Throughout 1966, Washington engaged in a serious information effort about operational nuclear issues, leading to the creation of two groups in December: the Nuclear Defense Affairs Committee (NDAC), open to all interested allies, and a restricted body, the Nuclear Planning Group (NPG), limited to seven members. This proved significant for the U.S. because it meant that it finally achieved a nuclear consensus with its allies on a question that was at the heart of transatlantic problems.[147] By late 1966, the fourteen had not only survived de Gaulle's institutional test and successfully sorted out a new France-NATO relationship, but they had also managed to make the Atlantic Organization more rational.[148]

Likewise, Paris was equally confident that it had successfully redefined its relations with NATO. Couve de Murville triumphantly stated "all is being progressively put in place for the establishment, on new bases, of France's military relations with her allies and the restoration of our full sovereignty."[149] De Gaulle appeared particularly optimistic that France's policy toward NATO would eventually act as a role model for other member-states. As he pointed out during the Council of Ministers meeting of 19 October, "it is clear that by leaving NATO, we are anticipating a deep change in the Atlantic Alliance, which was organized for the Cold War and thus called to change."[150]

Believing that the Cold War was obsolete only encouraged the French government to commit even more to its policy of East-West détente in late 1966. French leaders had come back from the Soviet Union convinced that the trip had produced important results. Couve de Murville emphasized to British Prime Minister Harold Wilson that although the Soviets had not offered any new policy toward European security, he had been impressed by their frame of mind.[151]

Even Quai d'Orsay officials, and, noticeably, Puaux, who were generally more wary of the Soviet Union than de Gaulle was, saw some grounds for optimism. They felt that the General's trip had highlighted certain nuances in Russian policy which, while not fundamental changes in attitude, had at least hinted at a move in France's direction. The common Franco-Soviet declaration at the end of the visit was based on the French text, the Soviets accepted French formulas and the priority given to détente, and they seemingly no longer saw the U.S. as their sole Western interlocutor.[152] French officials were also satisfied by the declaration on European security produced by the Warsaw Pact meeting in Bucharest in early July. The document included some Gaullist passages, with its tone of "Europe for the Europeans," and its call for the abolition of the military organizations.[153]

This optimism did not extend to all Quai d'Orsay officials, though, with many still doubting that the Kremlin leaders were really prepared to follow the General on the path to European détente. For Jacques Andréani, of the Foreign Ministry's Soviet desk, the Soviet regime remained "incapable at this stage of embarking on foreign policy ventures which would upset the careful balance it maintains in Eastern Europe and which would stimulate disequilibrium in the Soviet Union itself."[154] These doubts also extended to more practical aspects of Franco-Soviet cooperation, especially trade.

Pompidou expressed strong concerns during an Inner Council meeting on 17 October 1966: "We have to develop our trade with the Eastern bloc. But what worries me is that we are taking unilateral decisions. In fact it should be a tradeoff. We are being drawn in. We are giving twice."[155] The new ambassador in Moscow, Olivier Wormser, agreed with Pompidou. If the Soviets claimed that Franco-Soviet cooperation was given priority, in reality they were looking out for other economic partners as well. He believed that Moscow tended to view cooperation exclusively in terms of benefits, and it would demand intensive work to make the partnership more balanced.[156]

Some French officials, especially Wormser's predecessor in Moscow, Philippe Baudet, were even more skeptical of the Soviet Union. Baudet had never bought into the rapprochement with Moscow, claiming that both France and the Soviet Union only pretended to cooperate with each other. He also believed that the Soviet Union's nature could never allow it to adopt the role de Gaulle wanted it to play in his post–Cold War Europe. In his last report before leaving the Soviet capital, he argued that the Kremlin's hosts continued to see the policy of the status quo as the wisest, and presented the German problem in the same terms. Any agreement between French and Soviet policy would be temporary. As he powerfully stated: "I leave the Soviet Union with the deep conviction that there is no longer, if ever there was, and there will never be again, common measure between the European states and the Soviet Union. Disproportion exists everywhere: in dimensions, in population, in climate, in military power ... The Soviet Union is not really a state: it is a subcontinent, whose vital interests are in Asia and Europe, and for that reason it cannot be part of either an Asian or European system."[157] Baudet firmly rejected the notion that Moscow would accept a part in de Gaulle's modernized Concert of Nations.

In all likelihood, this report never made it to de Gaulle's desk. Driven by his optimistic belief that the Cold War was dissipating, the pursuit of East-West détente was now the cornerstone of his foreign policy: "I do not want my trip to the Soviet Union to have been in vain. There has to be some follow up. Franco-Soviet cooperation is a grand affair. It has to succeed ... In all domains, it needs to develop. Through this, we will have more exchanges and we will be able to overcome the politics of blocs," he confided to Peyrefitte on 22 September.[158]

The next day, during a meeting with Zorin, he inquired about his invitation to Brezhnev, Kosygin, and Podgorny to visit Paris—which had been accepted in principle—and noted that he hoped this could happen before the end of 1966.[159] After Kosygin agreed to come on his own in the first week of December, Franco-Soviet relations received another boost when Peyrefitte went to the Soviet Union in October, soon followed by the new minister of finance, Michel Debré. Moreover, France continued to pay attention to the Eastern European states when it welcomed the Bulgarian leader Todor Zhivkov in mid October.

Relations with the Kremlin leaders remained the priority for France in late 1966. The president provided a warm welcome for Kosygin, going as far as departing from protocol by meeting his visitor at the airport despite the fact he was not a head of state.[160] More importantly, the General went to great lengths to court the Soviet prime minister in order to enlist his country's cooperation for East-West détente. He repeatedly stressed the fact that the Vietnam War, by drawing America away from Europe and undermining its prestige, could create a new situation. The Soviet Union and France faced a unique opportunity "to organize a more European policy, which would be well perceived by many Western European states, and maybe even West Germany."[161]

That could only occur, however, if Paris and Moscow made concessions to Bonn, so as to end its subordination to Washington. De Gaulle wanted Kosygin to signal to Bonn that the division of Germany was not a permanent European feature.[162] Finally, during a more candid moment, the French president confided to Kosygin that he needed Soviet support for domestic reasons. A successful policy of cooperation with the Soviets in Europe could cut the grass under the feet of those in France who wanted closer ties with the U.S.[163] He counted on Moscow to act as a counterweight to Washington, thus protecting France's policy of independence.

In late 1966, de Gaulle appeared very confident about the perspectives for East-West détente in Europe. He needed Soviet support to satisfy his ambitions and was pleased that Kosygin had not categorically rejected the possibility of détente with West Germany. With the new grand coalition government in Bonn keen—as will be discussed later—to improve relations with the Eastern bloc, the General could foresee the emergence of a kind of Moscow-Paris-Bonn partnership. The latter would be vital to achieve his vision of a new European order, as he explained to Peyrefitte on 5 December 1966: "It is essential to push Germany towards a rapprochement with Russia. We have to disarm their reciprocated aggression. It is our game, it is the only one."[164]

This approach appeared clearly during a meeting between Brandt and the General, when the latter encouraged his German guest to follow the path of détente and added that France could help Bonn's position in the Eastern bloc.[165] Moreover, French leaders welcomed the fact that their allies were switching to the cause of "détente, entente and cooperation" during the NATO ministerial meeting in Paris in mid December.[166] With their partners seemingly adopting de Gaulle's theses on détente, French leaders felt vindicated in their view that the march toward an East-West rapprochement in Europe was an irreversible one.

The shadow of the Vietnam War, however, still loomed large over East-West relations, and increasingly French officials described it as the central obstacle to the policy of détente.[167] While not changing its stance toward Indochina in the aftermath of de Gaulle's Phnom Penh speech, Paris stepped up its criticism of Washington's actions in the region. During his meetings with Rusk on 3–4 October, Couve de Murville lectured his counterpart and ridiculed the idea that a guerrilla fighter could stop fighting before negotiating.[168] The General did not hesitate either to launch more salvos against his ally. In his end-of-year address to the French people, the French president denounced "an unjust war, as it results from a US intervention" and a "despicable war, as it leads a major nation to destroy a far smaller one."[169]

Nevertheless, the troubles in Vietnam could not convince de Gaulle to depart from his optimistic mood, one best emphasized during his press conference on 28 October 1966. In a real ode to France's independence, he condemned all those who wanted to subordinate his country to Moscow, Washington, or any supranational myth. Instead, France had withdrawn from NATO and all signs were pointing "to the re-emergence of our country as a great power."[170] The General added that France's rise as a Great Power served not just its own interests, but also the greater interests of humankind. By attacking American policy in Vietnam, by defending his country's right to break the superpowers' monopoly on nuclear weapons, France contributed to the creation of a more multipolar world that would eventually replace the Cold War's bipolar system.[171]

Led by a sort of euphoria, de Gaulle downplayed the Cold War as increasingly a feature of the past, claiming that "between these peoples [in the East] and ours [in the West], the Cold War appears obsolete in a time when a growing and friendly cooperation is being organized."[172] The policy of East-West détente had become such a priority for the General that it overshadowed other aspects of his European project. As he stated, nothing useful could be achieved in Europe, including a political union between the members of the EEC, as long as East and West did not solve their differences.[173] Additionally, the president's domestic position remained stable, with the economy still growing rapidly and public opinion supportive of his foreign policy initiatives.[174]

Conclusion

Throughout 1966, France pursued several major diplomatic initiatives. Besides withdrawing its forces from NATO and recovering its full sovereignty, Paris had taken steps toward fostering an East-West rapprochement in Europe and building a solid cooperation with the Kremlin leaders. Additionally, de Gaulle had powerfully denounced American actions in Indochina, thereby strengthening his prestige in the Third World. The French president was in a triumphant mood, convinced that the march toward détente and overcoming the Cold War order in Europe was irreversible, even if it would take time. He approached the coming year with optimism, noting that "guaranteed in its institutions, free in its foreign policy, experiencing economic growth and with a strong currency, France is walking towards a future of progress, independence, and peace."[175]

Yet, major developments in the international sphere would soon present new challenges to the Gaullist designs. Not only would France face increasing competition on the East-West détente scene, but it would become involved in difficult negotiations in its Western policy, be it in the monetary, trade, or EEC sphere. How all these questions unfolded would depend to a large extent on the attitude adopted by the new grand coalition government in Bonn, under Chancellor Georg Kiesinger. Erhard's successor quickly affirmed that he wanted to improve relations with the Soviet Union and its satellite states and that he perceived Franco-German cooperation as vital in that matter.[176] What was less clear, however, was whether Kiesinger intended to show real independence from Washington.

Chapter 5

ILLUSION OF INDEPENDENCE PART 1, JANUARY–JUNE 1967

Introduction

1966 was a high point for French diplomacy. After the withdrawal from NATO, the trip to the Soviet Union, and the solemn condemnation of American policy in Vietnam during the speech in Phnom Penh, de Gaulle seemed more confident than ever that France had reclaimed its Great Power status. He was also convinced that Europe was ripe for dramatic changes, opening up the possibility that the Cold War order might one day be overcome.

In 1967, however, the French president and his government faced major challenges. In addition to domestic difficulties, Paris faced a series of complex and interdependent negotiations—the Kennedy Round, the reform of the international monetary system, and the U.K. application to join the EEC. It needed to convince its Common Market partners to show more willingness to act independently vis-à-vis the United States. Additionally, France wanted to push the Soviet Union and the Eastern bloc to start a rapprochement with the new government in West Germany.

Behind all these trials lay the question of whether France could convert its newfound status into concrete influence over its partners and other states, despite having used two of its best diplomatic trump cards the previous year—the withdrawal from NATO and the trip to the Soviet Union. While France strove to be recognized as a major player on the international scene, it remained to be seen whether other states would listen to it.

New Challenges in the West

In March 1967, de Gaulle oversaw the departure of the last foreign troops from French territory. He believed France had won its showdown with NATO. By withdrawing French forces from the integrated military structure, he believed he was anticipating a long-term evolution that would ultimately make the military alliance obsolete. Until that happened, though, he did not object to the institutional compromise devised within the Atlantic Alliance. Whereas military questions would be handled by the fourteen in the Defence Planning Committee (DPC), France sat in the North Atlantic Council (NAC) to study matters of general significance.[1]

The moderate stance of neither appeasing nor attacking France, adopted by the fourteen under American impetus, added to the General's feeling of triumph. Rusk, in particular, encouraged the fourteen to deal with any obstruction, but also emphasized that they should welcome French participation in any NATO consultation.[2] This attitude helped to lessen some of the remaining differences between France and NATO. France and the U.S. reached an arrangement in March regarding the use of pipelines in peacetime. The essential Ailleret-Lemnitzer negotiations on the future role of French troops in the common defense had easily found common basis on military questions, but political issues still stalled an overall agreement.[3]

De Gaulle's optimism was not dented either by the fact that his allies were using France's withdrawal to inject renewed energy into the Alliance. On 9 May 1967, under the auspices of the DPC, NATO finally adopted flexible response as its strategy after more than four years of American lobbying.[4] Despite being an ambivalent strategy, masking rather than resolving existing differences, it nonetheless represented an important political success for the U.S. Flexible response marked "a decisive step towards ending the strategic disagreements within the Atlantic Alliance," and reinforced both NATO's cohesion and American leadership.[5] For the General, however, this result meant nothing since the U.S. had already de facto modified their nuclear strategy, and thus that of the Atlantic Alliance.[6]

Moreover, the French president failed to understand the challenge posed by his allies' attempt to consolidate NATO politically, specifically by making it more relevant in a context of détente in Europe. The U.S. had found valuable allies in the smaller states of the Alliance, especially Belgium, who feared that West Germany might one day follow France in its policies of independence. Who could forecast what would happen in 1969, when the North Atlantic Treaty was up for review and states were free to exercise the withdrawal clause? Under the impulse of its Foreign Minister Pierre Harmel, Belgium pushed for a study dedicated to the future role of the Alliance.[7]

Harmel hoped the exercise could fulfill three key objectives: keep all the members in the Alliance after 1969; define a collective political mission for the Alliance, in particular one that aimed at ending the East-West division in Europe; and finally, use this renewed emphasis on détente to convince France to stay in the Alliance after 1969.[8] On 16 December 1966, the North Atlantic Council formally authorized the Harmel exercise. The communiqué pointed out that the Council had "decided to undertake a large analysis of the changes that have taken place in the international sphere since the signing of the North Atlantic Treaty in 1949, in view of determining their influence on the Atlantic Alliance and to define the tasks to be accomplished in order to reinforce the Atlantic Alliance as an element of lasting peace."[9]

The Belgian initiative suited the U.S. because it represented a European, rather than American, initiative.[10] Moreover, as James Ellison argues, the Americans understood that backing Harmel's proposal presented real tactical benefits. They doubted that NATO could have a great impact in promoting détente. As an aide told Johnson, "on East-West matters, we must always remember that the limit on what we can do is largely set by changing attitudes in Moscow," but they saw the value of the Harmel Exercise in holding together the Atlantic Alliance in the face of de Gaulle's potentially destructive activities and the Soviet bloc's interest in improved East-West relations.[11]

Under American and Belgian guidance, the Harmel exercise slowly took shape, progressively emerging as a useful tool to underline NATO's continuing role in East-West affairs.[12] In February, the exercise moved forward when the Atlantic Council established a Special Group, headed by Secretary General Brosio and composed of government representatives, in charge of preparing a report. The following month, NATO states agreed that the Harmel exercise would be divided into four subgroups, each led by one or two rapporteurs, and respectively studying the following topics: East-West relations, under the chairmanship of German Secretary of State for Foreign Affairs Karl Schütz, and British Assistant Under Secretary for Foreign Affairs Adam Watson; intra-Alliance relations, led by former Belgium Prime Minister Paul-Henri Spaak; general questions of defense policy, with American Deputy Under Secretary of State Foy Kohler as rapporteur; and developments in regions outside the NATO Treaty area, under the responsibility of Dutch professor Constantyn Patijn.[13]

Furthermore, the Belgian government outmaneuvered its French counterpart. By not introducing politically sensitive questions in the first stages of the study, Brussels thought it could "avoid frightening off any hesitant governments" and give the "French as small a target as possible until the exercise is well under way."[14] This tactic worked successfully, as French officials initially expressed little concern about the Harmel exercise, claiming they wanted to receive additional information before taking a position.[15]

De Gaulle, additionally, essentially disregarded the threat posed by NATO's political and strategic consolidation because of his complete confidence in the eventual success of his pan-European strategy. Even though his previous attempts to establish an independent Western Europe had failed, he believed that this shortcoming would be overcome once East-West détente had brought about an end to the Cold War in Europe. Western Europe would then no longer need to be so dependent on American protection. Yet, by prioritizing East-West relations throughout 1966, the General had also largely ignored more immediate challenges in Western affairs. With key economic, tariff, and monetary negotiations reaching critical stages, it became more important than ever for Paris to convince its European partners to agree to a common stand, if only to counterbalance U.S. influence.

The French president's neglect of that latter objective came at a hefty price. This proved obvious during the 1966 monetary discussions within the G10, which witnessed significant shifts in the positions of the various key actors. Despite warnings from Jean Dromer, an advisor in the Elysée, to avoid a rigid stance, de Gaulle had opted to give his officials very restrictive instructions during an Inner Council meeting on 25 February. Officials were asked to emphasize the French commitment to gold as the only real international currency and to block any G10 discussions as long as the Anglo-Saxon powers maintained a significant balance-of-payments deficit.[16]

Conversely, the Johnson administration had adopted a more active stand toward the international monetary debates, pushing hard for the creation of a new reserve asset that could either substitute for or supplement gold. This proved an important turning point. Whereas the US had previously remained on the defensive when France called for a reform of the international monetary system, Washington now championed change while Paris opposed any contingency planning.[17] France's European partners, and West Germany especially, found themselves somewhere in the middle. They wanted to build on the gold exchange standard, not dismantle it. They wanted to control the international role of the dollar, but not destroy it.[18]

The tide soon turned against Paris as the G10 ministers convened in The Hague in late July 1966.[19] Under pressure from developing states, and keen to avoid supporting schemes to create money solely for large industrial nations, the G10 agreed to open discussions to all states and to hold joint meetings with the IMF. The concession was limited, however, since the G10 still underlined its special responsibility in any reform plan.[20]

Moreover, despite French warnings that contingency planning would offer an irresistible temptation to prematurely activate any agreement, the other European states sided with the U.S. They agreed that contingency planning would reassure other states that the likely future shortages in liquidity would not disrupt the world economy.[21] The Common Market partners further isolated Paris in fall 1966 when they seemingly accepted the fact that the removal of the American balance-of-payments deficit should not be a precondition to any reform of the international monetary system.[22]

The lack of European unity on monetary matters coincided with the EEC's attempt to find common ground in the last rounds of negotiation for the Kennedy Round. Tariff talks had resumed in Geneva on 14 September 1966 following the end of the "empty chair" crisis. Yet, the gaps between the parties—be it on agriculture, tariff disparities, or specific product groups—remained significant. Reaching an overall settlement could hardly be guaranteed before the 1962 Trade Expansion Act—which granted the White House authority to negotiate tariff reductions—expired on 30 June 1967; nor would it be easy for the European Community to maintain its unity as it approached negotiations in the final stages of the Kennedy Round.[23]

Moreover, European cohesion faced another significant challenge once the very divisive British question returned to the Community agenda in 1966. Throughout the year, London had issued multiple declarations that underlined its renewed interest in joining the Common Market. The French government feared it was facing a maneuver from its British counterpart that aimed at isolating France in preparation for British membership negotiations.[24]

The French were surprised by U.K. Prime Minister Harold Wilson's sudden announcement to the House of Commons, on 10 November, that "I intend to engage in a series of discussions with each of the Heads of Government of the six, for the purpose of establishing whether it appears likely that essential British and Commonwealth interests could be safeguarded if the UK were to accept the Treaty of Rome and join EEC," before concluding that "we mean business."[25] As Paris dreaded, Wilson's long-term strategy focused on making it difficult for de Gaulle to veto the U.K.'s entry, as he had done in 1963, by showing the U.K.'s sincere willingness to join the Community.[26]

The concurrent threat to European unity posed by the Kennedy Round, the international monetary system, and the likely British application to join the EEC convinced French officials in early 1967 that they needed to adopt a more coordinated approach. Dromer tried to draw de Gaulle's attention back to Western matters, arguing that these three negotiations were connected in that they presented the same fundamental challenge: "Can France convince its [EEC] partners, by persuasion, initiatives or veto, that Europe is ready to claim and achieve its independence, i.e. that it must free itself from the US and Anglo-Saxon supremacy?" Considering America's clout, Dromer insisted that France needed to stop "this generally defensive attitude whereby we fight on our own, with the neutrality of our partners of the Common Market" and instead "try and animate them so they veer in our direction."[27] Thus, he pushed for a new French strategy toward France's Western allies, one based less on unilateral attacks against American leadership and more on efforts to rally its European partners to its cause.

Dromer's suggestions resonated, starting with the approach toward international monetary reform. France had consistently opposed the Gold Exchange Standard because it conferred excessive privileges to the reserve currencies. This system also allowed the U.S. to continue financing its balance-of-payments deficit through the accumulation of dollars by foreign central banks, without having to resort to the same discipline that other states were held to.[28] By 1967, though, Paris knew it was isolated as most of the G10 states supported the creation of a new international reserve unit without removing the privileges of the reserve currencies.

France faced an arduous challenge to obtain European backing when bargaining with the U.S., with two important developments adding a further sense of urgency. The slow growth of global official gold reserves could not keep up with the increase of world trade, raising the possibility that a managed increase in liquidity might be needed before the U.S. balance-of-payments deficit was corrected.[29] Moreover, as argued by de Vries, the patience of the U.S. government was running out. On 17 March 1967, Fowler gave a particularly tough speech. Worried by the recession in the world economy and by the slowdown in the growth of world reserves, he urged an immediate agreement on a meaningful liquidity plan. He warned also that the U.S. might take unilateral action in the absence of an agreement, including suspending the conversion of official dollar balances held abroad into gold.[30]

This tense context prompted Minister of Finance Michel Debré to bring France's EEC partners together around a common proposal, or at least unite them in an effort to delay unwelcome reforms.[31] His first proposals received some support. During the meeting of finance ministers in The Hague in January 1967, he convinced his European partners to allow the EEC Monetary Committee to consider methods to improve international credit access.[32] He also convinced de Gaulle to change France's official instructions for the monetary negotiations, since Paris's partners had accepted the principle of a new international currency. While still committed to the central role of gold, France would compromise by tolerating increased resort to the IMF's credit facilities, the so-called Special Drawing Rights (SDR). In exchange, France called for a revision of IMF rules so as to give more clout to the European states and demanded that any credit granted be repaid within a predetermined time frame.[33]

This constructive approach enabled France to score an important, but temporary, victory during the meeting of EEC financial ministers in Munich on 17–18 April. Believing they deserved more influence in international monetary institutions, the six agreed "to seek a common position in the present discussions on the reform of the international monetary system and to maintain a close cooperation in the future" in order "to safeguard their legitimate interests."[34]

The six had reached a compromise agreement around the following objectives: the aim of the negotiations was to create "drawing rights" within the IMF, not a new reserve asset (a form of international money); the SDR would only be created if a lack of international liquidities was collectively acknowledged; and IMF voting rules would be revised to give the six a veto on key decisions.[35] The French welcomed these decisions; Debré insisted to officials involved in the joint IMF-G10 meetings that they needed to defend the Munich accords. He underlined the importance of preserving the cohesion of the European Community states.[36]

Munich seemingly demonstrated the EEC's influence in the international monetary sphere and provided an opportunity to flex its collective muscles, but the compromise was in fact rather fragile. It reflected a Franco-German agreement, whereby Paris promised to support further contingency planning while the Germans shifted their support from the creation of reserve assets to a new drawing right, but it had not erased all divisions among the six. Neither Italy nor the Netherlands, which favored the creation of reserve assets, had appreciated the Franco-German bilateral scheming.[37]

These internal differences came to the fore in the months following the Munich conference. Whereas Paris's partners remained firm on some principles, namely giving the EEC veto power and more influence within the IMF, they moved closer to accepting the creation of a new monetary instrument that could complement, if not replace, gold and the reserve currencies in the running of the international monetary system.[38] The European Community members, after all, could not invalidate the work of the joint G10-IMF meetings that took place between November 1966 and June 1967. They could not overlook the fact that the participants in these joint meetings were continuing to discuss the merits of both the drawing rights and the reserve units schemes.[39]

Paris's attempt to safeguard European cohesion showed more success in the final stages of the Kennedy Round negotiations. Two disputes, in particular, threatened to undo the talks: the Americans wanted free access to the European grain market, while the European Community wanted the U.S. to abolish the so-called American Selling Price (ASP) in the chemical sector, a system of tariffs on four classes of imports. Washington refused to do so without concessions from the EEC. Nonetheless, despite these obstacles, all parties wanted to reach an agreement and were ready to compromise in order to achieve some sort of package settlement.[40]

Lyndon Johnson firmly supported free trade. He believed that success on tariff talks could have a positive knock-on effect on Western cohesion: "If we could demonstrate our ability to move ahead in an economic partnership, especially with members of the Common Market, we could greatly improve the chances for a healthy NATO and for an increased international monetary cooperation."[41] French officials, likewise, wanted an accord as long as it remained balanced and in the interest of all parties. They believed that they could achieve such a result if the Community maintained a united front.[42] After a series of marathon sessions in Geneva, the negotiators reached a deal on 15 May. The Kennedy Round brought balanced and reciprocal rewards in the industrial sector, with tariff reductions averaging 36–39 percent, or slightly less than the original aim of 50 percent. Exporters in the agricultural field received few advantages, aside from an international agreement on wheat and food aid. Finally, the U.S. and the U.K. relented on the question of tariff disparities, accepting the validity of the EEC argument.[43]

The outcome of the Kennedy Round negotiations advanced French interests in two important ways. A positive end result in Geneva would benefit France's economy, whereas a breakdown, especially if blamed on French rigidity, could have disastrous economic and political consequences. At the same time, the GATT talks strengthened solidarity among the six.[44] French leaders sought to capitalize on this latter fact by contrasting the reasonable European proposals with the supposed negative pressure employed by their American interlocutors.[45]

This spin emerged clearly during de Gaulle's press conference of 16 May. Commenting on the Kennedy Round package, he stated, "I will only say that it seems to me that a certain impression of the six's solidarity vis-à-vis the outside world has been witnessed recently. In the economic domain, this is partly linked to the fact that, in the great tariff battle of Geneva, and even though we achieved an agreement based on reciprocal compensations, the more 'Atlantic' states, that is to say the US, the UK, and the Scandinavians, showed that their interests were very different than those of the Community."[46]

The Kennedy Round represented an important milestone for the EEC as the first negotiation conducted collectively by the Community. But, even its positive impact on European unity could not cancel the detrimental consequences of the British question returning to the Community's agenda. In January–March, Harold Wilson started his probing tour of the six member-states. He wanted to "establish the UK's sincerity in approaching the European Community" and "emphasized the political case in favor of British accession and enlargement, challenging the French view of the Community." At the same time, he hoped "his exposition of an enlarged Europe's 'strength and independence'" would "appeal to de Gaulle."[47]

Wilson's strategy failed to convince the General. While the president welcomed his interlocutor's emphasis on independence, he argued that British membership would completely alter the nature of the European Community, if only because of the agricultural question and the weakness of the pound.[48] The British currency presented a significant obstacle. Since Article 108 of the Rome Treaty committed members to help a partner experiencing a balance-of-payments crisis, this raised the possibility that the six would have to support the sterling exchange rate if the U.K. joined the EEC.[49] Debré could not imagine the U.K. adhering to the Common Market under the existing international monetary system.[50]

Additionally, other French officials opposed the principle of enlargement of the EEC and were suspicious of what they perceived as the Labour government's sudden conversion to the EEC's cause. Within the Quai d'Orsay's Direction des Affaires Economiques et Financières, which played an important role in the management of European affairs, the predominant view suggested that letting the U.K. into the Community would lead to the dissolution of the EEC and to the creation of a large zone of free trade instead.[51]

Although the immediate reactions of the French government to Wilson's visit seemed mostly unfavorable, de Gaulle still acknowledged that he needed a strategy that would avoid a repeat of the first British application to the EEC: "the key is not to be drawn into ever-lasting talks, like in 1962. But also to make clear that there is no easy solution, that the pure and simple entry is not so pure and simple," he explained during the Council of Ministers on 1 February.[52] If Paris could prevent the opening of membership negotiations with London, it could avoid resorting to a political veto as in January 1963. This approach, according to the French ambassador in Moscow, Olivier Wormser, might cause a crisis, but in all likelihood a far less serious one than occurred in 1961–1963.[53]

As France's Western strategy revolved around preserving the unity of the six, especially in the international monetary talks, avoiding a major crisis over the U.K. became paramount. De Gaulle tried to deter the British from filing an early application to join the EEC. Thus, during a meeting with Patrick Reilly, British ambassador in Paris, he argued that the overall economic situation did not favor any dramatic initiative and that there would still be the problem of how to fit the U.K. in the European Community in light of its close economic and political ties to the U.S.[54]

However, London—like Copenhagen, Dublin and Oslo soon after—ignored the General's advice, and officially announced its application to join the EEC on 2 May. French leaders initially reacted moderately. Most ministers opposed British membership and underlined the insurmountable problems posed by agriculture and the pound sterling. They insisted that the government needed to pay extra attention to how it presented its policy, if only to deal with a French public opinion favorable to the U.K. The General also believed that he could afford to wait. He seemed confident that the ball would be in France's court at the appropriate time.[55]

His press conference on 16 May reflected this calm approach. While de Gaulle avoided the spectacular style of January 1963 so as not to infuriate the other EEC members, he nonetheless sought to nip negotiations with London in the bud by emphasizing the problematic nature of a British membership. Sticking to a somewhat defensive posture, the French president described the Common Market as a sort of miracle that would fail to withstand a British entry. Instead of membership, he suggested an association between the U.K. and the European Community.[56]

The press conference hardly had the desired effect. The British, departing from their response in 1963, would not be deterred by de Gaulle's obstruction and based their strategy on the long-term hope that the application could outlast him.[57] Neither could the French president easily sway the other EEC states—which became apparent during the late May Rome meeting of the six heads of state. Originally planned to celebrate the tenth anniversary of the Rome Treaty, the meeting quickly shifted to the question of enlargement.

The Benelux states were adamant that Article 237 of the Rome Treaty legally obliged the EEC to start talks with the new applicants. France, however, wanted the six to first discuss the question of enlargement collectively before opening negotiations with the new candidates.[58] Unable to reach common ground, the six instead agreed on 26 June to request the Commission's opinion on enlargement—which was the first official stage in the process, but also a way to postpone any immediate decision on whether to open negotiations with the British. Moreover, while Couve de Murville "specifically vetoed the Belgian proposal to invite a British spokesman to outline the terms of the UK's membership bid to a specially convened meeting of the Council, he could not block the 'compromise' suggestion that the UK be allowed to make an opening statement at the 4-5 July meeting of the Western European Union [WEU] in The Hague."[59]

France faced an awkward balancing act: it needed to preserve European unity on international monetary matters, while simultaneously preventing the U.K. from joining the EEC. Paris banked on the renewed prospects of Franco-German cooperation after the stormy period of 1964–66 to provide a way out of this quandary. After all, the new West German grand coalition government, established in December 1966, had immediately sought to repair relations with France; consequently, the summit meeting on 13–14 January 1967 had proven very constructive.[60] French leaders welcomed this change of attitude, even if Couve de Murville warned that "time will tell if the Germans can better resist the Anglo-Saxon pressures."[61]

De Gaulle reacted with greater optimism: "They [the Germans] are getting closer to us. We have to use that to our advantage in the framework of the six, especially for monetary questions."[62] Certainly, Kiesinger and Brandt supported the British application to join the EEC, but wanted to avoid a conflict with France over the matter.[63] With regard to international monetary affairs, the Franco-German partnership played a decisive role in forging a common EEC position during the Munich meeting.[64] Obviously, Paris and Bonn had not ironed out all their differences. German officials still believed there were limits to Franco-German cooperation, and they were not ready to challenge the "supremacy" of the dollar.[65]

Yet, France believed the growing German-American tension that had built up in 1966–67—from the fall of the Erhard government in October to the first steps of the grand coalition—created an opportunity to draw Bonn away from Washington's orbit. Indeed, in the summer of 1966, a confrontation had erupted over offset payments for the British and American troops stationed in West Germany.[66] Erhard, facing an economic recession and budget troubles, had argued that he could not increase public spending to offset the costs of the British troops, while London, in the midst of a sterling crisis, had threatened to withdraw its troops unless it received full offset. The situation escalated when Erhard informed the U.S. in September that West Germany would not be able to fulfill its offset agreements, contributing two months later to the fall of his government.[67]

To complicate matters, U.S. Senator Mike Mansfield introduced a resolution on 31 August 1966 stating that "a substantial reduction of US forces permanently stationed in Europe can be made without adversely affecting either our resolve or ability to meet our commitment under the North Atlantic Treaty ..."[68] Lyndon Johnson understood that a British troop withdrawal from West Germany would increase domestic pressure in the U.S. for a similar move, which could accelerate the unraveling of the Atlantic Alliance. In order to deal with the offset crisis, Johnson opted to favor trilateral negotiations between West Germany, the U.S., and the U.K.[69]

The offset crisis drove Bonn to seek more independence from Washington. Conscious of what had happened to Erhard, Brandt believed West Germany could no longer act "like a girl who constantly has to be reassured by her boyfriend that he still loves her."[70] After waiting until late

January to resume the trilateral negotiations, Kiesinger made an unprecedented public critique of American foreign policy over the Non-Proliferation Treaty (NPT). He stressed that American and German interests were not always identical and that the time of unquestioning acceptance of U.S. leadership was over.[71] The German Chancellor's apparent deference to Paris, his criticism of the U.S., and the Munich monetary compromise seriously worried the American administration. Lyndon Johnson doubted whether he could still expect the traditional German policy of friendship toward the U.S.[72]

Yet, as Zimmermann argues, West Germany refrained from pushing the U.S. too far, as both sides avoided further damaging their relations. In a memo to Johnson on 23 February, Deputy National Security Advisor Francis Bator acknowledged the unlikelihood of getting a 100 percent military offset deal with the Germans. He added, however, that the U.S. could instead persuade the Germans to guarantee some financial compensation, such as a promise not to convert their dollars into gold. Despite some hesitations, Bonn recognized that there was no way around Washington. On 30 March, Bundesbank President Karl Blessing confirmed the German monetary non-conversion pledge to the U.S. treasury, defined by Bator as "by far the most important part of the US-German deal."[73]

As in 1963 and the aftermath of the Elysée Treaty, the stage was set for another round of the Franco-American struggle for West Germany's allegiance, which reached a high point during Konrad Adenauer's funeral in late April. After briefly speaking to Lyndon Johnson, de Gaulle met Kiesinger and urged him once again to resist Anglo-Saxon pressures. He stressed the fact that Paris and Bonn needed a common attitude vis-à-vis Washington and to stay together in all negotiations, especially in the international monetary sphere.[74]

Likewise, aware of the importance of the negotiations on monetary affairs, the NPT, and the Kennedy Round, the Americans encouraged the Germans to split with the French. Bator believed that this could be achieved as long as Johnson established friendly relations with Kiesinger and compromised over the trilateral negotiations.[75] Johnson showed some success insofar as he turned the tables on Kiesinger, pointing out his significant problems at home and that he needed Kiesinger's cooperation. On 28 April, the U.K., West Germany and the U.S. signed the trilateral agreement, removing a major thorn in their relationship.[76]

The battle between France and the U.S. over West Germany's allegiance persisted in May–June, shifting instead to international monetary affairs. The French repeatedly reminded their German colleagues of the importance of maintaining a common EEC position on the reform of the international monetary system.[77] In parallel, in a meeting with German Finance

Minister Kurt Schiller, U.S. Secretary of the Treasury Henry Fowler denounced France's unconstructive attitude, while Bator advised Schiller not to worry too much about accommodating the French. Schiller seemed unwilling, though, to take sides. He reminded his guests that Bonn wanted to act as an honest broker between Washington and Paris.[78]

The Paris-Bonn-Moscow Dynamic

If de Gaulle considered German support as important for his Western policy, he viewed it as even more essential for his detente strategy. In that regard, the January 1967 Franco-German summit added to his optimism by confirming the noticeable improvement in relations with the new coalition government in Bonn. Not only did Kiesinger confirm that he had renounced the Hallstein doctrine and the MLF, but he also accepted the General's analysis whereby German reunification could only happen through a rapprochement with the Eastern bloc. Bonn underlined its new approach by proclaiming its desire to establish diplomatic relations with all satellite states except East Germany.[79]

Brandt and Kiesinger also asked France to champion their Ostpolitik during talks with Eastern bloc leaders.[80] Aside from the question of the Oder-Neisse border, the January summit had largely convinced de Gaulle that "they [the Germans] are going through key changes. They realize that détente is the most promising path for them. They are getting closer to us."[81] Additionally, de Gaulle understood that if France supported Bonn's Eastern policies, this could help to insure German solidarity with France over Western matters, including monetary questions and the British application to the EEC.

Paris went out of its way to cooperate with Bonn and defend the Federal Republic's Eastern policy. Brandt and Couve de Murville agreed that their respective directeurs politiques should consult and look for possibilities of common action, and they encouraged their directeurs économiques to promote common industrial projects in Eastern Europe.[82] These regular meetings enabled the directeurs politiques to discuss their governments' latest initiatives, as well as to exchange their analyses of developments on the other side of the Iron Curtain.[83]

At the highest levels, France supported West Germany by defending its policies during meetings with Eastern bloc leaders, such as Zorin or Adam Rapacki, the Polish foreign minister. De Gaulle and Couve de Murville praised Bonn's new attitude on détente, the Hallstein doctrine, and the MLF as steps in the right direction. Furthermore, French leaders stressed that the West German government had taken these initiatives of its own accord, and that a negative Eastern bloc reaction would push Germany back into the arms of the U.S. Even though the French leaders did not deny the differences between their conception of détente and that of the West Germans, especially regarding borders, they still described Bonn as following in their footsteps.[84]

In the long term, de Gaulle believed a more open German policy toward the East, combined with a close alignment with France, strengthened the prospects of East-West détente in Europe. In particular, he expected the triangular relations between Bonn, Paris, and Moscow to play a central role in his goal of overcoming the Cold War order in Europe.[85] If West Germany and the Soviet Union could achieve a rapprochement—as France had done with both previously—and change their reciprocal perceptions of threat, the military blocs in Europe would lose their raison d'être. An American security guarantee in Western Europe would consequently become obsolete.[86]

The success of the General's grand design depended, therefore, on France's ability to convince Bonn and Moscow to improve their relations, which could then create the right conditions to transform the European security order. As he confided to Kiesinger, "the moment we both go to Moscow will be the big day."[87] He understood, though, that this would be no easy feat. As Couve de Murville cautiously noted, France could only do so much to mediate and improve German-Soviet relations.[88] More importantly, de Gaulle did not envision the partnership between Bonn, Paris, and Moscow as one between equals. Even if Germany finally achieved reunification, the General still expected it to play a subordinate role in his modernized Concert of Nations, leaving France and Russia as the central pillars.[89]

Conscious that they faced a difficult road ahead, French leaders still remained very optimistic about the eventual success of East-West détente in Europe. In the short term, they did not anticipate any major developments in East-West relations after the General's trip to the Soviet Union. As long as they witnessed movement in the "right direction," they could afford to be patient.[90] Couve de Murville summed up this attitude during his speech to the NATO ministerial meeting in Luxemburg, when he claimed détente had entered an irreversible phase and that the question was no longer to justify détente but to practice it.[91]

The French president and his collaborators did not worry about the more modest pace of their pan-European strategy, coming after the dramatic and frantic developments of 1966. They saw no reasons for concern so long as relations with the Soviet Union and Eastern Europe were improving in all spheres.[92] De Gaulle's visit to the Soviet Union, and the subsequent Franco-Soviet common declaration of 30 June 1966, had created a framework for cooperation that included the establishment of various trade commissions. The mixed Franco-Soviet commission first met in Paris between 26 and 31 January 1967 and both countries expected the following two years to be a learning process for these new bilateral structures.[93] Even though the French government switched to a low-key approach, it still planned important initiatives for the second half of 1967. Pompidou made sure to announce with great pomp de Gaulle's upcoming trips to Poland in early June and to Romania in the autumn, as well as his own trip to the Soviet Union in July.[94]

For all the French optimism, however, evidence pointed to Franco-Soviet relations undergoing a "cooling off" in this period. Wolton and Lefort rightly point out that the Soviet Union lost some of its interest in France once it left NATO and that Moscow felt frustrated by Paris's refusal to side with its policy toward West Germany.[95] The American ambassador in Paris, Charles Bohlen noted the same trend in a message to Rusk in spring 1967. He described the cooling off as the result of differences over the question of a European security conference, the NPT, and the natural strains caused by Paris's attempt to facilitate a rapprochement between Bonn and Moscow—but crucially, he reminded Rusk that "the Franco-Soviet affair was a hurry up business from the outset, and the concrete results have always panted along far behind the grandiose publicity."[96]

Indeed, de Gaulle expected long-term economic cooperation with the Soviet Union to have important political repercussions. He attributed great importance to the sociology of development: an improvement in economic standards inside the Soviet Union might encourage its population to push for freer and quieter living conditions—thereby strengthening the prospects of East-West détente.[97] But, the realities of Franco-Soviet trade cooperation—and for that matter trade cooperation with other Eastern bloc states—hardly matched expectations.[98] Trade with the Soviet Union only accounted for 1 percent of France's total foreign trade, and it seemed unlikely to increase further since the Russians had so little to sell.[99] As for the satellite states, Jacques Andréani, of the Quai d'Orsay's Soviet desk, argued that if France maintained good political relations with them, it would be "necessary for its economic role to match its political status if it were to really play an influential role. But this would be hard to achieve."[100] Despite improvements in 1966, France remained the fourth largest Western exporter to Poland, far behind the U.K. and West Germany.[101]

Furthermore, de Gaulle's vision for a post–Cold War Europe faced even greater obstacles in the Paris-Bonn-Moscow triangle. The French president never expected his grand design to succeed rapidly. He knew the Soviet Union and its allies would not immediately embrace West Germany's Ostpolitik.[102] He welcomed the new attitude of the West German government, but encouraged it to give up its illusions on borders and to make a move, short of recognition, toward East Germany.[103] Bonn seemed willing, within limits, to follow the advice of the General. Keen to create a climate in which the status quo could be changed peacefully, Brandt argued that "realities can be influenced for the better only if they are taken into account."[104]

West Germany accepted the Soviet Union's central role in any future German reunification, as Kiesinger explained in a 14 June 1967 speech to the Bundestag: "We all know that overcoming the division of our people can indeed only be achieved by an arrangement with Moscow."[105] Bonn also proposed a renunciation-of-force agreement to Moscow and sent officials to Bucharest, Prague, and Budapest in view of establishing diplomatic relations.[106] Finally, despite refusing to recognize East Germany and continuing to refer to it as the "East Zone," Kiesinger announced a series of proposals to improve communications with East Germany. This included practical steps such as improving travel possibilities, allowing the joining together of families, and expanding trade.[107]

French leaders welcomed these various initiatives, but they did not mean that West Germany was ready to accept the subordinate role envisioned by de Gaulle. Bonn's new Ostpolitik, according to Brandt, reflected a desire to take greater control over its own fate, rather than rely on others to speak on its behalf.[108] Even if it followed France's détente policy with great interest and attention, Bonn only expected limited gains from its cooperation with Paris. As Egon Bahr, Brandt's influential advisor on Ostpolitik, wrote in January 1967, common actions toward Eastern Europe could only go so far and Germany would need to take "decisive steps" with regard to the Eastern bloc at the bilateral level.[109]

In any case, West German moves to improve ties with the Eastern bloc soon faced significant opposition. The Soviet leaders were not initially hostile toward the new West German government. They believed that they could possibly benefit from Bonn's Ostpolitik and use it to undermine West Germany's alliance with Washington.[110] It did not take long for Moscow, however, and the more intransigent members of the Warsaw Pact, to shift to a more critical position. Attacking the new German policy as a tactical rather than a concrete change, Moscow and Warsaw denounced Bonn's attitude on nuclear weapons, its attitude on borders, and its failure to recognize East Germany.[111]

Soviet policy further stiffened after West Germany and Romania agreed to normalize relations on 31 January. The establishment of diplomatic relations between Bucharest and Bonn hit a raw nerve, stirring deep-rooted anxieties the masters of the Kremlin felt about the controllability of a sweeping European détente. The German-Romanian rapprochement reminded Moscow of the potential of détente to stimulate centrifugal forces within the Eastern bloc and of the threat posed by West German influence in Eastern Europe. Consequently, the Soviet leaders downplayed their maximal goal of isolating Bonn and lowering American influence, reverting instead to a more modest aim of consolidating control over Eastern Europe.[112]

East Germany, and its leader Walter Ulbricht, influenced the hardening of the Soviet position. Ulbricht feared that Hungary and Czechoslovakia would follow Romania's example and set up diplomatic relations with West Germany. As Garton Ash explains, "Ulbricht quickly moved to counter the new West German offensive ... Against the 'Hallstein doctrine' of Bonn, Pankow placed what journalists would label the 'Ulbricht doctrine', according to which no other Eastern bloc states should move faster than East Germany in setting up diplomatic relations with West Germany."[113] When the communist parties of Eastern and Western Europe, excluding Romania, met in April 1967 in Karlovy Vary, they rallied around Ulbricht's doctrine and all heaped abuse upon Bonn's policies.[114] This development did not convince Kiesinger to abandon his Ostpolitik, but it dampened his optimism, as well as that of French officials.[115]

Therefore, West Germany's unwillingness to play a subordinate role and the Soviet Union's refusal to embrace West Germany's new Ostpolitik posed important obstacles to de Gaulle's grand design, but Moscow's reluctance to participate in any European system presented an even more fundamental challenge. Opponents of the General, such as American Under Secretary of State George Ball, had dismissed his designs, arguing that the "Soviets see de Gaulle's power pretensions as a joke" and that they only wanted to exploit him for his divisive potential in the West.[116] Such criticism had some validity. Speaking to Ulbricht and Wladislaw Gomulka, secretary general of the Polish Communist Party, during a meeting in April 1967, Brezhnev gave the following very damning assessment of the French president:

> Take for example De Gaulle. Did we not manage, without any risk, to create a breach in imperialist capitalism? De Gaulle is our enemy and we know it. The PCF [Parti Communiste Français], narrow in its conceptions, tried to get us against de Gaulle. And what did we obtain however? A weakening of the position of the US in Europe. And it is not over. De Gaulle is a sly fox. He wants hegemony for France in Europe, and that is directed against us. But there, we have to act with flexibility. In any case, de Gaulle's European conceptions have no chance of succeeding because there are in Western Europe some strong countries that would never admit it. But the assessment, comrades, is it not favorable?[117]

The Brezhnev quote, as Soutou argues, strongly suggested that the Soviet leaders did not want to make the Franco-Soviet couple their main axis in Europe.[118] While Moscow showed more assertiveness in its relations with Paris, its policy toward Western Europe remained "actively reactive," constrained by the fear of a resurgent Germany and the risk of seeing an American withdrawal from Europe or NATO's collapse. In other words, the Kremlin leaders could not "truly embark on a Europe first policy that would treat Europe as a primary and ultimate focus, rather than a derivative of the superpower relationship."[119]

The Soviet reluctance to accept de Gaulle's vision for Europe coincided with the U.S. taking a more active commitment to the process of East-West détente, if only to restore its leadership in the West. Listening to his advisers, Lyndon Johnson outlined his European policy during a speech, on 7 October 1966, to the National Conference of Editorial Writers in New York. The American president called for progress on three fronts: modernizing NATO and strengthening the Atlantic Alliance, furthering the integration of the Western European Community, and accelerating progress in East-West relations. As for the latter point, he called for the immediate mending of the European division and added that it had to be "healed with the consent of the East European states and with the consent of the Soviet Union."[120] This renewed American focus on détente necessarily threatened France's attempt to develop a privileged dialogue with Moscow.

Despite the Vietnam War, Soviet leaders adopted in late 1966 a more open attitude with regard to dealing with the U.S. This applied to cultural exchanges, the outer space treaty signed in December, and of course the talks for the NPT. In the autumn, Rusk and Gromyko achieved a breakthrough over arms control and nuclear non-proliferation, with the American secretary of state presenting a treaty proposal to his NATO allies in December.[121] The upheaval in China caused by the Cultural Revolution, along with the growing Sino-Soviet tension, pushed Moscow to improve its ties with Washington. As Gromyko pointed out in his confidential report to the Politburo on 13 January 1967, good relations with the U.S. could act as a bulwark against the "adventurous schemes" of China.[122] The crisis in the Middle East later that year would only reinforce the preeminence of the superpowers.

Six Days that Shook the World

Indeed, the challenges faced by de Gaulle's grand design in transforming the European order would only be compounded by developments in the Third World. In early 1967, the General put extra-European affairs on the back burner, and that included the Vietnam War. He shied away from any major initiatives, simply sticking to his very critical stance toward

America that he had outlined during his Phnom Penh speech. He still denounced what he considered a terrible conflict and lamented its impact on the emerging détente in the world.[123] To further mark its disapproval of American actions, the French government withdrew its observer from the SEATO council meeting in Washington.[124]

Moreover, the French president stubbornly refused to take part in any mediation effort in this period. When U.S. Ambassador at Large Averell Harriman asked Jean Sainteny, a former French general delegate to North Vietnam, to act as an intermediary with Hanoi, de Gaulle fumed. He instructed Sainteny to not "become, in any way, a messenger for the US."[125] Why did he adopt this obstructive attitude, when he had repeatedly claimed that ending the Vietnam War would benefit détente? Several possible explanations can be posited. As Couve de Murville stated, France believed that a negotiated solution could only happen when the belligerents agreed on its objectives.[126]

As long as this remained unlikely, the General probably believed that he could have his cake and eat it too. He held Washington responsible for the conflict in Indochina, and without a foreseeable end in sight, he could constantly repeat a message that appealed to 80 percent of the French electorate. Such a position was especially useful in view of the upcoming parliamentary elections and because it struck a chord in the Third World.[127] Furthermore, de Gaulle noted that the U.S. was losing a lot of moral ground in Europe because of Vietnam and that this provided a golden opportunity for France to push for a more independent Europe along the Paris-Bonn-Moscow axis.

When the Third World did take center stage in 1967, it actually happened in the Middle East, rather than Vietnam.[128] For most of the decade, the relative calm in the region had meant limited Great Power interest, including from France. Since the end of the Algerian War, de Gaulle had focused on normalizing his Middle Eastern policy. On the one hand, he had loosened the privileged ties established with Israel by the Fourth Republic and rejected Israeli Prime Minister David Ben Gurion's offer of an alliance in 1963. On the other hand, Paris had successfully renewed relations with the Arab states, which had been broken after the Suez Crisis. The latter goal had been achieved without jeopardizing relations with Israel.[129] Israeli Foreign Minister Abba Eban noted that Israel's embassy in Paris continued to paint a favorable picture of French policy.[130] Until war changed the regional dynamics, France maintained a balanced approach in the region.[131]

The peaceful situation in the region started to unravel following a violent military coup in Damascus on 23 February 1966.[132] The new Ba'athist regime faced mounting opposition inside Syria and as a result it tried to pursue a foreign policy that would enhance its domestic standing. Hostility toward Israel and closer ties with Egypt were important aspects of such a foreign policy.[133] Before long, border incidents began to intensify between Israel and Syria, culminating with the 7 April 1967 air battle in which the Israeli Air Force downed six Syrian MiG-21 fighters.

Yet, as argued by William Quandt, if the tensions on the Syrian-Israeli border provided the fuel for the early stages of the crisis, the spark that ignited the fuel came in the form of erroneous Soviet reports to Egypt on 13 May that Israel had mobilized ten to thirteen brigades on the Syrian border. This prompted Egyptian President Gamal Abdel Nasser into action: on 14 May he sent troops into the Sinai Peninsula as a challenge to Israel. Two days later, the crisis escalated after Egypt made a request for the removal of the United Nations Emergency Force (UNEF), which had been acting as a buffer between the Israeli and Egyptian forces since 1957. Within 48 hours, UN Secretary-General U Thant responded positively to Cairo's demand.[134]

Paris at first did not seem unduly concerned by the crisis, even if it took note of the rising tension in the region. The General made it clear during a meeting with an Egyptian official on 9 May that a conflict was not desirable.[135] This did not mean, though, that French officials were expecting the situation in the region to escalate so quickly. When Hervé Alphand visited the Middle East between 6 and 16 May, meeting with various Syrian and Egyptian leaders, he assumed that his hosts were exaggerating when they warned that war was imminent.[136]

French officials took a number of precautionary measures, such as making several peace demarches in Cairo, Damascus, and Tel Aviv, while they waited for a better assessment of the situation. They did not object in principle to a meeting of the Security Council, although they regarded such a move as premature in the current situation.[137] French diplomats also confided to their British and American counterparts that the 1950 Tripartite Declaration remained the basis of their policy in the Middle East.[138] This acknowledgement opened up the possibility of close cooperation with the U.S. and the U.K., although the highest levels of the French government had not yet given their assent to this approach. American officials tried to capitalize on the regular meetings with their British and French colleagues by breathing new life into the Tripartite Declaration.[139] Moreover, they also suggested that the French, British, and American missions in Cairo, Damascus, and Tel Aviv should jointly deliver a tripartite note.

This strategy, however, soon backfired. The British government emphasized that it did not view the UN as the proper forum for action. The French Foreign Ministry reacted even more forcefully. It instructed the French ambassador in Washington to turn down the idea of daily meetings with his British and American colleagues, fearing that this would give the impression that the three powers were planning an intervention.[140]

Although French officials in Washington tried to reassure their British counterparts that they were still willing to sit down with them or the Americans, Paris had shifted its position and now opposed reviving the Tripartite Declaration. Fundamentally, France wanted to put some distance between itself and its allies, so as to avoid jeopardizing its relations with the Soviet Union and East-West détente. As Alphand confirmed to Bohlen, a formal meeting of the three Western powers without Russia would give the appearance of a "cold war."[141] The same Alphand confirmed to British officials that the French ambassador in Moscow had been instructed to sound out Soviet intentions.[142]

The hardening of the French position coincided with the serious escalation of the Middle Eastern crisis. Nasser's decision, on 22 May, to close the Straits of Tiran to Israeli ships forced the French government to adopt a clearer approach during the Council of Ministers meeting two days later. De Gaulle dominated the discussions. He imposed his view that the closure of the Straits did not constitute a casus belli, described war in the region as an absurdity, and claimed that the four Great Powers—France, the U.S., the U.K., and the Soviet Union—should cooperate to facilitate a settlement. He added that the situation had changed since 1957, when France had made a declaration favorable to freedom of navigation in the Gulf of Aqaba and had supported Israel's right to defend itself.[143] In 1967, the General regarded France as a Great Power with global responsibilities. In other words, de Gaulle had adopted a very dogmatic position in support of peace, which strove to maintain the equilibrium he had developed in the previous years with the Middle East.[144]

Moreover, global considerations shaped this approach at the expense of local circumstances. By presenting France as the defender of peace in the world, de Gaulle believed he could strengthen its claim to Great Power status. Four-power consultations appealed to the General because they seemed fundamentally consistent with his aristocratic conception of the international system. As he explained during a later Council of Ministers debate, "those problems [in the Middle East] cannot be solved internally. They must be solved internationally, which implies an agreement between the four [Great Powers]."[145] Through such a meeting, Paris wanted to underline its status and its right to take part in the settlement of the crisis,[146] but the meeting also reflected Paris's convictions that it faced a crisis with global rather than local significance and that the superpowers were hiding behind the belligerents.[147]

In the aftermath of the Council of Ministers meeting, the French president consistently advocated peace when he talked to officials from the region. He warned Egyptian Ambassador in Paris Abdel El-Naggar that a war would be terrible for Egypt and that he wanted talks among the four Great Powers to prevent them from taking sides.[148] He held the same line to Israeli Foreign Minister Eban, dispatched to Paris by his government, which worried about France's lack of public support.[149] The General cautioned Israel not to go to war, or at any rate not be the first one to shoot. He added that "today there are no Western solutions. The more Israel looks exclusively to the West, the less the Soviets will be ready to cooperate. It is essential that the four powers should concert their policies."[150]

This meeting had profound consequences for Franco-Israeli relations. Whereas Israel believed it was being abandoned by an ally in a time of dire need, de Gaulle wanted to prevent war and doubted that Israel needed to fear its Arab neighbors in a conflict. After meeting with Eban, he confided to Couve de Murville that Israel would surely start hostilities once it had obtained American support.[151]

Concomitantly with its warnings to the Middle Eastern local actors, France pressed the other three Great Powers to accept its proposal for consultations. Both London and Washington welcomed the suggestion of four-power discussions.[152] Moscow, however, turned down the offer, blaming Arab opposition, Washington's and London's pro-Israeli stances, and the U.S. war effort in Vietnam.[153] This Russian "no" was a major disappointment, considering the extent to which Paris had tried to court Moscow and preserve a close relationship, but was it really a body blow to de Gaulle's prestige, as suggested by U.S. Ambassador to the UN Arthur Goldberg?[154]

Based on the evidence, this latter assessment is overstated. Couve de Murville, as he told Bohlen, recognized that Soviet behavior was ambivalent and that the USSR sought to reduce Western influence in the Middle East, but at least Moscow had expressed a desire to maintain contacts with the Western powers. For the American ambassador, "Couve de Murville's general attitude showed ... that they still are hopeful that the Soviets will change their negative attitude and be willing to join in some form of negotiations."[155] Until then, as the crisis escalated and war appeared more and more imminent, France reverted to a detached and balanced stance. Following the Council of Ministers meeting on 2 June, the government solemnly stated its neutrality, warned it would condemn the state that fired the first shot, and called again on the Great Powers to settle the crisis.[156]

When war broke out on 5 June, it quickly prompted high-level cooperation between the Great Powers. True, French leaders resented the exclusive superpower dialogue that took place in the UN and aimed to agree on a cease-fire resolution, but at least Kosygin and de Gaulle stayed in regular contact during the war via the hot-line between the Elysée and the Kremlin.[157] Moreover, the reasonable attitudes adopted by the superpowers comforted the General that neither of them wanted the crisis to go too far.[158] With the threat of a major escalation out of the way, the French president saw a chance to push again for a Great Power agreement, thereby ensuring his country played an influential role. During the Council of Ministers meeting on 7 June, he argued that the Russians were surely embarrassed by their initial refusal to participate in high-level talks, and that it was up to France to remain "the champion of consultation between the four."[159]

Once the war ended on 10 June, France wasted no time outlining its vision for a lasting solution to the problems in the Middle East, which would require an agreement between all parties. Any settlement would have to address all the disagreements at hand, including navigation in the Gulf of Aqaba, the situation of Palestinian refugees, and the conditions of neighborly relations. France also emphasized that it could not accept a fait accompli as far as territorial borders were concerned.[160]

France also wanted to respect both the independence of Israel and the dignity of the Arab states, and seemed optimistic that it could have a positive influence on peace talks. As Alphand noted, "our attitude, wise and moderate, will enable us to play a useful role in the quest for peace."[161] On 14 June, France abstained on a Soviet Security Council resolution denouncing Israel as the aggressor, but accepted Moscow's proposal to convene a meeting of the UN General Assembly to discuss the aftermath of the conflict.[162]

Yet, within a week, France's optimism that it could play a positive role in mediating peace had given way to anxiety and finger pointing. Indeed, on 21 June, the French government issued a communiqué, prompted by de Gaulle, that solemnly denounced Israel for starting the conflict in the Middle East and blamed the spread of war on the American intervention in Vietnam. The communiqué also stressed that only an American withdrawal from Indochina could bring a peaceful solution to the current global situation.[163] This marked a significant change in tone.

Several developments likely dictated this shift. The French president genuinely feared the risks of further escalation in the aftermath of the war. The communist bloc, except Romania, had broken off relations with Israel, and the U.S. found itself temporarily cut off from the Arab world. In this atmosphere of growing danger, de Gaulle invited Kosygin to stop over in Paris for a meeting, as the latter was making his way to New York to address the UN. The talks, though, proved very unproductive. Kosygin pushed de Gaulle to abandon his neutral stance, but the General instead warned his guest of the dangers of escalation; he emphasized the potentially disastrous consequences for the superpower rivalry that was, in his view, responsible for the conflict.[164]

With positions hardening on both sides, the French president feared the reemergence of the Cold War in the Middle East.[165] To make matters worse, communist China detonated its first hydrogen bomb on 17 June, leading the General to alert Harold Wilson that this event, combined with the wars in Vietnam and the Middle East, threatened to create a very dangerous international context in which none of the Great Powers were truly in control.[166] Amid this troubled atmosphere, the 21 June communiqué reflected de Gaulle's sincere views about Israel's and the U.S.'s responsibility in the outbreak of the Middle Eastern conflict. He resented Israel for ignoring his advice and wrongly believed the U.S. government could have restrained Israel if it had wanted to.[167] De Gaulle essentially regarded Israel as a U.S. client and seemed convinced that Johnson had given Tel Aviv a green light to take preemptive action.[168]

Moreover, opportunistic reasons also pushed the General to criticize the U.S. and side more closely with the Soviet Union. As the Sous-Direction d'Europe Orientale of the Quai d'Orsay noted, "the events in the Middle East have highlighted the relative weakness of the Soviet Union vis-à-vis the US on the international stage."[169] Since the war had proved a major failure for the Soviet Union, it made sense to balance the American gain. At the same time, de Gaulle feared the emergence of a superpower condominium. The communiqué was strategically released two days before the start of the hastily arranged summit meeting (23–25 June) between Kosygin and Johnson in Glassboro, New Jersey, selected as a compromise venue because it was roughly equidistant from New York and Washington, D.C.

Unsurprisingly, France and the U.S. found themselves on opposite sides during the bitter postwar debates on the Middle East at the UN. The French government supported the non-aligned resolution, inspired by Yugoslavia, which called on Israel to withdraw its forces to the positions occupied before 5 June. This resolution, unlike the Latin American–inspired one supported by the U.S., presented many advantages for France, even if it was not perfect. The resolution dealt with essential issues, namely the withdrawal of troops and the resolution of key Arab-Israeli problems. If successful, it could help initiate talks, and it would give the Arab states a diplomatic victory, thus pushing them to take a less negative attitude on the main questions. Finally, siding more closely with the Arab states would ensure that the West preserved some influence in the Arab world and would prevent an exclusive dialogue between the latter and Moscow.[170]

The French attitude, however, left Israel and the U.S. in disbelief. The former was dismayed by France supporting a resolution whose authors mostly did not even have diplomatic relations with Israel. The Americans, for their part, complained that they regarded the French lobbying efforts at the UN for the Yugoslav resolution as a particularly unfriendly act. Washington could not understand why Paris seemed to be intent on upholding Soviet propaganda.[171] Ultimately, neither the Yugoslav resolution nor the Latin American one received enough votes. The diplomatic battle continued unabated throughout the summer and fall of 1967, with France adopting a harder and harder stance toward Israel.[172]

The Six Day War shook the Middle East and the world, seriously undermining de Gaulle's grand design in the process. On a basic level, Paris abandoned its balanced position toward the Middle East by moving closer to the Arab states and further away from Israel. Israel felt abandoned and cheated by France, although staunch Gaullists would later defend the French president's record by arguing he knew all along that Israel would win the war.[173]

Moreover, and on the back of the not-so-stellar results in the legislative elections of March—where the Gaullists barely held onto their majority in the Assemblée Nationale—the war in the Middle East undermined the General's popularity.[174] Large sections of the Quai d'Orsay disagreed with his policies and found it hard to accept that France supported the Soviet and Arab theses. As Vaïsse explains, the attitude of the government during the conflict also provoked a backlash among French people—more sympathetic to Israel—and marked the beginning of the slow yet significant erosion of de Gaulle's popularity.[175] Although he realized that a majority of French people backed Israel, the General seemed unfazed and justified his position by saying that "you do not pursue a policy by following public opinion. Public opinion always ends up following the policy, as long as it is good."[176]

De Gaulle's stance on the war did not help relations with his allies either, starting with West Germany. According to François Seydoux, French ambassador in Bonn at the time, the West Germans were strongly critical of the French approach: they "accused [de Gaulle] of having anti-American and anti-Israeli feelings. He was also accused of ignoring Germany, seeing it as not worthy enough to be associated to global responsibilities."[177] Moreover, the conflict also affected dynamics within NATO and further strengthened the organization to the detriment of France. As Harlan Cleveland, U.S. ambassador at NATO, pointed out after the June ministerial meeting in Luxemburg, "the whole spectrum has discernibly moved over toward pessimism about Soviet motivations, so that those ministers [of the member-states of NATO] who spoke of détente in [a] hopeful manner, felt constrained to balance their comments with [an] emphasis on maintaining the NATO deterrent as well."[178]

Last but not least, the war hurt France's global status. It proved a disappointment for the General, reminding him of "the lack of influence of

France in international affairs," as Wilson suggested to Lyndon Johnson on 23 June.[179] Undoubtedly, the Glassboro summit meeting was a reminder for de Gaulle of the continuing predominance of the superpowers on the international stage. While the talks between Kosygin and Johnson did not lead to any breakthrough, especially on Vietnam or the Middle East, they had taken place in a cordial atmosphere and had marked a first small step toward future arms control agreements. Moreover, the Glassboro meetings finally resumed the pattern of high-level summits between the superpowers, interrupted since 1961, and strengthened the hands of the "Americanists" in the Kremlin who wanted Moscow to deal in priority with Washington.

Yet, despite these various setbacks, de Gaulle could still take some comfort from the fact Kosygin had made two stops in Paris during the crisis. According to a CIA analysis, this did show the General was relatively successful "in his efforts to induce Moscow to give consideration to Paris and to prevent the 'superpowers' from negotiating without France";[180] and as de Gaulle commented about the results of Glassboro, "he [Kosygin] and Johnson agreed on nothing."[181]

Conclusion

The contrast between France's situation in mid 1967 and late 1966 was particularly striking, as the difficulties of converting status into influence became painfully apparent. In the West, and despite its best efforts, the U.K. application to the EEC had created acrimony between Paris and its Common Market partners, seriously undermining the French efforts to preserve cohesion among the six over international monetary matters.

In the field of East-West détente, the picture appeared no more promising. The Paris-Bonn-Moscow triangle had stalled, especially because of the lack of progress in West Germany's opening to the Eastern bloc. At the same time, the superpowers had acknowledged their need for closer contacts, be it over nuclear matters or to deal with major international crises, as confirmed by the Kosygin-Johnson Glassboro summit. Finally, the war in the Middle East had painfully confirmed some of the limits of France's influence on major international events and had even undermined de Gaulle's domestic position.

Gaullist foreign policy had not yet entered a period of inevitable decline by the mid 1967, since the fate of both France's détente policy in Europe and the negotiations within the Western world remained in the balance. But, it is equally fair to say that France approached a decisive period for its diplomacy in a weaker position and locked in a defensive stance.

Chapter 6

ILLUSION OF INDEPENDENCE PART 2, JULY–DECEMBER 1967

Introduction

De Gaulle's grand design faced its sharpest challenge in the second half of 1967 as it sought to pursue contradictory goals. France believed it could only turn Western Europe into a more independent player if it maintained European unity, especially over international monetary affairs, but that same cohesion was threatened by the Harmel exercise and the divisive British application to join the EEC. Moreover, an East-West rapprochement in Europe depended on France convincing West Germany and the Soviet bloc to significantly improve relations. Not to mention that Paris had already used its two best cards—the withdrawal from NATO and the opening to the Soviet Union—in its diplomatic game.

France confronted major obstacles at the start of summer 1967, but it was not devoid of options. For a start, de Gaulle's upcoming trip to Poland, the first visit of a Western leader to a satellite state, offered him a great opportunity to give renewed encouragement to the East-West rapprochement in Europe, and through that the possibility to maintain a certain leverage over Bonn. With West Germany on board, France could still find a way to fulfill its goals in the international monetary negotiations, as long, of course, as it found a way to deal with the British question.

July–August: The Calm before the Storm?

The diplomatic debates over the Middle East continued unabated in the UN throughout the rest of 1967, culminating with the Security Council adopting Resolution 242 on 22 November 1967. Approved by both the Arab and Israeli sides, the text spoke of a "just and lasting peace" within "secure and recognized boundaries," called for an end to "claims or states of belligerency," for an Israeli withdrawal "from territories occupied in the recent conflict," and for acknowledgment of all states' "sovereignty, territorial integrity and political independence." The resolution, however, did not lead to peace in the region. It merely papered over differences and was only accepted because each party interpreted the ambiguous text in its own favor.[1]

The UN discussions produced no fundamental change in France's approach toward the Middle East. France still condemned Israel's territorial gains and saw no prospect for an early regional settlement. De Gaulle maintained his view according to which Egypt's decision to close the Straits of Tiran had been regrettable, but Israel carried more blame because it had started the war.[2] He could not forgive Israel for ignoring his advice before the conflict, and wrongly accused the U.S. government of failing to restrain Israel.[3] If anything, France became increasingly critical of Israel in the fall as the latter moved closer to the U.S.[4]

The French government hardened its stance, despite the fact that the condemnation of Israel had caused great consternation among its allies and domestic public opinion.[5] French leaders sought to appease the concerns of their West German partners during the Franco-German summit in Bonn in July. De Gaulle explained to Kiesinger that France had disapproved of Israel's actions because it opposed war, not because it wanted to please the Soviets. He added that the Soviet Union had condemned Israel for its own reasons.[6] In regard to the domestic opposition, the General refused to let public opinion dictate his foreign policy choices, as he would make obviously clear with four famous words uttered in Montreal.

By defiantly proclaiming "Vive le Québec libre!" at Montreal's city hall on 24 July, de Gaulle caused serious uproar in Canada and throughout the world. Denouncing an unacceptable intervention in Canadian affairs, the federal government immediately cancelled the French president's planned stopover in Ottawa and the latter duly obliged. Although some commentators at the time, like U.S. Ambassador in Paris Charles Bohlen, questioned the General's sanity and motivations, his actions were not necessarily the improvised delusions of a senile or demented old man.[7]

As he confided to an aide-de-camp, de Gaulle wanted to state his support for the cause of the French Canadians. He sought out to prove that

France could "act without asking other countries' opinion, act on its own, independently, according to its own conscience."[8] He wanted to convince French citizens that an ambitious foreign policy, demonstrated by his recent controversial actions, was the only acceptable path for their country. As he explained during a television speech on 10 August, France's actions in the service of world peace—which, according to him, were widely approved in the world—required an independent stance that could not be affected by "foreign allegiances and the episodic impact of public opinion."[9]

Yet, despite the General's efforts to shelter his foreign policy from the vicissitudes of public opinion, he could not prevent the slow erosion of his support.[10] In part, this was simply the natural consequence of the wear and tear of Gaullism after nearly a decade in power, with the government losing steam and facing an opposition buoyed by its recent parliamentary successes.[11] In part, it also resulted from the unfavorable reactions to de Gaulle's positions on the Middle East and Quebec, meaning that for the first time public opinion had expressed serious hostility to two major foreign policy initiatives.[12] Finally, it reflected uneasiness with de Gaulle's refusal to acknowledge the results of the March parliamentary elections, leading Giscard to denounce "the solitary exercise of power."[13]

The growing criticism of the General's judgment, combined with wider domestic difficulties and a slowing economy, hardly placed France in an ideal position to confront external challenges, starting with the U.K.'s renewed push to join the EEC.[14] Whereas Paris appeared to be struggling, London moved ahead confidently, conscious of having submitted a stronger candidacy. Compared to its previous attempt in 1961–1963, the second application appeared far more enthusiastic, receiving broad support across the political spectrum and a substantial 488:62 majority in the House of Commons.

Moreover, in 1967, London was dealing with a very different Community than five years earlier. As Ludlow argues, "not only were the Community's policies that much more solidly established, but the UK seemed also to have accepted that the onus of adaptation lay with the applicant and not with the existing member states."[15] This crucially undermined France's central argument that enlargement would destroy the Community. With the five responding warmly to Foreign Secretary George Brown's speech to the WEU on 4 July, Paris faced an uphill battle to prevent London from joining the Common Market without resorting yet again to a divisive veto.

France's travails became apparent during the EEC Council of Ministers meeting in Brussels on 10–11 July, during which the six debated the British question. Couve de Murville presented an inspired case against enlargement, trying to impress on his interlocutors the wide range of obstacles to British entry rather than focusing on a specific reason. He highlighted the consequences for the Community, as the addition of new members would create an organization more akin to a wide Atlantic grouping and would impede the developing détente with the Eastern bloc—an argument repeated by de Gaulle a few days later during a meeting with British Ambassador to Paris Patrick Reilly.[16] Couve de Murville also underlined specific problems with the British candidacy, namely the weakness of sterling, the deficit of its balance of payments, and the incompatibility of British agricultural practices with the CAP.[17]

Despite the French foreign minister's great argumentative skills, the vigorous refutations by his five counterparts confirmed that few of his points had really struck home. Yet, the July meeting remained largely devoid of outright confrontation, with the "empty chair" crisis of 1965–1966 still very fresh in everyone's mind.[18] To avoid deadlock, the member-states requested a report from the Commission by September on the consequences of enlargement for the Community. This temporarily pushed the British question to the sidelines, as both sides hoped that positions might soften by the time the Commission produced its opinion.[19]

France welcomed that breathing spell, which along with other developments, soothed tension within the Western alliance. Indeed, France shifted to an annual authorization of overflight of its territory for its fourteen allies, rather than the month-to-month regime imposed in May 1966. Paris also signed the Ailleret-Lemnitzer agreement in August. This accord only confirmed what the French general had told his American counterpart many times. If war occurred, France would put its forces in a situation little different from that which existed before the withdrawal.[20] The negotiations over the international monetary system largely benefited from this relative thaw. The lesser tension allowed talks to take place in a more serene atmosphere, less affected by linkages with other areas of dispute within the Western world. More importantly, it meant Paris could focus on preserving the unity of the six over international monetary affairs without worrying about the divisive British question.

France gained from this more tranquil context, first at the meeting of the six finance ministers in Brussels on 4 July, and later on at the G10 meeting in London on 17–18 July.[21] Reviewing the latter gathering, Debré painted an optimistic picture for de Gaulle. While isolated the previous year at the G10 meeting in The Hague, Debré felt that France had this time held the six to a common stance. By staying united, he believed the six had obtained a veto over the future use of the Special Drawing Rights, as well as a guarantee that the SDR would be subject to a meaningful repayment obligation. This implied the SDR would become a form of credit as opposed to a new currency, as the United States desired.[22]

Debré's optimism did not extend to ignoring the existing differences between France and its Common Market allies. While all the EEC states wanted a greater say in the decision-making over the SDR, France seemed more adamant than its partners that the SDR should be like credit, and not like money.[23] But, Debré understood that any agreement over the international monetary system would be a compromise, and that was acceptable as long as the accord benefited France and strengthened the six's position within the IMF at the expense of the Anglo-Saxon powers.[24]

Moreover, two other developments facilitated an agreement. Four years of debate and the reduction of available liquidity had convinced French leaders that the feared collapse of the international monetary system was more imminent than they had thought.[25] Semantics also played a role in bringing together the contrasting French and Anglo-Saxon positions. Negotiations omitted the words that drew attention both to the U.S. preference for a new currency and the French option to create a more extensive credit facility.[26] The second G10 meeting in London on 26 August thus ended with the outline of a contingency plan that would be presented the following month at the annual IMF meeting in Rio. The plan called for the creation of a new monetary facility, subject to repayment clauses, that would require an 85 percent majority of votes within the IMF for its implementation—so giving the six a collective veto, as they represented 17 percent of the votes.[27]

Nonetheless, despite allowing some progress, the agreement had papered over many of the existing differences over monetary conceptions. With its ambiguous language, the London compromise hardly justified Debré's claim that it amounted to "a success for the French thesis" and that "the question of creating new money was discarded."[28] Instead, as Otmar Emminger, of the German Bundesbank, explained, the facility could be interpreted in different ways by the various parties involved, much like a zebra: "one could regard it as a black animal with white stripes or as a white animal with black stripes."[29] Since the outline had been couched intentionally in ambiguous terms, the most difficult negotiations still lay ahead.[30]

Once again, West Germany would play a crucial role in these talks, as highlighted by the continuing rivalry between France and Washington for Bonn's loyalty. This appeared clearly during Kiesinger's summer meetings with both de Gaulle and Johnson, where both presidents used similar techniques to swing Kiesinger to their cause. Johnson mentioned his confidence in de Gaulle, but added that he could not understand why the French president sometimes used such sharp language, whereas he personally refrained from negative statements about the General.

De Gaulle justified to Kiesinger his sharp language toward the U.S. as a way of opposing the pro-Atlanticist segments of French public opinion. The General pointed out that France felt no aversion to the U.S., but feared that the latter was a superpower that could not refrain from being dominant.[31] Both Paris and Washington specifically pressured Bonn on monetary matters. Fowler complained about French obstructionism in the negotiations and praised the compromises made by the U.S. He pushed Kiesinger to follow the American lead rather than stick with France. De Gaulle also stressed the need for the six to stay united in the negotiations if they wanted to defend their independence vis-à-vis the U.S.[32]

Moreover, West German leaders, always uneasy about having to choose between Paris and Washington, were divided on how to best support the U.K.'s candidacy to join the EEC. If Kiesinger wanted to avoid a confrontation with de Gaulle, Brandt preferred a blunter stance. He confided to his American counterpart Rusk that a French veto could have serious consequences for Franco-German relations.[33] Finally, both Paris and Washington could rely, or felt they could rely, on various cards to pressure their ally. If the U.S. could always play the security card, Couve de Murville, after the Franco-German summit of July, reminded Germany that it "now had to choose between either forcing the British application for admission [to the EEC] or aligning themselves to de Gaulle's policy of détente."[34]

Indeed, Paris believed that it could improve the prospects of German support on Western matters if it helped Bonn's Ostpolitik. In practice, however, the cooling off of Franco-Soviet relations undermined Paris's leverage over Bonn. Pompidou certainly welcomed the fact that in regard to the Vietnam War, the final communiqué of his July visit to Moscow marked the first occasion when France and the Soviet Union joined together to call for an end to foreign intervention and bombing.[35] This coincided with the regularization of relations between Paris and Hanoi, with François de Quirielle being accredited as the general French representative in Hanoi rather than an interim representative.[36] But on other key topics, the harmony was lacking and the French prime minister had far less to show for his visit.

While Brezhnev praised French policy toward the Middle East, he regretted France's failure to convince many African states to support the resolutions it endorsed during the UN debates.[37] On Europe, Kosygin also paid tribute to France's positive role in East-West relations, but he appeared very pessimistic as to the chances of progress for détente on the continent and expressed strong mistrust toward Bonn's Ostpolitik.[38] Pompidou, in a talk with Kiesinger a few days later, could only regret the Soviet government's inability to appreciate West Germany's new overtures.[39] This lack of momentum added further pressure on de Gaulle to deliver some breakthroughs during his extremely important trip to Poland—originally planned for June but postponed to early September because of the Six Day War.

The General considered the trip significant in itself, marking his first visit to a satellite state, but he also understood that the visit would only matter if it encouraged West Germany to normalize its relations with the states of the Eastern bloc. This would require flexibility from France's ally and de Gaulle did not hesitate to encourage Kiesinger to recognize the Oder-Neisse border because of the massive effect on Poland that would ensue.[40] In turn, Bonn also expected a lot from Paris. German leaders counted on French support in their quest to break the ice with the Eastern bloc. They repeatedly asked for the French government's help in the weeks preceding de Gaulle's visit.

Manfred Klaiber, West German ambassador to Paris, asked the French president if he could mention the problem of Germany's postwar borders "in a way that was not too 'demonstrative.'"[41] Limburg, a chargé d'affaires in the West German embassy in Paris, reiterated the point in a meeting with Jacques de Beaumarchais, the directeur politique of the Quai d'Orsay. He indicated that his government would be grateful if France could not only defend Bonn's Ostpolitik, but also emphasize that West Germany sincerely wanted to improve relations with Warsaw.[42]

Here lay both the crucial challenge and opportunity for France. On the one hand, the French government possessed — with this visit to Poland — a trump card in its relations with Bonn, one that might help convince its ally to cooperate in other political fields. On the other hand, the General would need to maintain a very difficult balancing act during his trip to Poland. In exchange for his support on the question of the postwar borders, he hoped that the Polish communist leaders would show more flexibility on the German question and greater independence vis-à-vis the Soviet Union. At the same time, for fear of antagonizing Bonn, de Gaulle could not side too openly with the Poles either;[43] nor could he afford to push Warsaw too far down the path of independence, for fear of angering Moscow.

September–October: Times of Tension

De Gaulle's trip to Poland, as pointed out by Couve de Murville, constituted an important step in his overall grand design "to disengage Europe from the bloc system and to accentuate the opening of Eastern Europe, while still recognizing the post-war borders."[44] He pursued multiple objectives by going behind the Iron Curtain. On a basic level, he wanted to promote French prestige and strengthen Franco-Polish relations. From a larger perspective, he believed his visit could stimulate the assertion of Polish national identity and provide additional impetus to the rapprochement between Western and Eastern Europe.

The trip was a resounding popular success, judging by the warm welcome the General received from Polish crowds, but proved to be a political failure. De Gaulle's public and private meetings with the austere and
inflexible Polish leaders, especially Secretary General of the Communist
Party Wladislaw Gomulka, contrasted starkly with his interactions with
the locals. When de Gaulle suggested to the Polish Parliament that security in Europe could only exist through détente and entente between states
rather than through futile opposition between two blocs, Gomulka offered
a polite but categorical denial. He rejected any alternative, praising the alliance with the Soviet Union as the "cornerstone of Polish foreign policy."[45]

The Polish leader proved as uncompromising behind closed doors, despite de Gaulle's best efforts. The French president made repeated pleas in
favor of German reunification, calling the current situation abnormal and
warning that European states would remain the pawns of superpower ri-
valries as long as they did not act in common. But, Gomulka simply replied that the Polish policy toward Germany was not only more dogmatic
than the Soviet policy, but the only valid policy. He added that France
could not expect concessions from Poland on that subject.[46]

The General lamented the limited results of his visit. He poured scorn
on a Polish government that "barely remembers Poland is in Europe" during the first Council of Ministers meeting after his return from behind
the Iron Curtain.[47] He still, though, put an optimistic spin on the trip by
defining it as a breakthrough from a longer-term perspective. By connect-
ing with the Polish people, he felt he had provided momentum for their
struggle to liberalize their regime and gain more independence from Moscow: "I know those regimes [in Eastern Europe] are totalitarian. But I am
sowing grains which maybe, with others, will blossom in twenty or thirty
years. I will not see them blossom. You might. The young Poles of today
will rattle the Soviet rule. It is written on the walls," de Gaulle confided to
Alain Peyrefitte, his then minister for education.[48] Since the French president considered that nothing could stop the inexorable march toward
East-West détente in Europe, he refused to give up on his pan-European
strategy simply because of the setback in Poland.[49]

Not all observers, however, shared the president's optimism. *Le Monde*
argued that while the trip had produced some interesting results, it had
also underlined the fundamental limits of French policy. De Gaulle could
not ignore the fact that the Eastern European states applauded France
when it weakened Western solidarity, but their leaders ran away when
asked to follow in France's footsteps.[50] This assessment would later reso-
nate with many scholars who agreed, albeit for different reasons, that de
Gaulle's trip to Poland had marked an important moment in the failure of
his European grand design.[51]

It is certainly difficult to disagree altogether with the previous claim. Poland had undermined the General's strategy because he had failed to achieve any of his major objectives aside from improving Franco-Polish relations, countering the impression he had patiently cultivated that France could make a difference in East-West affairs. De Gaulle had travelled to Poland with grand ambitions of furthering the cause of détente in Europe. He believed that he could only achieve this objective by keeping Poland, West Germany, and the Soviet Union committed to his vision of détente, a feat that required a very delicate balancing act.

Yet, by trying too hard to please all parties, the General ended up irritating all of them in equal measure. Any gratitude the General expected from West Germany by pleading the cause of its Ostpolitik in Poland was undone by his categorical declarations on the irreversible nature of the postwar borders. These created controversy in the West German press, contributing to the French president's relative loss of popularity in Germany, and could not guarantee any goodwill in return from the Polish leadership.[52] Even his invitation to Poland during a speech in Westerplatte, to "look a bit further, a bit bigger" and his advice on "obstacles that seem insurmountable today, you [Poland] will overcome without doubt. You know what I am referring to," hardly caused the desired impact.[53] Far from emboldened by de Gaulle's calls for Warsaw to show more independence from Moscow, his hosts reacted instead with embarrassment and irritation.

The Polish leaders were not the only ones expressing reservations toward de Gaulle's actions and speeches. Officially, Soviet leaders welcomed the French president's trip to Poland, with Zorin reassuring the General that "Moscow considers your trip to Poland as a major contribution to the developing normalization of European relations."[54] Privately, Soviet leaders were not so upbeat. While they did not oppose per se the Franco-Polish rapprochement, they resented the grandiose reception given to the General because they feared it could reinforce anti-communist movements in Poland. Additionally, despite Gomulka's show of loyalty, they feared the French attempts to underline Poland's national differences vis-à-vis the Soviet Union.[55]

The Polish trip represented an undeniable setback for de Gaulle's pan-European strategy and adversely impacted France's relations with other key players, especially West Germany and the Soviet Union. It did not, obviously, end France's attempts to overcome the Cold War order in Europe, as consultations and mutual visits with the countries of the Eastern bloc continued throughout 1967. Czech President Josef Lenart visited Paris in October 1967, and the same month the Soviet government hosted French Chief of Staff General Charles Ailleret. Yet, despite these meetings,

France's policy of East-West détente was stalling. The regular exchanges could not hide the fact that relations between France and the Eastern bloc states were becoming tenser and less trustful.

The growing inflexibility shown by the satellite states and Soviet attempts to restore discipline within the Eastern bloc played a key role in undermining France's objectives. As the satellite states seemed less willing to compromise, so their tone toward France became less lenient. Thus, an article on 13 September from *Prace,* the organ of the Czech trade unions, praised de Gaulle's visit to Poland but also sent an explicit warning to the French president: "The noble words of de Gaulle did not fool the sharp observer when it came to the little diplomatic subtleties by which he tried to tell his interlocutors about the need to express stronger national feelings. De Gaulle would obviously welcome what in the West they describe—in the relations between socialist states—as the 'policy of independence' towards the Soviet Union. It is also why there are some differences of opinions between France and Poland on the German problem."[56] The article reaffirmed the solidarity between the socialist states and the Soviet Union and reminded the General that French policy would only remain welcome insofar as it did not attempt to threaten this link.

Furthermore, France's détente policy suffered because of the cooling off of Franco-Soviet relations, which resulted in part from Moscow's hardening stance on European affairs. Soviet officials appeared wary, especially of West Germany, and far more interested in defending the status quo.[57] During their talks with their French counterparts, Soviet officials mainly focused on the question of a European security conference and a possible Franco-Soviet pact. They pushed such a conference since they believed it would confirm the status quo in Europe and allow them to undermine Western solidarity. Zorin not so subtly suggested to de Gaulle that April 1969, when the North Atlantic Treaty would be up for revision, could prove a favorable period to consider the question of European security in a different manner than through military blocs.[58]

The insistence with which Zorin pushed for a Franco-Soviet pact worried Secretary General of the Quai d'Orsay Hervé Alphand. He viewed it as evidence that Moscow only sought to detach France further from its allies in the Western world.[59] To make matters worse, the Soviet government remained deaf to all French calls for greater flexibility on East-West relations. During a meeting with Zorin, de Gaulle called on Moscow to improve its relations with Bonn because he believed this would have a vital impact in advancing the cause of détente. These pleas were to no avail.[60]

If the French government acknowledged the difficulties encountered by its policy of détente in late 1967, it tried not to seem unduly worried by the situation when discussing the matter with foreign counterparts, especially with the West Germans. Couve de Murville complained to Brandt about the rigidity of Soviet policy and expressed regret at the general immobilism in both East-West affairs and within NATO. He added that immobilism was an easier position to adopt, at least in the short term.[61]

Yet, the attempts at appeasing German concerns largely failed. The summer had brought renewed hopes for Bonn's Ostpolitik. Brandt was pleased by his successful trip to Romania and the exchange of trade missions negotiated between the Czechs and Germans by his personal representative Egon Bahr,[62] but these hopes quickly dissipated. After the minor successes of the summer, Bonn's Eastern policy once again came to a standstill in the fall because of the rigidity of the Eastern bloc, especially Poland and East Germany. West German officials agreed that aside from Yugoslavia, they could expect no key development with the satellite states in 1968.[63]

French officials shared the assessment of their German colleagues. Alphand, noticeably, seemed particularly pessimistic: "Everything is at a dead end: West Germany is not accepting either the post-war borders or the existence of East Germany, the Soviet Union prefers the status quo, and [Willy] Brandt still persists with the search for détente with Eastern Europe."[64] This unfavorable situation presented a fundamental challenge to de Gaulle's objective of overcoming the Cold War in Europe.

It also threatened Franco-German relations. If détente continued to stall, it would be an easy step for West Germany to question the usefulness of the Paris-Bonn link in regard to East-West matters and to be less cooperative over Western questions. This could only strengthen those in Germany who supported the U.K.'s entry into the EEC.[65] Moreover, without German support, France would face an uphill struggle to maintain European unity during its dealings with the U.S. This would be particularly damaging in late 1967 as crucial Western negotiations were fast approaching their final stages.

Indeed, the timid thaw within the Western Alliance in the summer rapidly faded away when fall came around, and this affected all spheres. It spilled into the Atlantic Alliance, rocked by increasing speculation as to whether France would remain a member of the North Atlantic Treaty after 1969.[66] Paris's ultimate intentions were unclear, but it made little secret of its growing animosity toward NATO. De Gaulle was already furious that he had not been consulted over the decision to restore an annual authorization for over flights;[67] his hostility only increased as he began to pay closer attention to the Harmel exercise.

Until fall 1967, France had downplayed the Harmel study. Even late in the summer, officials emphasized the limited progress of the four subgroups as well as their provisional conclusions.[68] This moderate approach changed in September, however, as French dissatisfaction threatened to turn into all-out opposition when the exercise moved toward its critical phase.[69] Only when the French government finally received, in early October, all four reports from the subgroups did it fully acknowledge the threat posed by the Harmel exercise. Two of the reports in particular—from the second subgroup on inter-allied relations and the fourth one on NATO's relations with the outside world—came across as real pleas against French policy.[70]

In parallel to the tension within NATO, the fragile consensus over the international monetary system came under increasing strain. Enough goodwill remained to reach a general agreement at the IMF's annual meeting in late September in Rio de Janeiro. The Fund's executive directors were instructed to submit a report by 31 March 1968 that proposed amendments for the activation of the SDR and new rules for the running of the IMF.[71] Even Debré initially expressed satisfaction with the agreement, convinced that the SDR constituted a new form of credit. He warned his colleagues that the SDR could only be activated if certain preconditions were met: the Anglo-Saxon powers would need to suppress their balance-of-payments deficits, the opening of the drawing rights would parallel a reform of the IMF, and new voting rules would be adopted to give the EEC states more influence.[72] Debré welcomed the Rio agreement initially, but its vagueness meant that it would not mark the end of negotiations over the international monetary system.

The SDR could only be effective if key differences between France and its partners were resolved. As Solomon explains, "some of the semantic compromises in the [Rio] outline had to be unmasked if the new language was to be clear and operational."[73] Furthermore, Debré's optimism soon gave way to rising suspicion. A few days after the London meeting in late August, he was already complaining to his American counterpart Fowler that some of the U.S. secretary of the treasury's recent declarations went against the agreed compromise.[74]

His doubts only increased after the Rio meeting. Despite his positive reaction to the compromise agreement, Debré quickly changed his mind when his collaborators emphasized its strong ambiguity and the Anglo-Saxons' desire to break the unity of Common Market ministers.[75] In particular, Italian Finance Minister Emilio Colombo had tended to break rank with his fellow European colleagues by dismissing the link between the study on the SDR and the IMF voting reform.[76]

The challenge of maintaining European unity on monetary affairs only became steeper when the European Commission published its opinion on the U.K. membership on 29 September. If the Commission supported the principle of enlargement and recommended the opening of negotiations, it nonetheless raised questions about the pound sterling.[77] France had at least managed to "make explicit links between the balance of payments and the reserve role of sterling, so drawing a clear political picture of a country whose extra-European obligations would render a European role difficult." The opinion had also "pointed out that the UK's extra-European interests would make it difficult for the UK to side with the six in IMF talks."[78]

Yet, despite those arguments on sterling, the general tone of the opinion appeared unfavorable to France, thereby emphasizing how much the debate on enlargement had changed since 1961–63. While the Commission had appeared lukewarm toward the first British application and sympathetic to the French efforts to defend the Community, by 1967 it had completely changed its position and was now prepared "to use its avis as a means of putting further pressure on the French to allow talks with the British, Danes, Irish and Norwegians to begin."[79] This presented a direct challenge to the French, whose whole strategy for the second UK application revolved around avoiding the start of official negotiations between the EEC and the applicants.

The differences between the two U.K. applications went even further. Like in 1962, when it also had to contend with Kennedy's "Great Partnership" proposal, France was fighting on various fronts that would have significant impact on the future of the Western world, but that was as far as the parallel went. While de Gaulle had approached the first U.K. application in late 1962 with strong domestic support, five years later he faced London's second candidacy with greater internal opposition to his policies. Paris's arguments had also often appeared as perfectly legitimate attempts to defend the Community during the 1961–1963 talks. In the 1967 negotiations, however, it found itself far more isolated than it had ever been before January 1963. This time around, the veneer of respectability seemed to be almost missing from its case against enlargement.[80]

Furthermore, France's position appeared fragile in the other negotiations, starting with NATO, where it faced a difficult dilemma. Paris understood that the Harmel exercise offered an opportunity for the U.S. to both strengthen the unity of the Atlantic Alliance and to lead the process of détente, thereby undermining France's impact on East-West affairs. Yet, since it coopted some of de Gaulle's ideas on détente, France risked contradicting its previous policies if it were to distance itself from the conclusions of the exercise.[81] As for international monetary affairs, under strong Anglo-Saxon pressure, Paris's partners in the Common Market increasingly accepted the idea that the SDR could become the outline of a real international currency detached from gold, as opposed to a form of credit.[82]

Finally, far from distinct, these three negotiations—over NATO, the EEC, and the international monetary system—were interconnected. This meant France needed an overall strategy, not just separate approaches for each issue: what tactics could it adopt to fulfill its objectives on each front, while avoiding any inherent contradictions? Indeed, France wanted on the one hand to preserve European unity so as to reform the international monetary system, limit Anglo-Saxon influence, and balance transatlantic relations. On the other hand, it wanted to undermine the Harmel exercise and block U.K. entry into the EEC, two goals inimical to the views of its Common Market partners. Obtaining successes in these three spheres would thus require a remarkable balancing act by de Gaulle and his government; in practice, they seemed very unsure about how best to achieve this.

Consequently, France adopted cautious tactics in all the various negotiations so as to keep its options open. It avoided a confrontation on the Harmel exercise in order to avoid jeopardizing European cohesion, preferring instead a carrot-and-stick approach to limit the impact of the exercise. De Gaulle sent a warning to his allies through a meeting with Secretary General of NATO Manlio Brosio. He reaffirmed France's loyalty to the Atlantic Alliance and its likely adherence to the North Atlantic Treaty after 1969, but he also stated that any attempts to "transform the Atlantic Alliance" or to turn the Atlantic Alliance into a political organization designed "to control and direct East-West relations"—an oblique reference to the Harmel exercise—could force France to reconsider its adherence to NATO.[83] At the same time, Couve de Murville took a more accommodating stance, seeking to coordinate policies with West Germany and convince it to water down the Harmel exercise. He insisted to Brandt that the exercise was a purely academic report, not an attempt to define a common foreign policy for all NATO states.[84]

Finding the most appropriate tactic to block the U.K. candidacy, however, proved more difficult. As Parr explains, de Gaulle seemed reluctant at this point to resort to a veto: on 5 October, he made the very unusual move of summoning U.K. Ambassador Reilly for a private meeting. He "urged Reilly to convince the British to drop the whole venture, arguing that the negotiations could not work and so there was no point in embarking upon them."[85] Despite de Gaulle's best wishes that the U.K. candidacy would simply fade away, London refused to give up.

This tactical uncertainty emerged even more clearly during the fascinating Inner Council meeting of the French cabinet that took place a few days later, involving only de Gaulle, Debré, Pompidou, Couve de Murville, and the French permanent representative to the EEC, Jean-Marc Boegner. All participants agreed that they opposed the U.K.'s membership in the EEC and that it would be best to avoid opening negotiations, but there was no consensus when it came to selecting a method to achieve that objective.[86]

Only in the aftermath of this meeting did French leaders adopt Debré's suggestion to closely tie the international monetary negotiations to the U.K.'s candidacy. Debré believed that because of the weakness of sterling, the U.K. could not ask for full membership in the EEC, and that the safety of its currency depended on a reform of both the IMF and the current international monetary practices.[87]

De Gaulle agreed that the sterling balances were a millstone around the U.K.'s neck and that once inside the EEC, the U.K. would resort to Article 108 of the Rome Treaty.[88] Additionally, the General felt that the Americans would exert pressure on the U.K. because of the weakness of sterling, meaning that the U.K. would become a Trojan horse.[89] With the help of the Commission's opinion and the autumn speculation over sterling, criticism of the weakness of the U.K. currency became the leitmotif of French diplomacy.[90]

This shift in strategy became obvious during the EEC Council of Ministers of 23–24 October. Unlike in the July discussions, where he had listed an impressive number of obstacles, Couve de Murville primarily focused on the U.K.'s economic problems. He argued that London needed to "completely transform its monetary situation and monetary system" and "turn the pound into a national currency."[91] Through this claim, France sought to "kill two birds with one stone." It wanted to prevent U.K. membership in the EEC by attacking the pound, but it also hoped to strengthen its call for the reform of the international monetary system by pushing London to end sterling's role as a reserve currency.

This strategy presented an additional advantage for Couve de Murville, as he explained during the French Council of Ministers meeting of 25 October. France was turning the debate into a referendum on whether the U.K. was ready to join the Common Market. This placed the onus on the U.K. to prove itself, rather than leave the weight of the decision on France.[92] Yet, Couve de Murville's optimism was not shared by all. Alphand feared what would happen once the other Common Market partners realized that France saw as "pointless the opening of any negotiations with the UK."[93]

November–December: Denouement

France stuck to its strategy of denouncing enlargement as potentially dangerous for the Community and stressed two preconditions before it would consent to opening talks with the U.K.: the six would have to agree on the problems presented by London's membership, while the U.K. would need to put its economy back in order. That would require equilibrium in its balance of payments and a solution to the sterling problem.[94] Couve de Murville emphasized the link between U.K. membership in the EEC and the international monetary negotiations. He relied on the Commission's opinion that stated "it is hard to imagine how, after UK accession, this currency [sterling] could continue to play a different role than the currencies of the other EEC states within the international monetary system."[95]

Despite all its efforts, the French government could not convince its Common Market partners. They acknowledged that the reserve role of sterling was problematic, but they would not agree that this should disqualify negotiations altogether.[96] The five also undermined France's call for the postponement of membership talks. They conceded that the U.K. economy needed to improve, but they believed this could take place in parallel with the membership talks, rather than be a precondition. The West Germans, in particular, felt that adhesion could prove a powerful incentive for economic modernization.[97] The persistence of the U.K. question not only threatened to jeopardize Community cohesion, but it also affected France's Western objectives in other fundamental ways. As long as London's second application remained at the forefront of Community affairs, it limited France's ability to cope with the final stages of the Harmel exercise.[98]

France's preoccupation with the European Community meant it could not completely focus on NATO at a crucial time when other member-states—especially the U.S. and Belgium—were playing an active behind-the-scenes role to give real value to the exercise on the future of the Alliance. Rusk and his Belgian counterpart Pierre Harmel knew they faced a potential dilemma if the French adopted an obstructionist approach: a report adjusted to French sensibilities could end up empty in content, while one too honest could give de Gaulle a pretext to withdraw from the Alliance.[99]

They eventually settled on a twofold strategy to overcome this quandary. They quietly spread the word to other allies about their determination to see the exercise through, so as to build up the unity of the fourteen in the face of possible French objections. Simultaneously, they tried to keep the French authorities on board by sounding them out discreetly and in a way that did not engage their prestige.[100] In parallel, Secretary General Brosio held regular meetings with the rapporteurs of the subgroups in order to discuss how to merge the subgroups' drafts into a final report and how to counteract possible French resistance. Brosio and his colleagues also underlined the need for balance: while they did not want the final report to unnecessarily exacerbate French feelings against the Alliance, they did not want to "water down" the final report either just to please the French.[101]

This twofold strategy enabled NATO, the U.S., and Belgium to outmaneuver the French during the November meetings of the Special Group on the Future Tasks of the Alliance. Roger Seydoux, French Permanent Representative to NATO, did not go down without a fight during the first meeting on 7–8 November. He denied that NATO could act as an agent of détente and initially opposed the proposed procedural format for the report that would mark the end of the Harmel exercise.[102] Yet, confronted with a determined group of fourteen states, he could only accept their favored procedural approach: Brosio received instructions to draft a final report that would be submitted at a second meeting scheduled on 22–23 November.[103]

Seydoux proved equally unsuccessful when it came to altering the content of the report. After managing to reject the previous seven drafts, he tried to remove all formulations that appeared incompatible with Gaullist views from the eighth version, especially on the general harmonization of policies among NATO states. His attempts, though, failed in the face of a hardened opposition from the fourteen, even if they did their best not to completely alienate France.[104] As the American permanent representative, Harlan Cleveland, summed up: "the broad consensus on key issues which began to take form in [the] subgroup sessions has begun to be converted into Alliance doctrine" and "confronted by this momentum, France appears to have made [the] decision that it prefers the embarrassment of compromises to the risk of rejection."[105] The road was open for the adoption of the Harmel Report during the NATO ministerial meeting in mid December.

The determination shown by the fourteen, combined with French public opinion, played an important role in narrowing France's margin of action. It also convinced Paris that it would be preferable to avoid a complete break with its NATO allies at a time when it risked acute isolation from its five Common Market partners over the possibility of a new veto of the U.K. candidacy.[106] Indeed, a few weeks later, Rusk reflected that France "undoubtedly went along" with the Harmel report in order to restore amity with the fourteen and avoid a NATO crisis, just as it was preparing to snub the U.K. in the EEC. The British also shared this view, believing that the French compromise on Harmel was designed to avoid "a war on two fronts."[107]

Indeed, France opted not to fight the Harmel report, but this amounted more to a tactical retreat than surrender. Realizing it could not gain full satisfaction on all fronts, France chose to prioritize the EEC—where it held more influence—and compromise with regard to NATO. This did not mean, however, that Paris was shifting to an accommodating line. Facing renewed adversity, de Gaulle abandoned the more cautious strategy used in the weeks before and shifted to a more aggressive stance. The U.K.'s decision, on 18 November, to devalue pound sterling provided him with a perfect opportunity to make the switch. The devaluation of sterling seemed a convenient excuse — much like the Nassau agreement in December 1962 — to deliver a unilateral veto. As in 1963, the General would use the stage provided by his semiannual press conferences to make his decision public.

During his press conference on 27 November, de Gaulle stressed the incompatibility between the Common Market on the one hand, and the U.K. economy, agriculture, and restrictions on free movement of capital on the other. He emphasized the gap between the Common Market and "the state of the pound sterling as highlighted, once again, by its devaluation …; with the state of the pound sterling also which, combined with its role as an international currency and the enormous external debts weighing on it, would not enable it right now to be part of the solid, connected, confident society where the franc, the mark, the lira, the florin and the Belgian franc are united." Instead of membership, the French president offered the U.K. an association agreement. Accepting London into the EEC was simply not possible because it would lead to "the breaking up of a community which was built, and works, according to rules that cannot tolerate such a monumental exception."[108]

The devaluation of sterling also created a tense atmosphere that gave more credence to French criticisms of the international monetary system. Within a few days, speculators who brought down one reserve currency began to turn their attention to the dollar. In the week between 20 and 27 November, the gold pool lost an unprecedented U.S. $641 million. The pool, created in 1961, had established a system whereby the Bank of England acted as controller of an international reserve stock of gold, fed by the central banks of the U.S., France, Belgium, West Germany, Italy, the U.K., Switzerland, and the Netherlands.[109]

The eight countries had agreed to sell or buy gold in the free market in order to maintain the official reserve price of $35.00.[110] However, as Hamilton argues, the gold pool mechanism struggled to steady the price of gold. Two problems, in particular, thwarted its management. The first was the speculation of private investors. The second was an increasing demand for gold for commercial and industrial purposes.[111] The situation became even more chaotic when it became public knowledge that France had secretly withdrawn from the gold pool.[112] France had left in June, but Paul Fabra, a financial journalist from *Le Monde* with close ties to the government, chose the week after the sterling devaluation to announce that Paris had dropped out from the pool.[113]

Furthermore, during his press conference, the French president took the opportunity to launch another scathing attack on the dollar. He condemned the fact that the U.S. balance-of-payments deficit favored American investments abroad, and seemed to welcome the current difficulties of the reserve currencies: "it is possible that the current storm, for which France is not responsible, and which swept away the exchange rate of the pound and is now threatening the dollar's rate, will lead in the end to the restoration of an international monetary system based on immutability, impartiality, and universality, which are the characteristics of gold."[114]

De Gaulle's more aggressive stance also included using his press conference to forcefully justify his foreign policy and the decisions that had caused serious domestic uproar in the previous months. After defending his defiant call of "Vive le Quebec Libre" in Montreal, the General shifted his attention to the recent conflict in the Middle East. While French policy hardened in the fall, becoming more sympathetic to the Arab states, the president went a step further during his press conference. Regretting the fact that Israel had transformed itself into a belligerent country since 1956, determined at all costs to expand its territory, he gauchely reminded his audience that the Jewish people remained a "peuple d'élite, sûr de lui-même et dominateur" (an elite people, self-confident and domineering).[115]

As with his January 1963 press conference, de Gaulle wanted to regain momentum by relying on the surprise effect and on defiant and unilateral initiatives. As in January 1963, his press conference in late November 1967 caused major uproar abroad and at home. Rusk, for example, complained to Charles Lucet, French ambassador in Washington, about the General's declarations on Israel, Quebec, and the dollar. Considering the great emotion these had caused in American public opinion, he added that "never had US-French relations reached such a cold and hostile point."[116]

Although there is no evidence that the French government manipulated the dollar-gold market to bring about its downfall, the U.S. government came to believe otherwise.[117] A CIA report written a few months later accused France of fanning the speculative flames by leaking unsettling financial news to the press and by encouraging other countries, especially China, Algeria, and other communist states, to convert their dollars into gold.[118] The situation became so tense that President Johnson complained to Senator Mike Mansfield about "the desire of the French and Soviets 'and all of our enemies' to get US gold and bring the dollar down."[119]

France's supposed attacks on the dollar went in parallel with its actual defiance toward NATO and security matters. An article by General Ailleret in the December 1967 issue of *Revue de Défense Nationale* caused major consternation among Paris's allies. Timed to coincide with the Harmel report,

Ailleret's piece stated that the French force de frappe could not be "oriented in a direction, against an a priori enemy, but had to be capable of intervening everywhere, or be tous azimuts."[120] The U.S. feared that this strategic doctrine amounted to a possible declaration of French military neutrality.[121]

French Minister for Armed Forces Pierre Messmer admitted that he had authorized the publication of the article—in effect confirming de Gaulle's involvement—and argued to American officials that the main purpose of Ailleret's piece was to convince the French public of the value of an independent nuclear capability.[122] While this may have been part of French calculations, Bozo is surely closer to the mark when he claims that the *tous azimuts* doctrine aimed to highlight French difference within the Atlantic Alliance and to transpose its opposition to Cold War blocs to the strategic field.[123]

Finally, France followed through with de Gaulle's veto of the U.K.'s second application to join the European Community. The tense EEC Council of Ministers meeting on 18–19 December confirmed the lack of agreement between member-states on enlargement. Couve de Murville argued that the U.K.'s economic woes should preclude the start of negotiations, Brandt called for talks to take place in parallel to the U.K.'s recovery, and their other colleagues rejected the view that economic revival should be a precondition for accession to the EEC.[124] So, although the five and the Commission wanted to start negotiations with London and the other candidates, they could not prevent France from imposing its will since enlargement decisions required unanimity.[125]

Therefore, de Gaulle was hoping for a repeat of January 1963, when his comprehensive offensive had vetoed U.K. membership to the EEC, shot down Kennedy's Great Partnership, and promoted the Franco-German axis with devastating effect. He believed that resorting to these more forceful methods could help France regain momentum in the West. However, the contrast between January 1963 and late 1967 was stark, both in terms of the European context and the relative impact of the General's initiatives. The diplomatic offensive of November–December 1967 came from a position of weakness and largely failed. After years of dealing with de Gaulle, Paris's allies seemed better equipped to deal with the challenge he posed as well as less willing to tolerate it anymore.

Indeed, in regard to EEC matters, Couve de Murville could certainly gloat about the fact that the December Council of Ministers meeting had ended in disagreement rather than the crisis wanted by the U.K.,[126] but that was a misreading of the situation. Sir Con O'Neill, British deputy undersecretary in the Foreign and Commonwealth Office, had already argued in summer 1967 that a French veto would "be par excellence the moment for not taking no for an answer."[127] He underlined the importance of having the friendly five on London's side: "the five must not acquiesce in the kind of position they adopted in January 1963: namely a reluctant acquiescence in the fact that the French attitude effectively terminated, or interrupted, the possibility of further negotiations with us. Thus, if the French say no, the five must continue loudly and determinedly, in season and out, to say yes."[128] The U.K. approach succeeded. Unlike in 1963, the five refused to let the question of enlargement die down. The decision to keep the candidacies on the Community agenda "reflected the fact that peace was unlikely fully to return to the EEC until la question anglaise had been answered in a fashion acceptable to the applicants, to the five and to the French."[129]

France's success in vetoing the U.K. application turned out to be even more pyrrhic when considering how it threatened to undermine European unity in other fields, starting with the international monetary negotiations. This posed a major problem with the future of the international monetary system largely uncertain in late 1967. After the sterling devaluation, the gold market began to stabilize somewhat, while support for the gold pool deteriorated. The European members of the group affirmed they would end their cooperation unless the U.S. took drastic measures to reduce its balance-of-payments deficit.[130] Yet, Paris could not take advantage of these conditions to promote its vision of a reform of the international monetary system.

By mid December—according to the CIA report previously mentioned—"the French government had become concerned about the deepening [monetary] crisis and subsequently had generally refrained from unsettling actions."[131] Its capacity to seriously damage the dollar was more limited by then, considering that it no longer possessed large dollar holdings in its external reserves.[132] Furthermore, it could not really count on the support of its European partners. While they agreed with Paris on certain core points, the five were moving closer to the U.S. interpretation of the August London agreement. To justify that shift, they used the pretext of the anti-American presentation of some of France's ideas.[133]

France's growing isolation thus left it in a vulnerable position, and one that only worsened because of additional internal and external developments. Domestically, the General's press conference of 27 November, in particular his words on the Jewish people, shocked French public opinion.[134] In the international sphere, the adoption of the Harmel report marked a symbolic turning point. Even though the report was vague, the NATO organization could now explicitly claim a competence in arms control policy and provide a multilateral framework to develop a détente policy.[135] As Vaïsse and Bozo both argue convincingly, this represented a great victory for the U.S. and its leadership. By "Atlanticizing" détente, NATO had said yes to détente and no to the dissolution of blocs, which was one of the central aims of the General's policy.[136]

Despite Couve de Murville's optimistic stance, de Gaulle's grand design to overcome the Cold War order was losing steam.[137] Not only were Franco-Soviet relations cooling off, but Paris now had to contend with a more cohesive NATO. Far from becoming more obsolete in an age of détente, as the French president had anticipated, the organization had managed to evolve. As President Johnson claimed, it was hard to escape the feeling that NATO had successfully defeated the French challenge.[138]

Conclusion

Throughout 1967, the French government had faced the challenge of interdependence and failed to devise a suitable answer. Politically, it could not find a balance between its desire to pursue independent goals—such as vetoing the U.K.'s application to the EEC—and its ambitions to unite Western Europe vis-à-vis the U.S. In the economic field, the French authorities realized that they could not destabilize the international monetary system without affecting their own economy. Equally, Paris lacked the influence to consolidate the East-West rapprochement once the Eastern bloc became more wary.

Thus, even if it was not completely buried by then, de Gaulle's grand design had been dealt a serious blow by external developments in 1967. If in 1966 the General had hoped that a weakened NATO and a more welcoming Eastern bloc would help to overcome the Cold War in Europe, a year later a strengthened Atlantic Alliance and a wary Warsaw Pact were showing no signs of withering away. Added to that, France was running out of options to make a difference on the international stage. The withdrawal from NATO, the trip to Moscow, and the conversion of dollars into gold were each like a single barreled shotgun. They could be used once, to potentially devastating effect, but once employed they could never be used again. By 1967, France had fired most of its weapons and had precious few left in its arsenal.

Chapter 7

THE FALL, JANUARY–AUGUST 1968

Introduction

On 15 March 1968, journalist Pierre Viansson-Ponté wrote in *Le Monde:* "What characterizes currently our public life is boredom. French people are bored. They are not involved in the great convulsions that are shaking the world … None of this affects us."[1] Little did he know that the students and workers of France would soon prove him very wrong. Until May 1968, however, France still appeared as a haven of stability and prosperity. The economy was growing, despite a slight slowdown in the previous year caused by the West German recession, and de Gaulle remained popular in spite of the uproar over Quebec and Israel. No one could have really anticipated the dramatic events of May 1968.

Instead, in early 1968, the urgent problem for de Gaulle was how to turn the situation around in regard to his foreign policy. 1967, as seen in the previous chapter, had ended with a series of setbacks for the French authorities. They had failed to prevent NATO from finding a renewed sense of purpose, with the adoption of the Harmel report that placed twin emphases on deterrence and détente. The question of enlargement within the EEC also refused to disappear, even after the veto of the U.K.'s application.

Moreover, even with the devaluation of sterling in November and the ensuing run on gold, France had failed to convince its European partners that they should follow its proposals to reform the international monetary system. The challenge in 1968 appeared very arduous: would France be more able to overcome the challenge of interdependence than it had in the previous year?

Changing Superpower Relations

1968 became a year of global upheaval, with unexpected and devastating consequences for the international system and de Gaulle's grand design. The Vietnam War provided the first shock in late January when Hanoi launched its surprise Tet Offensive. Although the attack failed to achieve its military objectives, its political shock waves went far beyond the Indochinese Peninsula. Aside from crystallizing domestic opposition to the conflict in the U.S., North Vietnam's determination convinced Lyndon Johnson that there could be no military solution, despite the presence of more than a half million American soldiers. On 31 March, during a televised speech, the U.S. president confirmed his desire to reduce the bombing campaign over North Vietnam and to start negotiations with Hanoi; Johnson also stunned the world when he announced his decision not to seek reelection.

Johnson's speech, praised by de Gaulle as "an act of reason and political courage," provided further fuel for France's efforts to mediate the conflict.[2] Indeed, in the weeks preceding the speech, French officials had privately and publicly expressed their desire to help end the war. On 28 February, the French government declared its support for UN Secretary-General U Thant's diplomatic initiatives and called on the U.S. to assume North Vietnam would deal in "good faith" if the bombing campaign came to an end.[3] Additionally, Quai d'Orsay officials informed their American counterparts of Hanoi's interest "in having Paris act as 'witness' to what it does in connection with the search for a negotiated solution"; officials also mentioned Hanoi's desire to see France "becoming more active" in the search for peaceful solutions.[4]

Moreover, as Journoud explains, the General resorted to informal diplomacy, before and after the Tet offensive, to make sure Paris appeared as an acceptable venue for any future peace talks. On 20 January, Doctor Roussel, the founder of l'Association Médicale Franco-Vietnamienne who was about to head to Hanoi, received an invitation to the Elysée Palace. To his surprise, the medical doctor received instructions from de Gaulle's diplomatic adviser, René de Saint-Légier de la Sausaye, to secretly sound out the North Vietnamese government and determine its interest in opening peace negotiations in Paris. Roussel's meeting with Prime Minister Pham Van Dong a few weeks later confirmed that Hanoi would not object to the choice of Paris. In April, de Gaulle also used a secret intermediary to convince Saigon to rally around the French capital as a venue for peace talks.[5]

Once Hanoi accepted Johnson's peace offers detailed in the 31 March speech, France's efforts became more public. On 18 April, Couve de Murville confirmed that his government would not object to Paris hosting the negotiations. By early May, all participants had settled on the French capital.[6] De Gaulle welcomed this decision as a symbolic victory. It seemed to be a sign that his views on the war were accepted throughout the world and could allow France to strengthen its influence in Southeast Asia.[7] It also marked "a triumph of his policy of independence and neutrality" as "Paris had become a 'neutral territory.'"[8]

Yet, despite the short-term boost for Paris, the U.S.'s decision to negotiate proved far more consequential for East-West relations. Even though they largely stalled in 1968, the Paris Vietnam negotiations facilitated a limited rapprochement between the superpowers. Soon after his 31 March speech, Johnson began his "campaign for a symbolically impressive summit, centered on questions of arms control, but encompassing other key areas of policy."[9]

Throughout 1967, Johnson had repeatedly tried to convince his Soviet counterparts to start Strategic Arms Limitation Talks (SALT). Undeterred by initial setbacks, his persistence was eventually rewarded. In a letter dated 21 June 1968, Kosygin wrote that he hoped it would be possible "to exchange views more concretely."[10] The timing of this reply was likely linked not only to the start of peace talks in Paris, but also the fact that the Soviet Union wanted a breathing spell because of the problems within its bloc—which will be detailed later in this chapter.[11]

Following the signing of the NPT on 1 July, the American push for SALT gathered momentum. The next day, U.S. Secretary of State Dean Rusk informed the Soviet ambassador in Washington, Anatoly Dobrynin, that Johnson wanted a meeting with Kosygin; on 25 July, Dobrynin handed Rusk a message from Kosygin "proposing that nuclear arms talks could start within a month or six weeks." In mid-August, Johnson finally received the long-awaited invitation to visit Moscow in October.[12] It seemed that the atmosphere of East-West relations had changed in profound ways by summer 1968.[13]

As will be explained later, the summit would fail to materialize due to external developments. It is possible that Moscow also came to believe that it would not be able to "achieve any meaningful agreements with the outgoing president," and preferred instead to "strengthen those political forces in the US opposed to arms spending."[14] Nonetheless, the modest changes introduced by Johnson in East-West relations came to have a long-term importance. They provided the foundations for Richard Nixon's foreign policy and a means of reducing the costs of containment by easing Cold War tensions.[15]

Dead End in the East ...

Changes in superpower relations and in U.S. policy toward Vietnam adversely affected de Gaulle's grand design. In the previous years, the escalating American involvement in Indochina had created an opportunity for France to establish a privileged dialogue with the Eastern bloc. The General hoped, through this rapprochement and East-West détente, to overcome the division of Europe. He believed that reduced tension could justify the departure of American troops stationed in Europe and that in return the Soviet Union would accept both the reunification of Germany and a lesser grip over the Eastern European states. These changed conditions would ultimately allow for the establishment of a new European security system. Yet, the prospects of such a vision became even more remote once Moscow turned back to Washington, rather than Europe, as its main interlocutor.

Moreover, de Gaulle's pan-European strategy had to contend not only with the thaw in superpower relations, but also with the continuing rigidity of Soviet policy. Moscow showed no willingness to unfreeze the situation in Europe, especially on the all-important question of its relations with Bonn. Rather than compromising, the Kremlin leaders denounced West German policies and their infringements in West Berlin, and again insisted on a long list of preconditions before they could sign any renunciation-of-force agreement.[16] In 1967–1968, the Soviet government simply refused to do business with its West German counterpart.[17]

Soviet rigidity undermined all parts of the Paris-Bonn-Moscow triangular partnership that the General hoped to establish in order to further European détente. It stalled West Germany's Ostpolitik. Apart from normalizing relations with Yugoslavia on 31 January 1968, thanks in part to French help, Bonn expected no other breakthrough in the foreseeable future.[18] West German officials believed that the current difficulties within the socialist camp meant the Soviet Union had no incentive to push for détente, since detente could risk promoting centrifugal tendencies within its bloc.[19] Moscow's obstructionism also complicated de Gaulle's attempts to convince both West Germany and the Soviet Union to adopt more forthcoming positions on East-West matters. Thus, during the Franco-German summit in mid February, the General urged Kiesinger to improve relations with the satellite states, especially Poland.[20] At the same time, he pleaded with Zorin to encourage his country to make a gesture toward West Germany.[21]

Zorin, however, refused to depart from well-known Soviet positions and ignored the call for help. The Kremlin leaders believed that the General followed his policies for his own reasons. They saw no reason to pay a political price to de Gaulle on Germany at a time when the grand coalition government in West Germany remained too divided to adopt a more forthcoming policy toward Eastern Europe.[22] The prospects for a serious triangular partnership between Paris, Bonn, and Moscow seemed pretty bleak in 1968.

Moscow's intransigence undermined Franco-Soviet relations as well. French frustrations with Soviet behavior had already been building up over a long period of time. As Jacques Andréani, a deputy director in the Quai d'Orsay on the Soviet desk, complained to an American embassy officer: "since then [Kosygin's trip to Paris in December 1966], the situation had changed" and "for some time now we [France] and Russia have been playing hide-and-seek with each other." He (Andréani) said that the Soviets kept saying "it is time we took a new step forward," but "they were extremely vague about what the step would be."[23] That Moscow increasingly gave priority to discussing measures that would perpetuate the status quo in Europe, in particular the project of a pan-European security conference, did nothing to improve Franco-Soviet relations.

The Soviet Union pushed for a European security conference so as to obtain formal recognition of the political and territorial status quo that had emerged after World War II, with the division of Germany as its cornerstone. While it was not a novel proposal, Soviet officials promoted it far more actively in 1968. They wanted to take advantage of the fact that 1969, which would mark the twentieth anniversary of the signing of the North Atlantic Treaty, was around the corner. During that period, NATO members could reconsider their membership in the Atlantic Alliance.[24] Gromyko, for example, hardly concealed his impatience during a meeting with French Ambassador in Moscow Oliver Wormser. Trying to pressure his French interlocutor, Gromyko insisted he wanted "to put an end to the position that consists in saying that the [European security] conference has to be well prepared."[25]

French officials hardly shared the sense of urgency of their Soviet counterparts. They did not object to discussing the topic of a European security conference, but they could not imagine it occurring in the near future because of the many existing unresolved questions, including determining its agenda and the exact list of participants.[26] These differences of perception emerged clearly during the two meetings held on the subject of the conference—between Couve de Murville and Zorin on 23 April and the talk on 8 May between the Quai d'Orsay's directeur politique, Jacques de Beaumarchais, with members of the Soviet embassy in Paris, Yuri Doubinin and Oberemko.

While the Soviets wanted to push ahead with preparatory work, the French believed instead that the conference should take place at a later stage in the détente process.[27] Even though the question of the European security conference did not play a vital role in Franco-Soviet relations, it highlighted an essential gap between the goals of both countries insofar as East-West détente was concerned. Paris hoped for a rapprochement between the two parts of Germany as part of a larger movement toward overcoming the Cold War in Europe, while Moscow openly promoted détente as a means to protect the status quo on the continent.

The Soviet defense of the status quo went hand-in-hand with its growing focus on strengthening the Warsaw Pact, rather than East-West relations, as confirmed by the theme developed by its various newspapers: "France should not expect anything in return from the socialist states for having withdrawn from NATO, as it was a unilateral decision in line with French national interest."[28] The focus on bloc solidarity signaled the doubts about European détente that affected the Kremlin leaders[29] and the events that unfolded in Czechoslovakia during 1968 only worsened those fears, compelling the Soviets to pay more attention to intra-bloc rather than inter-bloc developments.

Indeed, although dogmatic Stalinism had survived for a long time in Czechoslovakia, pressures for change finally pushed through in the 1960s in the direction of a less centralized economy. Antonin Novotny, the hard-line leader of the Czech Communist Party, opposed this trend and attempted a coup in December 1967 to roll back the reforms. Moscow, however, refused to back him, and consequently Alexander Dubcek replaced Novotny as secretary-general of the Czech Communist Party on 5 January 1968. Dubcek quickly introduced what he called "socialism with a human face," or an attempt to revitalize the country's polity and economy, which would gain public support and still remain within the perimeters of the post-1956 Soviet permissibility.[30] If the Soviet leadership initially tolerated this effort at self-renewal, as well as the public debate authorized by Dubcek after he suspended censorship, it soon expressed its first major reservations in late April.[31]

Paris closely monitored the development of the "Prague Spring" and alternated between optimism and anxiety. If de Gaulle welcomed Dubcek's election as "a victory for the supporters of liberalization," he also worried about the chain impact of these events elsewhere in Eastern Europe.[32] French officials acknowledged what was at stake in Czechoslovakia, but also their limited leverage. On the one hand, they believed a victory for the more liberal socialists could lead to far-reaching changes in the rest of the Eastern bloc.[33] On the other hand, France could do little to influence events and Couve de Murville made it clear that nothing should be done to encourage dissension in Eastern Europe.[34]

The French could only wait for further developments, but the signs coming out from Moscow were not promising. During a trip to the Soviet Union in late April, French Minister for Armed Forces Pierre Messmer received an ominous warning from his Soviet counterpart Marshal Andrei Gretchko: "We will not tolerate for long this Czech policy helped by the German *revanchards*. We will soon take the right dispositions to end this."[35]

The uncertainty surrounding the fate of the Czech experiment did not help France's relations with the other satellite states, although it did not stop meetings altogether. Jeno Fock, the president of the Hungarian Council of Ministers, visited Paris in late March, and de Gaulle headed to Romania in mid May. Despite his disappointing experience in Poland in autumn 1967, the General was too attached to détente to miss out on visiting Bucharest. He hoped, additionally, that the occasion could provide a "new momentum to the struggle of the peoples of Eastern Europe for the liberalization of their regimes and for greater independence vis-à-vis the Soviet Union."[36]

The trip was a major popular triumph, although, as will be mentioned later, it would also prove to be costly domestically for the General. The French president used all opportunities, both private and public, to hammer home his familiar message about détente. During a speech to the Great Romanian National Parliament on 15 May, he argued that Romania and France should cooperate amid the vast movement to overcome the Cold War order. Together they could help end the sterile division of Europe through détente, entente, and cooperation. In his private conversations with Romanian President Nicolae Ceauşescu, the General warned his host that Moscow should not be allowed to develop a full grip on Eastern Europe, because this could lead to a parallel increase in U.S. influence within the Western bloc. The satellite states needed to play a greater role for the sake of the continent's equilibrium.[37]

This rhetoric, however, could not alter the fact that the General faced growing constraints imposed by a less favorable international environment. Even the independent-minded Romanians worried about the impact of the trip, with the Romanian ambassador to Paris pleading with the French president to avoid saying anything that would exacerbate Bucharest's relations with Moscow.[38] De Gaulle agreed to be prudent. According to Wolton, "in his speech to the Romanian parliament [he] denounced the division of Europe into two blocs. But, he censured it after Ceauşescu asked him to do so. He removed the reference to hegemonies in the sentence 'to end the system of two blocs based around two hegemonies'. The Romanian president clearly did not want to embarrass the Soviets."[39]

Overall caution pervaded the whole trip, not just the speeches. As an American State Department analysis pointed out, Soviet concern over Romanian politics restrained both de Gaulle and Ceauşescu from pressing nationalist themes too far. Instead, the two leaders often "pointedly balanced homages to the Soviets ('a pillar of the continent') against the primary emphasis on bilateral friendship and foreign policy 'parallelism.'" Additionally, the current strains in Soviet-Czech relations, prompting the arrival in Prague on 17 May of Kosygin and a Soviet military delegation, no doubt further inhibited the General and Ceauşescu.[40]

By May 1968, France's détente policy was stuttering and close to a dead end. As Rey argues, the Gaullist idea of a greater Europe running from the Atlantic to Urals had at first pleased the Soviets, since they saw it as means of distancing the U.S. from Europe. By 1967–1968, however, it had begun to seriously disturb Moscow, as the General called on the Eastern European satellites to become more independent from their powerful ally.[41] Soviet rigidity, combined with the unrest in Czechoslovakia, had thus created an environment favorable to the status quo, one in which France appeared increasingly powerless to influence the course of East-West events. To make matters worse, France faced similar obstacles in its Western policies.

... And in the West

De Gaulle's grand design not only suffered from Soviet defensiveness, but also seemed outflanked in the West. As explained in previous chapters, NATO had successfully overcome the Gaullist challenge. It had used France's departure as an opportunity to strengthen its cohesion in the political, strategic, and military fields. Like Secretary General Manlio Brosio, many no longer feared that France would withdraw from the Alliance in 1969 when it would have the opportunity to do so.[42] Buoyed by the renewed sense of purpose provided by the Harmel report, NATO pushed for a more active role in East-West relations.

In March, Brosio gave the NATO council a series of questions to be studied by the permanent representatives; three of those—East-West relations, the situation in the Mediterranean, and a balanced reduction of forces—were investigated in depth.[43] Most member-states wanted to move away from the usual vague and sterile debates and actually give a concrete follow-up to the program of future tasks of the Atlantic Alliance, as set out in the Harmel report.[44]

This approach led to some tangible rewards for the Alliance. During the ministerial meeting in Reykjavik in late June, the member-states "issued a 'signal' to the USSR to help prepare future discussions on the possibility of mutual force reductions in Europe."[45] In other words, Paris's attempt to play a meaningful role in East-West relations not only faced competition from the emerging superpower rapprochement, but also from a NATO keen to promote a model of bloc-to-bloc détente.

Just as the Gaullist challenge against NATO had rallied the Europeans around American leadership and strengthened the Organization's cohesion, the major difficulties affecting the international monetary system threatened to lead to the same outcome. The serious speculation in the gold market that had followed the devaluation of sterling in November 1967 had created a crisis atmosphere that complicated France's objectives. Paris needed the support of its EEC partners to balance U.S. power and reform the international monetary system, but the latter's fragility made the Europeans more wary of embracing dramatic change. Moreover, the dispute over enlargement within the EEC had dealt a significant blow to European unity and undermined the prospects of cooperation over monetary matters. In 1968, France would prove no better at dealing with the problem of interdependence.

This applied first to the international monetary system, which soon became engulfed in further trouble despite Washington's best efforts. On New Year's Day, Lyndon Johnson issued Executive Order 11387—which included restrictions on loans made abroad and on the amount of capital that could be exported overseas—to correct the U.S. balance-of-payments deficit. Europeans in general favored these provisions and the foreign exchange markets responded enthusiastically at first to the American proposals, leading to a drastic reduction of gold pool losses in January.[46]

France reacted more ambivalently. Alain Prate, an economic adviser to de Gaulle, argued that the American program validated France's criticism of the frailty of an international monetary system based on the American balance-of-payments deficit. He added that it also offered a great opportunity for the European Community states. If united, the six could impose a new system that would be independent of the fluctuations of American policy and would guarantee greater European influence within the IMF. Prate, however, acknowledged that this was an unlikely scenario. Fear of the economic consequences that could follow a dislocation of the international monetary system would push Paris's partners toward unconditionally supporting the dollar.[47]

Prate's assessment reflected a wider pessimism about France's economy and status, which French Minister of Finance Michel Debré expressed in a letter to the General in early January. Considering that the expected growth rate of 5 percent for 1968 would just about cover national demands and individual aspirations, and that the drive toward industrial competitiveness was creating incompatibilities with a policy of full employment, Debré warned the president that France could expect a difficult year in 1968.

He added that America's New Year's Day program—which in his view let the Europeans bear the burden of American fiscal irresponsibility— would undermine European expansion unless the six coordinated their economic and monetary policy. Like Prate, and based on his own experience, Debré doubted that this would be feasible.[48] As he told Kosygin a few days later, if several states supported France's position in theory, in practice it was isolated in the struggle to reform the international monetary system.[49]

Despite this growing pessimism, French authorities still sought to establish a common European stand and in particular focused on Franco-German solidarity.[50] Throughout 1967, Franco-German entente had proven instrumental in preserving European unity over international monetary affairs along the following principles: the SDR were a form of credit rather than new currency reserves and their creation depended on several conditions being met, including a parallel reform of the IMF that would provide more influence to the six, and a restored equilibrium in the American balance of payments. Continuous support from West Germany, according to the Quai d'Orsay's Direction des Affaires Économiques et Financières, would be vital not only to help reform the IMF but also to preserve the EEC's cohesion.[51]

Guaranteeing a Franco-German entente became ever more urgent once Bonn started to shift its position. Under pressure from the U.S., and because of its important dollar surplus, West Germany slowly edged closer to the American position on international monetary questions. Debré's counterpart, Karl Schiller, argued in favor of an accelerated activation of the SDR. The German authorities were ready not only to accept the SDR as new currency reserves, rather than a form of credit, but also to subordinate their introduction to an improvement in the American balance-of-payments deficit, rather than its complete removal.[52]

Conscious of this development, Debré appealed directly to Schiller and suggested a detailed discussion of the monetary question during the upcoming February Franco-German summit.[53] Debré used the meeting to again warn Schiller that a premature use of the SDR would be dangerous for the future of the West's economy. He also arranged for closer cooperation between French and German experts before a meeting in Rome of the six European ministers of finance, which was to take place later in the month.[54]

Yet, despite Debré's best efforts, external events undermined his attempt to establish a common Franco-German position and by extension a common EEC position. The "Brandt affair," which erupted on 4 February, created unwelcome embarrassment. The incident broke out when a German press agency reported that Willy Brandt had publicly claimed that the Franco-German friendship was strong enough to overcome the rigid and anti-European conceptions of a head of state "thirsty for power."[55] Despite the many complaints and denials, this episode left scars at the highest levels and de Gaulle certainly gave the impression that he would not forget the insult easily.[56]

The Brandt affair, according to Alphand, marked the symbolic end of the "honeymoon" period with the Kiesinger government.[57] Yet, as Ludlow points out, the entente suffered also from persisting differences over the U.K.: "The dispute between France and its partners over whether or not the UK and its fellow applicants should be allowed to join the EEC did not fade away and become an unthreatening background controversy. Instead, an intense but ill-tempered debate about enlargement went on amongst the six for the whole of 1968 and the first half of 1969."[58]

Indeed, the British question refused to die down. It continued to dominate not only the EEC debates, but also Franco-German relations. Bonn urged Paris to be more flexible and offer London a perspective of entry into the EEC, if only to end the disarray within the Community.[59] If initially the French authorities opted to delay and procrastinate in the hope that the issue would simply disappear, tactical considerations pushed them to shift to a different approach. By making a gesture to Bonn on the British question, Paris hoped to improve its chances of preserving Franco-German entente on international monetary affairs.

After prolonged discussions, the summit of 15–16 February ended with a common Franco-German declaration. Both countries stated that they supported enlargement in principle, especially for the U.K., and suggested commercial arrangements with candidate states before membership actually became feasible.[60] According to Kiesinger, de Gaulle even apologized during the summit for the categorical language he customarily used toward the U.S. He blamed his tone on domestic factors and the need to get support from the French communists.[61]

It soon became apparent, however, that the declaration would not significantly soothe relations within the EEC. Discrepancies quickly surfaced between the French and German interpretations of the declaration—with Bonn hoping that it amounted to a major French concession, while Paris denied that it represented any significant change in attitude.[62] The other member-states were not impressed by the Franco-German initiative, and French behavior hardly helped. Couve de Murville's general lack of enthusiasm to conclude a deal with the applicants to the EEC made it very doubtful that France would be ready to go beyond a minimalist "arrangement."[63] This unwillingness to end the EEC stalemate impeded France's objectives in the international monetary sphere at a time when it faced many difficult challenges.

Thus, during the Rome meeting of the six ministers of finance on 26–27 February, France failed to get its partners to agree on a common stand. Apart from the shared desire to see a reform of the IMF that would give the EEC more influence, Debré doubted his colleagues' ambitions to resist growing Anglo-Saxon pressures. In parallel, the IMF Secretariat, following on the mandate it had received in Rio in September 1967, had presented in January a draft proposal for the activation of the SDR. Compared to the compromise agreement of the previous autumn, the draft project departed from the French position by presenting the SDR as a new form currency and by minimizing the proposals to reform the IMF.

France was very concerned by these deviations from the Rio compromise, but it was running out of time to undo them. France called for a G10 meeting in Stockholm in late March to debate the monetary proposal, hoping that the G10 would provide a more favorable forum than the IMF, where the Anglo-Saxon influence was more pronounced.[64] Debré realized that the French government was in a tight spot, and he seemed increasingly pessimistic as to the outcome of the international monetary negotiations. He viewed the IMF proposal as unacceptable, but hoped that an independent stance, like the threat of not signing any future agreement, might still allow France to sway its European partners.[65]

Dramatic events in the following weeks, however, radically altered the nature of the debate over the future of the international monetary system. After a calm period in January and February, speculative purchases of gold picked up substantially in early March. Financial circles became very worried about the long-term future of the existing gold price and disturbed by the failure of the U.S. to win the Vietnam War, as shown by the recent Tet Offensive. When Senator Jacob Javits called in late February for a suspension of the gold pool, speculation assumed a torrential quality.[66]

The massive losses in the gold pool reached a peak of almost $400 million on 14 March alone, forcing Fowler to telephone British Chancellor of the Exchequer Roy Jenkins to ask if the London gold market could be closed the following day.[67] Additionally, the U.S. government convened an emergency meeting in Washington over the weekend of 16–17 March with the Central Bank governors of the gold pool members.[68] The Bretton Woods system seemed in serious trouble, which vindicated many of the French criticisms. Yet, the accurate French predictions did not give Paris more influence; it was quite the opposite. Washington proved far more adept at exploiting this new crisis to its advantage, forging "new and more flexible arrangements for the development of the international monetary system."[69]

The American authorities realized they needed dramatic action to end this panic, but they also understood that the pressures of the monetary crisis could facilitate international agreements and a quick transition to the implementation of the SDR.[70] American officials were helped by the fact that the European governors did not have clear aims and mostly wanted to end this atmosphere of uncertainty.[71] Even in these favorable conditions, the U.S. authorities still had to choose a policy from their various options.

As Susan Strange explains, Washington could pick one of four options. First, it could hold the price and continue to lose gold, which would certainly require heavy and continued intervention. Second, it could give in to the pressure of the market and raise, perhaps even double, the official dollar price of gold. This option, however, raised many serious objections since the chief beneficiaries of such a policy would be the gold-producing states, including South Africa and the Soviet Union. Moreover, increasing the price of gold would be resented by the closest associates of the U.S., like Japan, Canada, and West Germany, who had agreed to hold onto dollars and not to ask for gold.

Third, the U.S. could "come off" gold, "close the gold window" unilaterally, and announce that dollars were no longer convertible into gold at any price. This would represent a capitulation to the forces of the market and would exacerbate failing confidence in the value of the dollar. This left the final compromise alternative of maintaining the official dollar-gold price unchanged for official transactions while allowing the private dollar-gold price to float.[72] All the governors present accepted the U.S. suggestion to follow up on the proposal made in November 1967 by Guido Carli, the governor of the Italian Central Bank: the creation of a "a two-tiered gold market in which the US would only supply central banks with gold at $35.00 an ounce, while gold would be allowed to float freely" on the private market.[73] The gold pool was also dissolved.

Given Washington's pressure and the limited choice between this two-tiered market and unilateral American action, the European central bankers had little choice but to cooperate. As Gavin points out, "a dollar float would have hurt their exports and helped US imports, and they would have had to run down their gold supply to maintain the exchange rate of the dollar."[74] Thus, while the U.S. reaffirmed the dollar as the linchpin of the international monetary system thanks to effective crisis decision-making, France in contrast found itself isolated because it was no longer a member of the gold pool.[75]

Indeed, Paris suffered because of its far less proactive and determined approach than the one adopted by Washington. Publicly, French officials appeared confident during the monetary crisis. Debré argued in an interview that the current troubles could favor a monetary emancipation of Europe. De Gaulle's solemn declaration at the end of the Council of Ministers on 20 March again vigorously denounced the abuses of the current international monetary system and called for a new mechanism based on gold.[76] Privately, however, French leaders were more resigned, as Debré did not really trust France's European partners: "the unity of Europe risks occurring only if we abandon our freedom. Given the attitude of our partners and, to say the word, subordination, we cannot accept this hypothesis. Our freedom is vital," he lamented to the General.[77]

Furthermore, various obstacles curtailed France's ability to successfully block any U.S.-led reforms of the international monetary system. Unlike in 1965, France could only boast a low level of dollar holdings and could no longer rely on a balance-of-payments surplus.[78] Additionally, the persistent divisions within the government over the best course to follow hardly helped either. If Debré received tacit support from de Gaulle for a more confrontational approach, Pompidou wanted France to follow the U.S. monetary theses.[79]

Finally, and most seriously, France faced a very difficult dilemma: if Paris refused the American proposals, it would maintain its freedom of action, but it would not be able to oppose the creation of a large dollar zone—one that would likely include many of its EEC partners. If it prioritized European unity, it risked paying an expensive price in the form of severe deterioration to the international monetary system and world inflation. In order to overcome this quandary, de Gaulle chose not to accept the failure of talks, but to try and "push negotiations [at Stockholm] to their limit."[80]

This strategy ultimately made no difference. The G10 meeting in Stockholm on 29–30 March ended in disappointment for France. Once his European colleagues showed more enthusiasm to debate activating the SDR as a new reserve currency, rather than trying to reform the international monetary system, Debré argued that he had no choice but to condemn the SDR and announce that his country would not sign the final communiqué.[81] In contrast, the U.S. government appeared thrilled with this historic agreement, which reaffirmed the SDR plan, the official $35.00 price for gold, and the need for cooperation to maintain the stability of the international monetary system.[82] When the governors soon after approved a proposed draft covering the SDR facility, France was the only large member of the Fund that did not vote in favor of it.[83]

Even though the decisions in spring 1968 would only prove a temporary reprieve for the Bretton Woods system, the European states believed that the price of rejecting their American ally would have been very steep.[84] They feared the consequences if the Bretton Woods system were to break down and understood that the U.S. remained the only country capable of holding it together.[85] Additionally, they could not ignore other pressures. There was always the risk that failing to cooperate with U.S. financial policies might trigger a U.S. departure or emasculation of its commitment to NATO. As David Calleo points out, "the main accumulators of exported dollars were West Germany and Japan, American military protectorates who absorbed their dollars as a kind of imperial tax."[86] In the case of West Germany, its dependence on world trade—especially with the U.S.—also made it more likely to follow modern solutions, rather than de Gaulle's conservative ideas on gold."[87]

Stockholm, thus, marked a significant setback for France, leading Debré to complain bitterly that "I was abandoned by our European partners" and that "the subordination to the US was total and humiliating."[88] Despite the disappointment, the French minister still hoped that the debate would continue, as he called for another meeting to discuss the monetary system.[89] Yet, this would rapidly prove to be a moot point. Stockholm was the "last fling of the French attempt to destroy the confidence in the dollar."[90]

From Paris to Prague

French foreign policy, by spring 1968, was losing all its momentum. The changing international environment, coupled with the challenge of interdependence for both France's Western and pan-European strategies, had clearly revealed a declining influence in external matters. Despite these difficulties, de Gaulle could at least take comfort from the fact that his country appeared sheltered from the widespread domestic unrest many parts of the world; that is, until the month long May 68 troubles shook France and nearly toppled the General.

The May events took everyone by surprise. Certainly, the Gaullist government faced a certain backlash after a decade in power, but it remained relatively popular. Economic indicators were a cause for concern. If the growth rate remained close to 5 percent per annum, France had suffered the previous year because of the West German recession, leading the unemployment figure to jump to 226,000 by January 1968.[91] Yet, these were worrying rather than dramatic signs and hardly forerunners of a revolution. At the end of April, France appeared—and came across as—stable and blessed with a strong currency. On 6 May, an article in *The Times* could still claim "France has never seemed so successful, so un-sheeplike, so prosperous—so different from the way she ought to be."[92] The following weeks would completely shatter this view.

The May 1968 events need to be understood as the result of part of the dramatic social, cultural, and economic changes that France experienced in the postwar era, including the accelerating rural exodus and urbanization, the rapid economic growth, and the emergence of mass media and of youth culture. This youth culture became more pronounced during the 1960s, as younger people struggled to find a place in what was still a rigid and traditional French society. They feared that the economic slowdown would limit their opportunities, they railed against the blossoming consumer society, and they pushed for a loosening of sexual mores.

Universities, which had struggled to cope with the explosion in the number of enrollments in higher education since the start of the decade, would prove to be the initial locations of unrest.[93] Nanterre's university, in particular, would turn out to be the epicenter. Isolated and located near shantytowns, the impersonal corridors of Nanterre were very fertile soil for the development of small far-left student movements that were intent on challenging the university's hierarchy, which they viewed as a pillar of the capitalist society. A libertarian wave of student protests, demanding the right to political activity and male access to female halls of residence, soon solidified into a political movement—the *mouvement du 22 Mars*.[94]

The growing unrest among students, along with the cycle of protests, repeated riots, and police repression, culminated in the forced closure of La Sorbonne on 2 May and the setting up of barricades in the Latin Quarter eight days later. Once the riot police decided to intervene in high-handed fashion during the night of 10 May to end to the protest, the May events took a more decisive turn. The "night of the barricades" and the images of police brutality crystallized public opinion in favor of the student movement and against the state. A large number of spontaneous strikes soon followed, which culminated in ten million people refusing to show up for work. France was suddenly in a state of paralysis and verging dangerously toward complete chaos.[95]

The social and economic crisis soon affected the political sphere as well, as both de Gaulle and Pompidou struggled to contain the generalized upheaval. As Bernstein and Milza point out, the president's initial response, a speech on 24 May in which he called for a referendum, failed to make any impact as it seemed so far away from the concerns of the strikers. The prime minister's approach hardly fared any better, as he organized a conference involving several representatives of the major trade unions. The Grenelle Accords, completed on the morning of 27 May, included a 35 percent increase of the minimum wage, a 10 percent increase of wages in two steps, and more trade union rights within firms. The grassroots members of the trade unions, though, opposed the agreement, and the strikes continued. The double failure of the General's and Pompidou's approaches gave the impression in late May that power was vacant, prompting center-left politician François Mitterrand to suggest on 28 May the establishment of a provisional government under the leadership of former Premier Pierre Mendès-France.[96]

Yet, de Gaulle refused to bow to the unrest and managed to turn the tables thanks to another dramatic gamble. His secret and unexpected departure from Paris on 29 May to visit General Massu in Baden-Baden created a real wave of panic throughout the country. The next day, taking advantage of his renewed position of strength, the French president announced in a radio speech that he would not stand down, denounced the forces of totalitarian communism, and called for new parliamentary elections.[97] The rapidly held ballot on 23 and 30 June produced a very clear victory for the Gaullist Party, as it won nearly 300 seats out of a total of 485. Even this stunning reversal, however, could not undo the fundamental damage that the May events had caused to the General, his government, and his foreign policy.

Indeed, since 1962 and the end of the Algerian War, de Gaulle had devoted most of his attention to the international stage and his ambitious agenda of restoring France's Great Power status and overcoming the Cold War bipolar order. Until 1967, when his positions on the Arab-Israeli conflict and Quebec had taken their toll, public attention had largely given its assent to the president's actions on the world stage. Although foreign policy did not play a crucial role in the outbreak of the events of May 1968, it contributed in a more indirect manner. It is not a complete stretch to suggest that the unrest and the strikes resulted to a certain extent from the General's tendency to prioritize international aims to the detriment of domestic concerns.[98] His decision to visit Romania in the middle of the crisis angered the public, who interpreted it as a further sign of his lack of interest in events at home.[99]

Moreover, as Patricia Dillon points out, "de Gaulle's efforts to constitute enormous reserves for the reform of the International Monetary System led to major tensions. Austerity measures were needed to maintain the external surplus, at a time when workers were keen on redistribution, rather than austerity."[100] This symbolized the widening gap between the General's aspirations for grandeur and prestige abroad and the more immediate and material concerns of the French population. As the 1960s progressed, a growing number of citizens began to openly doubt that France could truly achieve independence in the political, economic, or military fields.[101]

If de Gaulle's excessive focus on the international sphere played a part in the upheaval that shook France during May 1968, in turn the latter events forced a very significant readjustment of French priorities in the following month. Essentially, the wide social and economic unrest and the resulting need to restore stability forced the French government to turn inward. Only in the aftermath of the elections of 23–30 June, and after the formation of a new government headed by Couve de Murville on 10 July, could France even pay closer attention to the international scene. Even then, it could simply no longer focus as much on foreign policy as it had done in the previous years.

Furthermore, the social and economic disruptions damaged government unity, especially by breaking up the all-important de Gaulle-Pompidou tandem. Certainly, tensions had surfaced in the past, and supposedly the General had considered firing his prime minister after the March 1967 parliamentary elections. May 1968, however, created a major rift between the two leaders that would never really heal. Both men differed in their analysis of the troubles that had shocked France for a month. Whereas de Gaulle believed he was witnessing a crisis of civilization and a plea among the people for increased participation, Pompidou was convinced that France was not facing problems, but rather was victim of a certain boredom and taste for destruction.[102] Unsurprisingly, they also diverged in terms of their preferred solution: Pompidou thought new elections would be more appropriate than the drastic referendum advocated by the General.

From that point on, the split between prime minister and president led to growing mistrust, even after the disorder come to an end. Pompidou felt cheated by the way the General had kept him in the dark about his secret trip to Baden-Baden on 29 May and by the manner in which Couve de Murville came to replace him.[103] De Gaulle, in retrospect, came to hold his prime minister responsible for the May troubles. He believed that Pompidou's appeasement policies toward both students and workers—agreeing to reopen the Sorbonne on 11 May after the "night of the barricades" and signing the Grenelle Accords on 27 May—had helped to spread the crisis and dealt a serious blow to France's economy.[104]

Last, but certainly not least, May 68 shook the very foundations of Gaullist foreign policy, starting with its economic and monetary base as pointed out by Bernstein and Milza. May 1968 affected the budget, the commercial balance, and prices. The decisions taken at the Grenelle Accords led to a major increase in wages, as well as a growth of 19 percent of the monetary mass and a price rise of 7.2 percent in one year. This impacted the commercial balance, which went from being positive in 1967 to being strongly negative in 1968. France lost nearly 30 percent of its gold reserves, and the government would soon come under pressure to devalue the franc.[105] The Banque de France was forced to sell gold and to rely on its drawing rights at the IMF.[106]

The crisis also dealt a serious blow to the General's power and prestige. As new U.S. Ambassador to Paris Sargent Shriver explained, many of de Gaulle's diplomatic successes appeared less the result of France's intrinsic power and more the result of "[de Gaulle's] unique personal authority and audacity, coupled with [the] image of French prosperity and stability."[107] Amid the chaos in the streets of Paris, the General appeared for the first time utterly powerless to control the situation, and even his rhetorical powers, normally so trustworthy in times of need, deserted him. His speech on 24 May, calling for a referendum, had failed to calm the situation and led to further violence.[108] The troubles demystified the president, destroyed his aura, and raised questions about his ability to rise to difficult challenges. Throughout May, he looked more like an out-of-touch old man than the usual towering and imposing figure that people were used to.

In other words, the electoral turnaround could not undo the damage that the May 68 events had caused to France's image and status abroad, to de Gaulle's leadership, or to his own self-confidence. The May upheaval took its toll on the General, and he could never quite forgive himself for what he considered crucial lapses in judgment: abandoning leadership to Pompidou on 11 May, using the wrong tone for his speech on 24 May, and accepting Pompidou's request to call for new elections instead of a referendum on 30 May.[109] Even the turnaround of 29–30 May left a bitter taste in his mouth: "*ils* [French people] *ont eu peur du vide*" (they were scared of heights), he confided to Debré.[110]

The Gaullist regime survived, but the same could not quite be said for its ambitious foreign policy. The domestic crisis, coupled with the previous setbacks in its Western and pan-European policies, had effectively destroyed any hopes the General might have had of achieving his grand design. In previous years, the French positions on international monetary matters, the British entry to the EEC, and even the Kennedy Round had effectively been grounded on the fact that it ran an economically tight ship and could thus afford to be critical of those who did not. Following the May events, however, France suddenly found itself with budget deficits and a weakened currency, features for which it had criticized the Anglo-Saxon countries.

As Pompidou summed up eloquently: "The France of General de Gaulle was brought back to its real dimensions … No more war against the dollar. No more lessons given to the mighty of this world. No more leadership of Western Europe."[111] Moreover, as Couve de Murville pointed out to Debré, his successor at the Quai d'Orsay, "the stature of the General is no longer what it was, and all the reports of our ambassadors declare that our partners will not easily forget our internal difficulties."[112]

Moreover, it was hard to escape the fact that all the avenues for the French government to take ambitious action on the international scene seemed truly blocked by then: the EEC remained in a stalemate over the question of enlargement and France appeared powerless to stop NATO from taking a more active role in East-West affairs. It could do little more than criticize the Reykjavik "signal" on mutual force reductions and argue that it contributed to perpetuating the policy of blocs.[113] Relations with Washington had reached some sort of uncomfortable freeze. Paris could no longer condemn American policy in Vietnam since the latter had started peace talks, and it could no longer challenge the dollar hegemony.[114] In theory, pushing European détente was still an option, but even that objective seemed fraught with problems.

Even though Debré did his best to convince people otherwise, France could hardly escape the clear tension between claiming to fight totalitarian communism domestically and pushing for cooperation with the Eastern bloc externally.[115] Additionally, the future of France's policy of détente depended to a large extent on how events unfolded in Czechoslovakia, but it could hardly influence these developments, even when they became more ominous.

Indeed, the Soviet leaders became particularly alarmed by a number of developments in the early summer: the exclusion of former Secretary General Novotny from the central committee of the Czech Communist Party, the decision by the Prague authorities to end press censorship and to rehabilitate the victims of Stalinist purges, and, more worryingly, Czech liberal writer Ludvik Vaculik's issuance of the "2,000 words" manifesto on 27 June, which indicted twenty years of Communist Party dictatorship and demanded accelerated reforms. The sheer fact of the manifesto's publication convinced Moscow that Prague could not control the actions of the "counter-revolutionaries," leading Brezhnev to ominously warn in early July: "We cannot be and we will never be indifferent towards the fate of the building of socialism in other nations, towards the common cause of socialism and communism."[116]

Dubcek refused to make any major concessions, despite the pressures in July from all his Warsaw Pact partners—with the exception of Romania. He showed no inclination to either reimpose censorship or curb the intellectuals.[117] In these conditions, and before it could take any future steps forward in East-West relations, the Kremlin believed it had no choice "but to demonstrate to the world its incontrovertible resolve to maintain the neo-Stalinist regimes in Eastern Europe."[118] During the night of 20–21 August, Warsaw Pact troops entered Czechoslovakia and put an end to the Prague Spring.

This invasion was more than simply an "*incident de parcours*" (a hitch), to use Debré's clumsy take on the episode, and caused serious repercussions.[119] President Lyndon Johnson had to say goodbye to his summit in Moscow, while de Gaulle was forced to say goodbye to his grand design to overcome the Cold War order. East and West were not converging, despite his best hopes, nor were the Soviets prepared to abandon their grip on Eastern Europe. As Alphand summed up a few days later in his diary: "It is maybe indeed the end of a grand effort to reunite two worlds beyond ideology ... So the General's disappointment must be very profound, after the unrest of May and June, and the blows to the country's economy and finance, as well as to his morale."[120]

Conclusion

General de Gaulle remained president for another eight months after the crushing of the Prague Spring. He would eventually resign on 28 April 1969, after 53 percent of the electorate had disavowed his referendum on a planned reform of the Senate and of the regions. However, his ambitious foreign policy agenda—his quest to gain Great Power status for France and to overcome the Cold War order—had become a clear pipe dream by the time the Soviet troops entered Prague. The events of 1968 had painfully confirmed to the General, and to the rest of the world, the internal and external limits of his grand design.

May 68 not only shook France and its image abroad as prosperous and stable, but also de Gaulle's prestige. He could no longer count on his unique aura to pursue a dramatic foreign policy, nor did France have the available means.[121] Following the unrest, domestic problems, including the weakening franc, became the priority. The currency became involved in a major speculative crisis, which nearly resulted in devaluation in November, as France's total reserves dropped from $6.9 billion in April to just under $4 billion in November.[122] At the same time, Moscow's policy was very cautious and increasingly interested in a dialogue with Washington.

Certainly, de Gaulle's foreign policy was in trouble well before August 1968. The rapprochement with the Eastern bloc had only produced limited results.[123] France was isolated in the international monetary field. That said, even taking into account those difficulties, May 1968 and the crushing of the Prague Spring were particularly significant. They dramatically confirmed that French people were simply not ready to make the needed sacrifices for de Gaulle's ambitious foreign policy agenda, while Kremlin leaders were simply not ready to accept East-West détente if it involved a loosening of their control over the states of Eastern Europe.

Conclusion

On 9 September 1968, a few weeks after the Soviet tanks had rolled into Czechoslovakia, de Gaulle gave one of his semiannual press conferences. Unlike the one in January 1963 or even the one in February 1965, this press conference would not go down as a memorable piece of political theater or be defined by shocking declarations. Instead, the mood was austere and pensive, as if the General wanted to reflect on his legacy and achievements. Since 1958, he claimed, France had worked ceaselessly to end the division of Europe into two blocs. In that period, it had finalized reconciliation with West Germany; progressively withdrawn from NATO, which subordinated Europe to the U.S.; taken part in the EEC and prevented it from being absorbed into a larger Atlantic Community; and renewed relations with Eastern Europe.

The events in Czechoslovakia naturally deserved to be condemned because they appeared absurd in the context of détente, and marked the expression of Soviet hegemony in the Eastern Europe. Yet, the General ended on a positive note. The Czech desire to push for liberation confirmed that the French policy of détente was correct and in line with European realities. Unless a world conflict came to upset events, de Gaulle concluded that the evolution toward a rapprochement between both sides of Europe would prove inevitable.[1]

A few months later, de Gaulle resigned from office after French voters rejected by referendum his proposals to reform the Senate and to give power to regional councils. He left the Elysée Palace disappointed at his failure to see through to completion all his grand initiatives. In retirement, he remained out of the public eye, dedicating himself to his memoirs, which would cover his presidency. When he died in November 1970, he had only managed to complete the first of the three planned volumes, dealing with the 1958 to 1962 period. How he would have judged his foreign policy between 1963 and 1968 will remain forever unanswered.

This book, focusing on the latter period, has argued that de Gaulle pursued a coherent grand design, which, despite obvious flaws and contradictions, centered on two objectives. The first revolved around recovering France's independence, especially in the field of defense, and striving to recapture its lost Great Power status. The pursuit of *grandeur*, of an ambitious diplomatic agenda, was both a means and an end. For the General, misquoting *Hamlet*, to be great meant being able to sustain a great quarrel.[2] Only by striving for a higher goal and being ready to make the necessary sacrifices could France avoid decline. Additionally, grandeur implied the determination to be an actor, and not an object, a player, and not a stake.[3] De Gaulle never departed from the view that France needed to occupy a prime role on the world stage because its rightful status was to be a great power.

Even though he knew that France could not ultimately compete with the superpowers, especially in the military sphere, he also believed that it could compensate for some of its limitations through a creative and spectacular diplomacy. By relying on secrecy, surprise, and acute timing, the General could aggrandize the impact of his foreign policy initiatives. He could show that France still mattered.

Moreover, de Gaulle remained convinced that it was not only France's duty, but also its nature, to serve the interests of mankind. As he told Peyrefitte, "France's authority is moral ... Our country is different than others because of its disinterested and universal vocation ... France has an eternal role. That is why it benefits from an immense credit. Because France was a pioneer of American independence, of the abolition of slavery, of the rights of people to dispose of their own fate. Because it is the champion of nations' independence against all hegemonies. Everyone realizes that: France is the light of the world, its genius is to enlighten the universe."[4]

Thus, the second objective of de Gaulle's grand design sought to transform the international order and help to overcome the status quo inherited from the Cold War, especially in Europe. He always believed that a multipolar world would provide more stability than a system centered on the superpower rivalry. When he returned to power in 1958, he already possessed, as Soutou argues, a long-term blueprint to reshape European security. He did not approach it as a rigid guide for policy, nor as an agenda that he could pursue consistently. Between 1958 and 1962, when Europe had to contend with the Berlin crisis, he supported a firm stance against the Soviet Union, despite the fact that his long-term design involved a rapprochement with Moscow.[5]

Nonetheless, de Gaulle never lost sight of his grand design, which meant in practice that the various strands of his European policy often remained closely connected. This proved true when Paris used the withdrawal from NATO to further the cause of East-West détente. It also proved true when the attacks against the dollar moved in parallel to the growing criticism of American hegemony in other fields.

In the long run, the General hoped that his diplomacy could help overcome the Cold War and establish instead a pan-European security system, where American troops would eventually leave the continent. In return, the Soviet Union would abandon East Germany, allowing German reunification and a real détente in Europe, along with independence for the satellite states. The two main pillars of the system would be France and the Soviet Union, as nuclear powers, but security would be guaranteed by an interlocking set of checks and balances. Paris and Moscow would contain Bonn, while a closer union between the states of Western Europe would contain Soviet power. The U.S. would play its traditional role of underwriter and ultimate arbiter of the European order.[6]

Despite his global ambitions, the French president pursued a grand design that remained essentially Eurocentric. This did not prevent Gaullist rhetoric from pushing for a new model of relations between developed and developing states and for Paris to oppose the Third World becoming a new Cold War battlefield, but in practice, France's policies toward the non-European states were driven at least as much, if not more, by traditional Great Power interests and the need to maintain and extend its influence. Additionally, with the exception of Vietnam, the importance of the Third World in de Gaulle's grand strategy declined steadily after 1964. Even for Indochina, his approach increasingly became a derivative of his general outlook toward the U.S. once Washington escalated its involvement in the war.[7]

Even if the two aims of the General's foreign policy, restoring French independence and overcoming the Cold War order, appeared somehow incompatible, on closer inspection this contradiction proved more artificial than real. On the one hand, these twin objectives simply reflected de Gaulle's political philosophy, which stood at the confluence between two traditions, one liberal and revolutionary, the other realist and Machiavellian.[8] On the other hand, these two goals were played out in very different time frames. If restoring France's status constituted an immediate necessity, transforming the international status quo could only happen in the long term.

Furthermore, the General never believed that France could singlehandedly overcome the Cold War order, but instead felt that the bipolar competition was inevitably fading away in the 1960s. As he explained to New York Governor Nelson Rockefeller, he considered the Cold War an abnormal state of affairs, an aberration that would automatically give way to a more multipolar system. "It has never happened in modern times that one or two nations hold all the power. The US and the Soviet Union have all the means of power. All my life, I saw the power of the UK, France, Germany, Russia, Italy, and Japan before. It created equilibrium. Today, all has changed. Yet, France cannot accept that all the power in the world is shared between two countries. Deep down, all countries agree with us."[9] For de Gaulle, France could thus recapture its Great Power status if it embraced and placed itself at the vanguard of the anticipated profound changes in the international system. That was how he attempted to reconcile the two central pillars of his grand design.

However, the General's vision for France and for the world never came to be. His country could not quite achieve great power status, and while the Cold War order evolved and would eventually come to an end, it did so in ways different from those he had anticipated. The failure of the grand design came down to a variety of reasons. Certainly, de Gaulle faced major structural obstacles. On the one hand, France simply lacked the power to play the role that its president wanted. The economy performed well throughout the 1960s, but it nonetheless remained the Achilles heel of the General's popularity. Between 1964 and 1969, when people were asked specifically about economic issues, the discontented always outnumbered the satisfied.[10] Public opinion generally supported the goals of French foreign policy, but this could not prevent the widening gap between the president and his citizens, which would be dramatically highlighted by the events of May 1968. While de Gaulle aspired to grandeur and spoke of sacrifices, the rest of the population wanted more liberty and a redistribution of wealth.

On the other hand, the Cold War structure proved resilient and less prone to rapid and fundamental change than expected. The growing diffusion of the international order in the 1960s, combined with the desire of smaller states to gain more autonomy, certainly favored the emergence of a more multipolar world, but not to the point of really undermining the predominance of the superpowers. Rather than threaten the equilibrium, the various crises of the decade, such as the Six Day War, actually strengthened and underlined the latent bipolarity of the international system.[11] Moments of crisis convinced Moscow and Washington that they needed to cooperate more, if only to guarantee predictability in East-West relations.

At the same time, establishing feasible alternatives to Cold War or transatlantic structures was rather daunting, and Western European states were often willing or pressured to accept U.S. supremacy, like in the case of the international monetary system. As David Calleo argues, "throughout the Cold War, America's ability to create credit for depended on two conditions: first, there was no real substitute for the dollar as a reserve currency. And second, the principal accumulators of exported dollars were Germany and Japan, US military protectorates who absorbed their dollars as a kind of imperial tax. All things considered, the costs of accumulating the exported dollars was a cheap price for America's protection, and awkward to refuse. The United States was spending more on Europe's defense than the Europeans themselves."[12]

Furthermore, de Gaulle's grand design suffered from a series of flaws and contradictions.[13] As pointed out by many authors, he underestimated the role of ideology, in particular when it came to the communist bloc.[14] His plan for a new European security order effectively depended on the Soviet Union giving up its global ambitions and accepting a more traditional balancing role on the continent. Yet, the Kremlin leaders were not prepared at that time to follow that path. Additionally, the General's blueprint for overcoming of the Cold War order proved in many ways to be too complex. It could only succeed through an extraordinary concordance of events and changes, whereby all states would realize that it was in their interest to follow the Gaullist vision.[15]

In this respect, the General's diplomatic style posed a major problem. Apart from his tendency to overestimate his country's power and genius, too often wishful thinking deluded him into believing that France could become a role model for others. Bold initiatives could win praise, especially in the Third World, but this did not necessarily translate into influence. More often than not, de Gaulle's unilateral and spectacular method of action irritated and offended partners. As Bruno Kreisky, Austrian foreign minister, summed up in February 1963, "A great country must have three characteristics. It must have a healthy economy: that is your [France's] case. It must have a clear policy: you are one of the rare ones in that situation. It must be appreciated by others: this condition is not fulfilled; the Anglo-Saxon countries hate you; how do you want to pursue a great foreign policy, in today's world, if the Anglo-Saxon countries hate you?" [16]

Unsurprisingly, Paris's allies played a very significant role when it came to thwarting the General's plans. As the years went by, they became more adept at dealing with the Gaullist challenge. This became very obvious in 1967–1968, when a series of crucial negotiations for the future of the Western world—the second British application to join the EEC, the Harmel exercise for NATO, and the debates over the international monetary system—reached their conclusion. Facing a united and determined opposition, France found itself isolated and unable to have a significant impact on debates. It was forced to accept the Harmel report even though it felt uneasy with some of its conclusions. Had it rejected it, Paris would have found itself in contradiction with its commitment to East-West détente.

Similarly, taking advantage of the monetary crisis in March 1968, the U.S. managed to impose a series of changes that safeguarded the dollar as the central pillar of the global monetary system and only partially reformed the Bretton Woods arrangement. Again, France faced a choice between two evils. It could have cooperated with its European partners, but this would have entailed accepting a flawed system. Instead, it preferred to maintain its freedom of action in the hope that developments would turn in its favor and that other states would eventually accept the need to establish a new monetary mechanism.

As for the EEC, while Paris twice vetoed London's application to join the Common Market, this proved a pyrrhic victory in the long run. The five refused to let the British question die down after 1967, undermining in the process any chance that the European countries would be able to agree on a united position in other spheres. This was, in a nutshell, the challenge of interdependence that France could never quite overcome. How could it expect the other European Community states to follow its line on international monetary matters if it pursued goals related to NATO and the EEC that were inimical to their interests?

Thus, de Gaulle failed to achieve all the aims set out in his grand design, but his impact cannot be reduced to this sole fact. Although he courted controversy during his lifetime, even opponents would concede his enduring legacy. The General successfully ended the violent and divisive Algerian War, and he crucially helped to restore a sense of pride to France after the difficult years of the Fourth Republic. He left behind a country that was in a far stronger position domestically and had a more confident and assertive attitude externally. France did not quite become the global power that de Gaulle wanted, but he still gave it more influence.

It is another tribute to his importance that his presidential successors on the right and the left of the political spectrum have generally remained loyal to the central tenets of his foreign policy, even if they have not quite replicated his distinctive style. The Gaullist myth, furthermore, has continually grown in the four decades after his death, making him a figure of almost universal admiration.[17] His election as the greatest Frenchman of all time in a poll a few years ago can be seen as a further proof of this.

Moreover, the General also shaped the Western world in significant ways, albeit not always in the ways he intended. Undoubtedly, during the 1960s he dedicated a lot of his time to obstructing or wrecking initiatives. Hi most famous and spectacular move, the withdrawal from NATO's integrated military structure, was in part a negative reaction to his inability to reform the Atlantic Alliance. However, the French president also became the unwitting protector of Western unity. As surprising as this may sound in view of the previous arguments, it is less so when considering the actual impact of the French president rather than his intentions.

As Ludlow argues, the way in which he conducted policy and criticized the U.S. unintentionally helped to minimize the European challenge to American leadership. It therefore becomes possible to portray the would-be challenger of the Atlantic status quo as someone who actually made a generalized crisis within the Atlantic Alliance less likely than it would otherwise have been.[18] Additionally the Western world came out of the 1960s much stronger for having dealt with the test posed by de Gaulle. He often alienated allies by his methods, but he also put a spotlight on fundamental issues—in the economic, military, and political spheres—that could threaten the fabric of transatlantic relations if left unresolved.

Finally, the General left a lasting impression on the history of the Cold War. Although the conflict did not quite end in the way he had imagined, he nonetheless played an important role because of the fact that he outlined an alternative to the bipolar order. Through his trips to the Soviet Union, Poland, and Romania, he helped the cause of the rapprochement between the two divided blocs in Europe and imposed the principle that East-West détente should precede the reunification of Germany. De Gaulle's bold and pioneering policies would inspire subsequent leaders such as West German Chancellor Willy Brandt or U.S. President Richard Nixon, even if they did not necessarily share the same objectives. Nixon, in particular, admired and reveled in de Gaulle's company; he sought to emulate the General and was particularly fascinated by his penchant for personal diplomacy.[19]

Furthermore, he acted as a symbolic role model for the rest of the world with his nose-thumbing at the superpowers. As Gaddis argues, both China and France could act that way because of the disappearance of fear. By the 1960s, they had become sufficiently strong within the framework of their respective alliances that they no longer suffered from the insecurities that had led them to seek alliances in the first place.[20] But credit must also go to de Gaulle's ideas and prestige in that they contributed to an important transformation in the nature of the Cold War and even, to an extent, hasten its demise. It did not end in exactly the manner in which he had predicted. Yet, in the aftermath of 1989 his vision of a world without blocs and of a Europe stretching from the Atlantic to the Urals suddenly looked much less quixotic than it had two decades before.

ANNEXES

Annex 1. General de Gaulle's Popularity Index, July 1958–December 1965.
Source: Institut Français d'Opinion Publique.

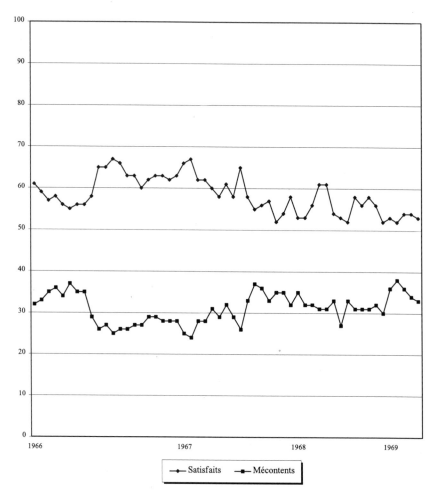

Annex 2. General de Gaulle's Popularity Index, January 1966–April 1969.
Source: Institut Français d'Opinion Publique.

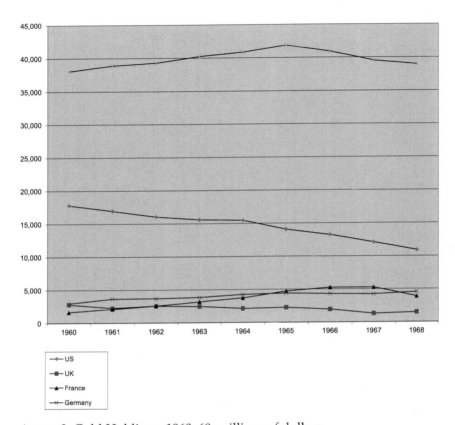

Annex 3. Gold Holdings, 1960–68, millions of dollars.
Source: Susan Strange, *International Economic Relations of the Western World, 1959–1971 vol. 2.*
1976, p. 296. London: Oxford University Press

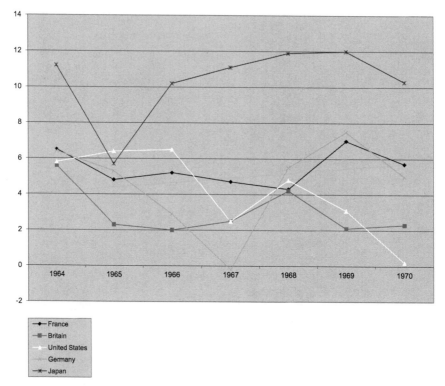

Annex 4. Real GDP Growth in OECD countries, 1964–1970, annual
percentage change.
Source: OECD Economic Outlook Database

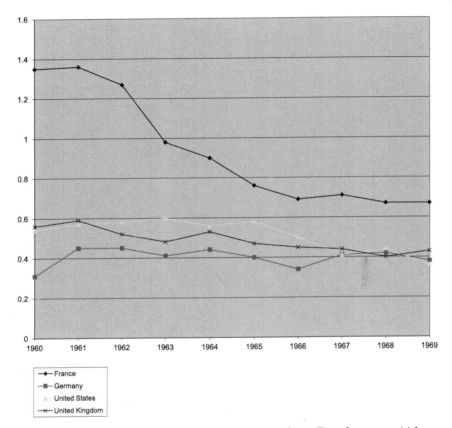

Annex 5. Net Official Development Assistance from Development Aid Committee Countries to Developing Countries, 1960–1969, as percentage of Gross National Income.

Source: OECD ODA statistics, http://www.oecd.org/dac/stats/idsonline

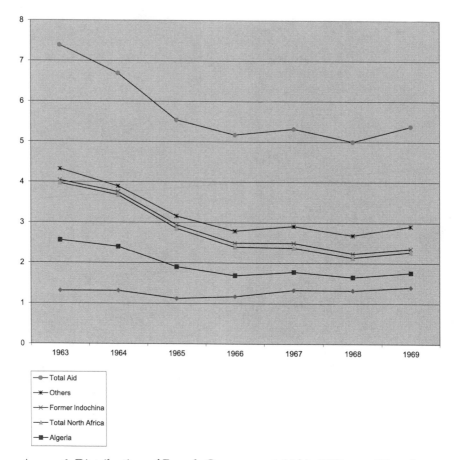

Annex 6. Distribution of French Government Aid in Billions of French Francs, 1963–1969.

Source: Gérard Bossuat, "French Development Aid and Co-Operation under de Gaulle". *Contemporary European History*, 12/4 (2003), p. 443

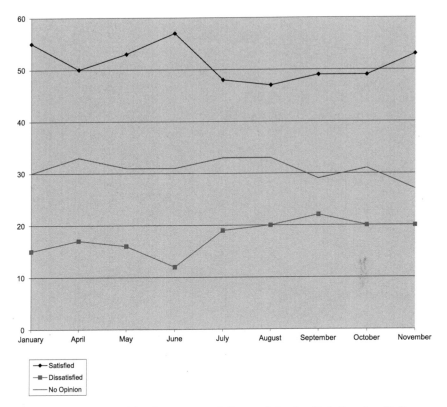

Annex 7. French Public Opinion and General de Gaulle's Foreign Policy, 1966.

Source: Institut Français d'Opinion Publique, *Les Français et de Gaulle* 1971, p. 260. Paris: Plon

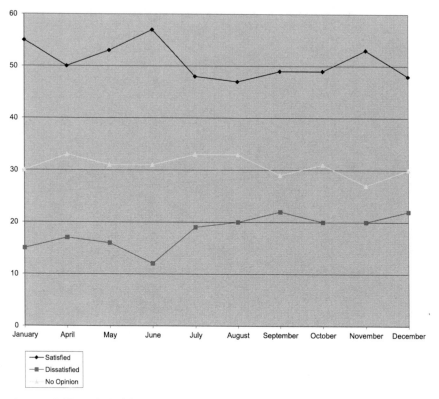

Annex 8. French Public Opinion and General de Gaulle's Foreign Policy, 1967.

Source: Institut Français d'Opinion Publique, *Les Français et de Gaulle* 1971, p. 260–1. Paris: Plon

ENDNOTES

Introduction

1. Nicolas Sarkozy, speech at l'Ecole Militaire, 11 March 2009, http://www.ambafrance-no.org/IMG/pdf/11_1_.03_Conclusion_colloque_Defense_Otan.pdf. The author is responsible for all translations from French to English.
2. N. Piers Ludlow, "The Protector of Atlantic Unity: De Gaulle's Unintentional Boost to the Atlantic Alliance" (unpublished paper presented to the LSE-Columbia workshop on transatlantic relations, April 2004).
3. See Annexes 1–2; between 1958 and 1969, de Gaulle's approval rating in France never went below 42 percent and remained close to 60 percent on average.
4. Paul-Henri Spaak, *Combats Inachevés: vol. 2 De l'espoir aux déceptions* (Paris: Fayard, 1969), p. 170.
5. Julian Jackson, *Charles de Gaulle* (London: Haus, 2003), pp. 55–57.
6. Charles de Gaulle, *Le Fil de l'Épée* (Paris: Berger-Levrault, 1944), pp. 44, 66.
7. Fredrik Logevall, *Choosing War: The Lost Chance for Peace and the Escalation of War in Vietnam* (Berkeley: University of California Press, 1999), p. 104; Erin Mahan, *Kennedy, De Gaulle, and Western Europe* (New York: Palgrave Macmillan, 2002), p. 27.
8. Marc Trachtenberg, *A Constructed Peace: The Making of the European Settlement, 1945–1963* (Princeton: Princeton University Press, 1999), p. 393; John Lewis Gaddis, *The Cold War: A New History* (New York: Penguin Press, 2005), p. 140.
9. See Richard Kuisel, *Seducing the French: The Dilemma of Americanisation* (Berkeley: University of California Press, 1993), p. 145.
10. See Hervé Alphand's testimony in Jean Lacouture, *De Gaulle: vol. 3* (Paris: Le Seuil, 1986), p. 344; Frank Costigliola, *France and the United States: The Cold Alliance Since World War II* (New York: Twayne Publishers, 1992), p. 136; Maurice Vaïsse, *La grandeur: politique étrangère du Général de Gaulle 1958–1969* (Paris: Fayard, 1998), p. 39.
11. Spaak, *Combats: vol. 2*, p. 170.
12. See Pierre Salinger's quote, in Jean Lacouture and Roland Mehl, *De Gaulle ou l'éternel défi: 56 témoignages* (Paris: Seuil, 1988), pp. 144, 152; Henry Kissinger quoted by Catherine Durandin, *La France contre l'Amérique* (Paris: Presses universitaires de France, 1994), p. 113; Andrew Moravcsik, *The Choice for Europe: Social Purpose and State Power from Messina to Maastricht* (Ithaca, N.Y.: Cornell University Press, 1998), p. 177.
13. See, for example, Dean Rusk, *As I Saw It: A Secretary of State's Memoirs* (London: Tauris, 1990), p. 240; John Newhouse, *De Gaulle and the Anglo-Saxons* (New York: Viking Press, 1970), p. 248; Éric Roussel, *Charles de Gaulle* (Paris: Gallimard, 2002), p. 738.

14. Vaïsse, *La grandeur*, p. 51; Stanley Hoffman, *Éssais sur la France: Déclin ou Renouveau?* (Paris: Editions du Seuil, 1974), p. 321; Edward Kolodziej, *French International Policy under De Gaulle and Pompidou: The Politics of Grandeur* (Ithaca, N.Y.: Cornell University Press, 1974), p. 56.

15. Ronald Granieri, "Franz Josef Strauß and the End of the Cold War," in *Visions of the End of the Cold War in Europe (1945–1990)*, ed. Frédéric Bozo, Marie-Pierre Rey, N. Piers Ludlow, and Bernd Rother (New York: Berghahn Books, 2012), p. 109.

16. Ball-Pearson meeting, 22 January 1964, National Archives Record Administration [NARA], Executive Secretariat, Secretary's and Under Secretary's Memoranda of Conversation, 1953–1964, Box 28.

17. Georges-Henri Soutou, "La décision française de quitter le commandement intégré de l'OTAN (1966)," in *Von Truman bis Harmel: Die Bundesrepublik Deutschland im Spannungsfeld von NATO und europäischer Integration,* ed. Hans-Joachim Harder (München: R. Oldenbourg, 2000), p. 188; Frédéric Bozo, *Deux Stratégies pour l'Europe: De Gaulle, les États-Unis et l'Alliance Atlantique, 1958–1969* (Paris: Plon, 1996), p. 16.

18. Among those who see de Gaulle's design as doomed to fail, see Thierry Wolton, *La France sous influence: Paris-Moscou, 30 ans de relations secrètes* (Paris: Grasset, 1997), p. 443; Among those who blame de Gaulle's failures on the international system, see Jean Charbonnel, *L' Aventure de la Fidélité* (Paris: Editions du Seuil, 1976), p. 126.

19. See paper prepared by the Ambassador to France (Bohlen), undated, document 27, FRUS, 1964–1968, Vol. XII.

20. See Vaïsse, *La grandeur*, pp. 23–24.

21. As de Gaulle claimed in February 1951, cited by Paul-Marie de la Gorce, *La France contre les Empires* (Paris: Editions Bernard Grasset, 1969), p. 210.

22. Marie-Pierre Rey, *La tentation du rapprochement: France et URSS à l'heure de la détente (1964–1974)* (Paris: Publications de la Sorbonne, 1991), p. 18.

23. Charles de Gaulle, *Lettres, Notes et Carnets: Tome II [LNC: II]* (Paris: Plon, 1980), De Gaulle to his mother, 20 December 1936, p. 442; Charles de Gaulle, *Discours et Messages: Tome V [DM:V]* (Paris: Plon, 1970), pp. 41–43, Reply to toast given by Nikolai Podgorny, 20 June 1966.

24. Charles de Gaulle, *DM: IV,* (Paris: Plon, 1970), p. 179, Press Conference, 31 January 1964.

25. David Calleo, "De Gaulle and the Monetary System: The Golden Rule," in *De Gaulle and the United States, 1930–1970: a centennial reappraisal,* ed. Nicholas Wahl and Robert Paxton (Oxford: Berg, 1994), p. 239.

26. Dana Allin, "De Gaulle and American Power," in *Charles de Gaulle's Legacy of Ideas,* ed. Benjamin Rowland (Lanham, M.D.: Lexington Books, c2011), p. 102.

27. Claude Mauriac, *Un autre de Gaulle: journal 1944–1954* (Paris: Hachette, 1970), p. 342, Tuesday 22 March 1949.

28. Vaïsse, *La grandeur,* pp. 39–40.

29. Charles de Gaulle, *DM: II* (Paris: Plon, 1970), p. 102, Speech in Rennes, 27 July 1947.

30. See De Gaulle, *DM: II,* p. 102, Speech in Rennes, 27 July 1947; De Gaulle-Wilson meeting, 3 April 1965, Ministère des Affaires Étrangères Français [MAEF], Cabinet du Ministre [CM], Couve de Murville [CdM], Vol. 379.

31. Bozo, *Deux Stratégies,* pp. 29–30.

32. Rey, *La tentation,* p. 17, claimed by de Gaulle in December 1954, cited by Gorce, *France contre les Empires,* p. 173.

33. Charles de Gaulle, *Memoirs of Hope: Renewal and Endeavor* (New York: Simon and Schuster, 1971), p. 201.

34. John Dumbrell, *President Lyndon Johnson and Soviet Communism* (Manchester: Manchester University Press, 2004), p. 26.
35. See Jeffrey Giauque, *Grand Designs and Visions of Unity: The Atlantic Powers and the Reorganization of Western Europe, 1955–1963* (Chapel Hill: University of North Carolina Press, 2002).
36. Thomas Zeiler, *American Trade and Power in the 1960s* (New York: Columbia University Press, c1992), p. 27.
37. For more on the international monetary system, see Robert Solomon, *The International Monetary System, 1945–1976: An Insider's View* (New York: Harper & Row Publishers, 1977), pp. 26–33; Diane Kunz, "The American Economic Consequences of 1968," in *1968: The World Transformed*, ed. Carole Fink, Philippe Gassert, and Detlef Junker (Cambridge, England and New York: Cambridge University Press, 1998), pp. 85–88; Francis Gavin, *Gold, Dollars, and Power: The Politics of International Monetary Relations, 1958–1971* (Chapel Hill: University of North Carolina Press, 2004), pp. 17–31; for the link between monetary and security issues, see, Hubert Zimmermann, *Money and Security: Troops, Monetary Policy, and West Germany's Relations with the United States and Britain, 1950–1971* (Cambridge: Cambridge University Press, 2001).
38. For more on the nuclear dilemma, see Bozo, *Deux Stratégies*; Helga Haftendorn, *NATO and the Nuclear Revolution: A Crisis of Credibility, 1966–1967* (Oxford: Clarendon Press, 1996); Constantine Pagedas, *Anglo-American Strategic Relations and the French Problem, 1960–1963: A Troubled Partnership* (London: Frank Cass, 2000); Jane Stromseth, *The Origins of Flexible Response: NATO's Debate Over Strategy in the 1960s* (Basingstoke: Macmillan in association with St. Antony's College, Oxford, 1988).
39. De Gaulle, *Memoirs of Hope*, p. 201.
40. Gorce, *France contre les Empires*, p. 209.
41. Memorandum for Eisenhower and Macmillan, 17 September 1958, MAEF, Secrétariat Général [SG], Entretiens et Messages [EM], Vol. 5.
42. Evidence seems to suggest that de Gaulle expected Eisenhower and Macmillan to reject his memorandum; see Alain Peyrefitte, *C'était de Gaulle: vol. 1* (Paris: Editions de Fallois-Fayard, 1994), p. 352; De Gaulle, *Memoirs of Hope*, p. 203.
43. See Gorce, *France contre les Empires*, pp. 103–04, 121. As early as 1944, de Gaulle had expressed his desire for a continental grouping that would extend to Africa and have the Channel, the Rhine, and the Mediterranean as its main arteries. By 1949, he began to refer to the necessity of a direct entente with West Germany.
44. For the *Plan Fouchet* see Giauque, *Grand Designs*; Georges-Henri Soutou, "Le général de Gaulle, le plan Fouchet et l'Europe," *Commentaire*, Vol. 13/52 (Winter 1990–1991).
45. Georges-Henri Soutou, "De Gaulle's France and the Soviet Union from Conflict to Détente," in *Europe, Cold War and Coexistence, 1963–1965*, ed. Wilfried Loth (London: Frank Cass, 2003), pp. 173–75.
46. For more on Eurafrique and on the ties between Algeria and de Gaulle's foreign policy in 1958–1962, see Irwin Wall, *France, the United States, and the Algerian War* (Berkeley: University of California Press, c2001).
47. Maurice Vaïsse, "'Une hirondelle ne fait pas le printemps': La France et la crise de Cuba," in *L'Europe et la Crise de Cuba*, ed. Maurice Vaïsse (Paris: A. Colin, 1993), pp. 104–05.
48. On the international dimension of the Algerian War, see Matthew Connelly, *Diplomatic Revolution: Algeria's Fight for Independence and the Origins of the Post-Cold War Era* (Oxford: Oxford University Press, 2002).
49. Vaïsse, *La grandeur*, pp. 42–43.

50. Oliver Bange, *The EEC crisis of 1963: Kennedy, Macmillan, de Gaulle and Adenauer in Conflict* (New York: St. Martin's Press in association with Institute of Contemporary British History, 1999), p. 42.

51. For more on this see N. Piers Ludlow, *Dealing with Britain: The Six and the First UK Application to the EEC* (Cambridge: Cambridge University Press, 1997).

52. For more on the Kennedy Round, see Zeiler, *American Trade*; Ernest Preeg, *Traders and Diplomats: An Analysis of the Kennedy Round of Negotiations under the General Agreement on Tariffs and Trade* (Washington: Brookings Institution, 1970); John Walker Evans, *The Kennedy Round in American Trade Policy: The Twilight of the GATT?* (Cambridge, M.A.: Harvard University Press, 1971).

53. Colette Barbier, "La Force Multilatérale," *Relations Internationales*, Vol. 69 (Printemps 1992), p. 3.

54. Kolodziej, *French International Policy*, p. 28.

55. Anthony Hartley, *Gaullism: The Rise and Fall of a Political Movement* (London: Routledge & Kegan Paul, 1972), pp. 196–97; Jean-Marie Soutou, *Un diplomate engagé: mémoires 1939–1979* (Paris: Editions de Fallois, c2011), p. 247.

56. Interview with Jean Charbonnel, Paris, 15 September 2004.

57. See Vaïsse, *La grandeur,* pp. 284–314 for a more in-depth look at the decision-making process; see also Paris to Foreign Office [FO], 13 May 1964, United Kingdom National Archives [UK-NA], Foreign Office [FO] 371/177865.

Chapter 1

1. Alain Peyrefitte, *C'était de Gaulle: vol. 2* (Paris: Editions de Fallois: Fayard, 1997), Meeting 7 January 1963, p. 16.

2. Mahan, *Kennedy, De Gaulle,* p. 27.

3. De Gaulle, *Memoirs of Hope,* p. 159; De Gaulle, *DM:IV,* p. 67.

4. Pierre Maillard, *De Gaulle et le Problème Allemand: Les leçons d'un grand dessein* (Paris: Guibert, 2001), p. 187; De Gaulle-Adenauer meeting 2, 21 January 1963, MAEF, CM, CdM, Vol. 375.

5. Benedikt Schoenborn, *La mésentente apprivoisée: De Gaulle et les Allemands, 1963–1969* (Paris: Presses Universitaires de France, 2007), p. 59.

6. Georges-Henri Soutou, *L'Alliance Incertaine: Les rapports politico-stratégiques franco-allemands 1954–1996* (Paris: Fayard, 1996), p. 253.

7. Quoted by Thomas Schreiber, *Les Actions de la France à l'Est, ou les Absences de Marianne* (Paris: Harmattan, 2000), p. 75.

8. De Gaulle, *DM:IV,* p. 69.

9. Ibid., p. 72.

10. Ibid., p. 71.

11. Peyrefitte, *C'était de Gaulle: vol. 1,* 23 January 1963, p. 367.

12. Couve de Murville-Kennedy meeting, 7 October 1963, MAEF, CM, CdM, Vol. 376; De Gaulle-Emmanuel Pelaez meeting, 8 February 1963, MAEF, CM, CdM, Vol. 375; Hervé Alphand, *L'étonnement d'être: journal, 1939–1973* (Paris: Fayard, 1977), Diary entry 26 August 1963, p. 407.

13. Robert Marjolin, *Architect of European Unity: Memoirs, 1911–1986* (London: Weidenfeld and Nicolson, 1989), p. 338.

14. For more details on the five's reactions, see Bange, *The EEC.*

15. Vincent Jauvert, *L'Amérique contre De Gaulle: histoire secrète, 1961–1969* (Paris: Seuil, 2000), pp. 103–05; Telegram from the Department of State to the Mission to the European Communities, 28 January 1963, Document 62, FRUS, 1961–1963, Vol. XIII.
16. Peyrefitte, *C'était de Gaulle: vol. 1*, p. 369.
17. N. Piers Ludlow, *The European Community and the Crises of the 1960s: Negotiating the Gaullist Challenge* (London: Routledge, 2006), p. 11; see also Bange, *EEC crisis*, pp. 229–30 or Edgar Pisani, *Le Général Indivis* (Paris: Albin Michel, 1974), pp. 110–13 for an account of the meeting.
18. Ludlow, *European Community*, p. 23.
19. Hervé Alphand interview with ABC, 30 January 1963, MAEF, Amérique, États-Unis 1952–1963, Vol. 358.
20. De Gaulle-Luns meeting, 16 March 1963, MAEF, CM, CdM, Vol. 375.
21. Ludlow, *European Community*, p. 23.
22. Jean-Marc Boegner to Couve de Murville, Telegram 566-578, 3 April 1963, Documents Diplomatiques Français [DDF], 1963, Tome I.
23. Boegner to Couve de Murville, Telegram 768-794, 10 May 1963, DDF, 1963, Tome I.
24. Speech to l'*Assemblée Nationale*, 24 January 1963, Fondation Nationale des Sciences Politiques [FNSP], Fonds Maurice Couve de Murville de Murville [CM] Carton 1.
25. Telegram from the Department of State to the Embassy in Germany, 23 January 1963, Document 60, and Summary Record of NSC Executive Committee Meeting No. 38 (Part II), 25 January 1963, Document 169, FRUS, 1961–1963, Vol. XIII.
26. Gavin, *Gold, Dollars, and Power*, p. 94.
27. Telegram from the Mission to the European Communities to the Department of State, 2 February 1963, Document 67, FRUS, 1961–1963, Vol. XIII.
28. Letter from President Kennedy to Chancellor Adenauer, 1 February 1963, Document 65, FRUS, 1961–1963, Vol. XIII; Trachtenberg, *Constructed Peace*, p. 374.
29. Schoenborn, *Mésentente apprivoisée*, pp. 38–39.
30. Ibid., pp. 50–54.
31. Peyrefitte, *C'était de Gaulle: vol. 2*, Meeting 24 April 1963, p. 228.
32. Vaïsse, *La grandeur*, p. 351 (in January 1963, 47 percent of French people approved of de Gaulle's policy toward the U.S., 17 percent disapproved, and 36 percent had no opinion); Institut Français d'Opinion Publique [IFOP], *Les Français et De Gaulle* (Paris: Plon, 1971), p. 277 (in February–March 1963, 44 percent approved of France's initiative to end negotiations with the U.K., 21 percent disapproved, and 35 percent had no opinion).
33. Bohlen to Rusk, Telegram 3900, 28 March 1963, John F. Kennedy Library [JFKL], National Security Files [NSF], Country Files [CO], Box 72. In a poll conducted in March, 42 percent were satisfied with de Gaulle as President, 40 percent were dissatisfied, and 18 percent were either indifferent or did not reply. 42 percent was de Gaulle's lowest approval rating since IFOP started its popularity poll in April 1959. See Annex 1.
34. Edmond Jouve, *Le Général de Gaulle et la Construction de l'Europe (1940–1966) Tome I* (Paris: Librairie générale de droit et de jurisprudence, R. Pichon et R. Durand-Auzias, 1967), p. 614. The dominant supplier provision would have allowed the U.S. president to eliminate tariffs for products for which the U.S. and the EEC combined for at least 80 percent of world exports. It would only have had a meaningful impact if the U.K. had been allowed to join the EEC.
35. Zeiler, *American Trade*, pp. 163–66.
36. JFKL, NSF, CO, Box 72, Geneva to Rusk, Telegram 1079, 18 March 1963.
37. Jean-Marc Boegner, *Le Marché Commun de Six à Neuf* (Paris: Armand Colin, 1974), p. 129.

38. Note 113 of Direction des Affaires Économiques et Financières, 26 April 1963, MAEF, Direction Économique, Coopération Économique 1961–1966, Vol. 930.
39. Brussels to State Department, Telegram 1704, 12 May 1963, NARA, Record Group [RG] 59, Central Foreign Policy Files [CFPF], 1963, Box 3911.
40. Evans, *Kennedy Round*, pp. 185–88.
41. Boegner to Couve de Murville, Telegram 768-794, 10 May 1963, DDF, 1963, Tome I.
42. Evans, *Kennedy Round*, p. 192.
43. Speech to l'*Assemblée Nationale*, 12 June 1963, FNSP, CM Carton 1.
44. Speech to l'*Assemblée Nationale*, 29 October 1963, FNSP, CM Carton 1.
45. Peyrefitte, *C'était de Gaulle: vol. 2*, Council of Ministers 21 August 1963, p. 32.
46. De Gaulle, *DM: IV,* Televised Speech 16 April 1964, pp. 204–05.
47. See De Gaulle to Couve de Murville, 1 May 1963, FNSP, CM Carton 8; De Gaulle-Pierson Dixon meeting, 23 November 1963, UK-NA, FO 371/172078.
48. See Haftendorn, *NATO*, pp. 39–41.
49. Bozo, *Deux Stratégies*, pp. 123–25.
50. Charles de Gaulle, *LNC: IX* (Paris: Plon, 1986), Note for Pompidou and Couve de Murville, 27 October 1963, p. 383.
51. Peyrefitte, *C'était de Gaulle: vol. 2*, Meeting 3 July 1963, p. 27.
52. Charles de Gaulle, *LNC: X* (Paris: Plon, 1987), De Gaulle to Pompidou, p. 43. On 27 April, French officers were also withdrawn from the inter-allied naval general staff.
53. See Paris to FO, 14 February 1964, UK-NA, FO 371/179064; Paris to FO, 13 March 1964, UK-NA, FO 371/179016.
54. Paris to FO, Telegram 299, 21 April 1964, UK-NA, FO 371/179064.
55. De Gaulle-Adenauer meeting 1, 22 January 1963, MAEF, CM, CdM, Vol. 375.
56. Couve de Murville-Kennedy meeting, 7 October 1963, MAEF, CM, CdM, Vol. 376.
57. Couve de Murville to François Seydoux, Telegram 3714-3729, 14 May 1964, MAEF, SG, EM, Vol. 21.
58. Spaak, *Combats: vol. 2*, p. 387.
59. Preeg, *Traders and Diplomats*, p. 69.
60. Council of EEC, Information Note, 13 May 1964, MAEF, Direction Économique, Cooperation Économique 1961–1966, Vol. 931.
61. De Gaulle-Lester Pearson meeting, 15 January 1964, MAEF, CM, CdM, Vol. 377.
62. Note of *La Direction des Affaires Économiques et Financières,* 7 February 1964, DDF, 1964, Tome I.
63. Francis Bator-Émile Noël meeting, 1 June 1964, Lyndon Baines Johnson Library [LBJL], Presidential Papers [PP], NSF, Subject Files [SF], Box 48.
64. Margaret Garritsen de Vries, *The International Monetary Fund, 1966–1971: The System Under Stress* (Washington, D.C.: The Fund, 1976), p. 25.
65. Susan Strange, *International Economic Relations of the Western World, 1959–1971* vol. 2 (London; New York: Oxford University Press, 1976), p. 213.
66. Ibid., pp. 214–15.
67. Peyrefitte, *C'était de Gaulle: vol. 2*, pp. 74–75.
68. Schoenborn, *Mésentente apprivoisée*, p. 120.
69. Christopher Chivvis, "De Gaulle and the Dollar," in *De Gaulle's Legacy of Ideas*, ed. Rowland, pp. 14–15. Rueff's thinking was profoundly shaped by the interwar years, with the Central European inflations of the 1920s, the rise of the Popular Front in France and the contemporaneous collapse of the franc Poincaré, and the collapse of the gold standard in the early 1930s, which he blamed primarily on the British efforts to push the burdens of postwar adjustments off onto other countries. Rueff saw a parallel between the Brit-

ish unwillingness to accept discipline in the 1920s and the United States' unwillingness in the 1960s.

70. Ibid., pp. 17–18.
71. For a good discussion of these divisions see Gavin, *Gold, Dollars, and Power*, pp. 76–77.
72. Peyrefitte, *C'était de Gaulle: vol. 2*, Meeting 18–19 September 1963, p. 78.
73. Giscard remarks at the IMF Annual Meeting, undated, S370, International Liquidity August–September 1963, Economic Subject Files, 1953–December 1963, Box 170, International Monetary Fund [IMF] Archives.
74. Solomon, *Monetary System*, p. 65.
75. Ibid., pp. 65–67.
76. Strange, *International Economic Relations*, pp. 217–19
77. Pierre Esteva, "Les relations monétaires extérieures de 1964 à 1966," in *De Gaulle en son siècle: vol. 3* [*DGESS III*], ed. Institut Charles de Gaulle (Paris: La Documentation française, 1992), p. 148; De Vries, *International Monetary Fund*, p. 37.
78. Alain Prate, *Les Batailles Économiques du Général de Gaulle* (Paris: Plon, 1978), p. 220.
79. See De Gaulle-Segni meeting, 20 February 1964, MAEF, SG, EM, Vol. 20; Speech to l'*Assemblée Nationale*, 28 April 1964, FNSP, CM Carton 1.
80. Couve de Murville-Kennedy meeting, 25 May 1963, MAEF, CM, CdM, Vol. 375.
81. Brussels to Rusk, Telegram 1817, 8 June 1963, NARA, RG59, CFPF, 1963, Box 3912.
82. Schoenborn, *Mésentente apprivoisée*, p. 93; see also Note, 13 November 1963, MAEF: Direction Économique, Papiers Olivier Wormser 1954–1966, Vol. 121.
83. De Gaulle-Roland de Margerie meeting, 4 June 1963, MAEF, CM, CdM, Vol. 375; Pierre Maillard-Herbert Blankenhorn meeting, 18 June 1963, Archives Nationales Françaises [ANF], 5ème République Archives de la Présidence De Gaulle [5AG1], Carton 161, Allemagne RFA.
84. De Gaulle-Heinrich Luebke meeting, 5 June 1963, and Pompidou-Erhard meeting, 4 July 1963, MAEF, CM, CdM, Vol. 375.
85. De Gaulle, *DM: IV*, p. 128–29
86. De Gaulle-Bohlen meeting, 5 November 1963, MAEF, SG, EM, Vol. 19.
87. De Gaulle-Erhard meeting, 22 November 1963, MAEF, SG, EM, Vol. 19.
88. De Gaulle-Klaiber meeting, 21 December 1963, MAEF, SG, EM, Vol. 19.
89. Evans, *Kennedy Round*, pp. 208–09; Preeg, *Traders and Diplomats*, p. 73.
90. Ludlow, *European Community*, p. 35.
91. Ibid., p. 37.
92. De Gaulle, *DM: IV*, pp. 176–77.
93. De Gaulle-Margerie meeting, 4 June 1963, MAEF, CM, CdM, Vol. 375; Peyrefitte, *C'était de Gaulle: vol. 2*, p. 231.
94. Maillard, *Problème Allemand*, pp. 194–97; Soutou, *L'Alliance Incertaine*, p. 255.
95. Note by French delegation to NATO, 10 June 1963, DDF, 1963, Tome I.
96. Maillard, *Problème Allemand*, p. 192.
97. De Gaulle-Adenauer meeting 2, 5 July 1963, MAEF, CM, CdM, Vol. 375; De Gaulle-Erhard meeting, 22 November 1963, MAEF, SG, EM, Vol. 19.
98. Couve de Murville-Ball meeting, 9 October 1963, MAEF, CM, CdM, Vol. 376.
99. De Gaulle, *DM: IV*, p. 119; see Couve de Murville's interview with *Notre République* in Anschuetz to Rusk, Airgram 972, 28 October 1963, NARA, RG59, CFPF, 1963, Box 3911.
100. Peyrefitte, *C'était de Gaulle: vol. 2*, Meetings 27 and 20 November 1963, pp. 48, 246.
101. Peyrefitte, *C'était de Gaulle: vol. 2*, Meeting 25 June 1963, p. 26.
102. See Bonn to FO, 17 December 1963, UK-NA, FO 371/172109. In October 1962, 61 percent of West Germans thought de Gaulle's policy was favorable for their country, and 6 per-

cent thought it was unfavorable; by November 1963, the numbers had dropped to 38 percent thinking it was favorable and 27 percent unfavorable.

103. Margerie to Couve de Murville, Telegram 1026-1040, 3 February 1964, MAEF, Asie-Océanie, Chine 1956–1967, Vol. 526.

104. De Gaulle, *DM: IV,* p. 153; Note 4 of *Direction Europe-Centrale,* 6 February 1964, DDF, 1964, Tome I.

105. Soutou, *L'Alliance Incertaine,* pp. 261–62; Note of *Sous-Direction d'Europe Centrale,* 17 September 1963, DDF, 1963, Tome II.

106. Memorandum of Conversation Erhard-Ball, 26 November 1963, Document 87, FRUS, 1961–1963, Vol. XIII.

107. For more on offset, see Zimmermann, *Money and Security,* pp. 162–66. Offset meant that the West German government agreed to purchase American armaments and undertake other monetary measures in order to cover the costs of the American troops stationed in Germany.

108. Schoenborn, *Mésentente apprivoisée,* pp. 68–69.

109. Carine Germond, "A 'Cordial Potentiality'? De Gaulle and the Franco-German Partnership, 1963-1969," in *Globalizing de Gaulle: International Perspectives on de Gaulle's Foreign Policies,* ed. Christian Nuenlist, Anna Locher, and Garret Martin (Lanham, M.D.: Rowman & Littlefield, 2010), p. 45.

110. See Wilfried Mausbach, "The United States, Germany, and French Peace Initiatives for Vietnam," in *The Search for Peace in Vietnam, 1964–1968,* ed. Lloyd Gardner and Ted Gittinger (College Station: Texas A&M University Press, c2004). For de Gaulle's policy toward Vietnam, see chapter 3.

111. Couve de Murville-Schroeder meeting 2, 8 June 1964, MAEF, SG, EM, Vol. 21; Joint Statement Following Discussions with Chancellor Erhard, 12 June 1964, http://www.presidency.ucsb.edu/ws/index.php?pid=26311&st=&st1=.

112. Mausbach, "The United States," pp. 176–77.

113. Peyrefitte, *C'était de Gaulle: vol. 2,* Meeting 23 June 1964, p. 257.

114. De Gaulle-Erhard meeting 1, 3 July 1964, MAEF, SG, EM, Vol. 22.

115. Couve de Murville-Schroeder meeting, 3 July 1964, MAEF, SG, EM, Vol. 22.

116. De Gaulle-Erhard meeting 1, 4 July 1964, MAEF, SG, EM, Vol. 22.

117. Couve de Murville-Schroeder meeting, 4 July 1964, MAEF: SG, EM, Vol. 22.

118. Peyrefitte, *C'était de Gaulle: vol. 2,* Meeting 7 July 1964, p. 262.

119. De Gaulle, *DM: IV,* p. 230.

120. Christian Aumale to Couve de Murville, Telegram 4951-4957, 24 July 1964, MAEF, Europe, Allemagne 1961–1970, Vol. 1604.

121. Alphand, *L'étonnement,* Diary entry 30 July 1964, p. 435.

122. Peyrefitte, *C'était de Gaulle: vol. 2,* Meeting 7 July 1964, p. 55.

123. De Gaulle-Manlio Brosio meeting, 3 September 1964, MAEF, SG, EM, Vol. 22.

124. Letter From the Ambassador to France (Bohlen) to the Assistant Secretary of State for European Affairs (Tyler), 14 September 1964, Document 33, FRUS, 1964–1968, Vol. XIII.

125. Memorandum of Discussion of the MLF at the White House, 10 April 1964, Document 16, FRUS, 1964–1968, Vol. XIII. For more on the MLF, see Bozo, *Deux Stratégies,* pp. 110–17 or Thomas Schwartz, *Lyndon Johnson and Europe: In the Shadow of Vietnam* (London: Harvard University Press, 2003), pp. 39–42.

126. Haftendorn, *NATO,* p. 132.

127. See Carine Germond, "La France et l'Allemagne face à l'Europe Politique dans les Années 1960," in *Le Couple France-Allemagne et les Institutions Européennes: Une postérité pour le Plan Schuman?,* ed. Marie-Thérèse Bitsch (Bruxelles: Bruylant, 2001), pp. 206–12.

128. Ludlow, *European Community*, p. 43; Note 185, 5 November 1964, MAEF, Direction Économique, Coopération Économique 1961–1966, Vol. 932.
129. Bohlen to Rusk, Telegram 2298, 21 October 1964, LBJL, PP, NSF, SF, Box 48.
130. See Couve de Murville-Rusk meeting, 7 April 1963, MAEF, CM, CdM, Vol. 375.
131. Bohlen to Rusk, Telegram 2004, 7 October 1964, NARA, RG59, CFPF, 1964–1966, Box
   1756.
132. Soutou, *L'Alliance Incertaine*, p. 278.
133. Couve de Murville to Margerie, Telegram 9200-9223, 26 October 1964, MAEF, SG, EM,
   Vol. 22.
134. Vaïsse, *La grandeur*, p. 575.
135. Bohlen to Rusk, Telegram 2354, 23 October 1964, LBJL, PP, NSF, CO, Box 170.
136. Idem.
137. Peyrefitte, *C'était de Gaulle: vol. 2*, Council of Ministers 21 October 1964, p. 265.
138. Couve de Murville-Paul Hasluck meeting, 4 November 1964, MAEF, SG, EM, Vol. 23.
139. De Gaulle-Adenauer meeting, 9 November 1964, MAEF, SG, EM, Vol. 23.
140. Ludlow, *European Community*, pp. 43–44.
141. Preeg, *Traders and Diplomats*, p. 87.
142. James Ellison, *The United States, Britain and the Transatlantic Crisis: Rising to the Gaullist
   Challenge, 1963–68* (Basingstoke: Palgrave Macmillan, 2007), p. 18.
143. Couve de Murville-Schroeder meeting, 9 December 1964, MAEF, CM, CdM, Vol. 378.
144. See Bonn to FO, Telegram 1153, 16 November 1964, UK-NA, FO 371/177867; Peyrefitte,
   C'était de Gaulle: vol. 2, pp. 269–70.
145. Bozo, *Deux Stratégies*, p. 118; Bohlen to Rusk, Telegram 2771, 6 November 1964, NARA,
   RG59, CFPF, 1964–1966, Box 1756.
146. Peyrefitte, *C'était de Gaulle: vol. 2*, 9 December 1964, p. 67.
147. Ibid., 16 December 1964, p. 67.
148. De Gaulle, *DM: IV*, p. 319.
149. See Paris to FO, 26 February 1965, UK-NA, FO 371/18293. According to *Le Figaro's* survey in February 1965, 44 percent were satisfied with the role France played on the international scene and 6 percent were dissatisfied with it. In February 1963, 36 percent were
   satisfied and 17 percent were dissatisfied. See IFOP, *De Gaulle*, p. 268; in May 1965, 16
   percent thought de Gaulle's attitude toward the U.S. was too harsh, 6 percent thought it
   was too conciliatory, and 50 percent felt it was as it should be.
150. Edward Morse, *Foreign Policy and Interdependence in Gaullist France* (Princeton: Princeton
   University Press, 1973), pp. 222–23.
151. Strange, *International Economic Relations*, pp. 223–24.
152. Giscard speech to IMF, 9 September 1964, UK-NA, PREM 13/2050. France was increasingly concerned with the risks of domestic inflation, and had implemented a *Plan de
   Stabilisation* in November 1963 to cool down an overheating French economy. See Serge
   Bernstein and Pierre Milza, *Histoire de la France au XXème Siècle: Tome IV, 1958–1974*
   (Bruxelles: Editions Complexe, 1992), pp. 149–50.
153. Strange, *International Economic Relations*, pp. 220–23; Solomon, *Monetary System*, pp.
   72–73.
154. De Vries, *International Monetary Fund*, p. 52.
155. Bozo, *Deux Stratégies*, p. 133. During the sixties, the French economy grew by an average of 5.8 percent *per annum*, against 2.9 percent for the U.K., 3.9 percent for the U.S.,
   and 4.9 percent for West Germany. Only Japan grew at a faster rate. See Annex 4; Henri
   Bourguignat, "Le général de Gaulle et la réforme du Système monétaire international:
   la contestation manquée de l'hégémonie du dollar," in *DGESS III*, ed. Institut Charles
   de Gaulle, p. 112.

156. Chivvis, "De Gaulle and the Dollar," p. 19.
157. De Gaulle, *DM: IV*, p. 332.
158. Ibid., p. 333; there is an interesting caveat, based on testimony from Giscard outlined in Schoenborn, *Mésentente apprivoisée*, p. 121. According to Giscard, he was summoned by de Gaulle just before the press conference. De Gaulle read his text to Giscard to get his opinion. When the General suggested a return to gold standard, Giscard disagreed, saying it would give the impression that de Gaulle's views were backward. De Gaulle then asked what he should offer instead. Giscard penned a new version, calling for a return to a new system based on gold, completed by a new international means of credit. De Gaulle accepted the new version. But during the press conference, the General lost track of the new text and switched to his old version in which he offered a return to the gold standard.
159. Calleo, "Golden Rule," pp. 240–41.
160. Prate, *Les Batailles*, p. 213.
161. On CRUs, see Gavin, *Gold, Dollars, and Power*, p. 80; Prate, *Les Batailles*, p. 219; and Solomon, *Monetary System*, p. 66.
162. Thomas Finletter to Rusk, Telegram 1247, 1 March 1965, LBJL, PP, NSF, CO, Box 171.
163. Couve de Murville to Pierre de Leusse, Circular Telegram 107, 22 May 1965, DDF, 1965, Tome I.
164. See De Gaulle, *LNC: X*, Personal note, 23 February 1965, p. 134; Alphand, *L'étonnement*, Diary entry 7 May 1965, pp. 452–33; Bozo, *Deux Stratégies*, p. 138.
165. Alphand, *L'étonnement*, Diary entry 7 May 1965, p. 452.
166. Bohlen to Rusk, Telegram 5335, 22 March 1965, LBJL, PP, NSF, CO, Box 171; Paris to FO, 25 March 1965, UK-NA, FO 371/184420.
167. De Gaulle-Wilson meeting, 2 April 1965, MAEF, CM, CdM, Vol. 379.
168. Telegram from the Embassy in France to the Department of State, 4 May 1965, Document 83, FRUS, 1964–1968, Vol. XIII.
169. Helen Parr, *Britain's Policy Towards the European Community, 1964–1967: Harold Wilson and Britain's World Role* (London: Routledge, 2006), p. 42. This was significant since at the time of the failure of the Fouchet Plan, Belgium and the Netherlands had posited U.K. membership in the EEC as a precondition for any European political union.
170. De Gaulle-Erhard meeting, 19 January 1965, MAEF, SG, EM, Vol. 23.
171. Germond, "L'Europe Politique," pp. 215–16.
172. See Bohlen to Rusk, Telegram 4580, 12 February 1965, LBJL, PP, NSF, CO, Box 170; or De Gaulle-Adolph Bentinck meeting, 9 March 1965, MAEF, SG, EM, Vol. 24.
173. Telegram From the Embassy in France to the Department of State, 4 May 1965, Document 47, FRUS, 1964–1968, Vol. XII; De Gaulle-Willy Brandt meeting, 2 June 1965, MAEF, CM, CdM, Vol. 379.
174. Lucet-Meyer-Lindenberg meeting, 25 March 1965, MAEF, CM, CdM, Vol. 379.
175. Note for the Prime Minister, 2 June 1965, MAEF, Direction Économique, Papiers Olivier Wormser 1954–1966, Vol. 122.
176. François Seydoux to Couve de Murville, Telegram 2071-2075, 29 March 1965, MAEF, Europe, Allemagne 1961–1970, Vol. 1605.
177. Ludlow, *European Community*, p. 60.
178. Ibid., p. 68.
179. N. Piers Ludlow, "From Words to Action: Re-interpreting de Gaulle's European Policy, 1958–1969," in *Globalizing de Gaulle*, ed. Nuenlist, Locher, and Martin, p. 68.
180. Ibid., p. 69.
181. Peyrefitte, *C'était de Gaulle: vol. 2*, 27.01.65, p. 281.

182. Moravcsik, *The Choice*, p. 228; Couve de Murville to Hallstein, 26 March 1965, MAEF, SG, EM, Vol. 24.
183. Marjolin, *Memoirs*, pp. 349–50.
184. Peyrefitte, *C'était de Gaulle: vol. 2*, Council of Ministers 14 April 1965, p. 281.
185. Maurice Couve de Murville, *Une politique étrangère, 1958–1969* (Paris: Plon, 1971), p. 331.
186. Note by Wormser, 11 June 1965, DDF, 1965, Tome I; Spaak, *Combats: vol. 2*, p. 406.
187. Bohlen to Rusk, Telegram number 4580, 12 February 1965, LBJL, PP, NSF, CO, Box 170; Ludlow, *European Community*, p. 58.
188. Maurice Vaïsse, "La politique européenne de la France en 1965: pourquoi 'la chaise vide,'" in *Crises and Compromises: The European Project 1963–1969*, ed. Wilfried Loth (Bruxelles: Bruylant, 2001), p. 214.
189. Vaïsse, *La grandeur*, p. 554–55.
190. John Newhouse, *De Gaulle*, p. 280.
191. Bozo, *Deux Stratégies*, p. 142.
192. Memorandum of Conversation Giscard-Deming, 8 July 1965, Document 50, FRUS, 1964–1968, Vol. XII.
193. Brunet Circular 166, 3 September 1965, MAEF. Direction Économique, Coopération Économique 1961–1966, Vol. 1020; Strange, *International Economic Relations*, p. 229.
194. Esteva, "Les relations monétaires," p. 149.
195. Solomon, *Monetary System*, pp. 74–79.
196. Alphand to Couve de Murville, Telegram 5234-5245, 4 October 1965, MAEF, Direction Économique, Coopération Économique 1961–1966, Vol. 1026; de Vries, *International Monetary Fund*, pp. 69–74; FO to Certain Missions, InTel 44, 7 November 1966, UK-NA, PREM 13/2050.
197. Bozo, *Deux Stratégies*, pp. 141–42, 146–47.
198. Note by De Gaulle, 5 July 1965, DDF, 1965, Tome II.
199. Telegram from the Mission to the North Atlantic Treaty Organization and European Regional Organizations to the Department of State, 18 December 1965, Document 118, FRUS, 1964–1968, Vol. XIII.
200. Bohlen to Rusk, Telegram 1433, 17 September 1965, NARA, RG59, CFPF, 1964–1966, Box 2186.
201. De Gaulle-Ball meeting, 31 August 1965, MAEF, CM, CdM, Vol. 381; Paris to FO, Telegram 483, 10 July 1965, UK-NA, PREM 13/1042.
202. De Gaulle, *DM: IV*, p. 383.
203. De Gaulle-Reilly meeting, 1 October 1965, MAEF, CM, CD, Vol. 381; De Gaulle-Heath meeting, 22 November 1965, MAEF, CM, CD, Vol. 381.
204. Peyrefitte, *C'était de Gaulle: vol. 2*, p. 292.
205. De Gaulle, *DM: IV*, pp. 377–81.
206. Ludlow, *European Community*, p. 73.
207. Peyrefitte, *C'était de Gaulle: vol. 2*, Meeting 13 July 1965, p. 293.
208. Bohlen to Rusk, Telegram 83, 6 July 1965, LBJL, PP, NSF, CO, Box 171.
209. Peyrefitte, *C'était de Gaulle: vol. 2*, Meeting 15 September 1965, pp. 299–300.
210. De Gaulle-Bentinck meeting, 18 October 1965, MAEF, CM, CdM, Vol. 381.
211. Speech to l'*Assemblée Nationale*, 20 October 1965, FNSP, CM Carton 2.
212. Ludlow, *European Community*, pp. 91–92.
213. Peyrefitte, *C'était de Gaulle: vol. 2*, Meeting 27 October 1965, p. 588.
214. Couve de Murville to Seydoux, Telegram 5930-5932, 24 December 1965, FNSP, CM Carton 9.

215. IFOP, *De Gaulle*, p. 164. In a survey conducted between 22 October and 5 November 1965, 76 percent thought de Gaulle had had a good influence on France's place in the world in the previous seven years, 7 percent thought he had had a bad influence, and 4 percent thought he had had no influence.
216. Bernstein and Milza, *France au XXème Siècle: Tome IV,* pp. 64–67.

Chapter 2

1. Alphand Interview with ABC, 30 January 1963, MAEF, Amérique, États-Unis 1952–1963, Vol. 358.
2. Paris to Rusk, Telegram 3283, 15 February 1963, JFKL, NSF, CO, 213.
3. Vaïsse, *La grandeur,* p. 413.
4. See Giscard-Khrushchev meeting, 27 January 1964, MAEF, Europe, URSS 1961–1965, Vol. 1931; Pompidou-Rudnev meeting, 10 February 1964, ANF, 5AG1, Carton 186, URSS; Couve de Murville to Moscow, Telegram 2445-2447, 20 February 1964, DDF, 1964, Tome I.
5. Wolton, *France sous influence,* p. 394.
6. Thomas Gomart, *Double Détente: Les relations Franco-Soviétiques de 1958 à 1964* (Paris: Publications de la Sorbonne, 2003), p. 384.
7. Couve de Murville to Dejean, Telegram 676-685, 15 January 1964, DDF, 1964, Tome I.
8. Couve de Murville-Rusk meeting, 7 October 1963, MAEF, CM, CdM, Vol. 376.
9. Telegram from the Embassy in the Soviet Union to the Department of State, 31 July 1963, Document 341, FRUS, 1961–1963, Vol. V; Michael Sodaro, *Moscow, Germany and the West from Khrushchev to Gorbachev* (London: I.B. Tauris, 1991), p. 51.
10. Roussel, *De Gaulle,* p. 738.
11. De Gaulle-Queen Juliana meeting, 16 March 1963, MAEF, CM, CdM, Vol. 375; De Gaulle-Margerie meeting, 4 June 1963, MAEF, CM, CdM, Vol. 375.
12. Couve de Murville-Ikeda meeting, 19 April 1963, MAEF, CM, CdM, Vol. 375.
13. De Gaulle-Vinogradov meeting, 29 January 1963, MAEF, SG, EM, Vol. 18; De Gaulle-Vinogradov meeting, 12 July 1963, MAEF, CM, CdM, Vol. 375.
14. De Gaulle-Queen Juliana meeting, 16 March 1963, MAEF, CM, CdM, Vol. 375.
15. Alphand, *L'étonnement,* Diary entry 4 May 1964, p. 429.
16. De Gaulle-Pearson meeting, 15 January 1964, MAEF, CM, CdM, Vol. 377; De Gaulle-Vinogradov meeting, 3 January 1964, MAEF, SG, EM, Vol. 20.
17. Note of *Sous-Direction Europe Centrale,* 2 March 1964, MAEF, Europe, URSS 1961–1965, Vol. 1931.
18. Julie Newton, *Russia, France and the Idea of Europe* (Basingstoke; New York: Palgrave Macmillan, 2003), p. 20.
19. Sodaro, *Moscow, Germany,* p. 49.
20. Laboulaye to Couve de Murville, Telegram 2613-2636, 17 May 1963, MAEF, Europe, URSS 1961–1965, Vol. 1931.
21. Dejean to Couve de Murville, Telegrams 3810-3834 and 3835-3836, 17 July 1963, DDF, 1963, Tome II.
22. Sodaro, *Moscow, Germany,* p. 49.
23. Newton, *Russia, France,* p. 56; Paris to FO, 19 July 1963, UK-NA, FO 371/169119.
24. George McGhee, *At the Creation of a New Germany: From Adenauer to Brandt, An Ambassador's Account* (New Haven: Yale University Press, 1989), p. 30.
25. Speech to *l'Assemblée Nationale,* 12 June 1963, FNSP, CM Carton 1.
26. Peyrefitte, *C'était de Gaulle: vol. 2,* p. 254.

27. Vaïsse, *La grandeur*, p. 566.
28. Vojtech Mastny, "Détente, the Superpowers and their Allies, 1962–64," in *Europe, Cold War*, ed. Loth, p. 217; Lescuyer to Couve de Murville, Telegram 88-91, 14 February 1963, DDF, 1963, Tome I.
29. Dejean to Couve de Murville, Telegram 655-662, 5 February 1963, DDF, 1963, Tome I.
30. Vinogradov to De Gaulle, 30 January 1963, MAEF, SG, EM, Vol. 18.
31. Couve de Murville to Alphand, Telegram 3133-3142, 9 February 1963, DDF, 1963, Tome I.
32. Mastny, "Détente," p. 228.
33. Current Intelligence Weekly Review, 25 January 1963, Document 284, FRUS, 1961–1963, Vol. V.
34. Mastny, "Détente," p. 218.
35. Editorial Notes, Documents 328 and 335, FRUS, 1961–1963, Vol. V; Khrushchev first suggested a non-aggression pact on 20 February.
36. De Gaulle, *DM: IV*, p. 123.
37. Peyrefitte, *C'était de Gaulle: vol. 2*, Council of Ministers 21 August 1963, p. 32.
38. William Glenn Gray, *Germany's Cold War: The Global Campaign to Isolate East Germany, 1949–1969* (Chapel Hill: University of North Carolina Press, 2003), p. 143; Anna Locher and Christian Nuenlist, "What Role for NATO? Conflicting Western Perceptions of Détente, 1963–65," *Journal of Transatlantic Studies*, Vol. 2/2 (2004), p. 189.
39. De Gaulle, *LNC: IX*, De Gaulle to Adenauer, 23 August 1963, p. 364.
40. De Gaulle-Adenauer meeting, 4 July 1963, MAEF, CM, CdM, Vol. 375.
41. Mahan, *Kennedy, De Gaulle*, p. 147; Couve, *Politique étrangère*, p. 193.
42. De Gaulle-Chang-Huan meeting, 2 September 1963, MAEF, CM, CdM, Vol. 376.
43. Rey, *La tentation*, p. 16.
44. See Locher, and Nuenlist, "What Role for NATO?," pp. 189–93.
45. See De Gaulle-Dixon meeting, 17 September 1963, MAEF, CM, CdM, Vol. 376; Paris to FO, Telegram 217, 10 September 1963, UK-NA, FO 371/172077.
46. François Seydoux to Couve de Murville, Telegram 380, 16 December 1963, MAEF, Service des Pactes [Pactes] 1961–1970, Vol. 270; Couve de Murville, *Politique étrangère*, p. 196.
47. Peyrefitte, *C'était de Gaulle: vol. 1*, Meetings 24 January 1963 and 13 March 1963, pp. 317, 320.
48. Baudet to Couve de Murville, Dépêche 940, 26 March 1963, DDF, 1963, Tome I.
49. Zhou Jianqing, "De Gaulle et le triangle sino-soviéto-américain," in *DGESS IV*, ed. Institut Charles de Gaulle, pp. 403–04.
50. For more on France's recognition of China, see Garret Martin, "Playing the China Card? Revisiting France's Recognition of Communist China, 1963–1964," *Journal of Cold War Studies*, 10/1 (2008), pp. 52–80.
51. De Gaulle, *LNC: IX*, 26 September 1963, pp. 374–75.
52. Instructions for de Beaumarchais, 11 December 1963, DDF, 1963, Tome II.
53. See Baudet to Couve de Murville, Telegram 2311-2316, 30 April 1964, MAEF, Europe, URSS 1961–1965, Vol. 1931; AFP Dépêche, 12 September 1964, MAEF, Europe, URSS 1961–1965, Vol. 1931.
54. De Gaulle-Vinogradov meeting, 18 June 1964, MAEF, Europe, URSS 1961–1965, Vol. 1931.
55. Dejean to Couve de Murville, Telegram 637-641, 9 February 1964, DDF, 1964, Tome I.
56. Dumbrell, *President Johnson*, pp. 35, 39; Anatoly Dobrynin, *In Confidence: Moscow's Ambassador to America's Six Cold War Presidents (1962–1986)* (New York: Times Books, Random House, c1995), pp. 119–26.

57. On credits, see Erhard to De Gaulle, 16 July 1964, MAEF, SG, EM, Vol. 22, and De Gaulle, *LNC: X*, De Gaulle to Erhard, 29 July 1964, pp. 80–81. On Palewski's trip see Baudet to Couve de Murville, Telegram number 4967-4977, 14 October 1964, DDF, 1964, Tome II.

58. Peyrefitte, *C'était de Gaulle: vol. 2*, Meeting 7 July 1964, p. 261.

59. De Gaulle, *DM: IV*, p. 155.

60. Gorce, *France contre les Empires*, p. 219.

61. See De Gaulle-Pearson meeting, 15 January 1964, MAEF, CM, CdM, Vol. 377; De Gaulle-Wilson meeting, 3 April 1965, MAEF, CM, CdM, Vol. 379.

62. National Security Action Memorandum No. 304, 3 June 1964, Document 4, FRUS, 1964–1968, Vol. XVII.

63. Michael Griffith, *The Ostpolitik of the Federal Republic of Germany* (Cambridge, Mass: MIT Press, c1978), pp. 120–21.

64. Schreiber, *Les Actions*, p. 91.

65. Couve de Murville, *Politique étrangère*, p. 197.

66. Joseph Rothschild and Nancy Wingfield, *Return to Diversity: A Political History of East Central Europe since World War II*, 2nd ed. (New York: Oxford University Press, 1993), pp. 162–63; Speech to *l'Assemblée Nationale*, 28 April 1964, FNSP, CM Carton 1.

67. Schreiber, *Les Actions*, p. 93.

68. Bouffanais to Couve de Murville, Telegram 219-222, 29 February 1964 and Telegram 562-567, 20 May 1964, DDF, 1964, Tome I; Burin des Roziers-Dimitriu meeting, 23 April 1964, ANF, 5AG1, Carton 183, Roumanie.

69. Telegram 1, 2 July 1964, UK-NA, FO 371/177619; Couve de Murville-Schroeder meeting, 3 July 1964, MAEF, CM, CdM, Vol. 378.

70. De Gaulle-Maurer meeting, 28 July 1964, MAEF, CM, CdM, Vol. 378.

71. Couve de Murville to French diplomatic representatives, Circular Telegram 90, 31 July 1964, DDF, 1964, Tome II.

72. Alphand, *L'étonnement*, p. 435.

73. De Gaulle, *LNC: X*, undated, p. 75.

74. Paris to FO, 14 March 1964, UK-NA, FO 371/177870.

75. Soutou, "De Gaulle's France," pp. 178–79.

76. Alphand, *L'étonnement*, Diary entry 1 January 1964, p. 420.

77. Dejean to Couve de Murville, Telegram 312-316, 18 January 1964, DDF, 1964, Tome I.

78. Wolton, *France sous influence*, pp. 406–07.

79. François Puaux, "L'originalité de la politique française de détente," in *DGESS V*, ed. Institut Charles de Gaulle, p. 433.

80. Paris to FO, Telegram 146, 24 February 1964, UK-NA, FO 371/177870.

81. De Gaulle-Podgorny meeting, 2 March 1964, MAEF, SG, EM, Vol. 20.

82. Couve de Murville to Margerie, unnumbered Telegram, 5 March 1964, DDF, 1964, Tome I; Pompidou-Ikeda meeting, 7 April 1964, MAEF, CM, CdM, Vol. 377.

83. Krag-Johnson meeting, 9 June 1964, NARA, RG59, CFPF, 1964–1966, Box 2188.

84. See Sodaro, *Moscow, Germany*, pp. 51–64; Douglas Selvage, "The Warsaw Pact and Nuclear Non-proliferation, 1963–65," http://www.wilsoncenter.org/topics/pubs/ACFB0E.pdf; see Benedikt Schoenborn, "Bargaining with the Bear: Chancellor Erhard's Bid to Buy German Reunification," *Cold War History*, 8/1 (2008).

85. Couve de Murville, *Politique étrangère*, p. 201; Interview with Jacques Andréani, Paris, 15 February 2006.

86. Thomas Wolfe, *Soviet Power and Europe: 1945–1970* (Baltimore: Johns Hopkins Press, 1970), pp. 256, 265. For more on the controversy over peaceful coexistence, see Newton, *Russia, France*, pp. 58–73.

87. Ilya Gaiduk, "The Soviet Union Faces the Vietnam War," in *La Guerre du Vietnam et l'Europe, 1963–1973*, ed. Christopher Goscha and Maurice Vaïsse (Paris: Bruylant, 2003), p. 193; Vladislav Zubok, *A Failed Empire: The Soviet Union in the Cold War from Stalin to Gorbachev* (Chapel Hill: University of North Carolina Press, 2007), pp. 196–98.
88. Wolfe, *Soviet Power*, pp. 280–81.
89. Newton, *Russia, France*, p. 59.
90. AFP Dépêche, 27 October 1964, MAEF, Europe, URSS 1961–1965, Vol. 1931.
91. Note of *Sous-Direction Europe Orientale*, 29 October 1964, MAEF, Europe, URSS 1961–1965, Vol. 1931; Bohlen to Rusk, Telegram 2607, 30 October 1964, NARA, RG59, CFPF, 1964–1966, Box 2188; Peyrefitte, *C'était de Gaulle: vol. 2*, Meeting 28 October 1964, p. 312.
92. Peyrefitte, *C'était de Gaulle: vol. 2*, p. 312.
93. Wolfe, *Soviet Power*, p. 288.
94. Note of *Directeur Politique* to Couve de Murville, 19 November 1964, MAEF, Europe, URSS 1961–1965, Vol. 1931.
95. Baudet to Couve de Murville, Telegram 6087-6122, 24 December 1964, DDF, 1964, Tome II.
96. Baudet to Couve de Murville, Telegram 99-105, 11 January 1965, MAEF, Europe, URSS 1961–1965, Vol. 1931.
97. Bonn to FO, Telegram 1153, 16 November 1964, UK-NA, FO 371/177867.
98. Georges-Henri Soutou, "La place de l'URSS dans la politique allemande de la France 1943–1969," in *Les tiers dans les relations franco-allemandes/Dritte in den deutsch-französischen Beziehungen*, ed. Christian Baechler and Klaus-Jürgen Müller (München: Oldenbourg, 1996), p. 59.
99. Peyrefitte, *C'était de Gaulle: vol. 2*, Meeting 18 November 1964, p. 62.
100. Speech to *l'Assemblée Nationale*, 3 November 1964, FNSP, CM Carton 1; Laboulaye to Couve, Telegram 5513, 7 November 1964, MAEF, Europe, URSS 1961–1965, Vol. 1931.
101. Alphand, *L'étonnement*, Diary entry 3 January 1965, p. 445.
102. Peyrefitte, *C'était de Gaulle: vol. 2*, meetings 6 and 12 January 1965, pp. 314–17.
103. Schreiber, *Les Actions*, p. 94.
104. Couve de Murville to French diplomatic representatives, Circular Telegram 174, 9 December 1964, DDF, 1964, Tome II.
105. De Gaulle-Mende meeting, 2 December 1964, MAEF, CM, CdM, Vol. 378.
106. Peyrefitte, *C'était de Gaulle: vol. 2*, meeting 4 January 1965, p. 313.
107. Philip Cerny, *The Politics of Grandeur: Ideological Aspects of de Gaulle's Foreign Policy* (Cambridge: Cambridge University Press, 1980), p. 179.
108. Draft note on Franco-Soviet relations, 5 January 1965, MAEF, Europe, URSS 1961–1965, Vol. 1931.
109. Couve de Murville to Baudet, Telegram 375-390, 8 January 1965, DDF, 1965, Tome I; Paris to FO, 29 January 1965, UK-NA, FO 371/182941.
110. De Gaulle-Vinogradov meeting, 25 January 1965, MAEF, CM, CdM, Vol. 379.
111. Soutou, "De Gaulle's France," p. 180.
112. De Gaulle, *DM: IV*, p. 341.
113. Idem.
114. Bohlen to Rusk, Telegram 4451, 5 February 1965, NARA, RG59, CFPF, 1964–1966, Box 2178.
115. See Soutou, "De Gaulle's France," pp. 173–75.
116. See Alphand, *L'étonnement*, Diary entry 3 January 1965, p. 445.
117. Bohlen to Rusk, Telegram 4916, 1 March 1965, NARA, RG59, CFPF, 1964–1966, Box 2186; Couve to Roger Seydoux, Telegram 2924-2928, 5 June 1965, DDF, 1965, Tome I.

118. Vaïsse, *La grandeur,* p. 424.
119. Kolodziej, *French International Policy,* p. 344.
120. Puaux-Doubinin meeting, 15 July 1965, MAEF, Europe, URSS 1961–1965, Vol. 1933.
121. De Gaulle-Mansfield meeting, 15 November 1965, MAEF, CM, CD, Vol. 381.
122. Peyrefitte, *C'était de Gaulle: vol. 2,* Meeting 13 October 1965, p. 303.
123. CIA Intelligence Info Cable, 25 August 1965, LBJL, PP, NSF, CO, Box 172.
124. Rey, *La tentation,* p. 38.
125. Couve de Murville to Baudet, Telegram 2370-2373, 16 February 1965, MAEF, Europe, URSS 1961–1965, Vol. 1931.
126. Bohlen to Rusk, Telegram 5046, 8 March 1965, NARA, RG59, CFPF, 1964–1966, Box 2188.
127. Newton, *Russia, France,* pp. 60–61.
128. Couve de Murville, *Politique étrangère,* p. 205.
129. Pompidou-Zorin meeting, 22 April 1965, MAEF, CM, CdM, Vol. 379.
130. Peyrefitte, *C'était de Gaulle: vol. 2,* Council of Ministers 28 April 1965, p. 318.
131. De Gaulle-Gromyko meeting, 27 April 1965, MAEF, CM, CdM, Vol. 379.
132. Soutou, "De Gaulle's France," p. 181.
133. Telegram from the Embassy in France to the Department of State, 24 April 1965, Document 46, FRUS, 1964–1968, Vol. XII.
134. Bozo, *Deux Stratégies,* p. 135; François Seydoux, *Dans L'Intimité Franco-Allemande: Une Mission Diplomatique* (Paris: Albatros, 1977), p. 45.
135. Telegram From the Embassy in France to the Department of State, 4 May 1965, Document 47, FRUS, 1964–1968, Vol. XII; Finletter to Rusk, Telegram 1247, 1 March 1965, LBJL, PP, NSF, CO, Box 171.
136. Courcel to Couve, Telegram 1984-1989, 12 May 1965, MAEF, SG, EM, Vol. 25.
137. Puaux-Doubinin meeting, 15 July 1965, MAEF, Europe, URSS 1961–1965, Vol. 1933.
138. Bohlen to Rusk, Telegram 6760, 28 May 1965, NARA, RG59, CFPF, 1964–1966, Box 2173.
139. Lucet-Ussachev meeting, 23 July 1965, MAEF, Europe, URSS 1961–1965, Vol. 1933.
140. Pompidou-Zorin meeting, 22 April 1965, MAEF, CM, CdM, Vol. 379.
141. Alphand, *L'étonnement,* Diary entry 7 May 1965, p. 452.
142. Bohlen to Rusk, Telegram 5591, 3 April 1965, NARA, RG59, CFPF, 1964–1966, Box 2180.
143. De Gaulle-Gromyko meeting, 27 April 1965, MAEF, CM, CdM, Vol. 379.
144. De Gaulle-Zorin meeting, 5 July 1965, MAEF, CM, CdM, Vol. 380.
145. Alphand, *L'étonnement,* Diary entry 17 July 1965, p. 459.
146. Bohlen to Rusk, Telegram 7298, 24 June 1965, NARA, RG59, CFPF, 1964–1966, Box 2173.
147. Note of *Sous-Direction Europe-Orientale,* 20 April 1965, MAEF, Europe, URSS 1966–1970, Vol. 2665.
148. Peyrefitte, *C'était de Gaulle: vol. 2,* Council of Minister 10 February 1965, pp. 317–18.
149. Account of Joxe's trip to Prague, 30 June 1965, DDF, 1965, Tome I.
150. Note of *Sous-Direction Europe Centrale,* 30 August 1965, DDF, 1965, Tome II; Bohlen to Rusk, Telegram 1191, 3 September 1965, LBJL, PP, NSF, CO, Box 172.
151. Couve de Murville, *Politique étrangère,* pp. 197–98.
152. De Gaulle-Cyrankiewicz meeting, 10 September 1965, FNSP, CM Carton 9.
153. Notes of *Sous Direction Europe Orientale,* 22 October 1965, MAEF, Europe, URSS 1961–1965, Vol. 1933.
154. Couve de Murville, *Politique étrangère,* p. 209.

155. See Maurice Couve de Murville entretien 7, 26 February 1988, MAEF, Archives Orales [AO] 29; Charles Lucet, entretien 5, 27 June 1986, MAEF, AO 26.
156. Couve de Murville-Brezhnev meeting, 1 November 1965, MAEF, SG, EM, Vol. 25.
157. Couve de Murville-Kosygin meeting, 31 October 1965, MAEF, SG, EM, Vol. 25.
158. Newton, *Russia, France,* p. 61.
159. CIA Intelligence Info Cable, 25 August 1965, LBJL, PP, NSF, CO, Box 172.
160. Mikhaïl Narinsky, "Le retrait de la France de l'organisation militaire de l'OTAN, vu de Moscou," in *De Gaulle,* ed. Vaïsse, p. 164.
161. De Gaulle-Heath meeting, 22 November 1965, MAEF, CM, CdM, Vol. 381; Marie-Pierre Rey, "De Gaulle, l'URSS et la sécurité européenne, 1958–1969," in *De Gaulle,* ed. Vaïsse, p. 223. First proposed during the Khrushchev period, the project of a European security conference was promoted again by the new Kremlin leaders.
162. Wolton, *France sous influence,* p. 415.
163. Couve-Schroeder meeting, 12 November 1965, MAEF, CM, CdM, Vol. 381.
164. Funkhouse to State Department, 13 December 1965, NARA, RG59, Bureau of Atlantic Affairs, Files of Robert J Schaetzel Deputy Assistant Secretary for Atlantic Affairs, Box 1.
165. De Gaulle-Zorin meeting, 12 January 1966, ANF, 5AG1, Carton 187, URSS.
166. According to IFOP, *De Gaulle,* p. 264, in 1963, 23 percent of the French population had a good opinion of the USSR, 30 percent neither good nor bad, 35 percent had a bad opinion, and 12 percent had no opinion; for 1964, the respective figures were 25 percent, 42 percent, 25 percent, and 8 percent; for 1965, 27 percent, 40 percent, 14 percent, and 19 percent.

Chapter 3

1. Interview with Jean Charbonnel, Paris, 15 September 2004; Gérard Bossuat, "French Development Aid and Co-Operation under de Gaulle," *Contemporary European History,* Vol. 12/4 (2003), pp. 451–53. For more on the divided public opinion, see Philippe Decraene, "Les Réactions de l'Opinion Publique Française à la Politique Tiers Mondiste du Général de Gaulle de 1962 à 1969," in *De Gaulle et le Tiers Monde,* ed. Institut Charles de Gaulle (Paris: A. Pedone, 1984), pp. 367–77.
2. Gorce, *France contre les Empires,* p. 260.
3. Ibid., p. 243.
4. De Gaulle-King Hussein meeting, 10 September 1963, MAEF, SG, EM, Vol. 19.
5. Couve de Murville-Kennedy meeting, 7 October 1963, MAEF, CM, CdM, Vol. 376.
6. See Vaïsse, *La grandeur,* p. 453, and Hartley, *Gaullism,* p. 205.
7. Couve de Murville, *Politique étrangère,* pp. 431–32.
8. De Gaulle, *DM: IV,* Speech in Lyon, 28 September 1963, p. 138.
9. Peyrefitte, *C'était de Gaulle: vol. 1,* Meeting 13 February 1963, p. 283.
10. Lacouture, *De Gaulle: vol. 3,* p. 422. In March 1963, a decree established a commission, presided over by former Minister Jean-Marcel Jeanneney, to write a study on the policy of cooperation with developing countries.
11. Vaïsse, *La grandeur,* p. 457; see Annex 6.
12. According to Pierre Pascallon, in "Les Aspects Économiques de la Politique Tiers Mondiste du Général de Gaulle de 1962 à 1969," in *De Gaulle et le Tiers Monde,* ed. Institut Charles de Gaulle, p. 189. Throughout the 1960s, France dedicated a higher percentage of its GNI to development aid than did the average member-state of the Develop-

ment Aid Committee of the Organisation for Economic Co-operation and Development (OECD). See Annex 5.

13. De Gaulle, *DM: IV*, p. 173; see also Peyrefitte, *C'était de Gaulle: vol. 2*, Meeting 16 September 1964, p. 517.

14. Paul Marie de la Gorce, "Trois changements essentiels," in *DGESS VI*, ed. Institut Charles de Gaulle, p. 74.

15. Toast to the Mexican President Adolfo Lopez Mateos, 27 March 1963, FNSP, CM Carton 1.

16. De Gaulle, *DM: IV*, Speech at the Mexican National Palace, 16 March 1964, p. 189.

17. De Gaulle-Mateos meeting, 16 March 1964, MAEF, SG, EM, Vol. 20. For more on this, see Pascallon, "Aspects Économiques," p. 175.

18. Pompidou-Eskhol meeting, 28 June 1964, MAEF, CM, CdM, Vol. 378.

19. Vaïsse, *La grandeur*, pp. 39–40; Couve de Murville, *Politique étrangère*, p. 446.

20. De Gaulle-Illia meeting, 4 October 1964, DDF, 1964, Tome II.

21. De Gaulle, *DM: IV*, 8 October 1964, p. 297.

22. Pompidou-Ikeda meeting, 7 April 1964, MAEF, SG, EM, Vol. 20.

23. De Gaulle, *DM: IV*, 12 September 1963, p. 133.

24. Costigliola, *Cold alliance*, p. 139.

25. De Gaulle-Rockefeller meeting, 3 October 1963, MAEF, CM, CdM, Vol. 376.

26. De Gaulle, *DM: IV*, p. 170.

27. Peyrefitte, *C'était de Gaulle: vol. 2*, Meeting 11 March 1964, p. 472.

28. Gorce, "Trois changements," pp. 73–74.

29. De Gaulle, *DM: IV*, 18 March 1964, p. 198.

30. Bossuat, "French Development Aid," p. 434.

31. Interview with Michel Habib-Deloncle, Paris, 15 December 2004.

32. Triboulet to Couve de Murville, 3 January 1963, FNSP, CM Carton 8.

33. For more on this internal struggle, see Raymond Triboulet, *Un Ministre du Général* (Paris: Plon, 1985), especially pp. 198–261. Information on the moves to destabilize Touré comes from an interview with Jean Charbonnel, Paris, 15 September 2004.

34. Bovey to State, Airgram 940, 29 October 1964, NARA, RG59, CFPF, 1964–1966, Box 2168.

35. Couve de Murville, *Politique étrangère*, p. 442.

36. Vaïsse, *La grandeur*, p. 462.

37. Bouhout El Mellouki Riffi, "De Gaulle et la coopération avec le Maghreb," in *DGESS VI*, ed. Institut Charles de Gaulle, p. 195.

38. On Algerian-French relations in the 1960s, see Jeffrey Byrne, "'*Je ne vous ai pas compris*': De Gaulle's Decade of Negotiation with the Algerian FLN," in *Globalizing de Gaulle*, ed. Nuenlist, Locher and Martin.

39. Roussel, *De Gaulle*, p. 768.

40. Note on French financial aid to Algeria, 13 November 1963, DDF, 1963, Tome II.

41. Semi-Bi Zan, "La coopération militaire franco-africaine au temps du général de Gaulle," in *DGESS VI*, ed. Institut Charles de Gaulle, p. 295.

42. Hartley, *Gaullism*, p. 238.

43. Roger Pfister, *Apartheid South Africa and African States: From Pariah to Middle Power, 1961–1994* (London; New York: I.B. Taurus Academic Studies, 2005), p. 49.

44. Claude Wauthier, *Quatre Présidents et l'Afrique, De Gaulle, Pompidou, Giscard d'Estaing, Mitterrand: Quarante ans de politique africaine* (Paris: Seuil, 1995), pp. 139–43, 144–45. Between 1961 and 1965, France sold 700M francs worth of weapons to South Africa, while the latter was a key source of uranium for Paris. See Note on Franco-South African economic relations, 28 April 1966 and Note, 9 May 1966, DDF, 1966, Tome I.

45. Cerny, *Politics of grandeur,* p. 203.
46. De Gaulle, *LNC: IX,* Draft before a Minister's Council, undated, p. 318.
47. Note on De Gaulle comments after his South American trip, 21 October 1964, DDF, 1964, Tome II.
48. Quoted by Pascallon, "Aspects Économiques," p. 194.
49. Charles Zorgbibe, "De Gaulle et le Tiers Monde: Orientations Générales," in *De Gaulle et le Tiers Monde,* ed. Institut Charles de Gaulle, p. 165; Cerny, *Politics of Grandeur,* p. 204.
50. Zorgbibe, "Orientations Générales," p. 165; Cerny, *Politics of Grandeur,* p. 204.
51. Vaïsse, *La grandeur,* p. 454.
52. Peyrefitte, *C'était de Gaulle: vol. 2,* Meeting 24 January 1963 and Council of Ministers 6 March 1963, pp. 462–63.
53. Wauthier, *Quatre Présidents,* p. 170.
54. Edmond Kwam Kouassi, "L'Afrique," in *DGESS VI,* ed. Institut Charles de Gaulle, p. 77.
55. Vaïsse, *La grandeur,* p. 480. However, the French president did continue to regularly receive African leaders. Interview with Jean Charbonnel, Paris, 15 September 2004.
56. Pfister, *Apartheid South Africa,* p. 49.
57. Among those who suggest Foccart's great influence on African policy, see Pierre Péan, *L'homme de l'ombre: Éléments d'enquête autour de Jacques Foccart, l'homme le plus mystérieux et le plus puissant de la Vème République* (Paris: Fayard, 1990); Wauthier, *Quatre Présidents;* Interview with Michel Habib-Deloncle, Paris, 15 December 2004.
58. Bossuat, "French Development Aid," p. 433.
59. De Gaulle, *LNC: IX,* De Gaulle to Couve de Murville, 22 October 1963, p. 380.
60. Note on French financial aid to Algeria, 13 November 1963, DDF, 1963, Tome II.
61. Zan, "La coopération militaire," p. 295.
62. Ibid., pp. 295, 299–301.
63. Paris to FO, Telegram 142, 20 February 1964, UK-NA, FO 371/177285; Peyrefitte, *C'était de Gaulle: vol. 2,* Meeting 26 February 1964, p. 471; Jacques Foccart, *Foccart parle: entretiens avec Philippe Gaillard* (Paris: le Grand livre du mois: Fayard: Jeune Afrique, c1995), p. 273.
64. Péan, *L'homme de l'ombre,* pp. 304–05.
65. Foccart, *Foccart parle,* p. 276; Wauthier, *Quatre Présidents,* p. 127.
66. Pierre-Michel Durand, "Les relations Franco-Américaines au Gabon dans les Années 60 ou la 'Petite Guerre Froide,'" in *Les Relations Franco-Américaines au XXème siècle,* ed. Pierre Melandri and Serge Ricard (Paris: L'Harmattan, 2003), especially pp. 120–24.
67. Bossuat, "French Development Aid," p. 454–55.
68. Hughes to Rusk, Research Memo INR-14, 4 April 1963, NARA, RG59, Records of Policy Planning Council, Box 252.
69. Vaïsse, *La grandeur,* pp. 503–04.
70. See, for example, Lacouture, *De Gaulle: vol. 3,* p. 445; Pierre Viansson-Ponté, *Histoire de la République Gaullienne: vol. 2* (Paris: Fayard, 1971), p. 79; Newhouse, *De Gaulle,* p. 256.
71. De Gaulle, *DM: IV,* 26 March 1963, p. 91.
72. De Gaulle-Bosch meeting, 1 February 1963, MAEF, CM, CdM, Vol. 375.
73. Peyrefitte, *C'était de Gaulle: vol. 2,* Meetings 27 March 1963 and 22 April 1963, p. 508.
74. De Gaulle-Rusk meeting, 8 April 1963, MAEF, CM, CdM, Vol. 375.
75. Peyrefitte, *C'était de Gaulle: vol. 2,* Council of Ministers 20 February 1963, p. 474.
76. Maurice Vaïsse, "De Gaulle et la guerre du Vietnam: de la difficulté d'être Cassandre," in *Guerre du Vietnam,* ed. Goscha and Vaïsse, p. 169.
77. Marianna Sullivan, *France's Vietnam Policy: A Study in French-American Relations* (Westport, Conn: Greenwood Press, 1978), p. 71.

78. De Gaulle-Pelaez meeting, 8 February 1963, and Couve de Murville-Martin meeting, 21 May 1963, MAEF, CM, CdM, Vol. 375. Note that the Geneva Accords gave France a residual role in the region, i.e., enabling it to send officers to train the Laotian National Army.

79. Logevall, *Choosing War,* p. 13.

80. See Lalouette to Couve de Murville, Dépêches 161 and 350, 2 March 1963 and 22 May 1963, MAEF, Asie-Océanie, Sud-Vietnam 1954–1964, Vol. 78. It seems that in April Lalouette had advised Diem that he should "gently" ask the Americans to leave, according to Marianna Sullivan's interview with Roger Lalouette, Versailles, 19 July 1972.

81. Paris to FO, 12 September 1963, UK-NA, FO 371/170107.

82. Note du *Secrétariat Général de la Présidence,* 20 June 1963, ANF, 5AG1, Carton 241, Sud-Vietnam; Note of *Direction des Affaires Politiques Asie-Océanie,* 6 September 1963, DDF, 1963, Tome II. The extent of Diem's peace feelers, as well as Lalouette's role and his exact intentions, are still subject to debate. See Mieczyslaw Maneli, *War of the Vanquished* (New York: Harper & Row, 1971); Logevall, *Choosing War;* Sullivan, *France's Vietnam Policy;* Gnoinska, Margaret, "Poland and Vietnam, 1963: New Evidence on Secret Communist Diplomacy and the 'Maneli Affair,'" http://www.wilsoncenter.org/topics/pubs/CWIHP_WP_45b.pdf.

83. Paris to FO, 12 September 1963, UK-NA, FO 371/170107; Note for Couve de Murville, 26 March 1963, MAEF, Asie-Océanie, Sud-Vietnam 1954–1964, Vol. 16.

84. De Gaulle, *LNC: IX,* Declaration concerning Vietnam, p. 367.

85. Armando Uribe, "Le général de Gaulle et l'Amérique Latine," in *De Gaulle et le Tiers Monde,* ed. Institut Charles de Gaulle, pp. 246–47; Peyrefitte, *C'était de Gaulle: vol. 2,* Meeting 29 August 1963, p. 476.

86. For more on the rapprochement with China, see Martin, "Playing the China card" and chapter 2, endnotes 47–52.

87. Peyrefitte, *C'était de Gaulle: vol. 2,* Meeting 11 December 1963, p. 483.

88. Philippe Devillers, "Le Général de Gaulle et l'Asie," in *De Gaulle et le Tiers Monde,"* ed. Institut Charles de Gaulle, p. 306.

89. Qiang Zhai, "China's Response to French Peace Initiatives," in *Search for Peace,* ed. Gardner and Gittinger, pp. 279–80.

90. De Gaulle, *DM: IV,* p. 180.

91. Paris to FO, 27 January 1964, UK-NA, FO 371/173687.

92. Paris to State, Airgram 1941, 13 February 1964, NARA, RG59, CFPF, 1964–1966, Box 2186.

93. Soledad Loaeza, "La visite du général de Gaulle au Méxique: le malentendu franco-méxicain," in *DGESS VI,* ed. Institut Charles de Gaulle, p. 508.

94. De Gaulle-Ambassadors to Latin America meeting, 3 June 1964, ANF, 5AG1, Carton 198, Voyage du Général de Gaulle en Amérique Latine.

95. De Gaulle, *DM: IV,* Speech in Santiago University, 1 October 1964, p. 277; De Gaulle-Valencia meeting, 23 September 1964, DDF, 1964, Tome II.

96. De Gaulle, *LNC: X,* De Gaulle to Debré, 18 September 1964, p. 88.

97. De Gaulle-Erhard meeting 1, 15 February 1964, MAEF, CM, CdM, Vol. 377.

98. Paris to FO, Telegram 114, 11.02.64, UK-NA, FO 371/177909.

99. For more on French peace initiatives, see Yuko Torikata, "Re-examining de Gaulle's Peace Initiative on the Vietnam War," *Diplomatic History,* 31/5 (2007), pp. 909–38.

100. De Gaulle, *DM: IV,* pp. 236–37.

101. Logevall, *Choosing War,* p. 104.

102. Laurent Césari, "Que reste-t-il de l'influence politique française en Indochine (1954–1966)?" in *Du Conflit d'Indochine aux Conflits Indochinois,* ed. by Pierre Brocheux (Bruxelles: Editions Complexe, 2000), p. 33.

103. Couve de Murville to Alphand, Telegram 2917-2920, 2 February 1964, DDF, 1964, Tome I.
104. Césari, "L'influence politique française en Indochine," in *Du Conflit d'Indochine*, ed. Brocheux, p. 33.
105. Alphand, *L'étonnement*, Diary entry 4 May 1964, p. 427.
106. De Gaulle-Huang Chen meeting, 19 June 1964, MAEF, SG, EM, Vol. 21; Couve de Murville-Huang Chen meeting, 21 July 1964, MAEF, SG, EM, Vol. 22.
107. Note of *Direction Asie-Océanie*, 17 June 1964, DDF, 1964, Tome I.
108. See Bohlen to Rusk, Telegram 2358, 15 November 1963, NARA, RG59, CFPF, 1963, Box 3910; Paris to FO, 4 June 1964, UK-NA, FO 371/177865; Pierre Journoud, *De Gaulle et le Vietnam: 1945–1969, la réconciliation* (Paris: Tallandier, c2011), p. 119.
109. Couve de Murville-Kennedy meeting, 7 October 1963, MAEF, CM, CdM, Vol. 376.
110. De Gaulle-Rusk meeting, 16 December 1963, MAEF, CM, CdM, Vol. 376.
111. Peyrefitte, *C'était de Gaulle: vol. 2*, Meeting 6 November 1963, p. 481.
112. Newhouse, *De Gaulle*, p. 260.
113. See, for example, Vaïsse, *La grandeur*, p. 527, Roussel, *De Gaulle*, p. 769, or Logevall, *Choosing War*, p. 131. According to one of Rusk's staffers, the Secretary of State's talk with Couve de Murville on 12 April was "extremely frank."
114. Rusk-Couve de Murville-Carrington meeting, 14 April 1964, MAEF, SG, EM, Vol. 21.
115. Ball to Rusk, Telegram 5876-5878, 5 June 1964, LBJL, PP, NSF, CO, Box 170.
116. De Gaulle, *DM: IV*, 17 March 1964, p. 192.
117. De Gaulle-Mateos meeting, 17 March 1964, MAEF, SG, EM, Vol. 20.
118. Loaeza, "La visite au México," p. 503.
119. De Gaulle-Stroessner meeting, 7 October 1964, DDF, 1964, Tome II.
120. Jova to State, Airgram 384, 16 November 1964, NARA, RG59, CFPF, 1964–1966, Box 2186.
121. Peyrefitte, *C'était de Gaulle: vol. 2*, Meeting 22 April 1964, p. 496.
122. De Gaulle-U Thant meeting, 21 July 1964, MAEF, SG, EM, Vol. 22.
123. Paye to Couve de Murville, Dépêche 204, 29 August 1964, DDF, 1964, Tome II.
124. Césari, "L'influence politique française en Indochine," p. 35.
125. Qiang Zhai, *China and the Vietnam Wars, 1950–1975* (Chapel Hill: University of North Carolina Press, 2000), p. 131.
126. Alphand, *L'étonnement*, Diary entry 31 August 1964, p. 438.
127. Couve de Murville-Hasluck meeting, 4 November 1964, MAEF, SG, EM, Vol. 23.
128. Peyrefitte, *C'était de Gaulle: vol. 2*, Dinner 8 December 1964, p. 499.
129. Alphand, *L'étonnement*, 3 January 1965, p. 445.
130. Devillers, "L'Asie," p. 310.
131. Declaration of the French government, 10 February 1965, MAEF, Asie-Océanie, Conflit Vietnam 1955–1975, Vol. 162.
132. For Couve de Murville's talks in the U.S., see MAEF, CM, CdM, Vol. 379.
133. Couve de Murville to Baudet, Telegram 3068-3073, 1 March 1965, MAEF, Europe, URSS 1961–1965, Vol. 1931.
134. Couve de Murville-Stewart meeting, 2 April 1965, MAEF, SG, EM, Vol. 24.
135. Peyrefitte, *C'était de Gaulle: vol. 2*, Meeting 7 April 1965, p. 502.
136. Ibid., Council of Ministers 14 April 1965, p. 503.
137. Couve de Murville speech to NATO Council, 12 May 1965, MAEF, SG, EM, Vol. 25.
138. Alphand, *L'étonnement*, Diary entry 7 May 1965, p. 452.
139. Costigliola, *Cold alliance*, p. 140.
140. De Gaulle-Shiina meeting, 20 July 1965, MAEF, CM, CdM, Vol. 380.
141. De Gaulle-Goldberg meeting, 31 December 1965, MAEF, CM, CdM, Vol. 381.
142. Alphand, *L'étonnement*, Diary entry 2 January 1966, p. 468.

143. Pierre Journoud, "Le Quai d'Orsay et le Processus de Paix, 1963–1973," in *Guerre du Vietnam,* ed Goscha and Vaïsse, pp. 387, 389.
144. Sanviti-Huyen Van Tam meeting, 29 July 1965, DDF, 1965, Tome II.

Chapter 4

1. De Gaulle, *DM: IV,* p. 445.
2. Peyrefitte, *C'était de Gaulle: vol. 2,* Meeting 21 December 1965, p. 613.
3. De Gaulle-Adenauer meeting, 10 March 1966, MAEF, CM, CdM, Vol. 382.
4. Bohlen to Rusk, Telegram 6146, 23 March 1966, LBJL, PP, NSF, CO, Box 177. This was a view shared by the main American source within the Quai. See Bohlen to Rusk, Telegram 5422, 3 March 1966, LBJL, PP, NSF, CO, Box 177.
5. Frédéric Bozo, "Chronique d'une décision annoncée: Le retrait de l'organisation militaire 1965–1967," in *La France et l'OTAN, 1949–1996,* ed. Maurice Vaïsse, Pierre Melandri, and Frédéric Bozo (Bruxelles: Editions Complexes, 1996), p. 337.
6. Note for Couve de Murville, 21 January 1966, MAEF, SG, EM, Vol. 26.
7. Charles Bohlen, *Witness to History* (London: Weidenfeld and Nicolson, 1973), p. 506.
8. Charles de Gaulle, *DM: V,* p. 19.
9. Compare Alphand, *L'étonnement,* Diary entry 28 February 1966, p. 473, with Lacouture, *De Gaulle: vol. 3,* p. 377. Pierre Messmer, French minister for armed forces at the time, agreed with Couve de Murville. Interview, Paris, 12 June 2003. Couve de Murville does admit that he had disagreed with de Gaulle on the modalities of the withdrawal. See Maurice Couve de Murville entretien 3, 22 July 1987, MAEF, AO 29.
10. Soutou, *L'Alliance Incertaine,* p. 291. For the Quai's note mentioned by Soutou, see Note of *Service des Pactes,* 17 January 1966, MAEF, Pactes 1961–1970, Vol. 261.
11. Bohlen to Rusk, Telegram 4867, 11 February 1966, LBJL, PP, NSF, CO, Box 172.
12. Spaak, *Combats: vol. 2,* p. 391.
13. De Gaulle, *LNC: X,* pp. 261–62.
14. See Bozo, *Deux Stratégies,* p. 155; Vaïsse, *La grandeur,* p. 350; Jean-Paul Brunet, "Le Retrait de la France de l'OTAN: La Scène Intérieure," in *France et l'OTAN,* ed Vaïsse, Melandri, and Bozo, pp. 393–94.
15. Interview with Jacques Andréani, Paris, 15 February 2006; Charles Lucet 4 and 5, Paris, 16 and 27 June 1986, MAEF, AO 26.
16. Alessandra Giglioli, "Le retrait de la France du commandement intégré de l'OTAN," http://www.nato.int/acad/fellow/98-00/giglioli.pdf, p. 16.
17. Soutou, "La décision française," pp. 186–87.
18. Frédéric Bozo, *La France et l'OTAN: de la guerre froide au nouvel ordre européen* (Paris: Masson, 1991), p. 104.
19. Soutou, "La décision française," p. 185.
20. Aide-mémoire to the NATO Allies, 29 March 1966, Documentation Française [DF], La Politique Étrangère de la France [PEF], Textes et Documents 1966–1967.
21. De Beaumarchais to Lucet, Telegram 1303-1309, 4 June 1966, MAEF, Amérique, États-Unis 1964–1970, Vol. 576.
22. Bohlen to Rusk, Telegram 6552, 6 April 1966, LBJL, PP, NSF, CO, Box 177.
23. Bozo, *Deux Stratégies,* p. 158.
24. Alphand, *L'étonnement,* Diary entry 31 March 1966, p. 476.
25. Giglioli, "Le retrait," p. 19.
26. Note of *Service des Pactes,* 23 April 1966, MAEF, CM, CdM, Vol. 339.
27. Alain Peyrefitte, *C'était de Gaulle: vol. 3* (Paris: Editions de Fallois Fayard, 2000), p. 189.

28. French aide-mémoire, 18 May 1966, DF, PEF, 1966–1967.
29. See Inner Council in Elysée, 2 June 1966 and Note by Charles de Gaulle, 4 July 1966, MAEF, Pactes 1961–1970, Vol. 263.
30. Telegram From the Embassy in France to the Department of State, 11 June 1966, Document 60, FRUS, 1964–1968, Vol. XII.
31. Rusk to Johnson, 12 June 1966, NARA, RG59, Records of Under-Secretary of State George Ball, 1961–1966, Box 21.
32. Thomas Schwartz "The de Gaulle challenge: The Johnson Administration and the NATO Crisis of 1966–1967," in *The Strategic Triangle: France, Germany, and the United States in the Shaping of Europe,* ed. Helga Haftendorn, Georges-Henri Soutou, Stephen Szabo, and Samuel Wells (Washington, D.C.: Woodrow Wilson Center Press; Baltimore: Johns Hopkins University Press, c2006), p. 136.
33. Bozo, *Deux Stratégies,* p. 163.
34. Peyrefitte, *C'était de Gaulle: vol. 3,* p. 191.
35. Devillers, "L'Asie," p. 314.
36. Maurice Couve de Murville, *Le Monde en Face: Entretiens avec Maurice Delarue* (Paris: Plon, 1989), p. 40.
37. French officials made these points to the Allies and to the public. See aide-mémoire from French government to the U.S. government, 11 March 1966, Document 142, FRUS, 1964–1968, Vol. XIII and Georges Pompidou speech to l'*Assemblée Nationale,* 13 April 1966, DF, PEF, 1966–1967.
38. For more on how the "empty chair" crisis ended, see N. Piers Ludlow, "The Eclipse of the Extremes. Demythologising the Luxembourg Compromise," in *Crises and Compromises,* ed. Loth, pp. 247–64.
39. Peyrefitte, *C'était de Gaulle: vol. 3,* Council of Ministers 13 April 1966, p. 185.
40. Ludlow, *European Community,* p. 109. For the details of the 11 May agreement, see Note of *Service de Coopération Économique,* 12 May 1966, DDF, 1966, Tome I.
41. Bohlen to Rusk, Telegram 7062, 22 April 1966, NARA, RG59, CFPF, 1964–1966, Box 2182.
42. Fessenden to Schaetzel, 25 May 1966, NARA, RG59, Bureau of European Affairs, Files of Robert Schaetzel, Deputy Assistant Secretary for Atlantic Affairs, Box 3.
43. Ludlow, *European Community,* p. 114.
44. Peyrefitte, *C'était de Gaulle: vol. 3,* p. 186, Council of Ministers, 9 March 1966.
45. Roussel, *De Gaulle,* p. 796; Johnson to Reuther, 7 March 1966, LBJL, Telephone Conversations, White House Series 6603.03, Citation 9841.
46. See, for example, Newhouse, *De Gaulle,* p. 285 and Bohlen to Rusk, Telegram 5542, 7 March 1966, NARA, RG59, CFPF, 1964–1966, Box 2179.
47. Bozo, *Deux Stratégies,* p. 163.
48. Interview with O.R.T.F. Radio, 23 April 1966, DF: PEF, 1966–1967.
49. Peyrefitte, *C'était de Gaulle: vol. 3,* p. 190.
50. Puaux Draft Circular, undated, MAEF, Pactes 1961–1970, Vol. 261.
51. Couve de Murville-Maurer meeting, 27 April 1966, MAEF, SG, EM, Vol. 27.
52. Couve de Murville-Gomulka meeting, 20 May 1966, MAEF, CM, CdM, Vol. 383.
53. US Embassy in Paris to Rusk, Telegram 6563, 6 April 1966, NARA, RG 59, CFPF, 1964–1966, Box 2173. Officially, the Soviet government welcomed the French withdrawal from NATO. In private, though, Moscow feared that it would increase West German influence within the Atlantic Alliance and could undermine the cohesion of the Warsaw Pact. See Baudet to Couve de Murville, Telegram 903-905, 18 March 1966, MAEF, Europe, URSS 1966–1970, Vol. 2665 and Note of *Sous-Direction d'Europe Orientale,* 13 May 1966, DDF, 1966, Tome I.

54. Meeting with Jan Druto, 11 June 1966, MAEF, CM, CdM, Vol. 383.
55. Couve de Murville-Gomulka meeting, 20 May 1966, MAEF, CM, CdM, Vol. 383.
56. Schreiber, *Les Actions*, pp. 102–03.
57. Couve de Murville, *Politique étrangère*, p. 227.
58. De Gaulle-Kliszko meeting, 13 May 1966, MAEF, CM, CdM, Vol. 383.
59. Étienne Burin des Roziers, "Le non-alignement," in *La politique étrangère du Général de Gaulle*, ed. Élie Barnavi and Saül Friedländer (Paris: Presses Universitaires de France, 1985), p. 72.
60. See Schreiber, *Les Actions*, p. 101.
61. Couve de Murville, *Politique étrangère*, p. 222.
62. See Andreas Wenger, "Crisis and Opportunity: NATO's Transformation and the Multi-lateralization of Détente, 1966–1968," *Journal of Cold War Studies*, Vol. 6/1 (2004), p. 31; Vaïsse, *La grandeur*, p. 390.
63. Vaïsse, *La grandeur*, p. 425.
64. Pompidou speech to *l'Assemblée Nationale*, 13 April 1966, DF, PEF, 1966–1967.
65. Couve de Murville-Schroeder-Rusk-Stewart meeting, 6 June 1966, MAEF, CM, CdM, Vol. 383.
66. Bernard Lefort, *Souvenirs et secrets des années gaulliennes, 1958–1969* (Paris: A. Michel, 1999), p. 149.
67. Peyrefitte, *C'était de Gaulle: vol. 3*, Council of Ministers 15 June 1966, p. 195.
68. De Gaulle-Zorin meeting, 29 April 1966, MAEF, CM, CdM, Vol. 382. For another example of de Gaulle's suspicions, in this case in the field of scientific cooperation, see Peyrefitte, *C'était de Gaulle: vol. 3*, Meeting 22 March 1966, p. 129.
69. De Gaulle-Adenauer meeting, 10 March 1966, MAEF, CM, CdM, Vol. 382. Similarly, de Gaulle told Ludwig Erhard that "Germany has nothing to fear" from his trip to Moscow. See De Gaulle, *LNC: X*, p. 306.
70. Interview with Jean Charbonnel, Paris, 15 September 2004.
71. See, for example, De Gaulle-Zorin meeting, 18 March 1966, MAEF, SG, EM, Vol. 26 and De Gaulle-Zorin meeting, 29 April 1966, MAEF, CM, CdM, Vol. 382.
72. De Gaulle-Krag meeting, 18 April 1966, MAEF, SG, EM, Vol. 27.
73. Telegram From the Embassy in France to the Department of State, 11 June 1966, Document 60, FRUS, 1964–1968, Vol. XII.
74. Soutou, "La décision française," pp. 194–96. The reference to the U.S. as the underwriter of Europe was featured in the briefing for De Gaulle's trip to Moscow, according to a Quai source. See De la Grandville-Funkhouse meeting, 9 July 1966, NARA, RG 59, Records of the Ambassador Charles Bohlen, Box 33.
75. Narinsky, "Le retrait," p. 166.
76. For a good example of de Gaulle's pessimistic assessment of West Germany, see De Gaulle, *LNC: X*, Exposé during the Council of Foreign Affairs on West Germany, pp. 246–49.
77. Bohlen to Rusk, Airgram 2425, 24 June 1966, NARA, RG 59, CFPF, 1964–1966, Box 2180.
78. Crouy-Chanel to Couve de Murville, Telegram 568-576, 8 June 1966, MAEF, Pactes 1961–1970, Vol. 272.
79. Wolfe, *Soviet Power*, p. 281.
80. See chapter 2, endnote 158.
81. For more on these debates, see Newton, *Russia, France*, pp. 58–73.
82. Ibid., pp. 73–75.
83. Narinsky, "Le retrait," pp. 165–67.
84. Durandin, *France contre l'Amérique*, pp. 98–99.

85. Zinaida Bieloussova, " La visite du général de Gaulle en URSS en Juin 1966," in *DGESS IV,* ed. Institut Charles de Gaulle, p. 394.

86. De Gaulle-Brezhnev-Kosygin-Podgorny meeting, 21 June 1966, MAEF, SG, EM, Vol. 27.

87. Peyrefitte, *C'était de Gaulle: vol. 3,* p. 197.

88. Franco-Soviet Common Declaration, 30 June 1966, see DF, PEF, 1966–1967.

89. René Andrieu, in Lacouture and Mehl, *De Gaulle ou l'éternel défi,* p. 221.

90. 63 percent of the French public supported the trip and only 5 percent were opposed to it, according to Gorce, *France contre les Empires,* p. 290.

91. Schreiber, *Les Actions,* p. 102. Interestingly, the French public developed a more favorable view toward the Soviet Union, see IFOP, *De Gaulle,* p. 264; whereas in 1964, 25 percent had a good opinion of the Soviet Union, 42 percent had a neither good or bad opinion, 25 percent had a bad opinion, and 8 percent had no opinion, by 1966 the numbers had changed to 35 percent, 31 percent, 13 percent, and 21 percent, respectively.

92. Rey, *La tentation,* p. 48.

93. See for example, De Gaulle, *LNC: X,* De Gaulle to Johnson, 5 February 1966, p. 250.

94. Couve de Murville-Maurer meeting, 27 April 1966, MAEF, SG, EM, Vol. 27.

95. Couve de Murville-Schroeder meeting, 21 July 1966, MAEF, CM, CdM, Vol. 384.

96. De Gaulle, *DM: V,* p. 23.

97. See Couve de Murville-Ceauşescu meeting, 28 April 1966, MAEF, SG, EM, Vol. 27; Couve de Murville-Rapacki meeting, 19 May 1966, MAEF, CM, CdM, Vol. 383, and Couve de Murville-Kallai meeting, 29 July 1966, MAEF, CM, CdM, Vol. 384.

98. See, for example, De Gaulle-Gandhi meeting, 25 March 1966, MAEF, SG, EM, Vol. 26; Malraux-Fawzi meeting, 23 March 1966, MAEF, CM, CdM, Vol. 382; and Report of Sainteny mission in Southeast Asia, 13 July 1966, MAEF, SG, EM, Vol. 27, which mentions that North Vietnamese Prime Minister Pham Van Dong expressed his respect for de Gaulle's statements on the Vietnam conflict.

99. Couve de Murville-Huang Chen meeting, 12 May 1966, MAEF, CM, CdM, Vol. 383.

100. Alphand, *L'étonnement,* p. 468.

101. Burin des Roziers-Chen meeting, 26 May 1966, ANF, 5AG1, Carton 226, Chine Populaire.

102. See US Embassy in Paris to State Department, Airgram 1845, 19 March 1966, NARA RG59, CFPF, 1964–1966, Box 2188.

103. François de Quirielle, *A Hanoï sous les Bombes Américaines: Journal d'un diplomate Français, 1966–1969* (Paris: Tallandier, 1992), p. 71. For de Gaulle's letter, see De Gaulle, *LNC: X,* De Gaulle to Ho Chi Minh, 8 February 1966, p. 251.

104. Note 149 of *Direction Asie-Océanie,* 14 May 1966, DDF, 1966, Tome I; De Quirielle, *A Hanoï,* p. 189.

105. See Note on Manac'h-Huynh Van Tam meetings, 6–7 June 1966, MAEF SG, EM, Vol. 27 and Manac'h-Nguyen Van Hieu meeting, 28 August 1966, MAEF, SG, EM, Vol. 28.

106. Quoted by Devillers, "L'Asie," p. 313.

107. Telegram From the Embassy in France to the Department of State, 7 March 1966, Document 136, FRUS, 1964–1968, Vol. XIII.

108. Claude Dulong, *La Dernière Pagode* (Paris: B. Grasset, 1989), p. 138; Torikata, "de Gaulle's Peace Initiative," p. 931.

109. Paris to FO, 29 June 1966, UK-NA, FO 371/185915; see Couve de Murville to Charles Malo, Telegram 272-273, 18 June 1966, DDF, 1966, Tome II.

110. Devillers, "L'Asie," p. 315.

111. Sainteny note, 7 July 1966, ANF, 5AG1, Carton 226, Chine Populaire.

112. Sullivan, *France's Vietnam Policy,* p. 101; Dulong, *Dernière Pagode,* p. 159.

113. Couve de Murville-Schroeder meeting, 21 July 1966, MAEF, CM, CdM, Vol. 384; De Gaulle, *DM: V*, Reply to Toast given by Haile Selassie, 27 August 1966, p. 69.
114. See De Gaulle-Church meeting, 4 May 1966, MAEF, SG, EM, Vol. 27.
115. Sullivan, *France's Vietnam Policy*, p. 92.
116. Couve de Murville-David meeting, 26 July 1966, MAEF, CM, CdM, Vol. 384.
117. De Gaulle-Lucet meeting, 25 July 1966, MAEF, SG, EM, Vol. 28.
118. Telegram From the Embassy in Ethiopia to the Department of State, 27 August 1966, Document 65, FRUS, 1964–1968, Vol. XII.
119. Kissinger-De la Grandville meeting, 23 January 1966, LBJL, PP, Confidential Files [CF], Box 8. Henri Froment-Meurice, a Quai official at the time, confirmed this point in an interview with the author, Paris, 24 April 2003.
120. Compare de Gaulle's meeting with Huang Chen and Couve de Murville's meeting with the same interlocutor. Whereas Couve de Murville highlighted the more limited American aims, de Gaulle underlined the similarity between France's and China's views, pointing to the "growing moral and diplomatic isolation of the US." See Couve de Murville-Chen meeting, 12 May 1966 and De Gaulle-Chen meeting, 16 May 1966, MAEF, CM, CdM, Vol. 383.
121. Journoud, "Quai d'Orsay," p. 393.
122. Couve de Murville, *Monde en face*, p. 40.
123. Anne Sa'adah, "Idées Simples and Idées Fixes: De Gaulle, the United States, and Vietnam," in *De Gaulle and the US*, ed. Wahl and Paxton, p. 307.
124. For the Phnom Penh speech, see De Gaulle, *DM:V*, pp. 74–78.
125. See Torikata, "de Gaulle's Peace Initiative," p. 934; Charles Lucet entretien 5, 27 June 1986, MAEF, AO 26; Note 500 of Direction des Affaires Politiques, Sous-Direction Asie-Océanie, 20 September 1966, DDF, 1966, Tome II.
126. Roussel, *De Gaulle*, pp. 801–05 ; Lefort, *Souvenirs et secrets*, p. 155.
127. Lacouture, *De Gaulle: vol. 3*, p. 436; Jean D'Escrienne, *Le Général m'a dit: 1966–1970* (Paris: Plon, 1973), p. 85.
128. Peyrefitte, *C'était de Gaulle: vol. 3*, Meeting 12 September 1966, p. 147.
129. Sullivan, *France's Vietnam Policy*, p. 91.
130. Inner Council in Elysée, 2 June 1966, MAEF, Pactes 1961–1970, Vol. 263.
131. De Gaulle-Lucet meeting, 25 July 1966, MAEF, SG, EM, Vol. 28; see also Katzenbach to Johnson, 10 December 1966, NARA, RG59, Executive Secretariat, NSC Meeting Files 1966–1968, Box 1.
132. Seydoux, *Mission Diplomatique*, p. 75.
133. De Gaulle-Erhard meeting 1, 21 July 1966, MAEF, CM, CdM, Vol. 384.
134. Vaïsse, *La grandeur*, p. 393. Erhard also wanted to appease the CDU's Gaullists after the electoral defeats of July 1966. See Schwartz, *Lyndon Johnson*, p. 109.
135. CIA report, 16 September 1966, LBJL, PP, NSF, Agency Files [AF], Box 36.
136. Charles de Gaulle, *LNC: XI*, (Paris: Plon, 1987), De Gaulle note, 11 October 1966, p. 28.
137. Frédéric Bozo, "The NATO Crisis of 1966–1967: A French Point of View," in *Strategic Triangle*, ed. Haftendorn, Soutou, Szabo, and Wells, p. 112.
138. Bozo, *Deux Stratégies*, p. 189.
139. Ibid., p. 170.
140. Giglioli, "Le retrait," pp. 21–22.
141. For a discussion of the debates within the U.S. government, see Wenger, "Crisis and Opportunity," pp. 34–39.
142. Schwartz, *Lyndon Johnson*, p. 104.
143. Bator to Johnson, 8 March 1966, LBJL, PP, NSF, CO, Box 177.

144. Memorandum From the President's Deputy Special Assistant for National Security Affairs (Bator) to President Johnson, 7 March 1966, Document 138, FRUS, 1964–1968, Vol. XIII. The U.S. government quickly realized it had to accept de Gaulle's decisions. As Johnson told Secretary of Defense Robert McNamara, "when a man asks you to leave his house, you don't argue; you get your hat and go." Lyndon Johnson, *The Vantage Point: Perspectives of the Presidency, 1963–1969* (London: Weidenfeld and Nicolson, 1972), p. 305.

145. Courcel to Couve de Murville, Telegram 961-964, 11 March 1966, DDF, 1966, Tome I.

146. See, for example, Wenger, "Crisis and Opportunity," pp. 34–61; James Ellison, "Defeating the General: Anglo-American Relations, Europe and the NATO Crisis of 1966," *Cold War History*, Vol.6/1 (2006), especially pp. 94–102.

147. See chapter 1, endnote 197; Bozo, *Deux Stratégies*, pp. 180–81.

148. Scope Paper, 7 December 1966, Document 223, FRUS, 1964–1968, Vol. XIII; Bozo, *Deux Stratégies*, p. 170.

149. Speech to *l'Assemblée Nationale*, 3 November 1966, FNSP, CM Carton 2.

150. Peyrefitte, *C'était de Gaulle: vol. 3*, p. 192.

151. Pompidou-Wilson meeting, 6 July 1966, MAEF, SG, EM, Vol. 27.

152. Circular Telegram 196, 12 July 1966, MAEF, Europe, URSS 1966–1970, Vol. 2665; Interview with Jacques Andréani, Paris, 15 February 2006.

153. Moscow to FO, Telegram 1325, 11 July 1966, UK-NA, PREM 13/902.

154. McBride to State Department, Telegram 2163, 16 August 1966, NARA, RG59, CFPF, 1964–1966, Box 2188.

155. Peyrefitte, *C'était de Gaulle: vol. 3*, p. 160.

156. Wormser to Couve de Murville, Telegram 5042-5057, 21 November 1966, MAEF, Europe, URSS 1966–1970, Vol. 2665. Debré, the French finance minister, feared that de Gaulle's opening to the Soviet Union would come to nothing unless there were a determined effort to implement policy at the higher levels. Franco-Soviet commercial exchanges only amounted to 2 percent of Franco-Soviet trade. See Reilly to Brown, 2 December 1966, UK-NA, FO 371/189114; Michel Debré, *Trois Républiques pour une France: mémoires tome IV* (Paris: Albin Michel, 1993), pp. 133–34.

157. Baudet to Couve de Murville, Telegram 3879-3938, 23 August 1966, MAEF, Europe, URSS 1966–1970, Vol. 2665.

158. Peyrefitte, *C'était de Gaulle: vol. 3*, p. 153.

159. De Gaulle-Zorin meeting, 23 September 1966, MAEF, CM, CdM, Vol. 384.

160. Wolton, *France sous influence*, p. 429.

161. De Gaulle-Kosygin meeting, 1 December 1966, MAEF, SG, EM, Vol. 29.

162. De Gaulle-Kosygin meeting 1, 2 December 1966, MAEF, SG, EM, Vol. 29.

163. De Gaulle-Kosygin meeting 1, 8 December 1966, MAEF, CM, CdM, Vol. 385.

164. Peyrefitte, *C'était de Gaulle: vol. 3*, Meeting 5 December 66, 206.

165. De Gaulle-Brandt meeting, 16 December 1966, MAEF, SG, EM, Vol. 29.

166. Alphand, *L'étonnement*, Diary entry 18 December 1966, p. 482.

167. See, for example, Franco-Soviet Communiqué, 8 December 1966, and Couve de Murville Interview, 16 December 1966, DF, PEF, 1966–1967.

168. Vaïsse, *La grandeur*, p. 534.

169. De Gaulle, *DM:V*, p. 130.

170. Ibid., p. 105.

171. Ibid.

172. Schreiber, *Les Actions*, p. 108.

173. De Gaulle, *DM:V*, p. 103.

174. Prate, *Les Batailles*, p. 164. GDP grew by 5.2 percent in 1966. IFOP, *De Gaulle*, p. 260. Support for de Gaulle's foreign policy was consistently high during 1966. See Annex 7.
175. De Gaulle, *LNC: XI*, Draft for a manifesto on general policy, undated, p. 50.
176. François Seydoux to Couve de Murville, Telegram 7063-7069, 13 December 1966, MAEF: Europe, Allemagne 1961–1970, Vol. 1608.

Chapter 5

1. Haftendorn, *NATO*, p. 59.
2. Telegram From the Department of State to the Mission to the North Atlantic Treaty Organization and European Regional Organizations, 6 April 1967, Document 245, FRUS, 1964–1968, Vol. XIII.
3. Bozo, *Deux Stratégies*, pp. 188–89. The Ailleret-Lemnitzer negotiations were stalled because of differences on the format—the U.S. still refused an exchange of letters—and the political content of the agreement. See Vice-Admiral d'Escadre to Pompidou, 24 March 1967, DDF, 1967, Tome I; see chapter 4, endnote 21 for discussion of the pipeline.
4. Lawrence Kaplan, "The US and NATO in the Johnson Years," in *The Johnson Years, volume three*, ed. Robert Divine (Kansas: University Press of Kansas, 1994), p. 134.
5. Stromseth, *Origins of Flexible Response*, p. 194; Bozo, *Deux Stratégies*, p. 182.
6. Bozo, *Deux Stratégies*, p. 183.
7. See Locher, and Nuenlist, "What Role for NATO?" pp. 193–94 for Pearson's ideas.
8. Interview with Pierre Harmel, Brussels, 2 April 2004.
9. NATO Council Meeting *Communiqué*, 16 December 1966, DF, PEF, 1966–1967.
10. Telegram From the Department of State to the Embassy in Belgium, 26 November 1966, Document 221, FRUS, 1964–1968, Vol. XIII.
11. Ellison, *Rising to the Gaullist Challenge*, pp. 111–12.
12. Circular Telegram From the Department of State to the Posts in the NATO Capitals, 11 February 1967, Document 236, FRUS, 1964–1968, Vol. XIII.
13. See NATO press release outlining the subjects studied by the four subgroups of the Special Group on the Future Tasks of the Alliance and their members, 13 April 1967, NATO Archives, Future Tasks of the Alliance [Harmel Report Documents], Vol. 2 Document 53; Helga Haftendorn, "The Adaptation of the NATO Alliance to a Period of Détente: The 1967 Harmel Report," in *Crises and Compromises*, ed. Loth, pp. 292–93.
14. Circular Telegram From the Department of State to the Posts in the NATO Capitals, 11 February 1967, Document 236, FRUS, 1964–1968, Vol. XIII.
15. Alphand-Eugene Rostow meeting, 14 February 1967, MAEF, Pactes 1961–1970, Vol. 276.
16. Dromer to De Gaulle 31 January 1966, and Note by De Gaulle, 25 February 1966, ANF, 5AG1, Carton 28, Affaires Économiques Conseils Restreints. De Gaulle believed gold was the only valid international currency and he dismissed plans to create any new international currency reserve units. Moreover, he felt that France's "isolation" was meaningless as long as its balance of payments was in good shape. See De Gaulle, *LNC: X*, Personal Note, 31 January 1966, p. 245.
17. ; chapter 1, endnote 196; Solomon, *Monetary System*, pp. 130–31; Morse, *Foreign Policy*, p. 236. France feared that the creation of reserve assets would just perpetuate American dominance under different conditions.
18. Strange, *International Economic Relations*, p. 230.

19. See Communiqué after the Hague G10 meeting, 26 July 1966, DF, PEF, 1966–1967; Brunet Circular Telegram 213, 1 August 1966, MAEF, Direction Économique, Coopération Économique 1967–1974, Vol. 884.

20. De Vries, *International Monetary Fund*, p. 99; Strange, *International Economic Relations*, p. 238. The IMF's involvement was a blow because France considered it a tool of U.S. domination and the dollar hegemony. See Jean-Yves Haberer, "Les relations monétaires extérieures de janvier 1966 à fin mai 1968," in *DGESS III*, ed. Institut Charles de Gaulle, p. 156.

21. Brunet Circular Telegram 213, 1 August 1966, MAEF, Direction Économique, Coopération Économique 1967–1974, Vol. 884; Solomon, *Monetary System*, pp. 133–34.

22. Debré, *Mémoires IV*, p. 164.

23. See Note 239 of Direction des Affaires Économiques et Financières, 15 December 1966, DDF, 1966, Tome II; Preeg, *Traders and Diplomats*, pp. 139–41; Evans, *Kennedy Round*, pp. 238–39; Zeiler, *American Trade*, p. 225.

24. Note 167 of Direction des Affaires Économiques et Financières, 22 September 1966, DDF, 1966, Tome II.

25. Harold Wilson, *The Labour Government, 1964–1970: A Personal Record* (London: Weidenfeld and Nicolson, 1971), p. 299. For more on the British decision to probe the six, see Parr, *Britain's Policy*, especially pp. 70–95.

26. Parr, *Britain's Policy*, p. 101.

27. Note by Dromer, 7 January 1967, ANF, 5AG1, Carton 29, Affaires Économiques Conseils Restreints.

28. Conference in *l'École Polytechnique*, 24 May 1967, FNSP, Fonds Michel Debré Ministre des Finances [4DE] Carton 72.

29. Strange, *International Economic Relations*, pp. 244–45.

30. De Vries, *International Monetary Fund*, p. 131.

31. Prate, *Les Batailles*, p. 222; Catherine Schenk, "Sterling, International Monetary Reform and Britain's Applications to Join the European Economic Community in the 1960s," *Contemporary European History*, Vol.11/3 (2002), p. 363; Note on Debré-French Ambassadors to the EEC states meeting, 9 January 1967, MAEF, Direction Économique, Coopération Économique 1967–1974, Vol. 886.

32. Communiqué of EEC Finance Ministers meeting in The Hague, 17 January 1967, S370, International Liquidity October 1966–January 1967, Economic Subject Files, October 1966–August 1967 1963, Box 173, IMF Archives; Hall to Southard, 27 March 1967, S370, International Liquidity March 1967, Economic Subject Files, October 1966–August 1967 1963, Box 173, IMF Archives.

33. Draft instructions for French delegates in international monetary meetings, 22 February 1967, ANF, 5AG1, Carton 29, Affaires Économiques Conseils Restreints.

34. EEC Official Communiqué, 18 April 1967, LBJL, Papers of Francis Bator [Bator], SF, Box 10.

35. Prate, *Les Batailles*, p. 224.

36. Instructions for French delegation in Washington, 21 April 1967, FNSP, 4DE Carton 6.

37. Strange, *International Economic Relations*, p. 247; Solomon, *Monetary System*, pp. 138–39; Bonn to State Department, Telegram 12594, 21 April 1967, LBJL, Private Papers, Henry Fowler [Fowler], Box 57.

38. Dromer to De Gaulle, 21 June 1966, ANF, 5AG1, Carton 32, Affaires Économiques.

39. De Vries, *International Monetary Fund*, p. 150.

40. For the tense 1967 negotiations, see Zeiler, *American Trade*, pp. 232–36; Preeg, *Traders and Diplomats*, pp. 159–92; Evans, *Kennedy Round*, pp. 265–73.

41. Johnson, *Vantage Point*, p. 312.

42. Note by Dromer, 7 January 1967, ANF, 5AG1, Carton 29, Affaires Économiques Conseils Restreints; Couve de Murville Circular Telegram 84, 21 March 1967, DDF, 1967, Tome I.
43. Zeiler, *American Trade*, pp. 237, 239; Couve de Murville Circular Telegram 132, 23 May 1967, DDF, 1967, Tome I.
44. Ludlow, *European Community*, p. 128.
45. See Couve de Murville-Brandt meeting, 28 April 1964, MAEF, SG, EM, Vol. 30.
46. De Gaulle, *DM: V,* p. 168.
47. Parr, *Britain's Policy*, pp. 111–13.
48. De Gaulle-Wilson meeting, 24 January 1967, MAEF, CM, CdM, Vol. 386.
49. Schenk, "Sterling, International Monetary Reform," p. 348; Gérard Bossuat, "De Gaulle et la seconde candidature britannique aux Communautés européennes 1966–1969," in *Crises and Compromises*, ed. Loth, p. 517.
50. Peyrefitte, *C'était de Gaulle: vol. 3*, Council of Ministers 1 February 1967, p. 267.
51. Couve de Murville, *Politique étrangère*, p. 418; Laurence Badel, "Le Quai d'Orsay, la Grande-Bretagne et l'élargissement de la Communauté (1963–1969)," in *Cinquante Ans après la déclaration Schuman: Histoire de la Construction Européenne*, ed. Michel Catala (Nantes: Ouest éditions, 2001), pp. 241, 247–50.
52. Peyrefitte, *C'était de Gaulle: vol. 3*, p. 267.
53. Wormser to Couve de Murville, 14 April 1967, FNSP, CM Carton 8.
54. Paris to FO, Telegram 255, 20 March 1967, UK-NA, Foreign and Commonwealth Office [FCO] 33/62.
55. See Peyrefitte, *C'était de Gaulle: vol. 3,* Council of Ministers 3 and 10 May 1967, pp. 268–72.
56. For the press conference, see De Gaulle, *DM: V,* pp. 156–74.
57. Parr, *Britain's Policy*, pp. 155, 160.
58. Conference of six Heads of State, 30 May 1967, FNSP, CM Carton 9.
59. CIA Memo, 1 August 1967, LBJL, PP, NSF, SF, Box 48; Boegner to Couve de Murville, Telegram 847-857, 27 June 1967, DDF, 1967, Tome I.
60. For the memorandums of conversation [memcons] of the summit, see MAEF, SG, EM, Vol. 29.
61. Peyrefitte, *C'était de Gaulle: vol. 3,* Council of Ministers 18 January 1967, p. 194.
62. Idem.
63. Note of the Direction des Affaires Politiques, Sous-Direction Europe Occidentale, 7 July 1967, DDF, 1967, Tome II. West German diplomacy walked a tightrope in regard to the British application to the EEC. The grand coalition wanted, on the one hand, to revive the Franco-German partnership and shared some of Paris's reservations about London's candidacy, especially over the weakness of the pound sterling. But, on the other hand, Bonn still supported London's accession in principle and did not want to be isolated from the other EEC members.
64. Katharina Böhmer, "'We Too Mean Business': Germany and the Second British Application," in *Harold Wilson and European Integration: Britain's Second Application to Join the EEC*, ed. Oliver Daddow (London: Cass, 2002), pp. 215–17; Solomon, *Monetary System,* p. 137.
65. Zimmermann, *Money and Security,* p. 223; Andreas Wilkens, "L'Europe en suspens. Willy Brandt et l'orientation de la politique européenne de l'Allemagne fédérale 1966–1969," in *Crises and Compromises*, ed. Loth, p. 327.
66. For a definition of offset see chapter 1, endnote 107.
67. See especially Zimmermann, *Money and Security*, pp. 192–207; Schwartz, *Lyndon Johnson*, pp. 115–21.
68. Quoted by Johnson, *Vantage Point,* p. 307.

69. Zimmermann, *Money and Security,* p. 209.
70. Memorandum of Conversation Rusk-Brandt, 8 February 1967, Document 235, FRUS, 1964–1968, Vol. XIII.
71. Dennis Bark and David Gress, *A History of West Germany, vol. 2* (Oxford: Blackwell, 1992), p. 99.
72. Schwartz, *Lyndon Johnson,* p. 152.
73. Zimmermann, *Money and Security,* pp. 220–27; Diane Kunz, *Butter and Guns: America's Cold War Economic Diplomacy* (New York: Free Press, 1997), p. 173–74.
74. De Gaulle-Kiesinger meeting, 25 April 1967, ANF, 5AG1, Carton 163, Allemagne RFA.
75. See Bator to Johnson, 21 April 1967, LBJL, PP, NSF, SF, Box 48; Bator to Rostow, 24 April 1967, LBJL, Bator, SF, Box 22.
76. Schwartz, *Lyndon Johnson,* p. 164. For trilateral negotiations, see Zimmermann, *Money and Security,* pp. 212–32.
77. Brunet-Neef meeting, 21 June 1967, MAEF, Direction Économique, Papiers Jean-Pierre Brunet [Brunet] 1966–1974, Vol. 53.
78. Memorandum of Conversation Fowler-Schiller, 19 June 1967, Document 129, FRUS, 1964–1968, Vol. VIII. For an example of Germans trying to act as brokers between Paris and Washington, see Bonn to State Department, Telegram 13443, 10 May 1967, LBJL, Private Papers, Fowler, Box 57.
79. De Gaulle-Kiesinger meeting 1, 13 January 1967, MAEF, SG, EM, Vol. 29.
80. See Couve de Murville-Brandt meeting 1, 13 January 1967, MAEF, SG, EM, Vol. 29.
81. Peyrefitte, *C'était de Gaulle: vol. 3,* Council of Ministers 18 January 1967, p. 194.
82. Couve de Murville-Brandt meeting 2, 13 January 1967, MAEF, SG, EM, Vol. 29.
83. See Beaumarchais-Meyer Lindenberg meeting, 17 February 1967, MAEF, CM, CdM, Vol. 387; Beaumarchais-Meyer Lindenberg meeting, 22 March 1967, MAEF, Direction Économique, Brunet 1966–1974, Vol. 54.
84. See Couve de Murville-Zorin meeting, 19 January 1967 and De Gaulle-Zorin meeting, 23 January 1967, MAEF, SG, EM, Vol. 29; Couve de Murville-Rapacki meeting, 26 January 1967, and De Gaulle-Rapacki meeting, 27 January 1967, MAEF, CM, CdM, Vol. 386.
85. See Garret Martin, "The Soviet Factor in Franco-German Relations, 1958–1969," in *A History of Franco-German Relations in Europe: From "Hereditary Enemies" to Partners,* ed. Carine Germond and Henning Turk (New York: Palgrave Macmillan, 2008), pp. 199–209.
86. On this idea of a triangular relationship, see Kolodziej, *French International Policy,* pp. 350–51; Newhouse, *De Gaulle,* p. 295; Bernard Ledwidge, "L'Europe de l'Atlantique à l'Oural: concepts et réalités," in *DGESS V,* ed. Institut Charles de Gaulle, p. 505; René Bloch, "L'Europe de l'Atlantique à l'Oural: concepts et réalités," in *DGESS V,* ed. Institut Charles de Gaulle, p. 513.
87. See Maillard, *Problème Allemand,* p. 231.
88. See Interview with French radio, 7 January 1967, FNSP, CM Carton 2.
89. For a discussion of the Concert of Nations, see chapter 4, endnote 74; the expression "multiple bilateralism" was coined by Georges-Henri Soutou during a conversation with the author.
90. Couve de Murville interview with *Le Figaro,* 30 January 1967, DF, PEF 1966–1967.
91. Paris to Couve de Murville, Telegram 8, 14 June 1967, MAEF, Pactes 1961–1970, Vol. 272.
92. Couve de Murville-Brandt meeting, 27 April 1967, MAEF, SG, EM, Vol. 30.
93. Rey, *La tentation,* p. 53.
94. Pompidou speech to *l'Assemblée Nationale,* 18 April 1967, DF, PEF, 1966–1967. Because of the Six Day War, the trip to Poland was later postponed to September 1967, and the one to Romania to May 1968.

95. Wolton, *France sous influence*, p. 443; Lefort, *Souvenirs et secrets*, p. 164.
96. Bohlen to Rusk, Airgram 1650, 19 April 1967, NARA, RG59, CFPF, 1967–1969, Box 2090.
97. Gorce, *France contre les empires*, p. 219.
98. Vaïsse, *La grandeur*, p. 433. French exports to the Soviet Union did increase by 105 percent in 1967, but the share of the Eastern bloc in overall French foreign trade remained limited, increasing from 2 percent in 1964 to 5 percent in 1968. See Gorce, *France contre les empires*, p. 215.
99. McBride to Rusk, Airgram 1255, 9 February 1967, NARA, RG59, CFPF, 1967–1969, Box 2089.
100. Bohlen to Rusk, Airgram 1436, 10 March 1967, NARA, RG59, CFPF, 1967–1969, Box 2089.
101. Note of MAEF, 26 May 1967, MAEF, Europe, Pologne 1966–1970, Vol. 2499. Only 2.4 percent of Polish imports came from France, compared to 6.4 percent for the U.K. and 2.7 percent for West Germany. Additionally, 1.6 percent of Polish exports went to France, compared to 6.4 percent to the U.K. and 5.4 percent to West Germany.
102. De Gaulle-Zorin meeting, 23 January 1967, MAEF, SG, EM, Vol. 29.
103. Paris to FO, Telegram 255, 20 March 1967, UK-NA, FCO 33/62.
104. Willy Brandt, *People and Politics: The Years 1960–1975* (London: Collins, 1978), pp. 168–69.
105. Timothy Garton Ash, *In Europe's Name: Germany and the Divided Continent* (New York: Random House, c1993), p. 54.
106. Beaumarchais-Meyer Lindenberg meeting, 10 January 1967, MAEF, Direction Économique, Brunet 1966–1974, Vol. 54.
107. Bark and Gress, *West Germany, vol. 2*, p. 101.
108. Brandt, *People and Politics*, pp. 168–69.
109. Wilkens, "L'Europe en suspens," p. 331.
110. Griffith, *Ostpolitik*, p. 141.
111. See endnote 84.
112. Newton, *Russia, France*, p. 79; Griffith, *Ostpolitik*, pp. 142–44; Wolfe, *Soviet Power*, p. 316.
113. Garton Ash, *In Europe's Name*, pp. 55–56.
114. Brandt, *People and Politics*, p. 172.
115. François Seydoux to Couve de Murville, Telegram 3955-3965, 30 June 1967, MAEF, Europe, Allemagne 1961–1970, Vol. 1608; Note of *Direction Europe Centrale*, 14 June 1967, MAEF, Europe, Allemagne 1961–1970, Vol. 1545.
116. Ball-Hasluck meeting, 13 April 1966, NARA, RG59, Bohlen, Box 34.
117. Erwin Weit, *Dans l'Ombre de Gomulka* (Paris: Robert Laffont, 1971), p. 188.
118. Georges-Henri Soutou, *La Guerre de cinquante ans: le conflit Est-Ouest 1943–1990* (Paris: Fayard, 2001), p. 472.
119. Newton, *Russia, France*, pp. 77–78.
120. Johnson speech to the National Conference of Editorial Writers in New York, 7 October 1966, LBJL, PP, NSF, Speech File, Box 5.
121. See Wolfe, *Soviet Power*, p. 267; Dumbrell, *President Johnson*, pp. 43–45.
122. Dobrynin, *In Confidence*, p. 162; Lucet to Couve de Murville, Telegram 297-305, 18 January 1967, DDF, 1967, Tome I.
123. De Gaulle, *DM: V,* Toast for Sihanouk, 21 February 1967, p. 147; De Gaulle speech to diplomatic corps, 1 January 1967, MAEF, Asie-Océanie, Conflit Vietnam 1955–1975, Vol. 163.
124. Manac'h to Lucet, Telegrams 706-707, 21 March 1967, MAEF, Asie-Océanie, Conflit Vietnam 1955–1975, Vol. 163.

125. Vaïsse, "De Gaulle et la guerre du Vietnam," p. 176.
126. Interview with French radio, 7 January 1967, FNSP, CM Carton 2.
127. Bohlen to Rusk, Telegram 10209, 10 January 1967, LBJL, PP, NSF, CO, Box 173.
128. For more on France and the Six Day War, see Garret Martin, "At Odds in the Middle East: Paris, Washington, and the Six-Day War," in *European-American Relations and the Middle East: From Suez to Iraq*, ed. Daniel Mockli and Victor Mauer (London: Routledge, 2010), pp. 62–76.
129. Samy Cohen, "De Gaulle et Israël: Le sens d'une rupture," in *Politique étrangère*, ed. Barnavi and Friedländer, pp. 193–95.
130. Eban Abba, *Personal Witness: Israel Through My Eyes* (London: Jonathan Cape, 1993), p. 339.
131. Vaïsse, *La grandeur,* p. 632. See, for example, Couve de Murville to Rochereau de la Sablière, Telegram 12-14, 19 January 1967, DDF, 1967, Tome I.
132. Recent literature on the Six Day War includes Michael B. Oren, *Six Days of War: June 1967 and the Making of the Modern Middle East* (New York: Oxford University Press, 2002) and Roland Popp, "Stumbling Decidedly into the Six-Day War," *Middle East Journal*, 60/2 (spring 2006), pp. 281–309.
133. For more on the coup in Damascus, see Mark Tessler, *A History of the Israeli-Palestinian Conflict* (Bloomington and Indianapolis: Indiana University Press, 1994), pp. 364–67.
134. William Quandt, *Peace Process: American Diplomacy and the Arab-Israeli Conflict since 1967*, third edition (Washington, D.C.: Brookings Institution Press, 2005), p. 24.
135. Mohamed Elsayed Gad, *Les relations franco-égyptiennes et le conflit israëlo-arabe, 1956–1970* (Lille: Atelier national de reproduction des thèses, 2004), p. 175.
136. Alphand, *L'étonnement*, p. 488.
137. Goldberg to Rusk, Telegram 5344, 18 May 1967, LBJL, PP, NSF, National Security Council Histories, Box 20; Roger Seydoux to Couve de Murville, Telegram 1043-1047, 15 May 1967, MAEF, Nations Unies et Organisations Internationales [NUOI], 1960–1969, Vol. 733.
138. See Circular Telegram from the Department of State to Certain Posts, 15 May 1967, Document 3, FRUS, 1964–1968, Vol. XIX. In 1950, Paris, London, and Washington had expressed their interest in the maintenance of peace between the Arab states and Israel and their opposition to an arms race and the use of force between any of the states in that region.
139. Washington to FO, Telegram 1710, 21 May 1967, UK-NA, PREM 13/1617.
140. See Washington to FO, Telegram 1723, 22 May 1967, UK-NA, PREM 13/1617; Alphand to Lucet, Telegram 964-967, 22 May 1967, MAEF, NUOI, 1960–1969, Vol. 733.
141. See Washington to FO, Telegram number 1742, 23 May 1967, UK-NA, PREM 13/1617; Telegram from the Embassy in France to the Department of State, 23 May 1967, Document 47, FRUS, 1964–1968, Vol. XIX.
142. Paris to FO, Telegram 484, 23 May 1967, UK-NA, PREM 13/1617.
143. Peyrefitte, *C'était de Gaulle: vol. 3*, pp. 276–77.
144. Lacouture, *De Gaulle: vol. 3*, p. 492.
145. Peyrefitte, *C'était de Gaulle, vol. 3*, p. 277.
146. Hafez Ismail, "La vision du général de Gaulle au conflit du Proche-Orient, 1967–1969," in *DGESS: VI*, ed. Institut Charles de Gaulle, p. 401.
147. Couve de Murville, *Politique étrangère*, p. 469.
148. De Gaulle-Naggar meeting, 25 May 1967, MAEF, CM, CdM, Vol. 387.
149. For the messages, see Eshkol to De Gaulle, 19 May 1967, and Eban to De Gaulle, 21 May 1967, MAEF, SG, EM, Vol. 30; Eban, *Personal Witness*, p. 370.
150. Eban, *Personal Witness*, pp. 372–75.

151. See Vaïsse, *La grandeur*, p. 634; Paul Marie de la Gorce, "La politique arabe du General de Gaulle," in *Politique étrangère*, ed. Barnavi and Friedländer, pp. 187–88; Cohen, "De Gaulle et Israël," pp. 196–99.

152. Lucet to Couve de Murville, Telegram 2724-2734, 24 May 1967, MAEF, NUOI, 1960–1969, Vol. 733; FO to Moscow, Telegram 1346, 25 May 1967, UK-NA, PREM 13/1618; Wilson to Johnson, 25 May 1967, LBJL, PP, NSF, CO, Box 106.

153. Wormser to Couve de Murville, Telegram 2069-2083, 28 May 1967, MAEF, NUOI, 1960–1969, Vol. 733.

154. Goldberg to Rusk, 28 May 1967, NARA, RG 59, Records of Secretary of State Dean Rusk [hereafter Rusk], Transcripts of Phone calls [hereafter Phone calls], Box 59.

155. Telegram from the Embassy in France to the Department of State, 2 June 1967, Document 133, FRUS, 1964–1968, Vol. XIX.

156. Official Declaration of French Council of Ministers, 2 June 1967, DF, PEF, 1966–1967.

157. Maurice Vaïsse, "Les crises de Cuba et du Proche-Orient dans les relations franco-soviétiques," in *De Gaulle*, ed. Vaïsse, p. 161. For the Kosygin-De Gaulle messages, see MAEF, SG, EM, Vol. 30.

158. De Gaulle-Nixon meeting, 8 June 1967, MAEF, CM, CdM, Vol. 387.

159. Peyrefitte, *C'était de Gaulle: vol. 3*, p. 278.

160. Speech to the National Assembly, 15 June 1967, and Speech to the UN, 22 June 1967, FNSP, CM Carton 2.

161. Alphand, *L'étonnement*, Diary entry 11 June 1967, p. 490.

162. Vaïsse, "Les crises de Cuba et du Proche-Orient," p. 157.

163. De Gaulle, *LNC: XI, Communiqué* at the end of the Council of Ministers, 21 June 1967, p. 119.

164. De Gaulle-Kosygin meeting, 16 June 1967, MAEF, CM, CdM, Vol. 387.

165. Speech to National Assembly, 15 June 1967, FSNP, CM Carton 2.

166. De Gaulle-Wilson meeting, 19 June 1967, MAEF, CM, CdM, vol. 387.

167. Bohlen to Rusk, Telegram 508, 11 July 1967, LBJL, PP, NSF, CO, Box 173.

168. Hartley, *Gaullism*, p. 240.

169. Quoted by Vaïsse, "Les crises de Cuba et du Proche-Orient," p. 159.

170. Alphand to Roger Seydoux, Telegram 634-637, 30 June 1967, MAEF, NUOI, 1960–1969, Vol. 734; Alphand to Roger Seydoux, Telegram 646-647, 2 July 1967, MAEF, NUOI, 1960–1969, Vol. 734; Couve de Murville, *Politique étrangère*, p. 473.

171. Roger Seydoux to Couve de Murville, Telegram 1864-1867, 30 June 1967, MAEF, NUOI, 1960–1969, Vol. 734; Lucet to Couve de Murville, Telegram 3381, 2 July 1967, MAEF, NUOI, 1960–1969, Vol. 734; Rusk to Goldberg, 3 July 1967, NARA, RG 59, Rusk, Phone calls, Box 59.

172. Vaïsse, *La grandeur*, p. 639.

173. D'Escrienne, *Le Général*, pp. 145–46; Gorce, "La politique arabe," p. 188. After visiting the military authorities of Israel and Egypt, Paul Marie de la Gorce had no doubt Israel would win any conflict, and he was told that de Gaulle shared this view.

174. On de Gaulle's domestic problems, see Bernstein and Milza, *France au XXème Siècle: Tome IV*, pp. 67–72.

175. Lefort, *Souvenirs et secrets*, pp. 196–97; Vaïsse, *La grandeur*, pp. 353–54. On 13 June, 57 percent of people were happy with de Gaulle's policies and 12 percent were unhappy; by 16 July, the numbers had dropped to 48 percent happy and 19 percent unhappy.

176. De Gaulle-Wilson meeting, 19 June 1967, MAEF, CM, CdM, Vol. 387; Peyrefitte, *C'était de Gaulle: vol. 3*, Council of Ministers 15 June 1967, p. 280.

177. Seydoux, *Mission Diplomatique*, p. 96; Maurice Vaïsse, "De Gaulle et Willy Brandt: deux non-conformistes au pouvoir," in *Willy Brandt und Frankreich*, ed. Horst Möller and Maurice Vaïsse (München: R. Oldenbourg, 2005), p. 108.

178. Telegram From the Mission to the North Atlantic Treaty Organization and European Regional Organizations to the Department of State, 17 June 1967, Document 258, FRUS, 1964–1968, Vol. XIII.
179. Soutou, *Guerre de cinquante ans*, p. 472; quoted by Roussel, *De Gaulle*, p. 829.
180. CIA memorandum on Middle East, 29 June 1967, LBJL, PP, NSF, Files of the Special Committee of the National Security Council, Box 3.
181. Peyrefitte, *C'était de Gaulle: vol. 3*, Council of Ministers 5 July 1967, p. 282.

Chapter 6

1. Henry Kissinger, *The White House Years* (London: Weidenfeld and Nicolson, 1979), p. 345.
2. De Gaulle-Hussein meeting, 4 July 1967, MAEF, CM, CdM, Vol. 388.
3. Bohlen to Rusk, Telegram 508, 11 July 1967, LBJL, PP, NSF, CO, Box 173.
4. Vaïsse, *La grandeur*, p. 639.
5. See Wallner to State Department, Airgram 312, 18 August 1967, NARA, RG59, CFPF, Box 2088. When asked for their views on France's position during the Arab-Israeli crisis, in June, 54 percent of the French public approved of their country's position, 18 percent disapproved, and 28 percent had no opinion; in July, when asked the same question, only 42 percent approved of France's position, 23 percent disapproved, and 35 percent had no opinion; in August, only 36 percent approved, 30 percent disapproved, and 34 percent had no opinion.
6. De Gaulle-Kiesinger meeting, 12 July 1967, MAEF, SG, EM, Vol. 31.
7. Telegram From the Embassy in France to the Department of State, 27 July 1967, Document 76, FRUS, 1964–1968, Vol. XII.
8. D'Escrienne, *Le Général*, p. 107.
9. De Gaulle, *DM:V*, p. 200.
10. See Annex 2. De Gaulle's numbers dropped from 65 percent satisfied, 26 percent dissatisfied, and 9 percent with no opinion in June, to 52 percent satisfied, 35 percent dissatisfied, and 13 percent with no opinion in October.
11. Bernstein et Milza, *France au XXème Siècle: Tome IV*, p. 74.
12. IFOP, *De Gaulle*, p. 281. In a survey on 4–8 August 1967, 18 percent approved of de Gaulle's position on the Quebec problem, 45 percent disapproved, and 37 percent had no opinion. See also Annex 8; Vaïsse, *La grandeur*, p. 354. Many ministers, including Pompidou and Couve de Murville, also disagreed with the General's actions on Quebec. See Peyrefitte, *C'était de Gaulle: vol. 3*, pp. 338–39, 349.
13. See Paris to State Department, Airgram 331, 23 August 1967, NARA, RG59, CFPF, 1967–1969, Box 2088.
14. Parr, *Britain's Policy*, p. 163.
15. Ludlow, *European Community*, p. 140.
16. Ellison, *Rising to the Gaullist Challenge*, p. 167.
17. Speech to the European Communities, 10–11 July 1967, FNSP, CM Carton 2.
18. Ludlow, *European Community*, p. 141.
19. Idem.
20. Bozo, "French Point of view," p. 115.
21. See Salle for Schweitzer, 5 July 1967, and G10 Communique for London Meeting, 18 July 1967, S370, International Liquidity July–August 1967, Economic Subject Files, October 1966–August 1967, Box 173, IMF Archives.
22. Telegram Debré to De Gaulle, 19 July 1967, FNSP, 4DE Carton 6. Reconstitution referred to the fact that the drawing rights, akin to forms of credit, ought to carry a repayment obligation.

23. Current Economic Developments, Issue 785, 2 August 1967, Document 136, FRUS, 1964–1968, Vol. VIII.
24. Note by *Secrétariat Général de la Présidence,* 23 August 1967, ANF, 5AG1, Carton 29, Affaires Économiques Conseils Restreints.
25. Morse, *Foreign Policy,* p. 241.
26. Strange, *International Economic Relations,* p. 246.
27. For the text of the agreement, see Communiqué after the London G10 meeting, 26 August 1967, DF, PEF 1966–1967.
28. Solomon, *Monetary System,* p. 142.
29. Idem.
30. De Vries, *International Monetary Fund,* p. 166.
31. See Memorandum of Conversation Johnson-Kiesinger, 15 August 1967, Document 263, FRUS, 1964–1968, Vol. XIII; De Gaulle-Kiesinger meeting, 13 July 1967, MAEF, SG, EM, Vol. 31.
32. See Memorandum of Conversation Rusk-Kiesinger, 15 August 1967, Document 227, FRUS, 1964–1968, Vol. XV; De Gaulle-Kiesinger meeting, 13 July 1967, MAEF, SG, EM, Vol. 31.
33. Compare Memorandum of Conversation Johnson-Kiesinger, 15 August 1967, Document 263, FRUS, 1964–1968, Vol. XIII with Memorandum of Conversation Rusk-Kiesinger, 15 August 1967, Document 227, FRUS, 1964–1968, Vol. XV.
34. CIA Memo, 1 August 1967, LBJL, PP, NSF, SF, Box 48.
35. Stoessel to Rusk, 14 July 1967, NARA, RG59, CFPF, 1967–1969, Box 2102.
36. De Quirielle, *A Hanoï,* p. 195.
37. Pompidou-Brezhnev meeting, 8 July 1967, MAEF, CM, CdM, Vol. 388.
38. Pompidou-Kosygin meeting 1, 4 July 1967, MAEF, CM, CdM, Vol. 388.
39. Pompidou-Kiesinger meeting, 12 July 1967, MAEF, SG, EM, Vol. 31.
40. De Gaulle-Kiesinger meeting, 12 July 1967, MAEF, SG, EM, Vol. 31.
41. François Seydoux to Couve de Murville, Telegram 4890-4893, 5 September 1967, MAEF: Europe, Pologne 1966–1970, Vol. 2500.
42. Note of De Beaumarchais, 18 August 1967, MAEF, Europe, Pologne 1966–1970, Vol. 2500.
43. Note by Tricot, 23 August 1967, ANF, 5AG1, Carton 182, Pologne. The grand coalition government in Bonn did not recognize the Oder-Neisse border, arguing instead that a final settlement of German-Polish borders would have to wait for a peace treaty. The government had to take into account the refugee parties who continued to hope that the land, which had been German prior to World War II and lost at the end of the war when Polish borders were moved to the West, could be recovered.
44. Peyrefitte, *C'était De Gaulle: vol. 3,* on the plane to Poland 6 September 1967, p. 293.
45. De Gaulle and Gomulka's speeches to the Polish Diet, 11 September 1967, DF, PEF, 1966–1967.
46. De Gaulle-Gomulka meeting, 11 September 1967, MAEF, CM, CdM, Vol. 388.
47. Peyrefitte, *C'était De Gaulle: vol. 3,* Council of Ministers 13 September 1967, p. 298.
48. Laszlo Salgo, "La politique européenne, de l'Atlantique à l'Oural, et la Hongrie," in *DGESS V,* ed. Institut Charles de Gaulle, p. 478; Peyrefitte, *C'était De Gaulle: vol. 1,* Meeting 9 September 1967, p. 47.
49. Rey, *La tentation,* p. 61.
50. *Le Monde* article, 13 September 1967, MAEF, Europe, Pologne 1966–1970, Vol. 2500.
51. See Lacouture, *De Gaulle: vol. 3,* p. 541 and Durandin, *France contre l'Amérique,* p. 101. On the one hand Vaïsse, *La grandeur,* p. 439 and Rey, *La tentation,* p. 61, claim that de Gaulle took a bold stance in favor of Polish independence that undoubtedly worried Mos-

cow; on the other hand, Wolton, *France sous influence*, p. 439 and Roussel, *De Gaulle*, pp. 843–44 see the trip as more of an embarrassment since "it was hard to find equivalents in the speeches in Poland which would credit the idea that de Gaulle maintained a good equilibrium between his policy towards the East and his policy towards the West."

52. Seydoux, *Mission Diplomatique*, p. 101.

53. De Gaulle's speech in Westerplatte, 10 September 1967, MAEF, Europe, Pologne 1966–1970, Vol. 2500; see Jarzabek, Wanda, "Rozmowa Charlesa de Gaulle'a z Wladyslawem Gomulka w czasie wizyty generala w Polsce we wrzesnu 1967 r" ("The four eyes conversation between Charles de Gaulle and Wladislaw Gomulka during the General's visit to Poland, September 1967"), *Dzieje Najnowsze* (*The Journal*), Vol. 32/4 (2000), p. 152.

54. Zorin-De Gaulle meeting, 4 October 1967, MAEF, SG, EM, Vol. 32.

55. Natalia Vassilieva, "L'URSS et le développement des relations de la France avec les pays d'Europe de l'Est (Pologne et Roumanie)," in *De Gaulle*, ed. Vaïsse, pp. 207–08.

56. Note of *Sous Direction Europe Orientale*, 18 October 1967, MAEF, Europe, Pologne 1966–1970, Vol. 2500.

57. Couve de Murville, *Politique étrangère*, p. 281.

58. Zorin-De Gaulle meeting, 4 October 1967, MAEF, SG, EM, Vol. 32.

59. Alphand-Zorin meeting, 20 September 1966, MAEF, Europe, URSS 1966–1970, Vol. 2666.

60. Zorin-De Gaulle meeting, 4 October 1967, MAEF, SG, EM, Vol. 32.

61. Couve de Murville-Brandt meeting, 17 October 1967, MAEF, CM, CdM, Vol. 389.

62. Memorandum of Conversation Rusk-Brandt, 15 August 1967, Document 225, FRUS, 1964–1968, Vol. XV.

63. François Seydoux to Couve de Murville, Telegram 6543-6547, 9 December 1967, MAEF, Europe, Allemagne 1961–1970, Vol. 1545.

64. Alphand, *L'étonnement*, Diary entry 22 October 1967, p. 494.

65. Note of *Sous-Direction Europe Centrale*, 22 November 1967, MAEF, Europe, Allemagne 1961–1970, Vol. 1608.

66. Leddy to Rusk, 11 September 1967, NARA, RG59, CFPF, 1967–1969, Box 2102.

67. De Gaulle, *LNC: XI*, De Gaulle to Pompidou, 15 September 1967, p. 134. According to Jean de la Grandville, then Director of the Quai d'Orsay's Service des Pactes, the French note of 31 August to the NATO embassies had not been properly cleared by the French government.

68. Note 348 of French delegation to North Atlantic Council, 20 July 1967, MAEF, Pactes 1961–1970, Vol. 276.

69. Frédéric Bozo, "Détente versus Alliance: France, the United States and the politics of the Harmel Report, 1964–1968," *Contemporary European History*, Vol. 7/3 (1998), p. 352.

70. Note du *Service des Pactes*, 5 October 1967, MAEF, Pactes 1961–1970, Vol. 276. For the negative French view on the draft report of the second subgroup, see Report by the Secretary of Sub-group 2 on the comments made after the draft report on the Ideological Foundation and Unity of the Alliance, 29 September 1967, NATO Archives, Harmel Report Documents, Vol. 5, Document 26.

71. For the agreement see Resolutions adopted in Rio, 29 September 1967, DF, PEF, 1966–1967.

72. Speech at the IMF Rio meeting, 26 September 1967, FNSP, 4DE Carton 73; Paris to Treasury, 4 October 1967, UK-NA, Treasury 312-2140.

73. Solomon, *Monetary System*, p. 143.

74. Debré to Fowler, 7 September 1967, LBJL, Bator, SF, Box 10.

75. Debré, *Mémoires IV*, p. 172.

76. Debré to Burin des Roziers, 2 October 1967, FNSP, 4DE Carton 6.
77. Parr, *Britain's Policy,* p. 164.
78. Ibid., p. 165.
79. Ludlow, *European Community,* p. 142.
80. N. Piers Ludlow, "A Short-term Defeat: The Community Institutions and the Second British Application to Join the EEC," in *Harold Wilson,* ed. Daddow, pp. 139–40.
81. Bozo, *Deux Stratégies,* p. 174.
82. Prate, *Les Batailles,* p. 225.
83. Cleveland to Rusk, Telegram 5, 15 October 1967, LBJL, PP, NSF, AF, Box 36.
84. Couve de Murville-Brandt meeting, 17 October 1967, MAEF, CM, CdM, Vol. 389.
85. Parr, *Britain's Policy,* p. 167.
86. Conseil sur les Affaires Économiques et Financières, 16 October 1967, ANF, 5AG1, Carton 29, Affaires Économiques Conseils Restreints.
87. Note of Debré, 14 September 1967, ANF, 5AG1, Carton 29, Affaires Économiques Conseils Restreints.
88. For an explanation of Article 108, see chapter 5 endnote 49.
89. Schenk, "Sterling, International Monetary Reform," p. 366.
90. Bossuat, "Seconde candidature britannique," p. 523.
91. Speech to the European Communities, 23 October 1967, FSNP, CM Carton 2.
92. Peyrefitte, *C'était de Gaulle: vol. 3,* p. 273. This was a change from De Gaulle's position in May. See chapter 5, endnote 55.
93. Alphand, *L'étonnement,* Diary entry 22 October 1967, p. 494.
94. Brunet-Lahr meeting, 2 November 1967, MAEF, Direction Économique, Papiers Jean-Pierre Brunet 1966–1974, Vol. 53.
95. Speech to *l'Assemblée Nationale,* 7 November 1967, FNSP, CM Carton 2.
96. Parr, *Britain's Policy,* p. 166.
97. Germond, "Cordial Potentiality," p. 53.
98. James Ellison, "Dealing with De Gaulle: Anglo-American Relations, NATO and the Second Application," in *Harold Wilson,* ed. Daddow, p. 180.
99. Memorandum of Conversation Rusk-Harmel, 27 September 1967, Document 267, FRUS, 1964–1968, Vol. XIII.
100. Circular Telegram From the Department of State to the Posts in the NATO Capitals, 4 October 1967, Document 268, FRUS, 1964–1968, Vol. XIII.
101. See Record of the Private Meeting of Permanent Representatives of countries furnishing Harmel exercise rapporteurs, 24 July 1967, NATO Archives, Harmel Report Documents, Vol. 8 Document 38; Record of meeting of rapporteurs of Sub-Groups for study on Future Tasks of the Alliance, 11 October 1967, NATO Archives, Harmel Report Documents, Vol. 9 Document 4.
102. Roger Seydoux to Couve de Murville, Telegram 459-462, 8 November 1967, MAEF, Pactes 1961–1970, Vol. 277.
103. Intelligence Note No. 904, 9 November 1967, Document 275, FRUS, 1964–1968, Vol. XIII.
104. Roger Seydoux to Couve de Murville, Telegram 673-675, 24 November 1967, MAEF, Pactes 1961–1970, Vol. 277. Note, Pierre Harmel also appealed to the French directly, taking into account some of their comments, as he pointed out during an interview, Brussels, 2 April 2004.
105. Telegram From the Mission to the North Atlantic Treaty Organization to the Department of State, 23 November 1967, Document 277, FRUS, 1964–1968, Vol. XIII.
106. IFOP, *De Gaulle,* p. 79. In a survey taken from 25 September–2 October, only 12 percent were in favor of leaving the Atlantic Alliance, 54 percent wanted France to stay in the Alliance, and 34 percent had no opinion. Bozo, "Détente versus Alliance," pp. 354–55.

107. Ellison, *Rising to the Gaullist Challenge,* p. 180.

108. De Gaulle, *DM:V,* p. 243.

109. Arran Hamilton, "Beyond the Sterling Devaluation: The Gold Crisis of March 1968," *Contemporary European History,* Vol. 17/1 (2008), p. 82.

110. See Raj Roy, "The Battle for Bretton Woods: America, Britain and the International Financial Crisis of October 1967–March 1968," *Cold War History,* 2/2 (2002), p. 47; Kunz, "American Economic Consequences," p. 95.

111. Hamilton, p. 82.

112. Solomon, *Monetary System,* p. 114.

113. Gavin, *Gold, Dollars, and Power,* p. 171; Paris to FO, Telegram 1161, 21 November 1967, UK-NA, PREM 13/1856.

114. De Gaulle, *DM:V,* p. 231.

115. De Gaulle, *DM:V,* pp. 232–33.

116. Lucet to Couve de Murville, Telegram 6405-6408, 7 December 1967, MAEF, Amérique, États-Unis 1964–1970, Vol. 577.

117. See Strange, *International Economic Relations,* p. 286.

118. CIA Intelligence Memorandum, 20 March 1968, LBJL, PP, NSF, CO, Box 174.

119. See footnote 6 of Memorandum From the President's Special Assistant (Rostow) to President Johnson, 15 December 1967, Document 158, FRUS, 1964–1968, Vol. VIII.

120. See General Charles Ailleret, "Défense 'dirigée' ou défense 'tous azimuts'?," *Revue de Défense Nationale,* December 1967.

121. Bozo, *Deux Stratégies,* pp. 183–84.

122. Wallner to Rusk, Telegram 7724, 11 December 1967, NARA, RG59, CFPF, 1967–1969, Box 1542.

123. Bozo, *Deux Stratégies,* p. 183.

124. Boegner to Couve de Murville, Telegram number 1641-1688, 20 December 1988, DDF, 1967, Tome II.

125. For the result of the meeting see Communiqué at end of EEC Council of Ministers, 19 December 1967, DF, PEF, 1966–1967.

126. Peyrefitte, *C'était de Gaulle: vol. 3,* p. 274.

127. Melissa Pine, *Harold Wilson and Europe: Pursuing Britain's Membership of the European Community* (London: I.B. Tauris & Co. Ltd., 2007), p. 21.

128. Idem.

129. Ludlow, *European Community,* p. 145.

130. Gavin, *Gold, Dollars, and Power,* pp. 172–73; Kunz, "American Economic Consequences," p. 96.

131. CIA Intelligence Memorandum, 20 March 1968, LBJL, PP, NSF, CO, Box 174.

132. Washington to FO, Telegram 3891, 8 December 1967, UK-NA, FCO 33/44.

133. See Note for Pompidou, 14 December 1967, ANF, 5AG1, Carton 33, Affaires Économiques ; Debré, *Mémoires IV,* p. 172.

134. Vaïsse, *La grandeur,* p. 640. According to Vaïsse, on p. 349, average approval for de Gaulle's foreign policy dropped three points in the second semester of 1967, from 52.6 percent to 49.5 percent.

135. Helga Haftendorn, "The NATO Crisis of 1966–1967: Confronting Germany with a Conflict of Priorities," in *Strategic Triangle,* ed. Haftendorn, Soutou, Szabo, and Wells, p. 96.

136. Bozo, *Deux Stratégies,* pp. 176–77; Vaïsse, *La grandeur,* p. 395.

137. Couve de Murville Interview with French Television, 14 December 1967, DF, PEF, 1966–1967.

138. Leprette to Couve de Murville, Telegram 6703-6708, 20 December 1967, MAEF, Amérique, États-Unis 1964–1970, Vol. 577.

Chapter 7

1. Viansson-Ponté, *République Gaullienne: vol. 2*, p. 388.
2. De Gaulle, *LNC: XI*, Note for the Council of Ministers, 3 April 1968, p. 210.
3. Sullivan, *France's Vietnam Policy*, p. 108.
4. Dean to Harriman, 9 February 1968, NARA, Files of Ambassador at Large Averell Harriman, 1967–1968, Box 2; Note number 76 of Direction des Affaires Politiques, Sous-Direction Asie-Océanie, 20 February 1968, DDF, 1968, Tome I.
5. Pierre Journoud, "La France, les États-Unis et la Guerre du Vietnam: L'Année 1968," in *Relations Franco-Américaines*, ed. Melandri and Ricard, pp. 186–89.
6. Lucet to Couve de Murville, Telegram number 2499, 3 May 1968, DDF, 1968, Tome I.
7. Ibid., p. 189.
8. Sullivan, *France's Vietnam Policy*, p. 109.
9. Dumbrell, *President Johnson*, p. 53.
10. Johnson, *Vantage Point*, pp. 480–85.
11. Wolfe, *Soviet Power*, p. 270.
12. Dobrynin, *In Confidence*, pp. 182–83.
13. Schwartz, *Lyndon Johnson*, p. 210.
14. Dobrynin, *In Confidence*, p. 182; Dumbrell, *President Johnson*, p. 82.
15. George Herring, "Tet and the Crisis of Hegemony," in *1968*, ed. Fink, Gassert, and Junker, p. 53.
16. For more details on Soviet criticisms of West German actions in Berlin and the preconditions for any agreement, see Note of *Sous-Direction Europe Orientale*, 5 February 1968, MAEF, Europe, URSS 1966–1970, Vol. 2666.
17. Garton Ash, *In Europe's Name*, p. 56.
18. Brandt to Couve de Murville, 5 February 1968, MAEF, Europe, Allemagne 1961–1970, Vol. 1609. Before both states established diplomatic relations, the French embassy defended West Germany's interests in Yugoslavia.
19. Seydoux to Couve de Murville, Telegram 1557-1561, 11 March 1968, DDF, 1968, Tome I.
20. McGhee, *At the Creation*, p. 247.
21. De Gaulle-Zorin meeting, 20 February 1958, MAEF, CM, CdM, Vol. 391.
22. FO to Paris, 19 April 1968, UK-NA, FCO 28/187; Paris to FO, 11 April 1968, UK-NA, FCO 33/119.
23. Wallner to State, Airgram 1751, 22 March 1968, NARA, RG59, CFPF, 1967–1969, Box 2104.
24. Note of *Sous-Direction Europe-Orientale*, 3 May 1968, MAEF, Europe, Organismes Internationaux et Grandes Questions Internationales 1966–1970, Vol. 2034.
25. Wormser to Couve de Murville, Telegram 1243-1246, 3 April 1968, MAEF, Europe, URSS 1966–1970, Vol. 2666.
26. Frank-Beaumarchais meeting, 13 March 1968, MAEF, CM, CdM, Vol. 391.
27. See Couve de Murville-Zorin meeting, 23 April 1968, MAEF, Europe, URSS 1966–1970, Vol. 2666; Note of *Direction des Affaires Politiques*, 8 May 1968, MAEF, SG, EM, Vol. 34.
28. Note of *Sous-Direction Europe-Orientale*, 3 May 1968, MAEF, Europe, Organismes Internationaux et Grandes Questions Internationales 1966–1970, Vol. 2034.
29. Newton, *Russia, France*, p. 79.
30. For more on the Prague Spring, see Mark Kramer, "The Czechoslovak Crisis and the Brezhnev Doctrine," in *1968*, ed. Fink, Gassert, and Junker; Rothschild and Wingfield, *Return to Diversity*, pp. 166–70.
31. Ibid., p. 170.

32. Lefort, *Souvenirs et secrets*, p. 231.
33. Frank-Beaumarchais meeting, 13 March 1968, MAEF, CM, CdM, Vol. 391.
34. Couve de Murville-Stewart meeting, 26 April 1968, MAEF, SG, EM, Vol. 33.
35. Pierre Messmer, *Après Tant De Batailles: Mémoires* (Paris: Editions Albin Michel, 1992), p. 299.
36. See Rey, *La tentation*, p. 61; Lefort, *Souvenirs et secrets*, p. 248.
37. See De Gaulle, *DM: V*, Speech to the Great National Assembly of Romania, pp. 281–82; De Gaulle-Ceauşescu meeting, 14 May 1968, MAEF, SG, EM, Vol. 34.
38. Paris to FO, 30 May 1968, UK-NA, FCO 33/46.
39. Wolton, *France sous influence*, p. 445.
40. Hughes to Rusk, Intelligence Note 377, 21 May 1968, NARA, RG59, CFPF, 1967–1969, Box 2091.
41. Marie-Pierre Rey, "'De Gaulle, French Diplomacy, and Franco-Soviet Relations as Seen from Moscow," in *Globalizing de Gaulle*, ed. Nuenlist, Locher, and Martin, p. 36.
42. Telegram From the Department of State to the Mission to the North Atlantic Treaty Organization, 22 February 1968, Document 291, FRUS, 1964–1968, Vol. XIII.
43. Note du *Service des Pactes*, 20 June 1968, MAEF, Pactes 1961–1970, Vol. 277.
44. See the example of Belgium in Note du *Service des Pactes*, 4 May 1968, MAEF, Pactes 1961–1970, Vol. 277.
45. Intelligence Note 512, 28 June 1968, Document 316, FRUS, 1964–1968, Vol. XIII.
46. Gavin, *Gold, Dollars, and Power*, p. 178.
47. Note by Prate, 3 January 1968, ANF, 5AG1, Carton 34, Affaires Économiques.
48. Debré to De Gaulle, 6 January 1968, FNSP, 4DE Carton 7.
49. Debré-Kosygin meeting, 11 January 1968, ANF, 5AG1, Carton 188, URSS. Debré implicitly suggested that a Soviet participation in the IMF could act as a counterweight to American dominance within the Organization!
50. Peyrefitte, *C'était de Gaulle: vol. 3*, p. 284.
51. Note of *Direction des Affaires Économiques et Financières*, 31 January 1968, MAEF, Direction Économique, Coopération Économique 1967–1974, Vol. 884.
52. Note by Prate, 8 February 1968, ANF, 5AG1, Carton 34, Affaires Économiques.
53. Debré to Schiller, 9 February 1968, ANF, 5AG1, Carton 48, Affaires Économiques.
54. Debré-Schiller meeting, 15 February 1968, ANF, 5AG1, Carton 164, Allemagne RFA.
55. Seydoux, *Mission Diplomatique*, p. 105; see also Vaïsse, "De Gaulle et Brandt," p. 110.
56. De Gaulle-Luebke meeting, 5 February 1968, MAEF, SG, EM, Vol. 33.
57. Alphand, *L'étonnement*, Diary entry 11 February 1968, p. 500.
58. Ludlow, *European Community*, p. 146.
59. Brunet-Lahr meeting, 16 January 1968, MAEF, Direction Economique, Papiers Jean-Pierre Brunet 1967–1974, Vol. 53.
60. For the summit conversations, see MAEF: CM, CdM, Vol. 391 and MAEF: SG, EM, Vol. 33. For the declaration, see 16 February 1968, DDF, 1968, Tome I.
61. Telegram From the Embassy in Germany to the Department of State, 23 February 1968, Document 292, FRUS, 1964–1968, Vol. XIII.
62. Pine, *Harold Wilson and Europe*, pp. 50–51.
63. Ludlow, *European Community*, p. 150.
64. Note by Prate, 27 February 1968, ANF, 5AG1, Carton 34, Affaires Économiques.
65. See Debré to Barre, 29 February 1968 and Debré to Couve de Murville, 3 March 1968, FNSP, 4DE Carton 7.
66. Roy, "Battle for Bretton Woods," p. 51.
67. Hamilton, "Beyond the Sterling Devaluation," p. 89.
68. Solomon, *Monetary System*, pp. 117–18.

69. Roy, "Battle for Bretton Woods," p. 56; Schwartz, *Lyndon Johnson*, p. 200.
70. Eugene Rostow report, 13 March 1968, LBJL, Bator, SF, Box 10.
71. Solomon, *Monetary System*, p. 120.
72. Strange, *International Economic Relations*, pp. 290–91.
73. Schwartz, *Lyndon Johnson*, p. 202.
74. Gavin, *Gold, Dollars, and Power*, pp. 182–84.
75. Morse, *Foreign Policy*, p. 243.
76. See *Le Monde* article, 17 March 1968, FNSP, 4DE Carton 28, and De Gaulle's official declaration, 20 March 1968, DF, PEF 1968–1969.
77. Debré to De Gaulle, 18 March 1968, FNSP, 4DE Carton 7.
78. CIA Intelligence Memo, 20 March 1968, LBJL, PP, NSF, CO, Box 174.
79. See Peyrefitte, *C'était De Gaulle: vol. 3*, Council of Ministers 20 March 1968, pp. 285–87 and Debré, *Mémoires IV*, p. 174.
80. Prate, *Les Batailles*, p. 226.
81. See Note by Prate, 29 March 1968, ANF, 5AG1, Carton 35, Affaires Économiques, and Final Debré speech at the G10 Stockholm meeting, 30 March 1968, FNSP, 4DE Vol. 74.
82. Memo for Johnson, 30 March 1968, LBJL, PP, White House Central Files, CO, Box 30.
83. De Vries, *International Monetary Fund*, p. 175.
84. Gavin, *Gold, Dollars, and Power*, p. 185.
85. Kunz, "American Economic Consequences," in pp. 104–05.
86. Quoted by Allin, "De Gaulle and American Power," p. 110.
87. Kunz, "American Economic Consequences," p. 108; Bonn to FO, Telegram 480, 21 March 1968, UK-NA, PREM 13/2091.
88. Peyrefitte, *C'était De Gaulle: vol. 3*, Council of Ministers 3 April 1968, p. 287.
89. Debré interview with ORTF, 1 April 1968, DF, PEF, 1968–1969.
90. Schwartz, *Lyndon Johnson*, p. 204.
91. Lacouture, *De Gaulle: vol. 3*, p. 666.
92. Patrick Brogan, "France: stable, prosperous, and infuriating," *The Times*, 6 May 1968, p. 9.
93. For statistics on the rising number of students, see the table in Jeremi Suri, *Power and Protest: Global Revolution and the Rise of Détente* (Cambridge, Massachusetts: Harvard University Press, 2003), p. 269.
94. Rod Kedward, *La vie en bleu: France and the French since 1900* (London: Allen Lane, 2005), p. 417.
95. There is a large and varied literature, including many memoirs, on the origins and events of May 1968. For a chronicle of the events, see Adrien Dansette, *Mai 68* (Paris: Plon, 1971); for a more analytical approach, Geneviève Dreyfus-Armand (ed.), *Les Années 1968: Le temps de la contestation* (Bruxelles: Editions Complexe, 2000) and Jacques Capdevielle and René Mouriaux, *Mai 68: l'entre-deux de la modernité': histoire de trente ans* (Paris: Presses de la fondation nationale des sciences politiques, 1988); for a more international perspective of the protest movements, see David Caute, *Sixty-eight: The Year of the Barricades* (London: Hamilton, 1988) and Suri, *Power and Protest*.
96. Bernstein and Milza, *France au XXème Siècle: Tome IV*, pp. 85–87.
97. For the speech, see De Gaulle, *DM:V*, pp. 292–93.
98. IFOP, *De Gaulle*, pp. 256–58, in August 1967, 22 percent thought that foreign policy was France's most important problem. This number dropped to 15 percent in May 1968 and 9 percent in September 1968.
99. Alphand, *L'étonnement*, Diary entry 19 May 1968, p. 503.
100. Patricia Dillon, "La stratégie monétaire internationale de Charles de Gaulle," in *DGESS III*, ed. Institut Charles de Gaulle, p. 137.

101. IFOP, *De Gaulle*, p. 282. Comparing 1965 and 1968, the number of people who thought France could achieve independence drop from 46 percent to 34 percent in regard to the political realm, from 41 percent to 26 percent for the economic sphere, and from 31 percent to 28 percent for defense.

102. This divergence emerges clearly in the Council of Ministers of 23 May. See Peyrefitte, *C'était De Gaulle: vol. 3*, pp. 533–40.

103. Georges Pompidou, *Pour rétablir une vérité* (Paris: Flammarion, 1982), especially pp. 188–204.

104. Peyrefitte, *C'était De Gaulle: vol. 3*, Meeting 14 June 1968, p. 578.

105. Bernstein and Milza, *France au XXème Siècle: Tome IV*, p. 151.

106. See Debré to Foccart, 28 May 1968, FNSP, 4DE Carton 7; Pompidou, *Pour rétablir une vérité*, p. 196; Vaïsse, *La grandeur*, p. 406.

107. Telegram From the Embassy in France to the Department of State, 28 May 1968, Document 79, FRUS, 1964–1968, Vol. XII.

108. De Gaulle could only recognize the failure of his speech, saying "J'ai mis à côté de la plaque," see Peyrefitte, *C'était De Gaulle: vol. 3*, Meeting 24 May 1968, p. 543.

109. Olivier Guichard, *Mon Général* (Paris: B. Grasset, 1980), p. 432.

110. Debré, *Mémoires IV*, p. 217.

111. Pompidou, *Pour rétablir une vérité*, p. 196.

112. Debré, *Mémoires IV*, p. 229.

113. Roger Seydoux to Debré, Telegram 1025-1033, 5 July 1968, MAEF, Pactes 1961–1970, Vol. 272 bis.

114. Shriver to Rusk, Telegram 18471, 24 July 1968, NARA, RG59, CFPF, 1967–1969, Box 2102; Paris to FO, Telegram 719, 12 July 1968, UK-NA, FCO 33/45.

115. Debré Interview with Paris-Presse-L'Intransigeant, 10–11 July 1968, DF, PEF, 1968–1969.

116. Note of Direction des Affaires Politiques, Sous-Direction Europe-Orientale, 11 July 1968, DDF, 1968, Tome II.

117. See especially Kramer, "Czechoslovak Crisis," pp. 133–51; Rothschild and Wingfield, *Return to Diversity*, p. 171.

118. Newton, *Russia, France*, p. 80; see also Zubok, *A Failed Empire*, pp. 207–09.

119. Debré, *Mémoires IV*, p. 259.

120. Alphand, *L'étonnement*, Diary entry 25 August 1968, p. 513.

121. Paris to FO, Telegram 719, 12 July 1968, UK-NA, FCO 33/45.

122. Solomon, *Monetary System*, pp. 151–55.

123. Vaïsse, *La grandeur*, p. 443.

Conclusion

1. De Gaulle, *DM: V*, pp. 333–35.

2. Quoted by Jackson, *De Gaulle*, p. 138.

3. D'Escrienne, *Le Général*, pp. 218–19; Vaïsse, *La grandeur*, pp. 682–83.

4. Peyrefitte, *C'était de Gaulle: vol. 1*, Meeting 13 February 1963, p. 283.

5. Soutou, "De Gaulle's France," p. 173.

6. Soutou, "La décision française," pp. 194–96.

7. Devillers, "L'Asie," p. 310.

8. Charbonnel, *L'Aventure*, p. 128.

9. De Gaulle-Rockefeller meeting, 3 October 1963, MAEF, CM, CdM, Vol. 376.

10. Jackson, *De Gaulle*, pp. 118–19.

11. Hoffmann, *Essais*, p. 371; Vaïsse, *La grandeur*, p. 676.
12. David Calleo quote from Allin, "De Gaulle and American Power," p. 110.
13. See, for example, Vaïsse, *La grandeur*, p. 679 for a detailed listing of these contradictions.
14. Lacouture, *De Gaulle: vol. 3*, p. 556.
15. Hoffmann, *Essais*, p. 375.
16. Quoted in Vaïsse, *La grandeur*, p. 680.
17. Jackson, *De Gaulle*, p. 143.
18. Ludlow, "Protector of Atlantic Unity."
19. Lanxin Xiang, "De Gaulle and the 'Eternal China,'" in *De Gaulle's Legacy of Ideas*, ed. Rowland, pp. 79–80.
20. Gaddis, *The Cold War*, p. 143.

BIBLIOGRAPHY

Archival Material

France

Archives Nationales: Paris

5ème République Archives de la Présidence De Gaulle [5 AG1]:

    Affaires Économiques: Cartons 32–35, 48.

    Affaires Économiques Conseils Restreints: Cartons 28–29.

    Allemagne RFA: Cartons 161–165.

    Biafra: Carton 211.

    Chine Populaire: Carton 226.

    Etats-Unis: Cartons 201, 204–205.

    Pologne: Carton 182.

    Roumanie: Carton 183.

    Sud-Vietnam: Carton 241.

    URSS: Cartons 186–188, 190.

    Voyage du Général de Gaulle en Amérique Latine: Carton 198.

Ministère des Affaires Etrangères (Quai d'Orsay): Paris

Afrique-Levant:

    Israël, 1966–1970.

Amérique:

    Etats-Unis, 1952–1963.

    Etats-Unis, 1964–1970.

    Voyage du Général de Gaulle en Amérique du Sud, 1964.

Archives Orales:

    AO 10 Roger Seydoux.

    AO 19 Jean-Marc Boegner.

    AO 21 Jean Laloy.

    AO 26 Charles Lucet.

AO 29 Maurice Couve de Murville.

AO 39 Jean-Pierre Brunet.

Asie-Océanie:

    Chine, 1956–1967.

    Conflit Vietnam, 1955–1975.

    Sud-Vietnam, 1954–1964.

Cabinet du Ministre:

    Couve de Murville, 1958–1968.

Direction Économique:

    Coopération Economique, 1961–1966.

    Coopération Economique, 1967–1974.

    Papiers Olivier Wormser, 1954–1966.

    Papiers Jean-Pierre Brunet, 1966–1974.

Europe:

    Allemagne, 1961–1970.

    Organismes Internationaux et Grandes Questions Internationales 1966–1970.

    Pologne, 1966–1970.

    Roumanie, 1961–1970.

    URSS, 1961–1965.

    URSS, 1966–1970.

Nations Unies et Organisations Internationales:

    NUOI, 1960–1969.

Secrétariat Général:

    Entretiens et Messages, 1956–1971.

Service des Pactes:

    Pactes, 1961–1970.

Fondation Nationale des Sciences Politiques—Archives d'histoire contemporaine: Paris

Fonds Maurice Couve de Murville, 1958–1989.

Fonds Michel Debré Ministre des Finances, 1966–1968.

Fonds Jean Sainteny, 1939–1978.

United States

National Archives Record Administration: College Park, Maryland

RG59 Department of State Central Files:

    Bureau of European Affairs, Files of Robert Schaetzel Deputy Assistant Secretary for Atlantic Affairs.

    Central Foreign Policy Files 1963.

    Central Foreign Policy Files 1964–1966.

    Central Foreign Policy Files 1967–1969.

Executive Secretariat:

NSC Meeting Files 1966–68.

Secretary's and Under Secretary's Memoranda of Conversation, 1953–1964.

Files of Ambassador at Large Averell Harriman, 1967–1968.

Records of Ambassador Charles Bohlen.

Records of Policy Planning Council.

Records of Secretary of State Dean Rusk, Transcripts of Phone Calls.

Records of Under-Secretary of State George Ball, 1961–1966.

John F. Kennedy Presidential Library, Boston, Massachusetts

John Fitzgerald Kennedy Archives.

President's Office Files.

National Security Files.

Personal Papers

Christian Herter.

George Ball.

C. Douglas Dillon.

White House Central Files.

Lyndon B. Johnson Presidential Library, Austin, Texas

Lyndon Baines Johnson Archives.

Confidential Files.

National Security Files.

Telephone Conversations.

Personal Papers

Francis Bator.

Henry H. Fowler.

White House Central Files.

United Kingdom

The National Archives (Previously Public Record Office): Kew, Surrey

FCO17: Foreign and Commonwealth Office, Eastern Department and successors.

FCO28: Foreign and Commonwealth Office: Northern Department and East European and Soviet Department.

FCO33: Foreign and Commonwealth Office, Western Department.

FO371: Foreign Office General Political Files.

PREM11: Prime Minister's Office Files, 1951–64.

PREM13: Prime Minister's Office Files, 1964–70.

International Organizations

International Monetary Fund
S 370: International Liquidity, 1953–1981.

North Atlantic Treaty Organization
Future Tasks of the Alliance—"Harmel Report" (1967), 9 volumes, available online http://www.nato.int/cps/en/natolive/80830.htm

Published Documents

Documentation Française: La Politique Etrangère de la France, Textes et Documents, multiple volumes, 1966–1969.

Documents Diplomatiques Français, multiple volumes, 1963–1968.

Foreign Relations of the United States, 1961–1963: Volume V, Soviet Union.

Foreign Relations of the United States, 1961–1963: Volume XIII, Western Europe and Canada.

Foreign Relations of the United States, 1964–1968: Volume VIII, International Monetary and Trade Policy.

Foreign Relations of the United States, 1964–68: Volume XII, Western Europe.

Foreign Relations of the United States, 1964–68: Volume XIII, Western European Region.

Foreign Relations of the United States, 1964–1968: Volume XV, Germany and Berlin.

Foreign Relations of the United States, 1964–1968: Volume XVII, Eastern Europe.

Foreign Relations of the United States, 1964–1968: Volume XIX, Arab-Israeli Crisis and War, 1967.

Memoirs

Alphand, Hervé. *L'étonnement d'être: journal, 1939–1973.* Paris: Fayard, 1977.

Boegner, Jean-Marc. *Le Marché Commun de Six à Neuf.* Paris: Armand Colin, 1974.

Bohlen, Charles. *Witness to History, 1929–1969.* London: Weidenfeld and Nicolson, 1973.

Brandt, Willy. *People and Politics: The Years 1960–1975.* London: Collins, 1978.

Burin des Roziers, Étienne. *Retour aux Sources: 1962, l'année décisive.* Paris: Plon, 1986.

Charbonnel, Jean. *L'Aventure de la Fidélité.* Paris: Editions du Seuil, 1976.

———. *A la gauche du Général.* Paris: Plon, 1996.

Couve de Murville, Maurice. *Une politique étrangère, 1958–1969.* Paris: Plon, 1971.

———. *Le Monde en Face: Entretiens avec Maurice Delarue.* Paris: Plon, 1989.

D'Escrienne, Jean. *Le Général m'a dit: 1966–1970.* Paris : Plon, 1973.

De Gaulle, Charles. *Le Fil de l'Epée.* Paris: Berger-Levrault, 1944.

———. *Discours et Messages, vols IV–V.* Paris: Plon, 1970.

———. *Memoirs of Hope: Renewal and Endeavor.* New York: Simon and Schuster, 1971.

———. *Lettres, notes et carnets, vols IX–XI.* Paris: Plon, 1986–1987.

De Quirielle, François. *A Hanoï sous les Bombes Américaines: Journal d'un diplomate Français, 1966–1969*. Paris: Tallandier, 1992.

Debré, Michel. *Entretiens avec le Général de Gaulle, 1961–1969*. Paris: Albin Michel, 1993.

———. *Trois Républiques pour une France, vol IV*. Paris: Albin Michel, 1993.

Dobrynin, Anatoly. *In Confidence: Moscow's Ambassador to America's Six Cold War Presidents (1962–1986)*. New York: Times Books, Random House, 1995.

Dulong, Claude. *La Dernière Pagode*. Paris: B. Grasset, 1989.

Eban, Abba. *Personal Witness: Israel Through My Eyes*. London: Jonathan Cape, 1993.

Foccart, Jacques. *Foccart parle: entretiens avec Philippe Gaillard*. Paris: le Grand livre du mois: Fayard: Jeune Afrique, 1995.

———. *Journal de l'Elysée, tomes I–II*. Paris: Fayart, 1997–1998.

Froment-Meurice, Henri. *Vu du Quai, 1945–1983*. Paris: Fayard, 1998.

Guichard, Olivier. *Mon Général*. Paris: B. Grasset, 1980.

Guy, Claude. *En écoutant de Gaulle: journal 1946–1949*. Paris: B. Grasset, 1996.

Johnson, Lyndon Baines. *The Vantage Point: Perspectives of the Presidency, 1963–1969*. London: Weidenfeld and Nicolson, 1972.

Macmillan, Harold. *At the End of the Day, 1961–1963*. London: Macmillan, 1973.

Maillard, Pierre. *De Gaulle et l'Europe: Entre la Nation et Maastricht*. Paris: Taillandier, 1995.

———. *De Gaulle et le Problème Allemand: Les leçons d'un grand dessein*. Paris: Guibert, 2001.

Maneli, Mieczyslaw. *War of the Vanquished*. New York, Harper & Row, 1971.

Marjolin, Robert. *Architect of European Unity: Memoirs, 1911–1986*. London: Weidenfeld and Nicolson, 1989.

Mauriac, Claude. *Un autre de Gaulle: journal 1944–1954*. Paris: Hachette, 1970.

Mauriac, François. *De Gaulle*. Paris: Bernard Grasset, 1964.

McGhee, George. *At the Creation of a New Germany: From Adenauer to Brandt, An Ambassador's Account*. New Haven; London: Yale University Press, 1989.

Messmer, Pierre. *Après Tant De Batailles: Mémoires*. Paris: Editions Albin Michel, 1992.

Peyrefitte, Alain. *C'était de Gaulle, vols 1–3*. Paris: Fayard, 1994–2000.

Pisani, Edgar. *Le Général Indivis*. Paris: Albin Michel, 1974.

Pompidou, Georges. *Pour rétablir une vérité*. Paris: Flammarion, 1982.

Rusk, Dean. *As I Saw It*. London: Tauris, 1990.

Seydoux, François. *Dans L'Intimité Franco-Allemande: Une Mission Diplomatique*. Paris: Albatros, 1977.

Solomon, Robert. *The International Monetary System, 1945–1976: An Insider's View*. New York: Harper & Row, Publishers, 1977.

Soutou, Jean-Marie. *Un diplomate engagé : mémoires 1939–1979*. Paris: Editions de Fallois, c2011.

Spaak, Paul-Henri. *Combats Inachevés, vol 2*. Paris: Fayard, 1969.

Triboulet, Raymond. *Un Ministre du Général*. Paris: Plon, 1985.

Weit, Erwin. *Dans L'ombre de Gomulka*. Paris: Robert Laffont, 1971.

Wilson, Harold. *The Labour Government, 1964–1970*. London: Weidenfeld and Nicolson, 1971.

Books

Amson, Daniel. *De Gaulle et Israël.* Paris: Presses Universitaires de France, 1991.

Ashton, Nigel. *Kennedy, Macmillan, and the Cold War: The Irony of Interdependence.* Houndmills; Basingstoke; Hampshire; New York: Palgrave, 2002.

Baechler, Christian and Klaus-Jürgen Müller, ed. *Les tiers dans les relations franco-allemandes/ Dritte in den deutsch-französischen Beziehungen.* Munchen: Oldenbourg, 1996.

Bange, Oliver. *The EEC Crisis of 1963: Kennedy, Macmillan, de Gaulle and Adenauer in Conflict.* New York: St. Martin's Press in association with Institute of Contemporary British History, 1999.

Bark, Dennis and David Gress. *A History of West Germany, vol. 2.* Oxford: Blackwell, 1992.

Barnavi, Élie and Saül Friedländer, ed. *La politique étrangère du Général de Gaulle.* Paris: Presses Universitaires de France, 1985.

Bernstein, Serge and Pierre Milza. *Histoire de la France au XXème Siècle: Tome IV, 1958–1974.* Bruxelles: Editions Complexe, 1992.

Bitsch, Marie-Thérèse, ed. *Le Couple France-Allemagne et les Institutions Européennes: Une postérité pour le Plan Schuman?* Bruxelles: Bruylant, 2001.

Bortoli, Georges. *Une si longue bienveillance: les Français et l'URSS 1944–1991.* Paris: Plon, 1994.

Bozo, Frédéric. *La France et l'OTAN: de la guerre froide au nouvel ordre européen.* Paris; Milan; Barcelone: Masson, 1991.

———. *Deux Stratégies pour l'Europe: De Gaulle, les États-Unis et l'Alliance Atlantique, 1958–1969.* Paris: Plon, 1996.

Bozo, Frédéric, Marie-Pierre Rey, N. Piers Ludlow, and Rother, Bernd, ed. *Visions of the End of the Cold War in Europe (1945–1990).* New York: Berghahn Books, 2012.

Brocheux, Pierre, ed. *Du Conflit d'Indochine aux Conflits Indochinois.* Bruxelles: Editions Complexe, 2000.

Capdevielle Jacques and René Mouriaux. *Mai 68: l'entre-deux de la modernité: histoire de trente ans.* Paris: Presses de la fondation nationale des sciences politiques, 1988.

Catala, Michel, ed. *Cinquante Ans après la déclaration Schuman: Histoire de la Construction Européenne.* Nantes: Ouest éditions, 2001.

Caute, David. *Sixty-eight: The Year of the Barricades.* London: Hamilton, 1988.

Cerny, Philip. *The Politics of Grandeur: Ideological Aspects of de Gaulle's Foreign Policy.* Cambridge: Cambridge University Press, 1980.

Chang, Gordon. *Friends and Enemies: The United States, China, and the Soviet Union, 1948–1972.* Stanford, California: Stanford University Press, 1990.

Cohen, Warren and Nancy Tucker, ed. *Lyndon Johnson Confronts the World: American Foreign Policy, 1963–1968.* Cambridge; New York: Cambridge University Press, 1994.

Connelly, Matthew. *Diplomatic Revolution: Algeria's Fight for Independence and the Origins of the Post-cold War Era.* Oxford: Oxford University Press, 2002.

Costigliola, Frank. *France and the United States: The Cold Alliance Since World War II.* New York: Twayne Publishers; Toronto: Maxwell Macmillan Canada; New York: Maxwell Macmillan International, 1992.

Craig, Gordon and Francis Loewnheim. *The Diplomats, 1939–1979.* Princeton, NJ: Princeton University Press, 1994.

Daddow, Oliver, ed. *Harold Wilson and European Integration: Britain's Second Application to Join the EEC*. London; Portland, OR: Cass, 2002.

Dansette, Adrien. *Mai 68*. Paris: Plon, 1971.

De La Gorce, Paul-Marie. *La France contre les Empires*. Paris: Editions Bernard Grasset, 1969.

De Vries, Margaret Garritsen. *The International Monetary Fund, 1966–1971: The System under Stress*. Washington, D.C.: The Fund, 1976.

Divine, Robert, ed. *The Johnson Years, vol. 3*. Kansas: University Press of Kansas, 1994.

Dreyfus-Armand, Geneviève, ed. *Les Années 1968: Le temps de la contestation*. Bruxelles: Editions Complexe, 2000.

Dumbrell, John. *President Lyndon Johnson and Soviet Communism*. Manchester: Manchester University Press, 2004.

Durandin, Catherine. *La France contre l'Amérique*. Paris: Presses universitaires de France, 1994.

Ellison, James. *The United States, Britain and the Transatlantic Crisis: Rising to the Gaullist Challenge, 1963–1968*. Basingstoke: Palgrave Macmillan, 2007.

Evans, John Walker. *The Kennedy Round in American Trade Policy: The Twilight of the GATT?* Cambridge, M.A.: Harvard University Press, 1971.

Fink, Carole, Philipp Gassert, and Detlef Junker, ed. *1968: The World Transformed*. Washington, D.C.; German Historical Institute; Cambridge, England; New York, N.Y.: Cambridge University Press, 1998.

Fontaine, André. *Un Seul Lit pour Deux Rêves: Histoire de la "Détente" 1962–1981*. Paris: Fayart, 1981.

Gad, Mohamed Elsayed. *Les relations franco-égyptiennes et le conflit israëlo-arabe (1956–1970)*. Lille: Atelier national de reproduction des thèses, 2004.

Gaddis, John Lewis. *The Cold War: A New History*. New York: Penguin Press, 2005.

Gardner, Lloyd and Ted Gittinger, ed. *The Search for Peace in Vietnam, 1964–1968*. College Station: Texas A&M University Press, 2004.

Garton Ash, Timothy. *In Europe's Name: Germany and the Divided Continent*. New York: Random House, c1993

Gavin, Francis, Gold, Dollars, and Power: *The Politics of International Monetary Relations, 1958–1971*. Chapel Hill: University of North Carolina Press, 2004.

Germond, Carine and Henning Turk, ed. *A History of Franco-German Relations in Europe: From "Hereditary Enemies" to Partners*. New York: Palgrave Macmillan, 2008.

Giauque, Jeffrey. *Grand Designs and Visions of Unity: The Atlantic Powers and the Reorganization of Western Europe, 1955–1963*. Chapel Hill: University of North Carolina Press, 2002.

Gomart, Thomas. *Double Détente: Les relations Franco-Soviétiques de 1958 à 1964*. Paris: Publications de la Sorbonne, 2003.

Goscha, Christopher and Maurice Vaïsse, ed. *La Guerre du Vietnam et l'Europe, 1963–1973*. Bruxelles; Paris: Bruylant, 2003.

Gray, William Glenn. *Germany's Cold War: The Global Campaign to Isolate East Germany, 1949–1969*. Chapel Hill: University of North Carolina Press, 2003.

Griffith, William. *The Ostpolitik of the Federal Republic of Germany*. Cambridge, M.A.: MIT Press, 1978.

Haftendorn, Helga. *NATO and the Nuclear Revolution: A Crisis of Credibility, 1966–1967*. Oxford: Clarendon Press, 1996.

Haftendorn, Helga, Georges-Henri Soutou, Stephen Szabo, and Samuel Wells, ed. *The Strategic Triangle: France, Germany, and the United States in the Shaping of Europe.* Washington, D.C.: Woodrow Wilson Center Press; Baltimore: Johns Hopkins University Press, c2006.

Harder, Hans-Joachim, ed. *Von Truman bis Harmel: Die Bundesrepublik Deutschland im Spannungsfeld von NATO und europäischer Integration.* München: R. Oldenbourg, 2000.

Hartley, Anthony. *Gaullism: The Rise and Fall of a Political Movement.* London: Routledge & Kegan Paul, 1972.

Hoffman, Stanley. *Éssais sur la France: Déclin ou Renouveau?* Paris: Editions du Seuil, 1974.

Institut Charles de Gaulle, ed. *De Gaulle et le Tiers Monde.* Paris: A. Pedone, 1984.

———. *De Gaulle en son siècle, vol 3–6.* Paris: La Documentation Française, 1992.

Institut Français d'Opinion Publique. *Les Français et De Gaulle.* Paris: Plon, 1971.

Jackson, Julian. *Charles de Gaulle.* London: Haus, 2003.

Jauvert, Vincent. *L'Amérique contre De Gaulle: histoire secrète (1961–1969).* Paris: Seuil, 2000.

Journoud, Pierre. *De Gaulle et le Vietnam: 1945–1969, la réconciliation.* Paris: Tallandier, c2011.

Jouve, Edmond. *Le Général de Gaulle et la Construction de l'Europe (1940–1966), Tomes I–II.* Paris: Librairie générale de droit et de jurisprudence, R. Pichon et R. Durand-Auzias, 1967.

Kedward, Rod. *La vie en bleu: France and the French since 1900.* London: Allen Lane, 2005.

Kolodziej, Edward. *French International Policy under De Gaulle and Pompidou: The Politics of Grandeur.* Ithaca: Cornell University Press, 1974.

Kuisel, Richard. *Seducing the French: The Dilemma of Americanisation.* Berkeley, C.A.: University of California Press, 1993.

Kunz, Diane, ed. *The Diplomacy of the Crucial Decade: American Foreign Relations During the 1960s.* New York: Columbia University Press, 1994.

———. *Butter and Guns: America's Cold War Economic Diplomacy.* New York: Free Press, 1997.

Lacouture, Jean. *De Gaulle, vol 3.* Paris: Le Seuil, 1986.

Lacouture, Jean, and Roland Mehl, ed. *De Gaulle ou l'éternel défi: 56 témoignages.* Paris: Seuil, 1988.

Lefort, Bernard. *Souvenirs et secrets des années gaulliennes, 1958–1969.* Paris: A. Michel, 1999.

Logevall, Fredrik. *Choosing War: The Lost Chance for Peace and the Escalation of War in Vietnam.* Berkeley: University of California Press, 1999.

Loth, Wilfried, ed. *Crises and Compromises: The European Project 1963–1969.* Baden-Baden: Nomos Verlag; Bruxelles: Bruylant, 2001.

———. *Europe, Cold War and Coexistence, 1953–1965.* London: Frank Cass, 2003.

Ludlow, N. Piers. *Dealing with Britain: The Six and the First UK Application to the EEC.* Cambridge: Cambridge University Press, 1997.

———. *The European Community and the Crises of the 1960s: Negotiating the Gaullist Challenge.* London: Routledge, 2006.

Mahan, Erin. *Kennedy, De Gaulle, and Western Europe.* Houndmills; Basingstoke; Hampshire; New York, N.Y.: Palgrave Macmillan, 2002.

Melandri, Pierre and Serge Ricard, ed. *Les Relations Franco-Américaines au XXème siècle.* Paris: L'Harmattan, 2003.

Mockli, Daniel and Victor Mauer, ed. *European-American Relations and the Middle East: From Suez to Iraq.* London: Routledge, 2010.

Möller, Horst and Maurice Vaïsse, ed. *Willy Brandt und Frankreich.* München: R. Oldenbourg, 2005.

Moravcsik, Andrew. *The Choice for Europe: Social Purpose and State Power from Messina to Maastricht.* Ithaca, N.Y.: Cornell University Press, 1998.

Morse, Edward. *Foreign Policy and Interdependence in Gaullist France.* Princeton, N.J: Princeton University Press, 1973.

Nelson, Keith. *The Making of Détente: Soviet-American Relations in the Shadow of Vietnam.* Baltimore: Johns Hopkins University Press, 1995.

Newhouse, John. *De Gaulle and the Anglo-Saxons.* New York: Viking Press, 1970.

Newton, Julie. *Russia, France and the Idea of Europe.* Basingstoke; New York: Palgrave Macmillan, 2003.

Nuenlist, Christian, Anna Locher, and Garret Martin, ed. *Globalizing de Gaulle: International Perspectives on French Foreign Policies, 1958–1969.* Lanham, M.D.: Rowman & Littlefield, 2010.

Pagedas, Constantine. *Anglo-American Strategic Relations and the French Problem, 1960–1963: A Troubled Partnership.* London; Portland, OR.: Frank Cass, 2000.

Parr, Helen. *Britain's Policy towards the European Community, 1964–1967: Harold Wilson and Britain's World Role.* London: Routledge, 2006.

Péan, Pierre. *L'homme de l'ombre: Eléments d'enquête autour de Jacques Foccart, l'homme le plus mystérieux et puissant de la Vème République.* Paris: Fayard, 1990.

Pfister, Roger. *Apartheid South Africa and African States: From Pariah to Middle Power, 1961–1994.* London; New York: I.B. Taurus Academic Studies, 2005.

Pine, Melissa. *Harold Wilson and Europe: Pursuing Britain's Membership of the European Community.* London: I.B. Tauris & Co. Ltd., 2007.

Prate, Alain. *Les Batailles Économiques du Général de Gaulle.* Paris: Plon, 1978.

Preeg, Ernest. *Traders and Diplomats: An Analysis of the Kennedy Round of Negotiations under the General Agreement on Tariffs and Trade.* Washington: Brookings Institution, 1970.

Rey, Marie-Pierre. *La tentation du rapprochement : France et URSS à l'heure de la détente (1964–1974).* Paris: Publications de la Sorbonne, 1991.

Rothschild, Joseph and Nancy Wingfield. *Return to Diversity: A Political History of East Central Europe since World War II, 2nd edition.* New York: Oxford University Press, 1993.

Roussel, Éric. *Charles de Gaulle.* Paris: Gallimard, 2002.

Rowland, Benjamin, ed. *Charles de Gaulle's Legacy of Ideas.* Lanham, M.D.: Lexington Books, c2011.

Schreiber, Thomas. *Les actions de la France à l'Est, ou les absences de Marianne.* Paris: Harmattan, 2000.

Schoenborn, Benedikt. *La mésentente apprivoisée: de Gaulle et les Allemands, 1963–1969.* Paris: Presses Universitaires de France, 2007.

Schwartz, Thomas. *Lyndon Johnson and Europe: In the Shadow of Vietnam.* London: Harvard University Press, 2003.

Sodaro, Michael. *Moscow, Germany and the West from Khrushchev to Gorbachev.* London: I.B. Tauris, 1991.

Soutou, Georges-Henri. *L'Alliance Incertaine: Les rapports politico-stratégiques franco-allemands 1954–1996.* Paris: Fayard, 1996.

———. *La Guerre de cinquante ans: le conflit Est-Ouest 1943–1990*. Paris: Fayard, 2001.

Strange, Susan. *International Economic Relations of the Western World, 1959–1971 vol. 2*. London; New York: Oxford University Press, 1976.

Suri, Jeremi. *Power and Protest: Global Revolution and the Rise of Détente*. Cambridge, M.A.: Harvard University Press, 2003.

Sullivan, Marianna. *France's Vietnam Policy: A Study in Franco-American Relations*. Westport, C.T.: Greenwood Press, 1978.

Trachtenberg, Marc. *A Constructed Peace: The Making of the European Settlement, 1945–1963*. Princeton: Princeton University Press, 1999.

Vaïsse, Maurice, ed. *L'Europe et la Crise de Cuba*. Paris: A. Colin, 1993.

Vaïsse, Maurice, Pierre Melandri, and Frédéric Bozo, ed. *La France et l'OTAN, 1949–1996*. Bruxelles: Editions Complexes, 1996.

Vaïsse, Maurice. *La grandeur: politique étrangère du Général de Gaulle 1958–1969*. Paris: Fayard, 1998.

Vaïsse, Maurice, ed. *De Gaulle et la Russie*. Paris: CNRS Editions, 2006.

Viansson-Ponté, Pierre. *Histoire de la République Gaullienne, vol 2*. Paris: Fayart, 1971.

Wahl, Nicholas and Robert Paxton, ed. *De Gaulle and the United States, 1930–1970: A Centennial Reappraisal*. Oxford: Berg, 1994.

Wall, Irwin. *France, the United States, and the Algerian War*. Berkeley: University of California Press, c2001.

Wauthier, Claude. *Quatre Présidents et l'Afrique, De Gaulle, Pompidou, Giscard d'Estaing, Mitterrand: Quarante ans de politique africaine*. Paris: Seuil, 1995.

Wolfe, Thomas. *Soviet Power and Europe: 1945–1970*. Baltimore: Johns Hopkins Press, 1970.

Wolton, Thierry. *La France sous influence: Paris-Moscou, 30 ans de relations secrètes*. Paris: Grasset, 1997.

Zeiler, Thomas. *American Trade and Power in the 1960s*. New York: Columbia University Press, 1992.

Zhai, Qiang. *China and the Vietnam Wars, 1950–1975*. Chapel Hill: University of North Carolina Press, 2000.

Zimmermann, Hubert. *Money and Security: Troops, Monetary Policy, and West Germany's Relations with the United States and Britain, 1950–1971*. Cambridge: Cambridge University Press, 2001.

Zubok, Vladislav. *A Failed Empire: The Soviet Union in the Cold War from Stalin to Gorbachev*. Chapel Hill: University of North Carolina Press, 2007.

Journal Articles, Online Papers, and Book Chapters

Allin, Dana. "De Gaulle and American Power," in *Charles de Gaulle's Legacy of Ideas*, ed. Benjamin Rowland. Lanham, M.D.: Lexington Books, c2011.

Badel, Laurence. "Le Quai d'Orsay, la Grande-Bretagne et l'élargissement de la Communauté (1963–1969)," in *Cinquante Ans après la déclaration Schuman: Histoire de la Construction Européenne*, ed. Michel Catala. Nantes: Ouest éditions, 2001.

Barbier, Colette. "La Force Multilatérale." *Relations Internationales* 69 (Spring 1992).

Böhmer, Katharina. "'We Too Mean Business': Germany and the Second British Application to the EEC, 1966–67," in *Harold Wilson and European Integration: Britain's Second Application to Join the EEC*, ed. Oliver Daddow. London: Cass, 2002.

Bossuat, Gérard. "De Gaulle et la seconde candidature britannique aux Communautés européennes 1966–1969," in *Crises and Compromises: The European Project 1963–1969*, ed. Wilfried Loth. Baden-Baden: Nomos Verlag; Bruxelles: Bruylant, 2001.

————. "French Development Aid and Co-Operation under de Gaulle." *Contemporary European History* 12/4 (2003).

Bozo, Frédéric. "Chronique d'une décision annoncée: Le retrait de l'organisation militaire 1965–1967," in *La France et l'OTAN, 1949–1996 Actes du colloque tenu à l'Ecole militaire, 8, 9 et 10 Février 1996 à Paris*, ed. Maurice Vaïsse, Pierre Melandri, and Frédéric Bozo. Bruxelles: Editions Complexes, 1996.

————. "Détente versus Alliance: France, the United States and the Politics of the Harmel Report, 1964–1968." *Contemporary European History* 7/3 (1998).

————. "The NATO Crisis of 1966–1967: A French Point of View," in *The Strategic Triangle: France, Germany, and the United States in the Shaping of Europe*, ed. Helga Haftendorn, Georges-Henri Soutou, Stephen Szabo and Samuel Wells. Washington, D.C.: Woodrow Wilson Center Press; Baltimore: Johns Hopkins University Press, c2006.

Brunet, Jean-Paul. "Le Retrait de la France de l'OTAN: La Scène Intérieure," in *La France et l'OTAN, 1949–1996 Actes du colloque tenu à l'Ecole militaire, 8, 9 et 10 Février 1996 à Paris*, ed. Maurice Vaïsse, Pierre Melandri, and Frédéric Bozo. Bruxelles: Editions Complexes, 1996.

Burin des Roziers, Étienne. "Le non-alignement," in *La politique étrangère du Général de Gaulle*, ed. *Élie Barnavi and Saül Friedländer*. Paris: Presses Universitaires de France, 1985.

Byrne, Jeffrey. "'Je ne vous ai pas compris': De Gaulle's Decade of Negotiation with the Algerian FLN," in *Globalizing de Gaulle: International Perspectives on French Foreign Policies, 1958–1969*, ed. Christian Nuenlist, Anna Locher, and Garret Martin. Lanham, M.D.: Rowman & Littlefield, 2010.

Calleo, David. "De Gaulle and the Monetary System: The Golden Rule," in *De Gaulle and the United States, 1930–1970: A Centennial Reappraisal*, ed. Nicholas Wahl and Robert Paxton. Oxford: Berg, 1994.

Césari, Laurent. "Que reste-t-il de l'influence politique française en Indochine (1954–1966)?" in *Du Conflit d'Indochine aux Conflits Indochinois*, ed. Pierre Brocheux. Bruxelles: Editions Complexe, 2000.

Chivvis, Christopher. "De Gaulle and the Dollar," in *Charles de Gaulle's Legacy of Ideas*, ed. Benjamin Rowland. Lanham, M.D.: Lexington Books, c2011.

Cogan, Charles. "'How Fuzzy Can One Be?': The American Reaction to De Gaulle's Proposal for the Neutralization of (South) Vietnam," in *The Search for Peace in Vietnam, 1964–1968*, ed. Lloyd Gardner and Ted Gittinger. College Station: Texas A&M University Press, 2004.

Cohen, Samy. "De Gaulle et Israël: Le sens d'une rupture," in *La politique étrangère du Général de Gaulle*, ed. Elie Barnavi and Saül Friedländer. Paris: Presses Universitaires de France, 1985.

Decraene, Philippe. "Les Réactions de l'Opinion Publique Française à la Politique Tiers Mondiste du Général de Gaulle de 1962 à 1969," in *De Gaulle et le Tiers Monde*, ed. Institut Charles de Gaulle. Paris: A. Pedone, 1984.

De la Gorce, Paul-Marie. "La politique arabe du Général de Gaulle," in *La politique étrangère du Général de Gaulle,* ed. Elie Barnavi and Saül Friedländer. Paris: Presses Universitaires de France, 1985.

Devillers, Philippe. "Le Général de Gaulle et l'Asie," in *De Gaulle et le Tiers Monde,* ed. Institut Charles de Gaulle. Paris: A. Pedone, 1984.

Durand, Pierre-Michel. "Les relations Franco-Américaines au Gabon dans les Années 60 ou la 'Petite Guerre Froide,'" in *Les Relations Franco-Américaines au XXème siècle,* ed. Pierre Melandri and Serge Ricard. Paris: L'Harmattan, 2003.

Ellison, James. "Dealing with De Gaulle: Anglo-American Relations, NATO and the Second Application," in *Harold Wilson and European Integration: Britain's Second Application to Join the EEC,* ed. Oliver Daddow. London: Cass, 2002.

———. "Defeating the General: Anglo-American Relations, Europe and the NATO Crisis of 1966." *Cold War History* 6/1 (2006).

Friedman, Max Paul. "Anti-Americanism and US Foreign Relations." *Diplomatic History* 32/4 (2008).

Gaiduk, Ilya. "The Soviet Union Faces the Vietnam War," in *La Guerre du Vietnam et l'Europe, 1963–1973,* ed. Christopher Goscha and Maurice Vaïsse. Bruxelles; Paris: Bruylant, 2003.

Gavin, Francis. "'The Interests of France and the United States Were Essentially the Same': Reassessing Franco-American Economic and Security Relations During the 1960s," in *Les Relations Franco-Américaines au XXème siècle,* ed. Pierre Melandri and Serge Ricard. Paris: L'Harmattan, 2003.

Germond, Carine. "La France et l'Allemagne face à l'Europe Politique dans les Années 1960," in *Le Couple France-Allemagne et les Institutions Européennes: Une postérité pour le Plan Schuman?* ed. Marie-Thérèse Bitsch. Bruxelles: Bruylant, 2001.

———. "A 'Cordial Potentiality'? De Gaulle and the Franco-German Partnership, 1963–1969," in *Globalizing de Gaulle: International Perspectives on French Foreign Policies, 1958–1969,* ed. Christian Nuenlist, Anna Locher, and Garret Martin. Lanham, M.D.: Rowman & Littlefield, 2010.

Giglioli, Alessandra. "Le retrait de la France du commandement intégré de l'OTAN." http://www.nato.int/acad/fellow/98-00/giglioli.pdf.

Gnoinska, Margaret. "Poland and Vietnam, 1963: New Evidence on Secret Communist Diplomacy and the 'Maneli Affair.'" http://www.wilsoncenter.org/topics/pubs/CWIHP_WP_45b.pdf.

Granieri, Ronald. "Franz Josef Strauß and the End of the Cold War," in *Visions of the End of the Cold War in Europe (1945–1990),* ed. Frédéric Bozo, Marie-Pierre Rey, N. Piers Ludlow, and Bernd Rother. New York: Berghahn Books, 2012.

Haftendorn, Helga. "The Adaptation of the NATO Alliance to a Period of Détente: The 1967 Harmel Report," in *Crises and Compromises: The European Project 1963–1969,* ed. Wilfried Loth. Baden-Baden: Nomos Verlag; Bruxelles: Bruylant, 2001.

———. "The NATO Crisis of 1966–1967: Confronting Germany with a Conflict of Priorities," in *The Strategic Triangle: France, Germany, and the United States in the Shaping of Europe,* ed. Helga Haftendorn, Georges-Henri Soutou, Stephen Szabo, and Samuel Wells. Washington, D.C.: Woodrow Wilson Center Press; Baltimore: Johns Hopkins University Press, c2006.

Hamilton, Arran. "Beyond the Sterling Devaluation: The Gold Crisis of March 1968." *Contemporary European History* 17/1 (2008).

Herring, George. "Tet and the Crisis of Hegemony," in *1968: The World Transformed*, ed. Carole Fink, Philipp Gassert, and Detlef Junker. Washington, D.C.; German Historical Institute; Cambridge, England; New York, N.Y.: Cambridge University Press, 1998.

Hoffman, Stanley. "The Foreign Policy of Charles De Gaulle," in *The Diplomats, 1939–1979*, ed. Gordon Craig and Francis Loewenheim. Princeton, N.J.: Princeton University Press, 1994.

Jarzabek, Wanda. "Rozmowa Charlesa de Gaulle'a z Wladyslawem Gomulka w czasie wizyty generala w Polsce we wrzesnu 1967 r" ("The four eyes conversation between Charles de Gaulle and Wladislaw Gomulka during the General's visit to Poland, September 1967"). *Dzieje Najnowsze (The Journal)* 32/4 (2000).

Journoud, Pierre. "La France, les Etats-Unis et la Guerre du Vietnam: L'Année 1968," in *Les Relations Franco-Américaines au XXème siècle*, ed. Pierre Melandri and Serge Ricard. Paris: L'Harmattan, 2003.

———. "Le Quai d'Orsay et le Processus de Paix, 1963–1973," in *La Guerre du Vietnam et l'Europe, 1963–1973*, ed. Christopher Goscha and Maurice Vaïsse. Bruxelles; Paris: Bruylant, 2003.

Kaplan, Lawrence. "The US and NATO in the Johnson Years," in *The Johnson Years, vol. 3*, ed. Robert Divine. Kansas: University Press of Kansas, 1994.

Kunz, Diane. "The American Economic Consequences of 1968," in *1968: The World Transformed*, ed. Carole Fink, Philipp Gassert, and Detlef Junker. Washington, D.C.; German Historical Institute; Cambridge, England; New York, N.Y.: Cambridge University Press, 1998.

Kramer, Mark. "The Czechoslovak Crisis and the Brezhnev Doctrine," in *1968: The World Transformed*, ed. Carole Fink, Philipp Gassert, and Detlef Junker. Washington, D.C.; German Historical Institute; Cambridge, England; New York, N.Y.: Cambridge University Press, 1998.

Locher, Anna, and Nuenlist, Christian. "What Role for NATO? Conflicting Western Perceptions of Détente, 1963–65." *Journal of Transatlantic Studies* 2/2 (2004).

Loth, Wilfried. "Français et Allemands dans la Crise Institutionnelle de 1965," in *Le Couple France-Allemagne et les Institutions Européennes: Une postérité pour le Plan Schuman?* ed. Marie-Thérèse Bitsch. Bruxelles: Bruylant, 2001.

Ludlow, N. Piers. "The Eclipse of the Extremes. Demythologising the Luxembourg Compromise," in *Crises and Compromises: The European Project 1963–1969*. ed. Wilfried Loth. Baden-Baden: Nomos Verlag; Bruxelles: Bruylant, 2001.

———. "A Short-term Defeat: The Community Institutions and the Second British Application to join the EEC," in *Harold Wilson and European Integration: Britain's Second Application to Join the EEC*, ed. Oliver Daddow. London: Cass, 2002.

———. "From Words to Action: Re-interpreting de Gaulle's European Policy, 1958–1969," in *Globalizing de Gaulle: International Perspectives on French Foreign Policies*, ed. Christian Nuenlist, Anna Locher, and Garret Martin. Lanham, M.D.: Rowman & Littlefield, 2010.

Martin, Garret. "Playing the China Card? Revisiting France's Recognition of Communist China, 1963–1964." *Journal of Cold War Studies* 10/1 (2008).

———. "The Soviet Factor in Franco-German Relations, 1958–1969," in *A History of Franco-German Relations in Europe: From "Hereditary Enemies" to Partners*, ed. Carine Germond and Henning Turk. New York: Palgrave Macmillan, 2008.

———. "At Odds in the Middle East: Paris, Washington, and the Six-Day War," in *European-American Relations and the Middle East: From Suez to Iraq*, ed. Daniel Mockli and Victor Mauer. London: Routledge, 2010.

Mastny, Vojtech. "Détente, the Superpowers and their Allies, 1962–64," in *Europe, Cold War and Coexistence, 1953–1965*, ed. Wilfried Loth. London: Frank Cass, 2003.

Mausbach, Wilfried. "The United States, Germany, and French Peace Initiatives for Vietnam," in *The Search for Peace in Vietnam, 1964–1968*, ed. Lloyd Gardner and Ted Gittinger. College Station: Texas A&M University Press, 2004.

Melandri, Pierre. "Le Général de Gaulle, la construction européenne et l'Alliance Atlantique," in *La politique étrangère du Général de Gaulle*, ed. Élie Barnavi and Saül Friedländer. Paris: Presses Universitaires de France, 1985.

Narinsky, Mikhaïl. "Le retrait de la France de l'organisation militaire de l'OTAN, vu de Moscou," in *De Gaulle et la Russie*, ed. Maurice Vaïsse. Paris: CNRS Editions, 2006.

Pascallon, Pierre. "Les Aspects Économiques de la Politique Tiers Mondiste du Général de Gaulle de 1962 à 1969," in *De Gaulle et le Tiers Monde*, ed. Institut Charles de Gaulle. Paris: A. Pedone, 1984.

Pommerin, Reiner. "La France, l'Allemagne et l'OTAN," in *La France et l'OTAN, 1949–1996 Actes du colloque tenu à l'Ecole militaire, 8, 9 et 10 Février 1996 à Paris*, ed. Maurice Vaïsse, Pierre Melandri, and Frédéric Bozo. Bruxelles: Editions Complexes, 1996.

Rey, Marie-Pierre. "L'URSS et l'Europe Occidentale de 1956 à 1975: de l'ignorance méfiante à la coopération." *Relations Internationales* 82 (Summer 1995).

———. "De Gaulle, l'URSS et la sécurité européenne, 1958–1969," in *De Gaulle et la Russie*, ed. Maurice Vaïsse. Paris: CNRS Editions, 2006.

———. "'De Gaulle, French Diplomacy, and Franco-Soviet Relations as Seen from Moscow," in *Globalizing de Gaulle: International Perspectives on French Foreign Policies*, ed. Christian Nuenlist, Anna Locher, and Garret Martin. Lanham, M.D.: Rowman & Littlefield, 2010.

Roy, Raj. "The Battle for Bretton Woods: America, Britain and the International Financial Crisis of October 1967–March 1968." *Cold War History* 2/2 (2002).

Sa'adah, Anne. "Idées Simples and Idées Fixes: De Gaulle, the United States, and Vietnam," in *De Gaulle and the United States, 1930–1970: A Centennial Reappraisal*, ed. Nicholas Wahl and Robert Paxton. Oxford: Berg, 1994.

Schenk, Catherine. "Sterling, International Monetary Reform and Britain's Applications to Join the European Economic Community in the 1960s." *Contemporary European History* 11/3 (2002).

Schoenborn, Benedikt. "Bargaining with the Bear: Chancellor Erhard's Bid to Buy German Reunification." *Cold War History* 8/1 (2008).

Schwartz, Thomas. "The de Gaulle Challenge: The Johnson Administration and the NATO Crisis of 1966–1967," in *The Strategic Triangle: France, Germany, and the United States in the Shaping of Europe*, ed. Helga Haftendorn, Georges-Henri Soutou, Stephen Szabo, and Samuel Wells. Washington, D.C.: Woodrow Wilson Center Press; Baltimore: Johns Hopkins University Press, c2006.

Selvage, Douglas. "The Warsaw Pact and Nuclear Non-proliferation, 1963–65." http://www.wilsoncenter.org/topics/pubs/ACFB0E.pdf.

Soutou, Georges-Henri. "Le général de Gaulle, le plan Fouchet et l'Europe." *Commentaire* 13/52 (Winter 1990–1991).

———. " La place de l'URSS dans la politique allemande de la France 1943–1969," in Les tiers dans les relations franco-allemandes/Dritte in den deutsch-franzosischen Beziehungen, ed. Christian Baechler and Klaus-Jürgen Müller. München: Oldenbourg, 1996.

————. "La décision française de quitter le commandement intégré de l'OTAN (1966)," in *Von Truman bis Harmel: Die Bundesrepublik Deutschland im Spannungsfeld von NATO und europäischer Integration,* ed. Hans-Joachim Harder. München: R. Oldenbourg, 2000.

————. "De Gaulle's France and the Soviet Union from Conflict to Détente," in *Europe, Cold War and Coexistence, 1953–1965,* ed. Wilfried Loth. London: Frank Cass, 2003.

Torikata, Yuko. "Re-examining de Gaulle's Peace Initiative on the Vietnam War." *Diplomatic History* 31/5 (2007).

Uribe, Armando. "Le général de Gaulle et l'Amérique Latine," in *De Gaulle et le Tiers Monde,* ed. Institut Charles de Gaulle. Paris: A. Pedone, 1984.

Vaïsse, Maurice. "'Une hirondelle ne fait pas le printemps': La France et la crise de Cuba," in *L'Europe et la Crise de Cuba,* ed. Maurice Vaïsse. Paris: A. Colin, 1993.

————. "La politique européenne de la France en 1965: pourquoi 'la chaise vide'?" in *Crises and Compromises: The European Project 1963–1969,* ed. Wilfried Loth. Baden-Baden: Nomos Verlag; Bruxelles: Bruylant, 2001.

————. "De Gaulle et la guerre du Vietnam: de la difficulté d'être Cassandre," in *La Guerre du Vietnam et l'Europe, 1963–1973,* ed. Christopher Goscha and Maurice Vaïsse. Bruxelles; Paris: Bruylant, 2003.

————. "De Gaulle et Willy Brandt: deux non-conformistes au pouvoir," in *Willy Brandt und Frankreich,* ed. Horst Möller and Maurice Vaïsse. München: R. Oldenbourg, 2005.

————. "Les crises de Cuba et du Proche-Orient dans les relations franco-soviétiques," in *De Gaulle et la Russie,* ed. Maurice Vaïsse. Paris: CNRS Editions, 2006.

Vassilieva, Natalia. "L'URSS et le développement des relations de la France avec les pays d'Europe de l'Est (Pologne et Roumanie)," in *De Gaulle et la Russie,* ed. Maurice Vaïsse. Paris: CNRS Editions, 2006.

Wenger, Andreas. "Crisis and Opportunity: NATO's Transformation and the Multilateralization of Détente, 1966–1968." *Journal of Cold War Studies* 6/1 (2004).

Wilkens, Andreas. "L'Europe en suspens. Willy Brandt et l'orientation de la politique européenne de l'Allemagne fédérale 1966–1969," in *Crises and Compromises: The European Project 1963–1969,* ed. Wilfried Loth. Baden-Baden: Nomos Verlag; Bruxelles: Bruylant, 2001.

Xiang, Lanxin. "De Gaulle and the 'Eternal China,'" in *Charles de Gaulle's Legacy of Ideas,* ed. Benjamin Rowland. Lanham, M.D.: Lexington Books, c2011.

Zhai, Qiang. "China's Response to French Peace Initiatives," in *The Search for Peace in Vietnam, 1964–1968,* ed. Lloyd Gardner and Ted Gittinger. College Station: Texas A&M University Press, 2004.

Zorgbibe, Charles. "De Gaulle et le Tiers Monde: Orientations Générales," in *De Gaulle et le Tiers Monde,* ed. Institut Charles de Gaulle. Paris: A. Pedone, 1984.

Zubok, Vladislav. "Unwrapping the Enigma: What was behind the Soviet Challenge in the 1960s," in *The Diplomacy of the Crucial Decade: American Foreign Relations During the 1960s,* ed. Diane Kunz. New York: Columbia University Press, 1994.

Unpublished Paper

Ludlow, N. Piers. "The Protector of Atlantic Unity: De Gaulle's Unintentional Boost to the Atlantic Alliance," presented to the LSE-Columbia workshop on transatlantic relations, April 2004.

Index

Acheson, Dean, 102
Adenauer, Konrad, 19, 22–23, 26, 32, 54–55, 98, 107, 134
Afghanistan, 87
Ailleret, General Charles, 116, 157, 167–68
Albania, 58
Alessandri, Jorge, 91
Algeria, 10, 76, 79–80, 82, 93, 167
Algerian War, 2, 10–11, 51, 74, 79, 85, 97, 114, 197
Alphand, Hervé, 59, 98, 142–43, 145, 158–59, 163, 181, 190
    meetings with Charles de Gaulle, 36, 42, 69–70, 101, 111
Andréani, Jacques, 118, 137, 175

Bahr, Egon, 138, 159
Ball, George, 1, 4, 36, 90, 117, 139
Bator, Francis, 117, 134–35
Baudet, Philippe, 60, 63–64, 118–19
Beaumarchais, Jacques de, 56, 116, 155, 175
Belgium, 6, 8, 28, 124, 164–66
Bentinck, Adolph, 49
Birrenbach, Kurt, 22
Blessing, Karl, 134
Bo, Mai Van, 112
Boegner, Jean-Marc, 21, 31, 48, 162
Bohlen, Charles, 5, 36, 43, 49, 68, 98, 100, 137, 143–44, 150
Bosch, Juan, 85
Botha, Pik, 80
Brandt, Willy, 116, 120, 133, 135, 138, 154, 159, 162, 168, 180–81, 198
Bretton Woods. *See* International Monetary System

Brezhnev, Leonid, 61–62, 71–73, 108–9, 119, 139, 154, 190
Brosio, Manlio, 36, 42, 68, 98–99, 116, 125, 162, 164–65, 178
Brown, George, 151
Bulgaria, 58, 63, 105, 119
Burin des Roziers, Étienne, 12
Burma, 87

Cambodia, 87–90, 112–14
Canada, 28, 150, 183
Carli, Guido, 183
Carstens, Karl, 22, 38
Cartier, Raymond, 74
Ceaușescu, Nicolae, 177
Charbonnel, Jean, 12
Chauvel, Jean, 84
Chen, Huang, 89, 111
Chile, 91
Christian Democratic Union (CDU), 22
Cleveland, Harlan, 147, 165
Collective Reserve Units (CRU), 42, 46
Colombo, Emilio, 160
Common Agricultural Policy (CAP), 9, 18, 21–23, 27, 30–31, 36–39, 43–45, 48–49, 103, 152. *See also* European Economic Community
Couve de Murville, Maurice, 12, 25, 28, 32, 34, 49, 56, 63, 70, 75, 79, 82, 86, 98, 112, 116, 133, 135–36, 144, 154–55, 159, 170, 187–89
    and the EEC, 20–21, 30, 38, 43–45, 49, 132, 151–52, 162–64, 168, 181
    and the Eastern bloc, 59, 63–64, 104–5, 111, 176

and NATO, 26, 35, 42, 47, 102, 104, 117,
    162
and the Soviet Union, 52, 61, 64, 67,
    70–72, 106, 108, 118, 175
and the Vietnam War, 85, 89–90, 92–93,
    102, 111, 113–14, 120, 141, 172
Cuban Missile Crisis, 10, 53
Cyrankiewicz, Josef, 70–71
Czechoslovakia, 54, 58, 63, 70, 139, 176–78,
    190–91

Debré, Michel, 88, 119, 128–29, 131, 152–53,
    160, 162–63, 179–85, 189–90
Defence Planning Committee (DPC), 124
Dejean, Maurice, 53–54, 60
De La Grandville, Jean, 26, 47
De Leusse, Bruno, 98
Denmark, 132, 161
D'Estaing, Valéry Giscard, 28, 40–41, 46, 52,
    70, 151
Détente, 9, 54, 56–57, 71, 73, 94, 97, 105, 107,
    110, 113, 126, 136, 138, 141, 143, 148, 152,
    154, 190–92, 194, 196, 198
    Franco-German relations and, 135–36,
        138, 154, 159
    French conception of, 55–56, 65, 68,
        108, 137
    French policy of, 66, 68, 110, 113, 115,
        118–22, 148, 156–59, 174–78
    NATO and, 124–25, 147, 161, 165,
        169–71
    between Superpowers, 55–56, 140
    the withdrawal from NATO and,
        104–5, 194
Diem, Ngo Dinh, 86, 90
Dillon, Douglas, 40
Dobrynin, Anatoly, 173
Dominican Republic, 43, 66, 85, 93
Dong, Pham Van, 172
Doubinin, Yuri, 69, 175
Dromer, Jean, 103, 126–28
Dubcek, Alexander, 176, 190

East Germany, 55, 58, 65, 67, 69, 107, 109,
    135, 138–39, 159, 194
Eban, Abba, 141, 144
Egypt, 142, 144, 150
Eisenhower, Dwight, 9
El-Naggar, Abdel, 144

Emminger, Otmar, 153
"Empty Chair" Crisis, 45–46, 48–50, 66,
    102–3, 127
En-lai, Zhou, 91, 111
Erhard, Ludwig, 23, 32–35, 37, 43, 88, 115,
    133
European Commission, 27, 37–39, 44–45,
    48–49, 103, 132, 152, 160–61, 163–64, 168
European Economic Community (EEC),
    8–11, 22–24, 28, 30–31, 33, 35, 37–41,
    102–3, 121–23, 127, 130, 159, 168–71, 192,
    196–97
    and the 'empty chair' crisis, 43–45,
        48–50, 66, 102–3
    and Franco-German relations, 30–31,
        33, 115, 133–35, 154
    and international monetary
        negotiations, 128–29, 132–34, 148–49,
        152–53, 160–64, 180–81, 184
    and the Kennedy Round, 11, 23–24, 28,
        31, 33, 37, 103, 127, 130
    and negotiations over UK's second
        application, 127, 131–33, 148–49,
        151–52, 154, 161–66, 178–81, 189
    and the veto against the UK's first
        application, 17–21
European Parliament, 44
Evian Accords, 11, 74, 80

Faure, Edgar, 56, 60, 87
Five. *See* EEC
Flexible Response, 9, 124
Foccart, Jacques, 78–79, 82–84
Fock, Jeno, 177
Force de frappe, 10, 17–18, 25, 37, 47, 55,
    74, 168
Forces Françaises d'Allemagne (FFA), 99,
    101, 115–16
Fornari, Giovanni, 49
Fouchet Plan, 10–11, 18, 32
Fowler, Henry, 46, 128, 135, 154, 160, 182
France, 1–13, 17–94, 97–121, 123–98
    conception of détente, 55–56, 65, 68,
        108, 137
    and the Eastern bloc, 59, 63–64, 70–71,
        105, 119, 155, 157, 176–77
    the establishment of diplomatic
        relations with Communist China, 12,
        33, 56, 87

and the EEC, 8–9, 20–22, 30–31, 37–39,
43, 45, 48–50, 102–3, 127, 131–32,
151–52, 160–64, 168, 181
and force de frappe, 10, 17–18, 25, 37,
47, 55, 74, 168
and the international monetary system
22, 28–29, 40–42, 46–47, 126–29,
134–35, 152–53, 160, 166–67, 169,
179–85
and the Kennedy Round, 23–24, 26–27,
37–38, 130
and NATO, 17, 26, 36, 47, 115–17, 124,
159–60, 162, 164–65, 167–68
and withdrawal from NATO, 26, 100–2,
152
and the Six Day War, 141–48, 150
and the Soviet Union, 51–55, 57–58, 60–
64, 67–69, 71–72, 92, 106–10, 118–19,
137, 144–45, 154, 157–58, 175–76
and the Third World, 74–84
and the United States, 3, 17, 32, 36, 38–
39, 91–94, 110, 112–13, 142, 144, 146
and the Vietnam War, 57, 66, 85–94,
110–13, 120, 141, 154, 172–73
and West Germany, 10–11, 17, 19,
22, 30–39, 43, 57, 62–63, 66–67, 88,
115–16, 133–35, 150, 154–55, 159,
180–81
French Community, 10–11, 74

Gabon, 79, 83
de Gaulle, General Charles, 1–7, 9–13,
17–94, 97–128, 130–59, 161–74, 176–81,
183–98
and Communist China, 9, 56, 60, 63–64,
70, 87, 89, 111
and the Eastern bloc, 9, 58–60, 63–66,
70–71, 105–6, 154–57, 176–77
and the EEC, 9, 17–19, 30–31, 43, 45–46,
48–50, 102, 131–32, 162–63, 166, 168
and the German question, 6, 65–66,
107–10
grand design of, 3–5, 19, 35, 51, 54,
65–66, 97, 104, 107–8, 136, 173–74,
192–98
and the international monetary system,
28, 41, 126, 167, 183
and the Kennedy Round, 23, 130
and NATO, 7, 9, 17–18, 26, 36, 47–48,
115–17, 124, 159, 162

and withdrawal from NATO, 26, 42, 47,
98–99, 101–4
personality of, 2–3
political philosophy, 5–7
and the Six Day War, 141–48, 150
and the Soviet Union, 6–7, 10, 19,
51–55, 57, 60–66, 68–69, 71–72, 103,
106–10, 118–20, 137, 144–45, 148, 174
and the Third World, 74–84, 86–88
and the United States, 3–4, 17–20, 32,
36, 39, 42–43, 91–94, 99, 110, 112–15,
141, 145–46, 150
and the Vietnam War, 57, 85–94, 102,
110–15, 120, 141, 145, 172–73
and West Germany 10, 17–20, 23, 25,
30–36, 39, 43, 58, 63, 67, 88, 120,
133–36, 150, 153–55, 174
General Agreement on Tariffs and Trade
(GATT). *See* Kennedy Round
German question, 64–65, 67–68, 107–10, 115,
120, 135–36, 138, 156, 174–75, 194, 198
Glassboro Summit, 146, 148
Goldberg, Arthur, 94, 144
Gold pool, 166, 169, 179, 182–83
Gold standard, 28, 212n69, 216n158
Gomulka, Wladislaw, 139, 156–57
Gretchko, Marshal Andrei, 176
Gromyko, Andrei, 54, 62, 67–69, 71, 108–9,
140, 175
Group of Ten (G10), 28–29, 40, 42, 46–7, 126,
128–29, 152–53, 182, 184

Habib-Deloncle, Michel, 78
Hallstein, Walter, 44–45
Hallstein Doctrine, 135, 139
Harmel, Pierre, 124–25, 164
Harmel exercise, 125–26, 149, 159–62,
164–65, 167, 169, 171, 178, 196
Harriman, Averell, 141
Hassel, Kaï-Uwe von, 33
Healey, Denis, 117
Heath, Edward, 72
Herter, Christian, 12
Hungary, 58, 63, 105, 138–39, 177

India, 87
Indochina, 34, 57, 75, 85–94, 110–14, 120–21,
141, 145, 174, 194
Intercontinental Ballistic Missiles (ICBM), 8
International Control Commission (ICC), 86

International Monetary Fund (IMF), 27–29, 40, 42, 46, 126, 129, 153, 160–61, 163, 179–82, 188
International Monetary System, 8, 46–47, 66, 123, 126–34, 166–67, 169–71, 178–79, 182–83, 187, 189, 191, 195–97
  and the American balance of payments deficit, 27, 40
  EEC unity and the, 128–29, 132–34, 148–49, 152–53, 160–64, 180–81, 184
  French views on the, 28–29, 40–42, 46, 128
Ireland, 132, 161
Israel, 80, 141–47, 150, 167, 171
Italy, 8, 28, 77, 101, 129, 166, 195

Japan, 28, 38, 77, 87, 183–84, 195–96
Javits, Jacob, 182
Jenkins, Roy, 182
Johnson, Lyndon Baines, 32, 37–38, 58, 99, 110, 125, 130, 140, 146, 153, 167, 172–73, 179
  and France's withdrawal from NATO, 102, 116–17, 170
  and the Soviet Union, 57, 146, 148, 173, 190
  and West Germany, 34, 37, 133–34, 153
Joxe, Louis, 70

Kennedy, John Fitzgerald, 3, 11, 17, 22, 26–27, 32–33, 55, 85, 90
Kennedy Round, 11, 21, 23–24, 26–27, 30–31, 33, 37–38, 49, 103, 123, 127, 129–30, 134
Khrushchev, Nikita, 52–55, 58–59, 61–62, 107
Kiesinger, Kurt Georg, 116, 122, 133–36, 138–39, 150, 153–55, 174, 181
Klaiber, Manfred, 31, 34, 155
Kliszko, Zenon, 106
Kohler, Foy, 125
Korry, Edward, 113
Kosygin, Alexei, 61–63, 71, 73, 109, 119–20, 144–46, 148, 154, 173, 177, 179
Krag, Otto, 107
Kreisky, Bruno, 196
Kuznetsov, Vasilii, 60

Lalouette, Roger, 86, 226n80
Laos, 77, 87–89
Latin America, 37, 62, 76, 84–85, 87–88, 90–91

Lemnitzer, General Lyman, 116
Lenart, Josef, 157
Lucet, Charles, 99, 113, 167
Luxembourg, 8

Macmillan, Harold, 9
Maillard, Pierre, 108
Manac'h, Étienne, 111–13
Maneli, Mieczyslaw, 86
Mansfield, Mike, 67, 133, 167
Mansholt, Sicco, 31, 44
Margerie, Roland de, 33
Mateos, Adolfo Lopez, 84–85, 90
Maurer, Ion, 59–60, 71, 105
May 1968, 185–89, 191, 195
M'Ba, Léon, 83
McNamara, Robert, 34, 47, 117
Messmer, Pierre, 83, 87, 168, 176
Mexico, 84–85, 87–88, 90
Meyer-Lindenberg, Hermann, 116
Mikoyan, Anastas, 61
Minh, Ho Chi, 111, 113
Mitterrand, François, 50, 75, 186
Monnet, Jean, 22
Morocco, 80
Multilateral Force (MLF), 11–12, 17–18, 36–39, 54, 62–63, 67, 69, 135

Nasser, Gamal Abdel, 142–43
National Liberation Front (NLF), 89, 94, 112
NATO Air Defense Ground Environment (NADGE), 101, 116
NATO's body in charge of production and logistic organization (HAWK), 116
NATO's Maintenance and Supply Organization (NAMSO), 116
Netherlands, 6, 8, 21, 28, 37, 40, 129, 166
Nhu, Ngo Dinh, 86
Nixon, Richard, 173, 198
Noël, Emile, 27, 103
Non-Proliferation Treaty (NPT), 134, 137, 140, 173
North Atlantic Council (NAC), 11, 124–25
North Atlantic Treaty Organization (NATO), 1, 12–13, 19, 22–23, 39, 45–46, 53, 56, 66, 93, 102–6, 108, 110, 112, 120–21, 123, 130, 136–37, 140, 147, 170, 173, 175–76, 184, 189, 192, 194, 197
  France's view of, 9, 26, 35–36

France's withdrawal from, 1, 9, 26, 32–33, 42–43, 47–50, 97–100
and the Harmel exercise, 125–26, 149, 159–62, 164–65, 167, 169, 171, 178, 196
and the MLF, 12, 37
and negotiations after France' withdrawal, 100–2, 115–17, 124
and nuclear strategy, 9, 25, 47, 117, 124
North Vietnam, 62, 86–87, 89–94, 102, 110–13, 141, 154, 172
Norway, 132, 161
Novotny, Antonin, 176, 190
Nuclear Defense Affairs Committee (NDAC), 117
Nuclear Planning Group (NPG), 117

Oder-Neisse frontier, 10, 65, 68, 135, 155
Offroy, Raymond, 88
O'Neill, Sir Con, 168
Organisation de l'Armée Secrète (OAS), 33
Organization of Africa Unity (OAU), 83
Ossola, Rinaldo, 29, 46
Ostpolitik, 135, 137–39, 154–55, 157, 159, 174

Pakistan, 87
Palewski, Gaston, 57
Partial Test Ban Treaty (PTBT), 25, 55–56, 86–87
Parti Communiste Français (PCF), 139
Patijn, Constantyn, 125
Paye, Lucien, 89
Pearson, Lester, 4
People's Republic of China (PRC), 33, 53, 60–61, 63–64, 70, 76, 84, 140, 146, 167, 198
and the establishment of diplomatic relations with France, 12, 56, 87
and the Soviet Union, 9, 55, 62, 140
and the Vietnam War, 48, 86–94, 110–12
Peyrefitte, Alain, 37, 62–63, 66, 87, 92, 119, 156
conversations with de Gaulle, 20, 28, 33, 36, 39, 48–49, 54, 58, 63, 76, 78, 82, 85–86, 90, 97, 106, 114, 119–20, 156, 193
Phouma, Prince Souvanna, 77
Podgorny, Nikolai, 61–62, 109, 119
Poland, 54, 58, 64–65, 70–71, 105, 137, 149, 154–59, 174, 177, 198

Pompidou, Georges, 17, 28, 38, 61, 68–69, 106, 116, 118, 137, 154, 162, 184, 186, 188–89
Portugal, 80–81
Prague Spring, 176, 190–91
Prate, Alain, 179
Puaux, François, 67, 69, 104–5, 118

Québec, 150–51, 167, 171, 187
de Quirielle, François, 154

Rapacki, Adam, 105, 135
Reilly, Sir Patrick, 131, 152, 162
Rockefeller, Nelson, 77, 194
Romania, 58–9, 64, 70–71, 104–5, 137–39, 145, 159, 177, 187, 190, 198
Roosa, Robert, 29
Rudnev, Konstantin, 52
Rueff, Jacques, 28, 41
Rusk, Dean, 20, 85, 90, 120, 124, 137, 140, 154, 164–65, 167, 173

Sainteny, Jean, 112–13, 141
Schiller, Kurt, 135, 180
Schroeder, Gerhard, 20–22, 34, 36, 68, 72, 101, 103, 113
Schütz, Karl, 125
Séquentiel Couleur Avec Mémoire (SECAM), 58, 62–63, 67
Selassie, Emperor Haile, 113
Seydoux, François, 147
Seydoux, Roger, 165
Shelepin, Aleksandr, 108
Shriver, Sargent, 188
Sihanouk, Prince Norodom, 87, 89, 114
Six. *See* EEC
Six Day War, 141–48
South Africa, 80–1, 84, 183
Southeast Asia Treaty Organization (SEATO), 85, 90, 141
South Vietnam, 85–6, 88–89, 91–94, 110–12, 172
Soviet Union, 6–10, 13, 19–20, 25, 30, 34, 38–39, 44, 51–73, 77, 84, 86–88, 91–94, 103–13, 118–23, 125, 136–50, 154–59, 167, 170, 173–78, 183, 190–96, 198
and debates about peaceful coexistence, 72, 108–9
and the Eastern bloc, 59, 105, 138–39, 176, 190–91

and France, 51–54, 57–58, 60–64, 66–69, 71–72, 107–10, 119–20, 137, 144–45, 148, 154, 157–58, 174–76
and the Six Day War, 144–48, 154
and the split with Communist China, 9, 55, 62, 140
and the United States, 25, 30, 54–55, 57–58, 108–9, 140, 144–46, 148, 173
and the Vietnam War, 62, 86
view of de Gaulle, 54, 61
and West Germany, 54, 61–62, 108–9, 138–40, 158, 174
Spaak, Paul-Henri, 2, 3, 24, 26, 63, 125
Special Drawing Rights (SDRs), 129, 152–53, 160–61, 180, 182, 184
Strategic Arms Limitation Talks (SALT), 173
Strauß, Franz Josef, 4
Suslov, Mikhail, 108
Sweden, 28
Switzerland, 28, 166
Syria, 141–42

Tan, Nguyen Huu, 111
Thant, U, 142, 172
Third World, 4–5, 11, 60, 63, 66, 68, 73–88, 90–92, 94, 110–11, 114, 121, 140–41, 194, 196
Touré, Sékou, 79
Trade Expansion Act (TEA), 11, 127
Treaty of Rome, 9, 45–46, 48–49, 127, 131–32, 163
Triboulet, Raymond, 78–79
Tunisia, 79–80

Ulbricht, Walter, 139
Ulrich, Maurice, 48
Union pour la Nouvelle République (UNR), 10–11
United Kingdom (UK), 11, 24, 25, 31, 43, 55, 68, 77, 84, 89, 111, 116, 130, 134, 137, 142–44, 195, 197
and its second application to join the EEC, 123, 127, 130–33, 148, 151, 154, 160–66, 168–69, 171, 181
France's veto of its first application to the EEC, 17–21, 23, 45
and the international monetary system, 28, 40, 47
United Nations (UN), 71, 79–80, 142, 144–47, 150, 154, 172

United Nations Emergency Force (UNEF), 142
United States, 4–5, 8–11, 17, 19–30, 32–44, 46–48, 50, 52–57, 59, 62–64, 66, 68–69, 71–72, 77, 82–85, 88–94, 99–102, 106–18, 120–28, 130, 132–35, 138, 140–48, 150, 152–54, 159, 161, 164–70, 172–74, 177–85, 188–89, 191–92, 194–98
and détente, 68, 125, 140
and Franco-German relations, 22–23, 32–33, 134–35, 153–54
and the international monetary system, 8, 22, 27–29, 40, 46–47, 126–28, 130, 134–35, 152–53, 161, 166–67, 169, 179–80, 182–85
and the Kennedy Round, 11, 23–24, 127, 130
and the MLF, 12, 36–39
and NATO, 47, 100–2, 116–17, 124–25, 130, 146, 152, 161, 164–65, 169–70
and nuclear strategy, 8–9, 47, 117, 124
and the Six Day War, 142–48, 150
and the Soviet Union, 25, 55, 57, 71, 125, 140, 144–46, 148, 173, 195
and the Vietnam War, 34, 40, 43, 48, 90–94, 110–12, 114, 120, 141, 172
view of de Gaulle, 3, 102, 117, 150, 188
and West Germany 22, 33–34, 37, 39, 63, 133–35, 153–54

Vietnam War, 34, 40, 43, 48, 62, 102, 121, 140–41, 144–46, 148, 174, 182
Franco-Soviet convergence on the, 57, 66–67, 109, 119, 154
French attempts to settle the, 86–89, 92–94, 110–12, 172–73
French views of American policy towards the, 85, 90–94, 112–115, 120, 123, 145, 190
Vinogradov, Sergei, 52–54, 57, 60, 62, 64, 67

Warsaw Pact, 58, 104, 118, 138, 170, 176, 190
Watson, Adam, 125
Western European Union (WEU), 132, 151
West Germany, 26, 28, 43–44, 49, 52–58, 62–63, 65–69, 86, 88, 107–10, 119–20, 123–24, 133–41, 147–50, 153–59, 162, 166, 174, 183–85, 192, 194–96
and the Eastern bloc, 58, 138, 159, 174

and the EEC, 8, 21–22, 30–31, 36–39,
    43–44, 154, 159, 180–81
and the FFA, 99–101, 115–16
and cooperation with France, 11, 22–23,
    32–39, 57–58, 63, 66–67, 72, 122, 133,
    135, 153–54, 180–81
summits with France, 30–31, 34–35,
    115–16, 133, 135, 150, 174, 191
and international monetary
    negotiations, 126, 134–35, 149,
    153–54, 159, 180–81
and the MLF, 36–39, 62–63, 67
and the Soviet Union, 54, 61, 122, 138,
    174

Westrick, Ludger, 33
Wilson, Harold, 58, 118, 127, 131, 146, 148
Wormser, Olivier, 38, 118, 131, 175

Yalta Conference, 7, 65
Yi, Chen, 91
Youlou, Fulbert, 82
Yugoslavia, 54, 58, 63, 146, 159, 174

Zhivkov, Todor, 119
Zorin, Valerian, 67–69, 72–73, 107–8, 119,
    135, 157–58, 174–75